BESTSELLING
BOOK SERIES

Paris For Dummies, 1st Edition

Cheat Sheet

Métro Stops for Paris Attractions

See the Métro map on the inside front cover and the RER map on the inside back cover to find the locations listed below.

Museums

Attraction	Métro Stop
Centre Georges Pompidou	1 : St-Paul
Musée d'Art et d'Histoire du Judaïsme	11: Rambuteau
Musée Carnavalet	1 : St-Paul
Musée de Cluny	10 : Cluny-La Sorbonne
Musée de l'Histoire de France	1,11 : Hôtel-de-Ville
Musée Jacquemart-André	9 : St-Philippe-du-Roule
Musée du Louvre	1 : Louvre-Rivoli
Musée des Médailles	1,7: Palais Royal
Musée d'Orsay	12 : Solférino.......RER Musée d'Orsay
Musée Picasso	1 : St-Paul
Musée Rodin	13: Varenne

Churches

Attraction	Métro Stop
Notre-Dame	4 : Cité
Sacré-Cœur	12 : Abbesses
Sainte-Chapelle	4 : Cité

Parks

Attraction	Métro Stop
Jardin du Palais-Royal	1, 7 : Palais-Royal
Jardin des Tuileries	1, 8, 12 : Concorde......1 : Tuileries
Jardin et Palais du Luxembourg	4, 10 : Odéon...RER Luxembourg...RER Port Royal
Place des Vosges	1 : St-Paul

Cemetery

Attraction	Métro Stop
Pére Lachaise	2, 3 : Pére Lachaise

For Dummies®: Bestselling Book Series for Beginners

Paris For Dummies,® 1st Edition

Cheat Sheet

Monuments and Architecture

Attraction	Métro Stop
Arc de Triomphe	1, 2, 6 : Charles de Gaulle-Étoile
Champs-Elysées	1, 8, 12 : Concorde....1, 13 : Champs-Elysées Clémenceau...1, 9 : Franklin D. Roosevelt...1 : George V....1, 2, 6 : Charles de Gaulle-Étoile
Conciergerie	4 : Cité
La Crypte Archéologique	4: Cité RER St-Michel-Notre-Dame
Eiffel Tower	8 : École-Militaire...6 : Bir-Hakeim...RER Luxembourg
Hotel des Invalides (Napoléon's Tomb)	8 : Latour-Maubourg...13 : Varenne...1, 13 : Champs-Elysées Clémenceau ...RER Invalides
Panthéon	10 : Cardinal Lemoine....RER Luxembourg
Place de la Bastille	1,5 : Bastille

Kids

Attraction	Métro Stop
Aquaboulevard	8 : Balard
Les Catacombes	4, 6 : Denfert-Rochereau
Cité des Sciences et de l'Industrie	7 : Porte de la Villette
Les Égouts	9 : Alma-Marceau....RER Pont-de l'Alma
Jardin d'Acclimation Bois de Boulogne	1 : Les Sablons
Jardin des Plantes	5, 10: Gare d'Austerlitz...7, 10: Jussieu
Parc Zoologique de Paris	8 : Porte Dorée

Historic Cafés & Bars

Attraction	Métro Stop
Brasserie	7: Pont Marie
Brasserie Lipp	4 : St-Germain-des-Prés
Café aux Deux-Magots	4 : St-Germain-des-Prés
La Closerie de Lilas	RER Port-Royal
Harry's New York Bar	3, 7, 8: Opéra

Hungry Minds™

For Dummies®: Bestselling Book Series for Beginners

Paris
FOR
DUMMIES®

1ST EDITION

Paris
FOR
DUMMIES®
1ST EDITION

by Cheryl A. Pientka

Hungry Minds™

HUNGRY MINDS, INC.

New York, NY ◆ Cleveland, OH ◆ Indianapolis, IN

Paris For Dummies,® 1st Edition

Published by:
Hungry Minds, Inc.
909 Third Avenue
New York, NY 10022
www.hungryminds.com
www.dummies.com

Library of Congress Control Number: 00-111134

ISBN: 0-7645-6289-4

ISSN: 1531-765X

Printed in the United States of America

10 9 8 7 6 5 4 3 2

1B/RX/QU/QR/IN

Distributed in the United States by Hungry Minds, Inc.

Distributed by CDG Books Canada Inc. for Canada; by Transworld Publishers Limited in the United Kingdom; by IDG Norge Books for Norway; by IDG Sweden Books for Sweden; by IDG Books Australia Publishing Corporation Pty. Ltd. for Australia and New Zealand; by TransQuest Publishers Pte Ltd. for Singapore, Malaysia, Thailand, Indonesia, and Hong Kong; by Gotop Information Inc. for Taiwan; by ICG Muse, Inc. for Japan; by Intersoft for South Africa; by Eyrolles for France; by International Thomson Publishing for Germany, Austria and Switzerland; by Distribuidora Cuspide for Argentina; by LR International for Brazil; by Galileo Libros for Chile; by Ediciones ZETA S.C.R. Ltda. for Peru; by WS Computer Publishing Corporation, Inc., for the Philippines; by Contemporanea de Ediciones for Venezuela; by Express Computer Distributors for the Caribbean and West Indies; by Micronesia Media Distributor, Inc. for Micronesia; by Chips Computadoras S.A. de C.V. for Mexico; by Editorial Norma de Panama S.A. for Panama; by American Bookshops for Finland.

For general information on Hungry Minds' products and services please contact our Customer Care department; within the U.S. at 800-762-2974, outside the U.S. at 317-572-3993 or fax 317-572-4002.

For sales inquiries and resellers information, including discounts, premium and bulk quantity sales and foreign language translations please contact our Customer Care department at 800-434-3422, fax 317-572-4002 or write to Hungry Minds, Inc., Attn: Customer Care department, 10475 Crosspoint Boulevard, Indianapolis, IN 46256.

For information on licensing foreign or domestic rights, please contact our Sub-Rights Customer Care department at 212-884-5000.

For information on using Hungry Minds' products and services in the classroom or for ordering examination copies, please contact our Educational Sales department at 800-434-2086 or fax 317-572-4005.

Please contact our Public Relations department at 212-884-5174 for press review copies or 212-884-5000 for author interviews and other publicity information or fax 212-884-5400.

For authorization to photocopy items for corporate, personal, or educational use, please contact Copyright Clearance Center, 222 Rosewood Drive, Danvers, MA 01923, or fax 978-750-4470.

Hungry Minds™ is a trademark of Hungry Minds, Inc.

About the Author

Cheryl A. Pientka is a freelance journalist and assistant literary agent. She's the co-author of both *Frommer's Paris From $80 a Day* and *France For Dummies*. A graduate of Columbia University Graduate School of Journalism and the University of Delaware, she lives in Paris when she's not in New York.

Dedication

For my father, Philip E. Pientka (1936–2000), the wind beneath my wings

Author's Acknowledgments

The author would like to thank the following on this side of the pond: Mary Anne Pientka and John Pientka, Sean Stevens, Jen and Henry at the Henry Dunow Literary Agency, Alicia Patterson Giesa, G and G, Jean-Christian Agid and Patricia Gaviria Agid, Alice Alexiou, Daniel Simmons, Kelly Regan, Kimberly Perdue, and Ron Boudreau. In Paris, thanks go to Siobhan Fitzpatrick and Margie Rynn, Karen Fawcett and Anne Deleporte.

Publisher's Acknowledgments

We're proud of this book; please send us your comments through our Hungry Minds Online Registration Form located at www.dummies.com.

Some of the people who helped bring this book to market include the following:

Editorial

Editors: Kathleen M. Cox, Kimberly Perdue, Kelly Regan

Copy Editor: Robert Annis

Cartographer: Elizabeth Puhl

Editorial Manager: Jennifer Ehrlich

Editorial Assistant: Michelle Hacker

Senior Photo Editor: Richard Fox

Assistant Photo Editor: Michael Ross

Cover Photos: The Image Bank, © Andrea Pistolesi (front cover); Odyssey/Chicago, © Robert Freick (back cover)

Production

Project Coordinator: Jennifer Bingham

Layout and Graphics: Amy Adrian, LeAndra Johnson, Heather Pope, Julie Trippetti

Proofreaders: John Bitter, Vickie Broyles, David Faust, Susan Moritz, York Production Services, Inc.

Indexer: York Production Services, Inc.

Special Help

Alissa Schwipps, Jennifer Young, Melissa Bennett

General and Administrative

Hungry Minds, Inc.: John Kilcullen, CEO; Bill Barry, President and COO; John Ball, Executive VP, Operations & Administration; John Harris, CFO

Hungry Minds Consumer Reference Group

Business: Kathleen A. Welton, Vice President and Publisher; Kevin Thornton, Acquisitions Manager

Cooking/Gardening: Jennifer Feldman, Associate Vice President and Publisher

Education/Reference: Diane Graves Steele, Vice President and Publisher; Greg Tubach, Publishing Director

Lifestyles: Kathleen Nebenhaus, Vice President and Publisher; Tracy Boggier, Managing Editor

Pets: Dominique De Vito, Associate Vice President and Publisher; Tracy Boggier, Managing Editor

Travel: Michael Spring, Vice President and Publisher; Suzanne Jannetta, Editorial Director; Brice Gosnell, Managing Editor

Hungry Minds Consumer Editorial Services: Kathleen Nebenhaus, Vice President and Publisher; Kristin A. Cocks, Editorial Director; Cindy Kitchel, Editorial Director

Hungry Minds Consumer Production: Debbie Stailey, Production Director

◆

The publisher would like to give special thanks to Patrick J. McGovern, without whom this book would not have been possible.

◆

Contents at a Glance

Cartoons at a Glance

By Rich Tennant

"Welcome to the Hotel d'Notre Dame. If there's anything else I can do for you, please don't hesitate to ring."

page 7

"It serves you right for requesting a lap-dance from someone doing the can-can."

page 279

"And how shall I book your flight to Paris — First Class, Coach, or Medieval?"

page 41

"Now THAT was a great meal! Beautiful presentation, an imaginative use of ingredients, and a sauce with nuance and depth. The French really know how to make a 'Happy Meal.'"

page 123

page 97

page 183

page 297

Cartoon Information:
Fax: 978-546-7747
E-Mail: richtennant@the5thwave.com
World Wide Web: www.the5thwave.com

Maps at a Glance

Table of Contents

Introduction

●●●

*I*f you've never been to Paris, you may be amazed to find so much to like! As this book went to press, scaffolding that had been covering much of the city in preparation for the new century was being torn down. Many of the city's monuments and historical buildings shine anew following recent renovations. The Opéra Garnier, and the Centre Georges Pompidou have reopened. Workers are widening the quays along the Seine for more foot traffic, and the arches on the stately Pont Neuf have been restored and reinforced. A dynamic theater and music scene, terrific exhibits at galleries, and new museums under construction (or in the planning stages) all point to the fact that Paris is a city of culture. One look in store windows attests that the city is also a paradise for fashion and objets d'art. Paris is a gathering place — adults meet in cafés to discuss their day, while young people congregate around place d'Italie and the Bastille to inline skate or ride their *trotinettes* (scooters).

If you haven't been to Paris in a dog's age, you're in for some changes. First of all, the city's a lot more friendly. Forget that stereotype about rude Parisians; many more people are willing to try out their English to help visitors, and service at stores and in restaurants is more warm and friendly. Monuments have been restored — Pont Neuf and Notre-Dame shine in their original alabaster color now that centuries of grime have been scrubbed away. And you find the city has entered the twenty-first century in some ways more than its American counterparts. Everywhere people talk on cell phones. You won't see a conductor in the Métro's brand new Meteor line — the train drives itself. Architecture has a decidedly futuristic flair — like that of the buildings of the Cité des Sciences et de l'Industrie, a park and museum complex that includes a huge sphere on which movies are shown, and the giant Bibliothéque Nationale de François Mitterand that is shaped to resemble an open book. It all demonstrates France's eagerness to embrace the future.

But in some things Paris remains timeless — the city's beauty takes your breath away — the graceful rounded beaux arts buildings, willowy arching bridges, the spires and domes of famous churches and cathedrals, and the pink light of the setting sun reflecting off the river that is its heart.

About This Book

Consider this a textbook of sorts that you won't have to read from front to back, and certainly one you won't be tested on! Basically, *Paris For Dummies* presents you with to-the-point information on Paris that's fun and easy to access. I include very basic information about the city for readers who have never visited, but listings have been chosen to include something of interest for the seasoned traveler to Paris as well.

Conventions Used in This Book

Again, *Paris For Dummies* is a reference book, meaning you may read the chapters in any order you wish. I use some standard listings for hotels, restaurants, and sights. These listings allow you to open the book to any chapters and access the information you need quickly and easily.

Other conventions used in this book include the following:

- ✔ The abbreviations for credit cards: AE (American Express), DC (Diner's Club), MC (MasterCard), and V (Visa).

- ✔ Hotels, restaurants, and attractions are listed in alphabetical order so that moving among the maps, worksheets, and descriptions is easier.

- ✔ I include the Paris *arrondissement,* or administrative district, in each address to give you a better idea of where each place is located. Paris is divided into 20 *arrondissements,* which are indicated by an ordinal number from first (in the very center of Paris, abbreviated *1er* in French) to 20th (on the outer edges of the city, abbreviated *20e* in French). They appear after the street address in each citation in this book. For example, "123 bd. St-Germain, 6e," indicates the building numbered 123 on the Boulevard Saint Germain in the 6th *arrondissement.* To get an idea of where each *arrondissement* is located, consult the "Paris at a Glance" map in Chapter 1. Street abbreviations used throughout the book include not only *bd.* (boulevard), but also *rue* (street) and *av.* (avenue).

- ✔ Also to help you orient yourself, I give the nearest subway (or Métro) stop for all destinations (for example: Métro: Pont Marie).

- ✔ Two prices for everything are provided — first in the local currency (the franc) and second in U.S. dollars, rounded to the nearest dime. Though exchange rates can and will fluctuate daily, and the rate probably won't be the same when you visit, the price conversions in this book were calculated at the rate of 7 francs to one U.S. dollar.

All hotels and restaurants in this book are rated with a system of dollar signs to indicate the range of costs for one night in a double-occupancy hotel room or a meal at a restaurant, from "$" (budget) to "$$$$$" (splurge). Check out the following table to decipher the dollar signs. For more specific guidelines, consult Chapter 7 for hotels and Chapter 14 for restaurants.

Cost	Hotel	Restaurant
$	Under 700F ($100)	Under 125F ($17.90)
$$	700–1000F ($100–$143)	125– 200F ($17.90– $28.60)
$$$	1000–1500F ($143–$215)	200– 300F ($28.60– $42.90)
$$$$	1500–2100F ($215–$300)	300– 500F ($42.90– $71.45)
$$$$$	Over 2,100F ($300)	Over 500F ($71.45)

Foolish Assumptions

As I wrote this book, I made some assumptions about you and what your needs might be as a traveler. Maybe this is your first trip to Paris. Or maybe you visited so long ago that you went to the Jeu de Paume to see Impressionist masterpieces and wouldn't know that you can see them today at the Musée d'Orsay. Or maybe you're traveling to Paris on business and have only a day or two to spend in the city.

Whatever the reason, this book is for all of you — those who are itching to discover Paris, and those who want to know what the big deal is. You want a book you can look at on the go, a book that won't have you wading through pages of information to get to the news you can use. Yet you still want descriptions of the best accommodations and ideas of where to eat in the city's more than 2,000 restaurants. You want opinions, you want the straight scoop, and you want some fun. *Paris For Dummies* is for you.

How This Book is Organized

Paris For Dummies is divided into seven parts and two appendixes. If you read the parts in sequential order, they can guide you through all the advance planning aspects of your trip and then get you off and running after you're in the City of Light.

- ✔ The four chapters that comprise **Part I: Getting Started** introduce Paris and touch on everything you need to consider before planning a trip. You find out the pros and cons of each season, develop a realistic budget, and discover a host of options available to travelers with special needs or interests.

- ✔ In **Part II: Ironing Out the Details,** I get down to the nitty-gritty of trip planning, and answer questions such as: Should you use a travel agent or go it alone? What kind of accommodations should you use in Paris? Why don't you have to pay full price at hotel chains? I list of some of the city's best moderately priced hotels (with a few super-budget and some deluxe resorts thrown in for good measure), as well as advise you how to tie up those frustrating last-minute details that can unnerve the most seasoned of travelers.

✔ Chapters 10– 12 make up **Part III: Settling In to Paris,** and I get you oriented in Paris in no time — from navigating your way through customs, getting to your hotel from the airport and discovering Paris, neighborhood by neighborhood. You find out how to use the city's terrific transportation system, why you shouldn't rent a car here, and what to know when you hail a cab. You make sense of the franc, ferret out where you can go, and find out where to turn if your wallet gets stolen.

✔ Paris is known for its fine food, and **Part IV: Dining in Paris** helps you choose the best restaurants for your taste and budget. I provide everything from moderatrely priced to *haute-cuisine* restaurants, delicious dining options, one and all, so you can discover that a fine meal is truly an art in itself. Chapter 15 also provides you with options for those occasions when you don't have the time, or the desire, for a full-course meal.

✔ **Part V: Exploring Paris** has everything you need to know about Paris's top sights — how to get to them, how much they cost, and how much time to devote to them, as well as handy indexes by sight, type, and neighborhood to make them easier to find. I include kid- and teen-specific sights, as well as information on orientation and other tours, a shopper's guide to Paris, four recommended itineraries, and five great day trips if you're in the mood to get out of town.

✔ Nothing is more beautiful than Paris at night when the city's monuments are lit up — like a stage set where anything can happen. In **Part VI: Living It Up after Sundown,** I give you information on everything from theater, opera, ballet, and live music to night-clubs, bars, and those spectacles for which Paris has come to be known — the cabarets. You uncover how to find out what's going on and where you can getreduced-rate tickets. You even get the lowdown on how Parisians dress for a visit to a classy bar.

✔ And finally, you arrive at **Part VII: The Part of Tens** — what Dummies book would be complete without it? Included is a quick collection of fun tidbits: a digest of reading suggestions, and my recommendations for the best places to relax with a picnic, a very Parisian pastime!

Icons Used in This Book

This icon is a catchall for any special hint, tip, or bit of insider's advice that may help make your trip run more smoothly. Really, the point of a travel guide is to serve as one gigantic "tip," but this icon singles out the nuggets o' knowledge you may not have run across before.

This icon pegs the best bargains and juiciest money-saving tips. You may find a particularly value-conscious choice of hotel or restaurant, a discount museum or transportation pass, or simply a way to avoid spending more than you have to.

 When you need to be aware of a rip-off, an overrated sight, a dubious deal, or any other trap set for an unsuspecting traveler, this icon alerts you. These hints also offer the low-down on the quirks, etiquette, and unwritten rules of the area so you may avoid looking like a tourist and instead, be treated like a local.

 This icon, in addition to flagging tips and resources of special interest to families, points out the most child-friendly hotels, restaurants, and attractions. If you need a baby-sitter at your hotel, a welcoming relaxed atmosphere at a restaurant, or a dazzling site that delights, instead of bores, your child, look for this icon. I include information regarding larger, family-sized rooms at hotels and restaurants that serve meals that go easy on your little one's tummy.

 Sometimes a great hotel, restaurant, or sight may be a bit out of the center or require a bit of effort to get to. I let you in on these secret little finds, and you can rest assured, I don't include any spots that aren't truly worth the energy. I also use this to peg any resource that's particularly useful and worth the time to seek out.

Where to Go from Here

To Paris! The "city of lights" is for everyone, and *Paris For Dummies* shows you just how accessible it can be. I present you with a selective list of the best hotel, dining, and touring options along with insider info to help you make informed decisions. Follow the advice laid out here, and you'll want to return to Paris again and again. Because, as the author Honoré de Balzac once said, in Paris there will always remain an undiscovered place, an unknown retreat, and something unheard-of.

Part I
Getting Started

The 5th Wave   By Rich Tennant

"Welcome to the Hotel d'Notre Dame. If there's anything else I can do for you, please don't hesitate to ring."

In this part . . .

Are you a stranger to Paris? Or has it been a lo-o-o-o-ng time since you last visited? Then (re)introduce yourself to the city and whet your appetite for finding out more about it. In Chapter 1, you get an overview of Paris and why you should pay it a visit. Chapter 2 makes it easier to decide when to visit — and why some times may be better than others to go. In Chapter 3, you discover how to plan a reasonable budget based on prices in Paris and get some cost-cutting tips. You find specially targeted advice in Chapter 4 for families, seniors, travelers with disabilities, and gay and lesbian travelers.

Chapter 1

Discovering the Best of Paris

● ●

In This Chapter

▶ Explaining why Paris is a wonderful place to visit

▶ Condensing Paris history into a nutshell

● ●

So you're planning a visit to Paris, and everyone is regaling you with their favorite memories of visiting the "City of Lights." You discover that the **Louvre Museum** is just as incredible as you've always heard, that the views from the **Eiffel Tower** are stunning, and that crossing a footbridge across the Seine at sunset is one of the world's most romantic strolls. You hear about mouth-watering meals in palatial settings and great bargain places not far from the river. Perhaps friends and family tell you about drinking coffee in historic cafés or window shopping where *haute couture* was born. You quickly discover that every story is different. Why? Because Paris is more of an experience than a mere city and every visitor experiences it in an entirely individual way. You have every right to feel excited.

Perhaps, however, you feel more nervous than excited. After all, consider the language difference, and aren't Parisians known for their rudeness to tourists? I put your mind at ease in this chapter, giving a face to the place that's the heart of all of France.

Taking In All the Spectacular Sights

For most people, the real reason to visit Paris is to see those quintessentially French attractions for which the city has come to be known. Are the sights really as great as returning travelers say? Yes, yes, and yes. The **Eiffel Tower** continues to grace the city skyline with its lacy presence. To celebrate the Millenium year, it was rigged to sparkle with twinkling lights for ten minutes once an hour; you can still see this beautiful light display throughout 2001. **Notre-Dame** is now the original ivory color its builders intended — centuries worth of dirt has been cleaned off. The **Louvre** has even more exhibits — in fact, you can see its new primitive art exposition near the Denon Wing until 2004 when the **Musée Branly** is scheduled to open and take over that collection. Take a tour boat down the Seine and see the towers of Notre-Dame highlighted against the sky as lights from bridges older than the United States cast reflections in the water. Or watch the sunset from one of the footbridges across the Seine. Consult Chapters 16 and 17 for the best sights to see and things to do in Paris.

Wining and Dining and Wining Some More

Parisians are on an eternal quest for the perfect meal and make a pastime of sharing that information with their friends. And what wonderful meals they have to choose from! In the last decade, the city has seen the rise of "baby bistros" — restaurants opened by celebrity chefs that offer simpler and less expensive meals than those served at their deluxe establishments. Even the talented young apprentices of these celebrity chefs have opened their own restaurants.

Paris dining runs the gamut, from ultra-fancy high cuisine to hearty home cooking — and all fabulous. Dine under the stained glass ceiling at **Bofinger** — Paris's quintessential belle-epoque brasserie — while waiters in long aprons deftly make a fuss over you. Or nurse a drink at **Brasserie Lipp,** where author Ernest Hemingway penned many a short story. You soon find that you aren't just sitting down to a meal, but entering the life of a thriving city. Chapters 13, 14, and 15 give you the lowdown on Paris dining, including the addresses of some of the best restaurants, and tell you how to fill up quickly when you don't have time for a three-course meal.

Introducing Ground Zero for High Fashion

Shopping in Paris has never been better. A recent upswing in France's economy has seen many new stores open and others expand. Paris has a well-deserved reputation as a bastion of over-the-top luxury; all you have to do is head for the 8th *arrondissement* (district, abbreviated 8e) to see why. At the same time, the young and trendy are heading to the Sentier area in the third *arrondissement* (3e) for the season's funkiest looks at lower prices. At press time, a strong dollar and a falling euro meant that the city was much more affordable for non-European Union visitors. Chapter 19 tells you all you need to know about shopping in Paris.

Sampling Culture, Both Day and Night

Paris is a great place to pursue culture — the recent multimillion dollar renovations of the **Opéra Garnier** and the **Châtelet,** home to Théâtre Musical de Paris, are just some examples of the interest residents take in enlightening themselves. Even if your French is rusty or not up to par, you have alternatives to French-language plays with many avant-garde productions and English-language theater. See Chapters 22 and 23 for more info.

Painting the Town at Clubs and Cabarets

Paris is an ongoing party, and you find that each neighborhood makes a different contribution to the nightlife scene. The **Marais** is the center of gay clubs and bars as well as some of the best dance clubs; the **Bastille** attracts bohemian types and clubgoers. The side streets of the **Champs-Elysées** are home to upscale bars and discos, and a new generation of trendsetters is turning **Pigalle** into a rock music lovers' paradise. Jazz lovers find it easy to club-hop around **Les Halles** or on the **Left Bank.** The naughty cancan dancers are still drawing the crowds at the **Lido, Crazy Horse Saloon,** and **Moulin Rouge** clubs, though the torch singers that made these clubs famous have given way to glitzy light shows, special effects, and recorded music. One thing hasn't changed: Flesh is plentiful and on display everywhere. Chapters 23 and 24 tell you how to dance the night away or catch a show.

Going Green in the Parks and Gardens

From flowers to plants to city views to puppet shows to pony rides and museums — Paris has parks for every taste and interest. Whichever parks you decide to visit, you can relax in the beauty and serenity of planted gardens, splashing fountains, and arrow-straight paths — and kids love them. Chapter 17 steers you toward the best green spaces in town. Stunning beauty doesn't stop at the city limits, either; in Chapter 21 you find side trips like **Versailles, Fontainebleau,** and **Giverny** that offer their own sprawling splendor.

Paris at a Glance

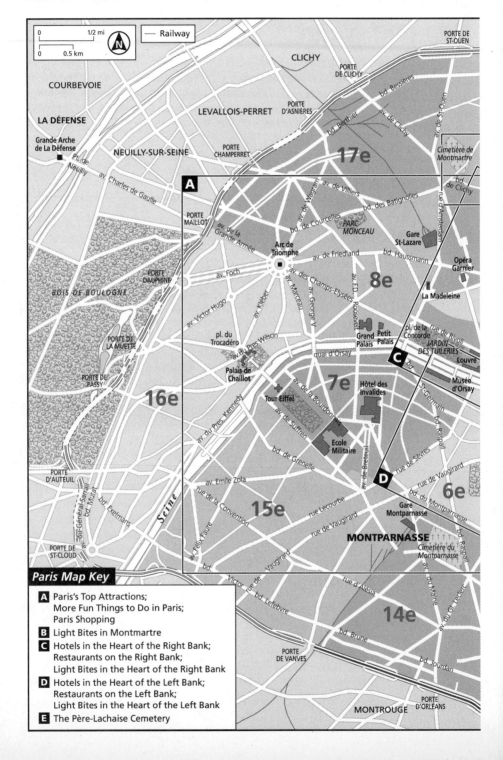

PORTE DE
ST-OUEN

COURBEVOIE

CLICHY

PORTE
DE CLICHY

LA DÉFENSE

LEVALLOIS-PERRET

PORTE
D'ASNIÈRES

bd. Bessières

bd. Berthier

av. de Clichy

bd.
de Clichy

rue d'Amsterdam

Cimetière de
Montmartre

Grande Arche
de La Défense

NEUILLY-SUR-SEINE

PORTE
CHAMPERRET

17e

Pt. de
Neuilly

av. Charles de Gaulle

A

av. de Villiers

av. de Wagram

bd. des Batignolles

PORTE
MAILLOT

av. de la
Grande Armée

bd. de Courcelles

PARC
MONCEAU

Gare
St-Lazare

Arc de
Triomphe

av. de Friedland

bd. Haussmann

Opéra
Garnier

BOIS DE BOULOGNE

PORTE
DAUPHINE

av. Foch

av. des Champs-Élysées

av. F.D. Roosevelt

8e

La Madeleine

av. Victor Hugo

av. Kléber

av. Marceau

av. George V

pl. de la
Concorde

rue de Rivoli

JARDIN
DES TUILERIES

PORTE DE
LA MUETTE

pl. du
Trocadéro

av. du Prés. Wilson

Grand
Palais

Petit
Palais

C

Louvre

PORTE DE
PASSY

Palais de
Chaillot

quai d'Orsay

bd. St-Germain

Musée
d'Orsay

16e

Tour Eiffel

av. de la Bourdonnais

7e

Hôtel des
Invalides

bd. Raspail

av. du Prés. Kennedy

av. de Suffren

av. de Breteuil

rue de Sèvres

6e

PORTE
D'AUTEUIL

Ecole
Militaire

bd. de Grenelle

D

rue de Vaugirard

bd. du Montparnasse

Seine

av. Emile Zola

rue de la Convention

15e

rue Lecourbe

rue de Vaugirard

Gare
Montparnasse

bd. Raspail

bd. Général-Sarrail

bd. Murat

bd. Exelmans

MONTPARNASSE

Cimetière du
Montparnasse

av. du Maine

PORTE DE
ST-CLOUD

av. Félix Faure

bd. Victor

rue de Vaugirard

rue d'Alésia

14e

bd. Lefebvre

bd. Brune

av. du Gal.-Leclerc

PORTE
DE VANVES

bd. Jourdan

MONTROUGE

PORTE
D'ORLÉANS

Paris Map Key

A Paris's Top Attractions;
More Fun Things to Do in Paris;
Paris Shopping

B Light Bites in Montmartre

C Hotels in the Heart of the Right Bank;
Restaurants on the Right Bank;
Light Bites in the Heart of the Right Bank

D Hotels in the Heart of the Left Bank;
Restaurants on the Left Bank;
Light Bites in the Heart of the Left Bank

E The Père-Lachaise Cemetery

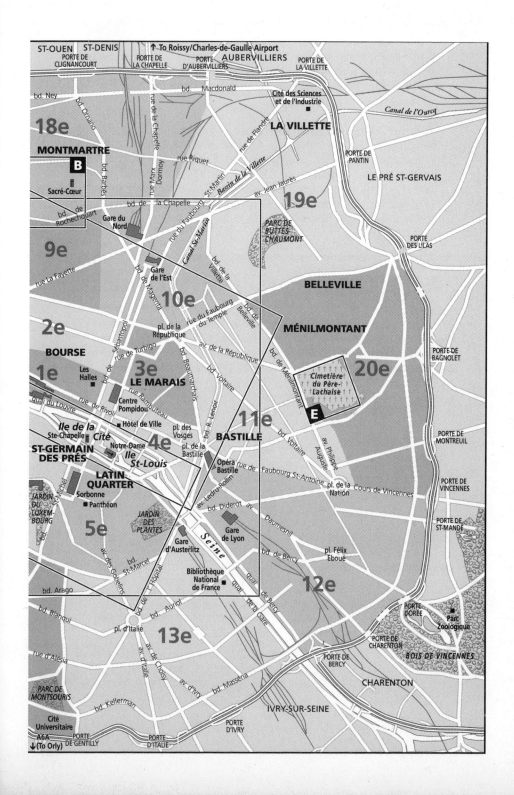

News Flash: The People Are Nice!

Why are the French now so inclined to speak English and be polite? Perhaps they're tired of having a reputation for rudeness that compares to that of New Yorkers. Whatever the reason, it only makes a visit to the city more appealing.

Whether Paris dominates the future as brilliantly as it did the past remains to be seen. Yet a city that has survived brutal wars, revolution, occupation, and political disarray has demonstrated a strength and resiliency that should sustain it well into the next millennium. And the fact that Paris is much more friendly and open not only benefits the city, but the country, which, with 72 million yearly visitors, is the world's most visited destination.

A brief history, from Parisii to Parisians

Paris was settled by the Parisii tribe on the Ile de la Cité, in the third century B.C. They were peaceful fishermen who traded with other tribes along the length of the river and with those traveling on the main north-south trading road connecting the Mediterranean with northern Europe. Unfortunately, the road made it convenient for invaders to attack the Parisii; the first and most successful were the Romans led by Julius Caesar in 52 B.C. They stayed 500 years, and the settlement became known as Lutetia Parisiorum ("Lutèce" in French). You can still see their public baths at the Musée National du Moyen Age/Cluny Museum in the heart of the Latin Quarter.

Years of barbarian invasions eventually weakened the Romans' hold over the territory, until in the 400s, the Franks from the east were able to successfully take over. In 508, Clovis, king of the Franks, chose Paris as his capital. Abandoned as a capital 250 years later, it wasn't until 987 that Hugues Capet was proclaimed king of France, and Paris again became a capital city. To celebrate the city's importance, the two Gothic masterpieces — the cathedral of Notre-Dame and Sainte-Chapelle (holy chapel) — were built on the Ile de la Cité, and across the river on the Left Bank, the Sorbonne University was born. Under Louis XIV, the Sun King, who ruled for 72 years, the monarchy's power reached its height. Though he added monuments and splendor to the city, by establishing his court at Versailles he alienated the citizenry and prepared the ground for the French Revolution.

During the reigns of Louis XIV and Louis XV, Paris dominated the Western world, nourishing some of Europe's greatest architects and intellectuals, but the financial strain of pomp, glamour, and military conquest had drained its treasury.

On July 14, 1789, a mob stormed the Bastille, and three days later at the Hôtel de Ville, Louis XVI was forced to kiss the new French tricolor. On July 14, 1790, the Festival of the Federation was celebrated on the Champs de Mars. About 300,000 people attended a mass at which the king swore an oath of loyalty to the constitution. Yet radical factions grew. On August 10, 1792, revolutionary troops and a Parisian mob stormed the Tuileries, taking the king prisoner, and in 1793 he and Queen Marie Antoinette were beheaded in the place de la Concorde. Robespierre presided over the Reign of Terror from 1793 until his arrest on July 27, 1794. A reaction ushered in the Directory (1795-99), which ended with Napoléon's coup. In 1804, at Notre-Dame, Napoléon crowned himself emperor and his wife, Joséphine, empress; he then embarked on a series of military campaigns against surrounding countries until he was defeated at the Battle of Waterloo in 1815. During his reign, he gave Paris many of its most grandiose monuments, notably the Arc de Triomphe and the Bourse. His greatest gift, however, was the Louvre, which he set on its course to becoming an art museum. Here, he displayed the art he had "acquired" in his many military campaigns; it later became the core of the museum's collection.

The look that most of us associate with Paris was created in the nineteenth century. Napoléon landscaped the view from the Louvre, extending the perspective past the Tuileries and the place de la Concorde to the Champs-Elysées and the Arc de Triomphe. He also built fountains, cemeteries, and the arcades along the rue de Rivoli. From 1852 to 1870, Napoléon's nephew, Napoléon III, reshaped Paris with the aid of Baron Haussmann, who razed whole neighborhoods and laid out boulevards and avenues and 24 parks.

The Eiffel Tower *(La Tour Eiffel)*, built for the 1889 expo (World's Fair) as a temporary structure, was allowed to remain standing, the tallest structure in the world at the time. Paris opened its first Métro line in 1900. By the turn of the century, Paris had 27,000 cafés, about 150 café concerts, and thousands of restaurants.

In the 100 years since then, Paris has seen two world wars, in which more than 10 million soldiers died, and four years of German occupation. Tens of thousands of soldiers lost their lives fighting the end of colonial French rule around the world. In 1968 in Paris, students took to the streets, rebelling against France's antiquated educational system; the government flirted unsuccessfully with textbook socialism in the 1980s, and in 1989, France celebrated two great birthdays: the bicentennial of the French Revolution and the centennial of the Eiffel Tower. Former Paris Mayor Jacques Chirac won the presidency in 1995 upon a promise to jump-start the economy, but growth remained stagnant, and the president was forced to "cohabit" with Prime Minister Lionel Jospin, the leader of the opposition, when Jospin called for elections in 1997. In 1998, France hosted the World Cup soccer championships and surprised the world by winning. People have said that the celebration on the Champs-Elysées rivaled only that of DeGaulle's Liberation in 1944. Two years later, the French team, the Bleues, won the Euro Cup, making the team the only World Cup champions to simultaneously hold the Euro Cup. At press time, Jospin's popularity was waning and Chirac was back on top as the French economy recovered. Dilemmas included the falling euro, rising gas prices, and a referendum that would give the island of Corsica more independence.

Chapter 2

Deciding When to Go

● ●

In This Chapter

▶ Choosing the best season to visit

▶ Finding events that suit your interests

● ●

In this chapter, I play devil's advocate, giving you the pros and cons of each season to help you decide when you can make the most of your visit. I also compile a calendar of the most memorable events in Paris; you may want to consider planning your trip to coincide with one of these festivals, sporting events, or celebrations.

The Secret of the Seasons: What to Expect

Most residents find Paris ideal in spring and autumn, when the weather is kind, the crowds reasonably sized, and Parisian life at a steady hum. In reality, Paris is great any time of year. In winter you can find plenty of things to do inside — you can fill an entire trip with visits just to the Louvre, and don't forget the January sales — and in summer you can bask in daylight that lasts until 10 p.m. The timing of your visit to Paris depends on what kind of experience you want to have.

Table 2-1 presents the average temperatures in Paris to help you as you plan your trip.

Table 2-1		Average Daytime Temperatures for Paris									
Jan	**Feb**	**Mar**	**Apr**	**May**	**June**	**July**	**Aug**	**Sept**	**Oct**	**Nov**	**Dec**
38°F	39°	46°	51°	58°	64°	74°	76°	61°	53°	45°	40°
3°C	4°	8°	11°	14°	18°	28°	29°	16°	12°	7°	6°

Spring

George Gershwin wrote "I love Paris in the springtime," and with good reason. Spring in Paris brings an abundance of clear, fresh days. The parks and gardens of Paris (as well as those at Versailles; Fontainebleu; and at Claude Monet's home, Giverny; see Chapter 21) are at their colorful, fragrant best in early May. The crowds of visitors don't kick in until summer vacation, so lines are relatively short at the top sightseeing attractions; and airfares have yet to reach their summertime highs.

But keep in mind that April in Paris is *not* as temperate as Gershwin would have you believe. Count on the weather being very fickle, so pack for warm, cold, wet, dry, and every other eventuality (bring layers and don't even *think* about coming without an umbrella). Also, nearly every Monday in May is a holiday in France, so stores may be closed and other venues affected.

Summer

Wonderfully long and sultry days are summer's hallmark — I'm talking 6 a.m. sunrises and 10 p.m. sunsets — so you're afforded additional hours to wander and discover. You can find discounts of 30 to 50 percent in most stores during July, one of the two big months for shopping sales. Hotel room rates are less expensive during the summer low season, and during August, parking is free in much of the city.

But remember that an influx of tourists during the summer, coming to take advantage of the low season, means long lines at museums and other sites. Because most Parisians take their vacations in August, you either find the city wonderfully tranquil in August — or a ghost town. The city's cultural calendar slows down, and you may have to walk an extra block or two to find a shop or newsstand that's open. Although the city does not entirely shut down in August, some shops and restaurants still close for the entire month. And if you go to Paris in August with thoughts of practicing your French, think again. French may be the foreign language you're least likely to hear in August.

Fall

Paris crackles back to life come September, one of the most exciting times of the year, when important art exhibitions open along with trendy new restaurants, shops, and cafés. Airfares drop from summertime highs. And with days in the 60s and 70s and nights in the 50s, the weather is still pleasant.

But keep in mind that finding a hotel at the last minute in the fall can be difficult due to the number of business conventions and trade shows happening in the city (be sure to book ahead). Also, transportation strikes of varying intensities traditionally occur during the fall — some may go virtually unnoticed by the average traveler, but others can be a giant hassle.

Winter

You can find great airfare deals during the winter; airlines and tour operators often offer unbeatable prices on flights and package tours. Lines at museums and other sights are mercifully short. And if shopping is your bag, you can save up to 50 percent during the January sales.

But remember that although Paris winters may look mild on paper, residents know that the season is gray (sometimes the sun doesn't shine for weeks), dreary, and often bone-chillingly damp. And look out for those wind tunnels that lash up and down the city's grand boulevards. Bring a warm, preferably waterproof, coat.

Hitting the Big Events: A Paris Calendar

When you arrive, check with the **Paris Tourist Office** (☎ **08-36-68-31-12**; a charge of 2.23F per minute) and buy *Pariscope* (a weekly guide with an English-language insert from *Time Out Paris*) or *L'Officiel des Spectacles* for dates, places, and other up-to-date information. For a refresher course in the ways and means of Paris addresses, as well as the basics of the French franc (F), see the Introduction.

January

La Grande Parade de Montmartre. A big, noisy parade on the square called place Pigalle on New Year's Day makes even the mildest hangover throb, but grin and bear it for the fun and flash — today Paris is more Rose Bowl than City of Lights. Watch the majorettes and high school bands, as well as elaborate floats, traverse through the city streets. The parade begins at 2 p.m. (so you can sleep in) in the place Pigalle, 18e (the 18th *arrondissement* or neighborhood), and ends at the place Jules-Joffrin, 18e. January 1.

Commemorative Mass for Louis XVI. Yes, Parisians hold a mass for a king their ancestors beheaded more than 200 years before. The event draws a full turnout of aristocrats and royalists, along with some far-right types. It's held at the Chapelle Expiatoire, 29 rue Pasquier, 8e. Sunday closest to January 21.

Chinese New Year Festival. Though Paris's Chinatown in the 13e is mostly high-rise apartment buildings, you can easily find good street life and many excellent restaurants. Residents go all out for the parade, featuring dragons, dancers, and fireworks. Depending on the Chinese calendar, the holiday falls between January 21 and February 19.

18 Francs à 18 Heures. This popular annual midwinter film promotion allows you admission to the showing closest to 6 p.m. of any film in town for 18F ($2.60). Date varies.

February

Foire à la Feraille de Paris. The yearly antiques and secondhand fair is held in the Parc Floral de Paris in the Bois de Vincennes (12e). Call the Paris Tourist Office for exact dates.

Salon de l'Agriculture. The country fair comes to Paris with hundreds of farmers displaying animals and produce. Regional food stands offer tastes of all parts of France, and the atmosphere is friendly and quintessentially French. At the Parc des Expositions de Paris, Porte de Versailles, 15e. For more information, call ☎ 01-43-95-10-10. Last week of February to first week of March.

March

Salon de Mars. This high-caliber annual art and antiques fair displays mostly seventeenth-, eighteenth-, and nineteenth-century antiques and paintings. In the Espace Eiffel Branly, near the Eiffel Tower. Admission is 50F ($7.15). Late March.

Foire du Trone. Tacky and fun, this annual carnival has a Ferris wheel, rides and games, hokey souvenirs, and fairground food. At the Pelouse de Reuilly in the Bois de Vincennes. Late March to end of May.

La Passion à Ménilmontant. Professional actors and residents of the neighborhood perform the Passion Play (the events leading up to and including Christ dying on the cross) for a month around Easter. The play is staged at the Théâtre de Ménilmontant in the 20e. The event is a local tradition that's been observed since 1932. Call ☎ 01-46-36-98-60 for schedules and ticket prices. Mid-March to mid-April.

April

Le Chemin de la Croix (Stations of the Cross). Follow the Archbishop of Paris from the square Willette in Montmartre up the steps to the basilica of Sacré-Coeur where he leads people in prayers, which commemorate the passion and death of Jesus Christ. Good Friday, 12:30 p.m.

Paris Marathon. One of the most popular athletic events during the year, this race runs past a variety of the city's most beautiful monuments. Held on a Sunday, the marathon attracts enthusiastic crowds. Mid-April. Call the Paris Tourist Office for exact dates.

Foire de Paris. A great place to bargain hunt and people watch, this huge annual fair signals the start of spring with hundreds of stands selling excellently-priced food and wine, and a variety of clothing and household goods. At the Parc des Expositions at the Porte de Versailles. Late April to early May.

Grandes Eaux Musicales et les Fêtes de Nuit de Versailles. The sounds of Bach, Mozart, or Berlioz are brought to life at the magnificent fountains in the gardens of the Château de Versailles. The Grandes Eaux Musicales are held every Sunday from mid-April to mid-October, and every Saturday and national holiday from June through August. The Grandes Fêtes are a spectacular sound and light show with fireworks that are held one Saturday in June, three Saturdays in July, one Saturday in August, and two Saturdays in September. Château de Versailles, Versailles. Log onto www.chateauversailles.fr for more information.

May

May Day. Banks, post offices, and most museums are closed on May 1, the French version of Labor Day, but you can watch a workers' parade that traditionally ends at the place de la Bastille. Call the Paris Tourist Office for more information. May 1.

French Open. Tickets are hard to come by for this tennis tournament, one of the biggest events on Paris's calendar. The French Open is held in the Stade Roland Garros in the Bois de Boulogne on the western edge of the city. Unsold tickets — those not reserved for corporate sponsors — go on sale two weeks before the competition starts. The stadium is at 2 av. Gordon Bennett, 16e. Call the French Federation of Tennis at the stadium for more information (☎ **01-47-43-48-00**) or visit the Web site at www.fft.fr. Last week in May and first week in June.

June

Fireworks at La Villette. Once a year, by invitation, a famous architect or designer plans a fireworks celebration, which takes place along the banks of the canal de l'Ourcq between the modern museums and gardens of the Musée de Musique and the Cité des Sciences et del'Industrie. Call the Paris Tourist Office for more information. Mid-June.

Festival Chopin à Paris. The Orangerie in the beautiful Bagatelle gardens on the edge of the Bois de Boulogne is the backdrop for this much-loved annual series of daily piano recitals. Mid-June to mid-July.

Fête de la Musique. The entire country becomes a concert venue in celebration of the first day of summer, and you can hear everything from classical to hip hop for free in squares and streets around Paris. A big rock concert usually happens in the place de la République and a fine classical concert generally takes place in the gardens of the Palais-Royal. June 21.

The Paris Air Show. One of the most distinguished aviation events in the world takes place in odd-numbered years at Le Bourget Airport just outside Paris. Visitors can check out the latest aeronautic technology on display. Call the Paris Tourist Office for more information. June 2001.

Gay Pride. Art exhibits and concerts as well as a fantastic parade are held in the Marais and in other Paris streets, including the boulevard St-Michel. Call the Centre Gai et Lesbien for dates ☎ **01-43-57-21-47.** Late June.

July and August

Bastille Day. Citywide festivities begin on the evening of July13, with street fairs, pageants, and feasts. Free *bals* (dances) are open to every-one and held in fire stations all over the city. (Some of the best *bals* are in the fire station on the rue du Vieux-Colombier near the place St-Sulpice, 6e; the rue Sévigné, 4e; and the rue Blanche, near the place Pigalle, 9e.) Though the *bals* are free, drinks cost. On July 14, a big mili-tary parade starts at 10 a.m. on the Champs-Elysées; get there early if you hope to see anything. A sound-and-light show with terrific fire-works is held that night at the Trocadéro; rather than face the crowds, many people watch the fireworks from the Champs de Mars across the river, from hotel rooms with views, or even from rue Soufflot, in front of the Panthéon. July 13 and 14.

Tour de France. The most famous bicycle race in the world always ends in Paris on the Champs-Elysées. Spectators need special invita-tions for a seat in the stands near place de la Concorde, but you can see the cyclists further up the Champs-Elysées, and, depending on the route (which changes each year), elsewhere in the city, too. Check the newspapers the day before. Late July or early August.

September

Journées Portes Ouvertes. Off-limits palaces, churches, and other offi-cial buildings throw open their doors to the public for two days. Long lines can put a damper on your sightseeing, so plan what you want to see and show up early (with a good book, just in case). Get a list and a map of all the open buildings from the Paris Tourist Office. Weekend closest to September 15.

Festival d'Automne. This arts festival held around Paris is recognized throughout Europe for its innovative programming and the high quality of its artists and performers. Obtain programs through the mail so that you can book ahead for events you don't want to miss. Write to the Festival, 56 rue de Rivoli, 75001 Paris, or call ☎ **01-53-43-17-00.** September 15 to December 31.

October

Fêtes des Vendanges à Montmartre. Celebrate the harvest of the wine produced from Montmartre's one remaining vineyard, Clos Montmartre, and watch as the wine is auctioned off at high prices to benefit local charities. (Word of advice: DON'T bid! The wine isn't very good.) Locals dress in period costumes, and the streets come alive with music. First or second Saturday of October.

FIAC (Foire Internationale d'Art Contemporain). One of the largest contemporary art fairs in the world, the FIAC has stands from more than 150 galleries, half of them foreign. As interesting for browsing as for buying, the fair takes place in Espace Eiffel Branly, near the Eiffel Tower. Early October.

November

Lancement des Illuminations des Champs-Elysées. The annual lighting of the avenue's Christmas lights makes for a festive evening, with jazz concerts and an international star who pushes the button that lights up the avenue. For more information, call the Paris Tourist Office. Late November.

December

La Crèche sur le Parvis. Each year a different foreign city installs a life-sized Christmas manger scene in the plaza in front of the Hôtel de Ville (City Hall). The crèche is open daily from 10 a.m. to 8 p.m. December 1 to January 3.

Chapter 3

Planning Your Budget

●●

In This Chapter

▶ Developing a workable budget

▶ Uncovering hidden expenses

▶ Using ATMs, credit cards, traveler's checks, and cash

▶ Cutting costs and how to do it

▶ Estimating costs in Paris

●●

"*Soit raissonable*" (be reasonable), the French say, and being reasonable is the key to budgeting a trip to Paris. A good way to figure out a budget is to mentally walk through the trip, from the moment you leave to the minute you get back home (figure in your transportation to and from the airport). Then add in the flight cost (see Chapter 5 for tips on how to fly to Paris for less), the price of getting from the Charles-de-Gaulle or Orly airports to your hotel, your hotel rate per day, meals, public transportation costs, admission prices to museums and the theater, and other entertainment expenses. Afterward, add on another 15 to 20 percent for good measure. To help you record your estimates, I include several budget worksheets; look for our very own "yellow pages" at the end of the book.

Adding Up the Elements

Cities are rarely cheap or expensive across the board; Paris tends to be pricey for dining, but reasonable for accommodations, so booking a good hotel shouldn't be a problem. Here are some guidelines for what you're likely to spend while in Paris:

✔ **Lodging:** Before you start shelling out money for lodging, think about how much time you'll actually be spending in your room. For between 300–500F ($42.90–$71.45), you can rent a clean but functionally furnished hotel room with a private bathroom and cable TV. These kinds of budget rooms are normally comfortable and have the basic furnishings and décor, but are supplied with thin, but serviceable, towels and a less-than-stellar array of toiletries. If you're feeling extravagant, and are willing to spend 700F ($100) and up to live in luxury, the upper-tier hotels offer more services, such as room service and air conditioning.

✔ **Transportation:** The Paris Métro has been the model for subways around the world since its inauguration in 1900 — simply put, the Métro is one of the best transit systems around in terms of price and efficiency. Getting across town in less than a half hour is no problem and the cost is lower if you purchase one of several discount tickets available, such as a *carnet* of ten tickets. (See Chapter 11 for options and prices.)

As for cars — well, expect your heart to be in your throat the entire time you drive in Paris — unless, of course, you thrive on labyrinthine one-way streets, a dearth of parking spaces, hellish traffic, and driving among the statistically worst drivers in Europe. If you want to rent a car to see other parts of France or make a day trip outside of Paris, do it on your way out of the city. (See Chapter 9 for addresses and phone numbers of Paris car rental agencies.)

✔ **Restaurants:** The French consider dining out one of the finer joys in life, and they pay for it. You can expect to do so as well. An average Parisian dining experience — a three-course dinner in a popular eatery — runs about 200 to 250F ($28.60 to $35.70) per person. You can find restaurants serving satisfying two-course meals for as little as 125F ($17.90) and wonderful ethnic food and sandwich shops that help you save even more money. Dining reasonably in Paris isn't an impossibility if you know where to look, and Chapters 14 and 15 help you do just that.

✔ **Attractions:** Entry fees to museums and other sights can add up quickly; after referring to the money-saving advice in Chapters 16 and 17, make a list of must-dos to get a feel for how much money to set aside.

✔ **Shopping:** Paris is a shopping paradise, and French shopkeepers arrange their wares in windows so enticing they give new meaning to the phrase *faire du leche-vitrines* (window licking). You can find some great deals during the semi-annual sales which are held in January and July, but remember that a steep 20.6 percent tax (TVA) is added to most goods. If you live outside the European Union, you are usually entitled to get back part of the tax, if you meet certain requirements. See Chapter 19 for more information.

✔ **Nightlife:** Don't forego the spectacles at the Lido or Moulin Rouge if you've always wanted to see them, just know beforehand that they charge a small fortune for entry and alcoholic beverages. Plan on seeing the show without dinner, and come out with a wallet that's a bit heavier. Budget big, too, if you plan to visit clubs and other nightspots; nightclubs and bars are not cheap.

Keeping a Lid on Hidden Expenses

Remember the tipping rules and you can save money in Paris. In restaurants, the tip is already included (the 15 percent is already figured into the bill), and though technically unnecessary, a small additional tip for satisfactory service (10F/$1.45 for a moderately priced meal) is considered appropriate. Also, don't tip a bartender for each round of drinks — instead leave 5 to 10F (70¢ to $1.45) at the end of the night. Hotel service personnel should get 5F per luggage item or service performed, and taxi-cab drivers generally are tipped 10 percent of the fare. If an usher shows you to your seat in a cinema or theater, tip 5F.

Also, don't think a café is a cheaper alternative to a restaurant. A simple meal of *croque monsieur* and *pommes frites* (a toasted ham-and-cheese sandwich with french fries) accompanied by a beer or soda can set you back $15 or $20. You can get a much tastier meal at the same price or less at a restaurant.

Choosing ATMs, Credit Cards, Traveler's Checks, or Cash

Money makes the world go round, but dealing with an unfamiliar currency can make your head spin. In Paris, you pay for things in francs and centimes, meaning you must convert your own currency into French francs (see Chapter 12 for detailed information about French money). When it comes to getting cash in Paris, should you bring traveler's checks or use ATMs? How easy is it to pay with a credit card? You find the answers in this section.

Using ATMs: They're everywhere

Before you leave, make a note of the following Web sites: www.visa.com/pd/atm (Visa) and www.mastercard.com/atm (MasterCard), which identify the locations of cash machines all over Paris. Most of the major banks in Paris, such as Credit Lyonnais, Credit Agricole, Banque Nationale de Paris (BNP), Banque Populaire, Credit Commercial de France (CCF), Credit du Nord, and even some branches of the post office have automatic cash distribution machines. But you won't be able to check your balance or transfer funds, so keep track of your withdrawals while you travel.

Make sure your ATM card has a 4-digit personal identification number (PIN). French bank cards are issued with PINs of four digits, but most French ATMs still accept PINs of up to six digits. To withdraw cash, your

PIN has to be made up of just numbers (French ATMs usually don't have alphanumeric keypads). If your PIN is a combination of letters and numbers, use a telephone dial to figure out the numeric equivalent.

 Finally, remember that each time you withdraw cash from an ATM, your bank hits you with a fee, sometimes as much as $5. Check how much your bank charges before leaving home. On top of this fee, the bank from which you withdraw cash may also include its own fee. Thus, it makes sense to take out larger amounts of money every two to three days rather than small denominations again and again. Also, remember that your bank places a limit on the amount of money you can take out per day, usually between 1500– 3000F ($214.30– $430). Again, check with your bank before you leave for the maximum amount.

Paying by credit card

You can use credit cards to buy virtually anything in France, as long as it costs a minimum of 100F ($14.30). You can also get cash advances from your Visa and MasterCard at any bank.

 As is the case in life, expect a downside. American Express and Diner's Club are not widely accepted at small restaurants, shops, and budget hotels in Paris. You also pay interest on cash advances the moment you receive the cash. And finally, many credit card companies have begun tacking on additional fees for foreign currency transactions — sometimes up to 4 percent, on top of the 1 percent service charge they already take. Worse, according to Lee Dembart, a writer for *The International Herald Tribune,* is that credit card companies don't expect you to notice the charge. "Recognizing the additional fee requires that the consumer know what the exchange rate was on the day the charge came through and then do the math," he writes, "steps most people don't take. You can find the official rate for dates in the past at www. oanda.com."

If you don't know how much your credit card charges for currency conversion, ask them. If the rate isn't acceptable, consider switching — **MBNA America** (☎800-932-2775; www.mbna.com), a Delaware-based credit card issuer, still charges only 1 percent for currency conversion.

Leaving home without traveler's checks

Because most cities now have banks with 24-hour ATMs, traveler's checks, previously one of a globetrotter's best friends, have become less necessary these days. Many people find it increasingly difficult to find places that cash traveler's checks. And when you do, well, who wants to stand in a line?

What things cost in Paris

What Things Cost in Paris	U.S.$
Taxi from Charles de Gaulle Airport to the city center	31.45
Taxi from Orly Airport to the city center	24.30
Public transportation for an average trip within the city (from a Métro *carnet* of 10)	.80
Local telephone call	.34
Glass of wine	2.60
Coca-Cola (at a café)	3.45
Cup of coffee	2.15
Roll of ASA 100 color film, 36 exposures	7.75
Admission to the Louvre	6.45
Movie ticket	7.90
Concert ticket (at the Salle Pleyel)	11.15

You can easily exchange traveler's checks in U.S. dollars for French francs in Paris, but don't expect to use them directly at many budget establishments; change them for francs at a bank or change outlet and use cash instead. Also, keep in mind that many establishments do not accept traveler's checks in French francs and that, of the places that do accept traveler's checks in U.S. dollars, you normally get a poor exchange rate. If you're still interested in purchasing traveler's checks, you can get them at almost any bank. Make sure to keep a record of their serial numbers, separately from the checks of course, so you're ensured a refund in an emergency. (See Chapter 9 for companies that offer traveler's checks and their phone numbers.)

Your best bet is to buy traveler's checks before leaving home as well as some French currency — about $50 to $100 worth — unless you don't mind waiting at the exchange offices at the Paris airports.

Cutting Costs

Throughout this book, Bargain Alert icons highlight money-saving tips and/or great deals. Here are some additional cost-cutting strategies:

1. **Fly during the week rather than on weekends.**

   Also, you can save on airfare and dining if you **travel during the off-season,** the period from approximately October to March.

2. Try a package tour.

For many destinations, you can book airfare, hotel, ground transportation, and even some sightseeing just by making one call to a travel agent or searching the Internet, for a lot less than if you tried to put the trip together yourself. (See Chapter 5 for specific companies to call.)

3. Pack light.

You won't need a cart or a taxi to carry your load.

4. Take the cheapest way into the city from the airport.

You can save around $30 by taking a train or bus instead of a cab from Roissy– Charles-de-Gaulle, and about $15 from Orly.

5. Book your hotel room early.

Those at the best prices fill up quickly.

6. Negotiate the room price, especially in the low season.

Ask for a discount if you're a student or over 60; ask for a discount if you stay a certain number of days.

7. Reserve a room with a kitchen.

It may not seem like much of a vacation if you do your own cooking and dish-washing, but you can save a lot of money by not eating in restaurants three times a day. Even if you only make breakfast and pack an occasional bag lunch, you may have a little extra cash for those souvenirs and gifts for your family and friends back home. And you won't need to fret about a hefty room service bill.

8. Stay at a hotel that doesn't insist you take breakfast.

Breakfast can add another $5 a day to your bill. Make sure you aren't being charged for it. Instead, buy a croissant or a *pain au chocolat* (bread filled with chocolate) from a *boulangerie* (bread bakery) for about $2.

9. Make lunch your main meal.

Many restaurants offer great deals on a fixed-price (*prix fixe*) lunch. After two or three courses at midday, you won't want a big dinner.

10. Try the ethnic neighborhoods.

You can get terrific Chinese food in the 13e arrondissement between the place d'Italie and the Porte de Choisy; and the 10e, 18e and 20e have North African, Turkish, Vietnamese and Thai. Couscous is on the menu at many restaurants and is usually an inexpensive offering.

11. Remember that the plat du jour is usually the cheapest main dish at a budget restaurant.

12. Remember that wine is cheaper than soda.

Also, some mineral waters are less expensive than others. Ask for tap water (*une carafe d'eau*), which is free.

13. Know the tipping rules.

Service is usually included at restaurants; don't double-tip by mistake.

14. Have drinks or coffee at the bar.

You pay twice as much when you're seated at a table.

15. Use the Métro or else walk.

Buy a *carnet* of 10 Métro tickets at a time— a single ticket costs $1.35, while a carnet ticket is 85¢. Better yet, if you know you're going to be in Paris from one to five consecutive days, buy a **Paris Visite pass,** good for unlimited subway and bus travel.

16. If you plan to visit two or three museums a day, buy the Carte Musées et Monuments (Museum and Monuments) Pass.

The pass costs 80F ($11.45) for one day, 160F ($22.90) for three days, and 240F ($34.30) for five days.

17. Take advantage of the reduced admission fee at museums.

The reduced price usually applies after 3 p.m. and all day Sunday.

18. For discounts on fashion, try the rue St-Placide in the 6e arrondissement.

Look for stylish inexpensive clothes at Monoprix or Prisunic located all over the city.

19. Buy half-price theater and other performance tickets.

You can find them at one of the kiosks by the Madeleine, on the lower level of the Châtelet– Les Halles Métro, or at the Gare Montparnasse.

20. At clubs, avoid weekends if you want to save money.

Also, you can save money by sitting at the bar instead of at a table. Some clubs are cheaper than others, and some are cheaper during the week.

Finally, in general, **always ask for discount rates.** Membership in AAA, frequent flyer plans, trade unions, AARP, or other groups may qualify you for savings on car rentals, plane tickets, hotel rooms, even meals. Ask about everything; you may be pleasantly surprised.

Chapter 4

Tips for Travelers with Special Interests or Needs

*B*e it the food, the history, the breathtaking art and architecture, or that inimitable French joy of living (*joie de vivre*), France ranks among the most visited of all tourist destinations, and more resources than ever make it available — and enjoyable — to all. How-to guides, tour companies for disabled travelers, and English-speaking baby sitters are only some of the ways that travelers with special needs are making the most of Paris these days. In this chapter, I tell you about those and others.

Taking the Family Along

Don't let anyone talk you out of taking your kids to Paris. The City of Lights is full of attractions worthy of your children's attention, and they only benefit from the experience — probably longer than you do! Parks and playgrounds abound, as well as kid-specific sights and museums, along with interesting boat rides and bike tours. Paris is also safer than most big American cities.

If you plan your trip well in advance, your kids may get a kick out of learning the language from one of the many French–language videotapes on the market. Books like Ludwig Bemelmans's *Madeline* series, Albert Lamorisse's *The Red Balloon,* and Kay Thompson's *Eloise in Paris* are great for kids under 8 years of age. You can order them from the Forum Français, in Wellesley, MA (☎ **781-239-0658**; Fax: 781-237-9083, Internet: www.forumfrancais.com), or the Librairie Francaise, New York, NY

(☎ **212-581-8810;** Fax: 212-265-1094). Older teens may appreciate Ernest Hemingway's *A Moveable Feast,* Victor Hugo's *Les Miserables,* and Rose Tremain's *The Way I Found Her.*

Preview some of the museums that you want to visit (see the sidebar "Ten Web sites to browse with your children" later in this chapter) by checking out their Internet sites. Children under 18 years old are admitted free to France's national museums (though not necessarily to Paris's city museums). If you stay long enough, consider a day trip to Disneyland Paris, easily accessible by public transportation. (See Chapter 21 for more information.)

If your children are under 12 years old and you are traveling by rail through France, check out the **Carte Enfant Plus.** Available at any SNCF (French National Railroads) station, it offers a 50-percent discount for the child and up to four adult travel companions. The card costs 330F ($47.15) and is good for a month, but only a limited number of seats are available, and the discounts aren't offered for periods of peak travel or on holidays. Reserve in advance.

Finally, a word of advice: Although the French people love kids and welcome them just about everywhere, they do expect them to be well-mannered. Proper behavior is expected everywhere, especially in restaurants and museums. French children are taught at an early age to behave appropriately in these settings, and French adults expect the same from your kids.

Bringing along baby

You can arrange ahead of time for such necessities as a crib, bottle warmer, and, if you're driving, a car seat (small children are prohibited from riding in the front seat). Find out if the place you're staying stocks baby food; if not, take some with you for your first day and then plan to buy some. Plenty of choices are available from Nestlé to Naturalia.

Transportation in Paris isn't as stroller friendly as in the United States. Be prepared to lift your child out of the stroller to board buses and climb up and down stairs and/or walk long distances in some Métro stations. The upside to all of this is that you and your child can stroll in some of the world's prettiest parks and gardens.

Locating some helpful resources

If you need a baby sitter, consider one of the following agencies that employ English-speaking caregivers. **Ababa,** 8 av. du Maine, 15e (☎ **01-45-49-46-46**), **Allo Maman Poule?,** 7 villa Murat, 16e (☎ **01-45-20-96-96**), or **Kid Services,** 17 rue Molière, 9e (☎ **01-42-61-90-00**). Specify when calling that you need a sitter who speaks English.

Ten Web sites to browse with your children

Checking out some of the following Web sites with your children ahead of time is a wonderful way to introduce them to the sites they will find in Paris. For more information about each of these attractions, refer to the chapters given below.

Cité des Sciences et de l'Industrie (see Chapter 17) `www.cite-sciences.fr`

La Villette (see Chapter 17) `www.la-villette.fr`

Musée d'Orsay (see Chapter 16) `www.musee-orsay.fr`

Palais de la Découverte (see Chapter 17) `www.palais-decouverte.fr`

Musée de Louvre (see Chapter 16) `www.louvre.fr`

Centre Georges Pompidou (see Chapter 16) `www.centrepompidou.fr`

Disneyland Paris (see Chapter 21) `www.disneylandparis.com`

Les Catacombes (see Chapter 17) `www.multimania.com/houze`

Eiffel Tower (see Chapter 16) `www.tour-eiffel.fr`

Parc Zoologique de Paris (see Chapter 17) `www.mnhn.fr`

The books *Family Travel* (Lanier Publishing International) and *How to Take Great Trips with Your Kids* (The Harvard Common Press) are full of good, general advice that can apply to travel anywhere. Another reliable tome with a worldwide focus is *Adventuring with Children* (Foghorn Press).

You can also check out *Family Travel Times,* published six times a year by Travel with Your Children, 40 Fifth Ave., 7th floor, New York, NY 10011 (☎ **888-822-4FTT** or 212-477-5524; Internet: `www.familytraveltimes.com`). It includes a weekly call-in service for subscribers. Subscriptions are $39 a year. A free publication list and a sample issue are available on request.

Searching Out Bargains for Seniors

While in Paris, don't be shy about asking for senior discounts, and always carry a form of identification that shows your date of birth. Also, mention that you're a senior citizen when you first make your travel reservations. People over the age of 60 qualify for reduced admission to theaters, museums, and other attractions, as well as other travel bargains like the **Carte Senior,** which entitles holders to an unlimited number of train rides and reductions of 20 to 50 percent on train trips (except during holidays and periods of peak travel). The Carte Senior also allows some discounts on entrance to museums and historic sites. It's valid for one year, costs 285F ($40.70), and you can buy it at any SNCF station. Be prepared to show an ID or a passport as proof of age when you buy the card.

If you're over 50 and not already a member, join the **American Association of Retired Persons** (AARP), 601 E St. NW, Washington, DC 20049 (☎ 800- 424-3410; Internet: www.aarp.org) for discounts on hotels, airfares, and car rentals. As a member, you're eligible for a wide range of special benefits, including *Modern Maturity* magazine and a monthly newsletter.

You get discounts on hotel and auto rentals, as well as a magazine that's partly devoted to travel tips, if you join the nonprofit **National Council of Senior Citizens,** 8403 Colesville Rd., Suite 1200, Silver Spring, MD 20910 (☎ 301-578-8800; Internet: www.ncscinc.org). Annual dues are $13 per person or couple.

Members of **Mature Outlook,** P.O. Box 9390, Des Moines, IA 50306 (☎ 800-265-3675), receive discounts on hotels and a bimonthly magazine. Annual membership is $19.99, which includes discounts and coupons for discounted Sears merchandise.

Available by subscription ($30 a year), *The Mature Traveler,* a monthly newsletter on senior citizen travel, is a valuable resource. A free sample can be had by sending a postcard with your name and address to GEM Publishing Group, Box 50400, Reno, NV 89513 or by e-mailing your information to maturetrav@aol.com. GEM also publishes *The Book of Deals,* which lists more than 1,000 senior discounts on airlines, lodging, tours, and attractions around the country; you can purchase it for $9.95 by calling ☎ 800-460-6676. *101 Tips for the Mature Traveler* is another useful publication and is available from **Grand Circle Travel,** 347 Congress St., Suite 3A, Boston, MA 02210 (☎ 800-221-2610; Internet: www.gct.com).

Hundreds of travel agencies currently specialize in senior travel, one of which is Grand Circle. However, many of the vacations are of the tour-bus variety, which may cramp the style of an independent senior. One bonus of these tour-bus packages is that free trips are often thrown in for organizers of groups of 20 or more. Obtain travel information from **SAGA International Holidays,** 222 Berkeley St., Boston, MA 02116 (☎ 800-343-0273), which offers inclusive tours and cruises for those 50 and older.

Check at newsstands for the quarterly magazine *Travel 50 & Beyond,* and at bookstores for The *50+ Traveler's Guidebook* (St. Martin's Press), *The Seasoned Traveler* (Country Roads Press), or *Unbelievably Good Deals and Great Adventures That You Absolutely Can't Get Unless You're Over 50* (Contemporary Books).

Accessing Paris: Advice for Travelers with Disabilities

Unfortunately, the features that make Paris so beautiful — uneven cobblestoned streets, quaint buildings with high doorsills from the Middle Ages, and sidewalks in some areas narrower than a wagon — also make it a nightmare if you use a walker or wheelchair. According to French law, newer hotels with three stars or more are required to have at least one wheelchair–accessible guest room. Unfortunately, most of the city's older, budget hotels, which are exempt from the law, occupy buildings with winding staircases, or elevators smaller than phone booths, and are generally not good choices for handicapped travelers.

And, as it is for people with strollers, Paris's public transportation system isn't the most accessible to folks with mobility problems. Few Métro stations have elevators, and most feature long tunnels, some with wheelchair–unfriendly moving sidewalks, and staircases. Escalators often lead to a flight of stairs, and many times when you climb up a flight of stairs, you're faced with another set of stairs leading down. Wheelchair lifts are currently not standard equipment on city buses, nor do they "kneel" closer to the curb to make the first step lower.

But don't let these inconveniences change your mind about visiting Paris.

Before your trip to Paris, contact the **French Government Tourist Office** for the publication (with an English glossary) *Touristes Quand Même*. It provides an overview of facilities for the disabled in the French transportation system and at monuments and museums in Paris and the provinces.

You can also get a list of hotels in France that meet the needs of disabled travelers by writing to **L'Association des Paralysés de France,** 22, rue de Père Guérion, 75013 Paris (☎ 08-00-85-49-76).

You can contact the **Groupement pour l'Insertion des Personnes Handicapées Physiques** (Help for the Physically Handicapped), Paris Office, 98 rue de la Porte Jaune 92210 St-Cloud (☎ 01-41-83-15-15) and **Les Compagnons du Voyage** of the **RATP** (Paris public transportation) (☎ 01-45-83-67-77; Internet: www.ratp.fr/voy_q_eng/f_travel_eng.htm) for help in planning itineraries using public transportation.

The newly built line 14 of the Métro is wheelchair accessible, as well as the stations Nanterre-Université, Vincennes, Noisiel, Saint-Maur-Créteil, Torcy, Auber, Cité-Universitaire, Saint-Germain-en-Laye, Charles-de-Gaulle–Étoile, Nanterre-Ville, and several others. Bus 91, which links the Bastille with Montparnasse, is wheelchair accessible, as are new buses on order. Some high-speed and inter-city trains are also equipped for wheelchair access, and a special space is available in first class (at the price of a second-class ticket) for wheelchairs, though you must reserve well in advance.

A good English language guide for disabled travelers is *Access in Paris*, which you can obtain by calling ☎ **020-1250 3222** or writing to **RADAR**, Unit 12, City Forum, 250 City Road, London EC1V 8AF. It costs £13.95 (approximately $9.50).

More options and resources for disabled travelers are available than ever before. Check out *A World of Options*, a 658-page book of resources for disabled travelers, which covers everything from biking trips to scuba outfitters around the world. The book costs $35 and can be ordered from **Mobility International USA,** P.O. Box 10767, Eugene, OR, 97440 (☎ **541-343-1284,** voice and TYY; Internet: www.miusa.org). Another place to try is **Access-Able Travel Source** (Internet: www. access-able.com), a comprehensive database of travel agents who specialize in disabled travel, and a clearinghouse for information about accessible destinations around the world.

Travelers with disabilities may also want to consider joining a tour that caters specifically to them. One of the best operators is **Flying Wheels Travel,** P.O. Box 382, Owatonna, MN 55060 (☎ **800-535-6790;** Fax: 507-451-1685). They offer various escorted tours and cruises, as well as private tours in minivans with lifts. Another good company is **FEDCAP Rehabilitation Services,** 211 W. 14th St., New York, NY 10011. Call ☎ **212-727-4200** or fax them at 212-727-4373 for information about membership and summer tours.

Vision-impaired travelers can contact the **American Foundation for the Blind,** 11 Penn Plaza, Suite 300, New York, NY 10001 (☎ **800-232-5463**), for information on traveling with seeing-eye dogs.

Living the High Life: Tips for Gay and Lesbian Travelers

They don't call it 'Gay Paris' for nothing — Oscar Wilde and James Baldwin lived here, and Gertrude Stein settled here with Alice B. Toklas. Same-sex couples are treated with polite indifference from hotel clerks to servers. France is one of the world's most tolerant countries toward gays and lesbians, and has no laws that discriminate against them. Technically, sexual relations are legal for consenting partners aged 16 years old and over. However, one doesn't come of legal age in France until 18 years of age.

Paris's gay center is the Marais, which stretches from the Hôtel de Ville to the place de la Bastille, The biggest concentration of gay bookstores, cafés, bars, and clothing boutiques is here, as well as the best source of information on Parisian gay and lesbian life — the **Centre Gai et Lesbien,** 3 rue Keller, 11e (☎ 01-43-57-21-47; Métro: Bastille). The center is a source of information, and staff coordinate the activities and meetings of gay people around the world. The center is open daily 2 to 8 p.m.

Another helpful source is **La Maison des Femmes,** 163 rue Charenton, 12e (☎ 01-43-43-41-13; Métro: Charonne), which has a café and a feminist library for lesbians and bisexual women. It holds meetings on everything from sexism to working rights and sponsors informal dinners and get-togethers. Call Monday, Wednesday, or Friday from 3 to 8 p.m. for more information.

Gay magazines that focus mainly on cultural events include *Illico* (free in gay bars, about 12F/$1.70 at newsstands) and *e.m@le* (available free at bars and bookstores). *Lesbia* is available for women. You can find these and others at Paris's largest and best-stocked gay bookstore, **Les Mots à la Bouche,** 6 rue Ste-Croix-la-Bretonnerie, 4e (☎ 01-42-78-88-30; Métro: Hôtel-de-Ville). Open Monday to Saturday 11 a.m. to 11 p.m., Sunday 3 to 8 p.m., the store carries both French- and English-language publications.

For advice on HIV issues, call **F.A.C.T.S.** (☎ 01-44-93-16-69) Monday, Wednesday, and Friday 6 to 10 p.m. The acronym stands for Free Aids Counseling Treatment and Support, and the English-speaking staff provides counseling, information, and doctor referrals.

Part II
Ironing Out the Details

The 5th Wave   By Rich Tennant

"And how shall I book your flight to Paris— First Class, Coach, or Medieval?"

In this part . . .

Wondering how to get to Paris and where to stay once you're there? Then look no further than these chapters. Chapter 5 helps you get to your city on your own or using a travel agent and discusses the pros and cons of package tours. Chapter 6 breaks down the most central Paris neighborhoods where you may want to stay and lets you know just what kind of room you get for your money. In Chapter 7, you discover how to get the best room at the best rate, how to surf the Web for good hotel deals and find out where to turn if you arrive without a reservation. Located in Chapter 8 are descriptions and rates for my 40 favorite hotels — cross-indexed by price and location; and in Chapter 9, you get some advice about those last-minute details that can frustrate even the most frequent flyers.

Chapter 5

Getting to Paris

• •

• •

*P*lanning a trip abroad used to be a science so exact that only travel agents, with their numerous contacts and extensive experience, could get you fantastic trips and low prices. These days, the Internet — with its online travel agents, airline, lodging, and car rental Web sites, along with a myriad of information about your destination — has drastically changed travel planning. Still, don't negate entirely the idea of the travel agent — there *are* times that an agent will be better for handling your arrangements than you will be. That's why you need to decide what kind of travel best suits you — are you an independent traveler, or do you prefer the comfort of a tour group where everything is planned for you? In this chapter, I show you how to get to Paris simply and easily — whether you do it yourself or have someone do it for you.

Using a Travel Agent

A travel agent can help you find a bargain airfare, hotel, or rental car, but these days many people are choosing to forego this route entirely in favor of acting as their own agents by using the Web. If you have a complicated itinerary with multiple stops and not much time to plan, a travel agent may be your best bet. Also, a good travel agent knows how to balance price with value. Travel agents can tell you how much time you should budget for a destination, find a cheap direct flight, get you a better hotel room for the same amount of money you would have spent otherwise, and even give restaurant and sightseeing recommendations.

To make sure you get the most out of your travel agent, do your homework. Read about your destination and pick out some accommodations and attractions that you think you'd like. Visit travel-planning Web sites like Expedia and Travelocity.com for the latest airfares and special hotel promotions. Does your travel agent know about them? Let him or her know that you've got a good feel for what's out there and what it costs, and ask for further deals and discounts. Your travel agent still has access to more resources than even the most complete Web travel site (though the Web is quickly catching up) and should be able to get you a better price than you could get on your own. An agent can also issue your tickets and vouchers right on the spot, and if he or she can't get you into the hotel of your choice, can recommend a good alternative.

Remember, however, that travel agents work on commission. You don't pay it; the airlines, hotels, resorts, and tour companies do. Because of this payment, some travelers have turned to the Web to avoid agents who push vacations designed to net them the highest commission. If you have plenty of time — and it does take some time — go ahead and explore your Web options. I provide some helpful travel sites (See the section "Who flies there . . ." later in this chapter) to get you on your way.

Understanding Package and Escorted Tours

What kind of traveler are you? Do you like listening to a tour guide tell you about a city's important sights, or would you rather discover those sights and lesser known attractions on your own? Do you like avoiding the stress of getting to unfamiliar places, or do you prefer to make an adventure of finding your way in a foreign destination? Is meeting people one of your goals, or do you shrink at the idea of sharing so much time with strangers? How you answer these questions will let you know whether you'd enjoy an escorted tour.

The most inclusive kind of travel, an *escorted tour* spells out nearly everything in advance: your flights, your hotel, your meals, your sight-seeing itineraries, and your costs. It's the least independent way to travel, but some travelers find the escorted tour to be liberating — no hassles with public transportation, no deciphering maps, and the comfort of knowing what you're getting.

Others fervently despise escorted group tours, feeling that they're being herded from one sight to the next, missing the element of surprise and individuality that independent travel affords.

Package tours are a happy medium between hooking up with a group and going it alone, and they're enormously popular because they save you a ton of money. In many cases, a package tour bundles the price of airfare, hotel, and transportation to and from the airport into a "package" that you buy, and the good news is that the package often costs less than the hotel alone would have, if you had booked each item separately. That's because packages are sold in bulk to tour operators, who resell them to the public at a cost that drastically undercuts standard rates.

Many travelers confuse the package tour with the escorted tour. On an escorted tour, every detail of your trip is prearranged, from the flight to the hotels, meals, sightseeing, and transportation. Package tours, on the other hand, bundle various elements of the trip — perhaps your flight and hotel, or your flight and a rental car, for example. But once you arrive at your destination, your time is your own.

So what's the catch? Packages vary widely. Some offer a better class of hotels than others. Some offer the same hotels for lower prices. Some offer flights on scheduled airlines, while others book charters. In some packages, your choice of accommodations and travel days may be limited. Some packages let you choose between escorted vacations and independent vacations; others allow you to add on just a few excursions or escorted day trips (also at lower prices than you can locate on your own) without booking an entirely escorted tour. Each destination usually has one or two packagers that are cheaper than the rest because they buy in even greater bulk. If you spend the time to shop around, you'll save in the long run.

The best place to start your search is the travel section of your local Sunday newspaper. Also check the ads in the back of national travel magazines like *Arthur Frommer's Budget Travel, Travel & Leisure, National Geographic Traveler,* and *Condé Nast Traveler.* **Liberty Travel** (☎ 888-271-1584 to find a travel agent near you; www.libertytravel.com), one of the biggest packagers in the Northeast, often runs a full-page ad in the Sunday papers. You won't get much in the way of service, but you will get a good deal. **American Express Vacations** (☎ 800-241-1700; www.leisureweb.com) is another option. They're pros at bundling flights on big-name carriers with accommodations in mid-priced hotels.

Another good resource is the airlines themselves, which often package their flights with accommodations. (See "Who flies there . . ." later in this chapter for airline Web addresses and phone numbers.)

If money is most certainly an object, it's hard to beat the deals offered by **New Frontiers,** 12 East 33rd St., New York, NY 10016 (☎ 800-366-6387 in the United States or 212-779-0600; Fax: 212-770-1007; another branch is at 5757 West Century Blvd., Suite 650, Los Angeles, CA 90045 (☎ 800-677-0720 in the U.S. or 310-670-7318; Fax: 310-670-7707). New Frontiers has its own airline, Corsair (one of the few that fly direct from the United States into Orly Airport, eight miles south of Paris), and a recent roundtrip flight bought five days in advance in the middle of summer cost just $498 before tax. But there's always a catch: The plane was older, with small, uncomfortable seats; meals were small and of poor quality; and the flight was jam-packed.

The French Experience, 370 Lexington Ave., Suite 812, New York, NY 10017 (☎ **212-986-3800**), offers several fly–drive programs through different regions of France (the quoted price includes air fare and a rental car). You can specify the type and price level of hotels you want. The agency arranges the car rental in advance, and the rest is up to you. Some staff can seem unfriendly, but persevere for good deals.

American Express Vacations, P.O. Box 1525, Fort Lauderdale, FL 33302 (☎ **800-241-1700**), is perhaps the most instantly recognizable tour operator in the world. Its offerings in Paris and the rest of Europe are probably more comprehensive than those of any other company, and include package tours as well as independent stays.

Making Your Own Arrangements

So you want to plan the trip on your own? This section tells you all you need to know to research and book the perfect flight.

Who flies there from the U.S. and Canada

Web sites and phone numbers for the major airlines serving Paris are in the list that follows. These sites offer schedules, flight booking, and package tours; most have Web pages where you can sign up for e-mail alerts that list weekend deals and other late-breaking bargains.

Air Canada (☎ 800-630-3299; www.aircanada.ca) flies from Halifax, Montreal, Toronto, and Vancouver.

Air France (☎ 800-237-2747; www.airfrance.com) flies from Atlanta, Boston, Chicago, Cincinnati, Houston, Los Angeles, Miami, New York City, Philadelphia, and Washington, D.C.

American Airlines (☎ 800-433-7300; www.aa.com) flies from Boston, Chicago, Dallas, Los Angeles, New York City, and Miami.

British Airways (☎ 800-247-9297; www.british-airways.com) flies from Atlanta, Baltimore, Boston, Charlotte, Chicago, Cincinnati, Detroit, Houston, Los Angeles, Miami, Orlando, Philadelphia, Phoenix, Newark, New York, San Diego, San Francisco, Tampa, and Washington, D.C.

Continental Airlines (☎ 800-525-0280; www.continental.com) flies from Houston and Newark.

Delta Air Lines (☎ 800-221-1212; www.delta.com) flies from Atlanta, Cincinnati, and New York and shares flights with Air France from Los Angeles, Philadelphia, and San Francisco.

Iceland Air (☎ 800-223-5500; www.icelandair.com) flies from Baltimore, Boston, Minneapolis, and New York.

Northwest/KLM (☎800-225-2525; www.nwa.com) flies from Detroit, Memphis, and Minneapolis.

TWA (☎ 800-221-2000; www.twa.com) flies from New York City and St. Louis.

United Airlines (☎ 800-241-6522; www.united.com) flies from Chicago, Los Angeles, San Francisco, and Washington, D.C.

USAirways (☎ 800-428-4322; www.usairways.com) flies from Charlotte, Philadelphia, and Pittsburgh.

Who flies there from the United Kingdom

These airlines serve Paris from the United Kingdom:

Air France (☎ 0845-0845-111; www.airfrance.com) flies from London and Manchester.

British Airways (☎ 0845-773-3377; www.britishairways.com) flies from Edinburgh, Glasgow, London, and Manchester.

British Midland (☎ 0870-6070-555; www.britishmidland.com) flies from Leeds, London, and Manchester.

Who flies there from Australia and New Zealand

These airlines fly to Paris form Australia and New Zealand:

Qantas (☎ 13-13-13 anywhere in Australia; www.qantas.com) flies from Sydney.

AOM (☎ 61-92-23-44-44; www.flyaom.com) flies from Sydney.

Tips for getting the best airfare

Passengers within the same cabin on an airplane rarely pay the same fare. Rather, they pay what the market will bear. As a leisure traveler, you should never, *ever* pay full fare. The top price is for business travelers who need fares with unrestricted flexibility. They buy their tickets a few days or a few hours in advance, need to be able to change itineraries at the drop of a hat, and want to be back home for the weekend. Flying unrestricted coach class from New York to Paris on a major airline can cost more than $1,500 during the summer high season. In the middle of winter, unrestricted fares can go for $1,200.

Most vacation travelers can get a great fare by buying a ticket with restrictions. Book your tickets at least 14 days in advance, travel Tuesday through Thursday, and stay over one Saturday night, and you can nab the airline's lowest available fare, typically about $650 in summer, $400 in winter, a huge savings over the full unrestricted fare.

Periodically, airlines lower prices on their most popular routes. Check your newspaper for advertised discounts, check the Web, or call the airlines directly and ask if any *promotional rates* or special fares are available. You almost never see a sale during the peak summer vacation months of July and August, or during the Thanksgiving or Christmas seasons. Note, however, that the lowest-priced fares are often nonrefundable, require advance purchase of one to three weeks and a certain length of stay, and carry penalties for changing dates of travel.

Check airfares from secondary or alternative airports. If you live in a city that's close to more than one international airport, check prices on flights going to Paris from all of them. For example, travelers living in the Philadelphia area should not only check out prices from Philadelphia International, but from Newark and Baltimore–Washington International, as well. You may find lower prices or special promotions not offered from the airport you regularly use.

Consolidators, also known as bucket shops, are also good places to find low fares. Consolidators buy seats in bulk from the airlines and sell them back to the public at prices below even the airlines' discounted rates. Their small, boxed ads usually run in the Sunday newspaper travel section at the bottom of the page.

Before you pay, however, ask for a confirmation number from the consolidator and then call the airline itself to confirm your seat. If the airline can't confirm your reservation, DON'T BOOK with the consolidator. There are plenty of others from which to choose. Also be aware that bucket shop tickets are usually nonrefundable or carry stiff cancellation penalties, often as high as 50 percent to 75 percent of the ticket price.

Council Travel (☎ 800-2-COUNCIL; www.counciltravel.com) and **STA Travel** (☎ 800-781-4040; www.sta-travel.com) are two consolidators that cater especially to young travelers, but their low prices are available to people of all ages. **1800-AIRFARE** (☎ 800-AIR-FARE; www.1800airfare.com) also offers deep discounts on many airlines, with a four-day advance purchase. *Rebaters,* such as **Travac** (☎ 877-872-8221 or 212-630-3310), rebate part of their commissions to you.

You can also try booking a seat on a *charter flight* for savings. Discounted fares have knocked down the number available, but they can still be found. Most charter operators advertise and sell their seats through travel agents. Before deciding to take a charter flight, however, check the restrictions on the ticket. Two well-known operators that sell tickets directly to the public are **Travac** (☎ **877-872-8221** or 212-630-3310) and **Council Charters,** 205 E. 42nd St., New York, NY 10017 (☎ **212-822-2800**).

Look into *courier flights.* Couriers relinquish their luggage allowance in return for a deeply discounted ticket. Flights are often offered at the last minute, and you may have to arrange a pretrip interview to make sure you're right for the job. **Now Voyager,** open Monday through Friday from 10 a.m. to 5:30 p.m. and Saturday from noon to 4:30 p.m. (☎ **212-431-1616;** www.nowvoyagertravel.com), flies from New York. If you don't want to fly as a courier, Now Voyager also offers non-courier discounted fares.

Finally, try joining a travel club, such as **Moment's Notice** (☎ **718-234-6295;** www.moments-notice.com) or **Sears Discount Travel Club** (☎ **800-331-0257**; ask for code T5D29), to get discounted prices on air-fares. You pay an annual membership fee to get the club's hotline num-ber. Of course, you're limited to what's available, so you have to be flexible.

Booking Your Ticket Online

Online travel sites are among the most visited on the Web. The top agencies, including Expedia and Travelocity.com, offer an array of tools that are valuable even if you don't book online. You can check flight schedules, hotel availability, car rental prices, or even get paged if your flight is delayed. For each of them, the drill is basically the same: You enter your departure city, destination, and travel dates, and the site generates a list of flights, noting the lowest fare. Some sites even search for lower fares leaving from different airports or on different days.

Most online travel sites now have extensive security policies and pro-tect against credit card theft with the most advanced encryption tech-nologies. To be assured you're in secure mode when purchasing with a credit card, look for an icon (such as padlocks in Netscape or Internet Explorer) at the bottom of your Web browser. Most sites also offer toll-free numbers if you prefer to book over the phone.

If the thought of all that comparison shopping gives you a headache, then two options await you. Head for **Smarter Living**'s newsletter serv-ice (www.smarterliving.com), where every week you get a cus-tomized e-mail summarizing the discount fares available from your departure city. They track more than 15 different airlines, so it's a worthwhile time saver (but keep in mind the majority of low fares quoted are for travel available the weekend immediately following the e-mail). If you'd prefer to let the computer do the work for you, call up

Qixo.com (www.qixo.com), an airfare search engine that checks almost a dozen separate travel sites, (including the biggies like Expedia and Travelocity.com) to find the lowest fares for the dates you have in mind.

Here's the lowdown on what you can expect from the top online sites for discount travel fares:

✔ **Expedia** (www.expedia.com) lets you book flight, hotel, and rental cars on one itinerary. Its hotel search offers crisp maps to pinpoint most hotel properties, and you can click on the camera icon to see images of many rooms and facilities. Expedia also offers a service similar to that of Priceline — you name the price for a flight or a hotel room and submit your credit card information. If your price is matched, Expedia makes the reservation and charges your card. Keep in mind, however, that like many online databases, Expedia focuses on the major airlines and hotel chains, so you may not get the lowest prices out there.

✔ **Travelocity.com** (www.travelocity.com) has international flight, hotel, and rental car booking; airfare sales; deals on cruises and vacation packages; multimedia "visits" to destinations, as well as a Fare Watcher that alerts you by e-mail whenever the fare to the city of your choice changes by $25 or more. It also has a Best Fare Finder feature that, after it finds the lowest fare you've requested, searches for better deals by plugging in times that are a little earlier or a little later than those on your itinerary.

✔ **Priceline** (www.priceline.com) lets you name your price for domestic and international airline tickets. Select a route, dates, and a preferred rate; make a bid for what you're willing to pay; and guarantee with a credit card. If the hotels and airlines in Priceline's database have a fare that's lower than your bid, your credit card is automatically charged. You can't say what time you want to fly — you have to accept any flight leaving between 6 a.m. and 10 p.m. on the dates you choose, and you may have to make one stopover. No frequent flyer miles are awarded, and tickets are nonrefundable and can't be exchanged for another flight. So, if your plans change, you're out of luck. Priceline can be good for travelers who have to take off on short notice (and who are thus unable to qualify for advance purchase discounts).

✔ But be sure to shop around first — if you overbid, you are required to purchase the ticket, and Priceline pockets the difference between what it pays for a ticket and what you bid.

✔ **Cheap Tickets** (www.cheaptickets.com), **Lowestfare.com** (www. lowestfare.com), **Go4Less** (www.go4less.com), and **Last Minute Travel** (www.lastminutetravel.com) are just four sites that sometimes offer exclusive deals not available through more mainstream channels.

Chapter 6

Deciding Where to Stay

· ·

· ·

*U*pon your first visit to Paris, your expectations about what a hotel room should look like are probably based on what you see in your own country.

Rooms tend to be smaller than you would expect, even in expensive places (unless you opt for a modern chain hotel). Parisian doubles are almost never big enough to hold two queen-size beds, and the space around the bed probably won't be big enough to put more than a desk and perhaps a chest of drawers. Welcome to Europe; the story is the same in London, Rome, and most other continental capitals where buildings date back two, three, or sometimes four centuries, when dimensions — and people! — were smaller.

Parisian hotels also vary widely in their plumbing arrangements. Some units come with only a sink; others are equipped with a toilet and either a shower or tub. Private bathrooms with tubs often have hand-held shower devices — so pay attention to where you aim — shower curtains are a rarity. The trend these days is to renovate small hotels and put a small shower, toilet, and sink in each room.

As for acoustics, they tend to be unpredictable in old Parisian hotels. Your quarreling neighbors may be as annoying as street noise, so bring earplugs, or ask for a room in the rear of the hotel. Also, most budget hotels in Paris do not have air-conditioning, but fortunately, their solid stone walls tend to keep out the summer heat.

Determining the Kind of Place That's Right for You

More than 2,200 hotels are located in Paris — chain hotels, deluxe palace–like accommodations, hotels that cater to business travelers, budget hotels, and mom-and-pop establishments. To find the hotel that's right for you, you need to weigh five variables: price, location, room size, amenities, and the least tangible, but perhaps most desired of them all — a charming Parisian ambience. If the first variable, price, poses no problem, then you can have it all: great location, huge room, super perks, and sumptuous surroundings. Most travelers, however, need to make some compromises.

If you're only going to use your room as a place to sleep, you won't miss twice-daily maid and turn-down service. And you won't miss having a restaurant on the premises if you plan to eat at some of the great bistros, cafés, and other eateries recommended in Chapters 13 and 14. Perhaps your biggest priority is being within walking distance of all the main sights. Or maybe all you really want is a room that's clean, comfortable, and typically Parisian in character.

Before you commit to a hotel, however, keep in mind that Paris offers additional options for lodging.

Nothing beats living in Paris as a Parisian. In your own apartment you can conduct cooking experiments, taste fine wines that would be too expensive in a restaurant, and entertain new friends. Although the daily rate can be higher than a budget hotel, the room will be larger and you can save money on meals.

The most practical way to rent an apartment is through an agency. Most agencies require a seven-day minimum stay, and some offer discounts for longer stays. I've found that apartments vary quite a bit in size, location, and amenities. At the bottom end — about 500F ($71.40) per day — you'll find yourself in either a small, centrally located studio, or a larger studio in an arrondissement a bit far from the center of Paris. Apartments usually feature a convertible couch, an armchair or two, a bathroom with a tub or shower, and a tiny kitchenette with a refrigerator, stove, coffeemaker, and maybe a microwave oven. Dishes, cutlery, pots and pans, telephone, TV, iron, vacuum cleaner, linen, and sometimes a washing machine are also provided. Pay a bit more — 700F to 800F ($100 to $114.30) per day — and you get a more centrally located one-bedroom apartment. As with anything else, higher prices pay for larger, more luxurious spaces.

If you bring the kids with you to Paris, your best option may be the *aparthotel,* a hybrid between an apartment and a hotel where you can have the autonomy of an apartment with some of the amenities of a hotel. Like hotels, they have 24-hour reception desks, satellite TV, housekeeping services, kitchenettes, and laundry. For a family of four, a one-bedroom apartment is a good-value alternative to two double rooms in a cheap hotel. And if you use your kitchenette to prepare even half of your own meals in Paris, you can reap huge savings on your dining bill.

And don't write off *home exchanges.* The money that you save by swapping can be substantial. Contact Trading Homes (www.trading-homes.com) or check out *FUSAC* (France USA Contacts, P.O. Box 115, Cooper Station, New York, NY 100276 ☎ **212-777-5553;** Fax: 212-777-5554), a Paris-based publication that contains listings of apartments in Paris available for rental and exchange. Listings are available in the United States for $10 an issue or $90 a year.

Location, Location, Location: Where Should You Stay?

You're coming to Paris to see the city, and you need accommodations that put you in the middle of everything. Not a short Metro ride away, but smack dab in the center. Toss aside any book that recommends a well run little hotel next to the **Gare du Nord** or an adorable *pensione* near place d'Italie. They're too far away for you.

You want to be able to walk out your door and be within walking distance of at least two major sights. The river should be a short stroll away. Therefore, you absolutely need a hotel in one of the first eight districts. Period. The next chapter has already done the hard work for you, since every single one of the recommended hotels is located in arrondissements 1 through 8. Pick one of them, and you're guaranteed a decent address.

With the field narrowed to central Paris, you next have to decide which neighborhood you want. The city is made up of a patchwork of districts, and each has a distinctive style and character. Your Paris experience is determined greatly on what neighborhood you choose. (See Chapter 10 for more information.) Here's a run-through.

Right Bank

The Right Bank of the River Seine is home to the **Marais** and **Opéra** neighborhoods, as well as the **Louvre, Champs-Elysées,** and technically, the two islands that sit in the middle of the Seine, **Ile de la Cité** and **Ile St-Louis.**

You can't get any more central than the first arrondissement, unless you want to spend the night in the river. **The Louvre, Tuileries Gardens, Place de la Concorde, Palais Royal, Place Vendôme** — some of Paris's most important sights — are within a five-minute walk of each other, and haute couture shopping abounds nearby on **rue Faubourg St-Honoré.** The area is well connected by buses and the Métro, and is an ideal location in terms of convenience, though more crowded with tourists and less atmospheric than the nearby Marais. So if you plan to stay in the Louvre neighborhood, keep these things in mind:

- ✔ The Louvre and other major sights are close, and the rest of Paris is easily accessible.
- ✔ You may meet more tourists than Parisians.
- ✔ The area isn't known for its cheap hotels, so you may have to sacrifice ambience if you're on a budget.
- ✔ Restaurants tend to cater to the tourist crowd and may be more expensive, or of lesser quality, than elsewhere.

Opéra (2e)

The Opéra district, dominated by the newly renovated **Opéra Garnier,** is convenient to boulevard Haussmann's big department stores (**Galéries Lafayette, Au Printemps**), American Express, and most Right Bank sights. But the **Bourse** (Paris stock exchange) and **grands boulevards** make the area more business-oriented, and you get fewer glimpses of essential Parisian daily life (such as outdoor food markets and neighborhood shops) than in the more residential districts. So, if you plan to stay here, keep these things in mind:

- ✔ If you're a shopping addict, you're close to big department stores.
- ✔ If you like ballet and opera, you're in the right place.
- ✔ You're near the main American Express office on rue Scribe.
- ✔ You see fewer slices of French life than in residential neighborhoods.
- ✔ The area is not tranquil and pretty, nor is it an atmospheric neighborhood for strolling and hanging out.
- ✔ Cafés, restaurants, and snack bars tend to be higher-priced.

Le Marais (3e, 4e)

Now one of the hippest neighborhoods in Paris, **Le Marais** (translated as the swamp) fell into decay for years after its seventeenth-century aristocratic heyday. Paris's old Jewish neighborhood is here around the **rue des Rosiers,** and the **rue Vieille-du-Temple** is home to numerous gay bars and boutiques. Attractions include the **Musée Picasso,** stuffed with treasures that the artist's estate had to turn over to the French government in lieu of astronomical inheritance taxes, the wonderful **Pompidou Center** modern art museum, and the beautiful **place des Vosges,** a former royal residence. So if you plan to stay in Le Marais, keep these things in mind:

✔ Stores are open and the neighborhood is hopping on Sundays.

✔ Some of the best Jewish food in the city can be found here.

✔ If you're a light sleeper, Le Marais may be too loud.

✔ The narrow sidewalks and cobblestoned streets are difficult for travelers with limited mobility.

The Islands (1er, 4e)

Paris has two islands, which lay side-by-side in the middle of the Seine: Ile de la Cité and Ile St-Louis. Although the Ile de la Cité seems to have it all — **Notre-Dame, Sainte-Chapelle,** and the **Conciergerie,** where Queen Marie Antoinette was sentenced to death in 1793 — it also has all the tourists, too. The tiny Ile St-Louis, on the other hand, is a little more peaceful. Gorgeous town houses, leafy courtyards, and tiny shops that deal in antiques dealers provide atmosphere galore. The location is superb, with the **Marais** directly across the river on the Right Bank, and the **Latin Quarter** on the Left. The Islands are the costliest arrondissement in which to rent or buy an apartment in Paris. So if you plan to stay here, keep these things in mind:

✔ Every spot is picture-postcard perfect.

✔ Notre-Dame, Sainte-Chappelle, the Latin Quarter, and the Marais are within easy walking distance.

✔ Paris's best ice cream shop, **Berthillon,** is located on the Ile St-Louis.

✔ The islands get overrun with visitors — especially in spring and summer.

✔ Prices are higher at cafés, shops, and restaurants.

✔ Few hotels are located here.

Champs-Elysées (8e)

The 8e is the heart of the Right Bank, and its prime showcase is the Champs-Elysées. Here you find the fashion houses, the most elegant hotels, expensive restaurants and shops, and the most fashionably attired Parisians. A renovation has broadened sidewalks, added rows of trees and new streetlights, and overhauled legends such as the **Hotel Georges V** (now the Four Seasons Georges V). The 8e features many of the city's best, grandest, and most impressive places and attractions. It has the most splendid square in all of France (**place de la Concorde**), the grandest hotel in France (**the Crillon**), the most impressive triumphal arch (**L'Arc de Triomphe**), the world's most expensive residential street (**avenue Montaigne**), the oldest Métro station (**Franklin-D-Roosevelt**), and the most ancient monument in Paris (the 3,300-year-old **Obelisk of Luxor**). So if you plan to stay in the Champs-Elysées, keep these things in mind:

- You're never at a loss for something to do or see.

- Many stores are open on Sunday.

- Budget hotels and eateries (that aren't fast-food establishments) are scarce.

- The neighborhood can be impersonal due to the rampant commercialism.

- Some of the stores and fast food places are the same as those you find in your hometown mall.

Left Bank

The Left Bank is home to that eternal symbol of Paris, the **Eiffel Tower,** as well as to the **Latin Quarter** and **St-Germain-des-Prés** neighborhoods.

Latin Quarter (5e)

The Latin Quarter is the intellectual heart and soul of Paris. Bookstores, schools, churches, night clubs, student dives, Roman ruins, publishing houses, and expensive boutiques characterize the district. The famous learning institution, the Sorbonne is also located within the Latin Quarter. The quarter is actually called "Latin" because of the language Sorbonne students and professors once spoke together there. However, the Latin Quarter of the past is gone forever now. Changing times have brought Greek, Moroccan, and Vietnamese immigrants, among others, hawking souvlaki, couscous, and spring rolls, and owning clothing stores. Sights include the **Panthéon,** the **Jardin du Luxembourg,** and the **Musée de Cluny.** So if you plan to stay in the area, keep these things in mind:

- Students and tourists keep restaurant prices down.

- You're close to the Seine, the Jardin du Luxembourg, and the Roman ruins.

- Room size is often tighter than in other neighborhoods.

- Eateries are mediocre.

St-Germain-des-Prés (6e)

The heart of Paris publishing, and home to the famous **École des Beaux-Arts (School of Fine Arts),** St-Germain-des-Prés encompasses everything anyone can love about the Left Bank for many travelers. Strolling the boulevards of the 6e, including St-Germain, you can window shop some of the chicest designers and art galleries around — but the secret of the district lies in discovering its narrow streets and hidden squares. Nearby main attractions include the Jardin du Luxembourg, and the fabled (and you pay for it) **Café de Flore** and the **Deux Magots.** So if you plan to stay in the area, keep these things in mind:

✔ You're in the middle of the Left Bank's best cafés and shops.

✔ You're near the Jardin du Luxembourg and the Seine.

✔ Establishments of all kinds are pricier than those in the nearby Latin Quarter.

✔ Comparatively few major sightseeing attractions are at your doorstep.

Eiffel Tower and Invalides (7e)

The city's most famous symbol, the Eiffel Tower, dominates the 7e, a district of stately government buildings (including the Prime Minister's residence), traditional bourgeois shops, and some of the most magnificent mansions in Paris. Even visitors with no time to thoroughly explore the 7e take the time to at least rush to its second major attraction, the **Musée d'Orsay,** the world's premier showcase of nineteenth-century French art and culture. **Napoléon's Tomb** and the **Musée de l'Armée** are also in the 7e, as well as the **Musée Rodin,** housed where the sculptor lived until his death in 1917. Overall, the 7e makes a great base if you want to be central, but still favor peace and quiet at night. On the other hand, it can feel rather dull if you want to go out on the town, and Métro stations are far apart. So if you plan to stay here, keep these things in mind:

✔ You're near the Eiffel Tower and the Musée d'Orsay.

✔ The area is quiet at night, meaning nightlife is practically nonexistent.

✔ Métro stations are farther apart than those in other neighborhoods.

Understanding Prices: What You Get for Your Money

Prices for the hotels recommended in Chapter 8 are designated with dollar signs — the more you see, the more expensive the hotel. The number of dollar signs corresponds to the hotel's rack rates (full rate) from the cheapest double room in low season to the most expensive in high season. The most noticeable difference between hotels in the budget bracket and the most expensive hotels is better amenities and services, followed by a more luxurious décor. None of the hotels listed here is a "dump"; the places recommended are decent and reputable. Naturally, the luxury level in a 2000F room is substantially higher than in a 500F one.

Here's how the dollar-sign system works:

$ (Under $100) — The low end of the scale represents the true budget hotels. Don't expect a lot of space or extras: You won't get room service, and though you may get a TV, it may only receive French channels. You can expect a clean, private bathroom with shower or tub, and the room will offer a basic level of comfort. Low price aside, the décor can evoke true Parisian charm — though it may be slightly dated or old-fashioned.

$$ ($100–$143) — Moving up a level, the rooms are roughly the same size as those in the first category. The décor is a big step up, however, and the overall comfort is substantially higher. While there won't be a concierge, the front desk usually helps you make dinner reservations if you ask. Some creature comforts — air conditioning, satellite TV, and in-room hair dryers — can be expected. A step above budget, the loving care that hoteliers put into their properties is clearly visible here. You can find many real bargains for a reasonable price.

$$$ ($144–$215) — The middle-range hotels offer rooms that are slightly larger than those in the first two categories. The décor tends to be more luxurious, often featuring at least some antique furnishings, and more amenities (better toiletries, perhaps more English-language channels on TV). There probably won't be a restaurant, but limited room service is probably available. There also won't be a concierge, but the front desk can help you make reservations for dinner or entertainment.

$$$$ ($216–$300) — These hotels feel like luxury hotels, though not the sky's-the-limit kind. Room size is much bigger, concierges are on hand to assist you, 24-hour room service is available, and décor is much more luxurious, with antiques and quality fabrics the norm. Expect a restaurant or other in-house facilities, though probably no fitness center.

$$$$$ (over $300) — Here you get much more than a room: You get an experience. Service is impeccable, décor features quality down to the last knick-knack, and rooms are enormous compared to the typical European standard. The hotel's restaurant may be overseen by a one- or two-star Michelin chef, and the fare is often both excellent and pricey. Usually a fitness center and/or pool is available for guest use. These hotels do everything with more style than their less-expensive counterparts.

Chapter 7

Booking Your Room

● ●

In This Chapter

▶ Beating the rack rates

▶ Getting the best room at the best rate

▶ Surfing the Net for hotel deals

▶ Landing a room if you arrive without a reservation

● ●

*A*fter you decide on the type of lodging that's best for you and the neighborhood where you'd like to stay, you need to get down to the nitty-gritty of paying the least amount possible for accommodation. Paris tends to have reasonable hotel rates, and many of its hotels offer additional special deals; in this chapter, I tell you how to go about finding them. You can use the money saved on your room for dinners in quality restaurants, spectacular entertainment, and perhaps a day trip or two out of the city (see Chapter 21).

The Truth about Rack Rates (and Why You Don't Have to Pay Them)

The *rack rate* is the maximum rate that a hotel charges for a room. It's the rate you'd get if you walked in off the street and asked for a room for the night. You sometimes see the rate printed on the fire/emergency exit diagrams posted on the back of your door.

Hotels are happy to charge you the rack rate, but you don't have to pay it! At chain hotels and at other luxury hotels, you can often get a good deal by simply asking for a discounted rate. Your odds improve drastically if you're staying for more than just a few nights.

 Keep in mind, however, that bartering for a cheaper room isn't the norm in Paris budget hotels. Most establishments are small and privately owned; they post their rates in the reception area and may not be willing to negotiate. To be fair, they may not be able to afford to let rooms go for less.

Tips for Getting the Best Room at the Best Rate

In all but the smallest accommodations, the rate you pay for a room depends on many factors — chief among them being how you make your reservation. A travel agent may be able to negotiate a better price with certain hotels than you can get by yourself. (That's because often the hotel gives the agent a discount in exchange for steering his or her business toward that hotel.)

Reserving a room through the hotel's 800-number may also result in a lower rate than if you called the hotel directly. On the other hand, the central reservations number may not know about discount rates at specific locations. For example, local franchises may offer a special group rate for a wedding or family reunion, but they may neglect to tell the central booking line. Your best bet is to call both the local number and the 800-number and see which one gives you a better deal.

Room rates also change with the season, as occupancy rates rise and fall. If a hotel is close to full, it is less likely to extend discount rates; if it's close to empty, it may be willing to negotiate. Room prices are subject to change without notice, so the rates quoted in this book may be different than the actual rate you receive when you make your reservation. Be sure to mention membership in AAA, AARP, frequent-flyer programs, and any other corporate rewards programs when you make your reservation. You never know when it might be worth a few dollars off your room rate (though in truth, this usually only works at chain hotels; family-run establishments rarely have such arrangements with large organizations).

The best room in the house, please

Once you've made your reservation, asking one or two more pointed questions can go a long way toward making sure you have the best room in the house.

Always ask for a *corner room*. They're usually larger, quieter, closer to the elevator, and have more windows and light than standard rooms, and don't always cost any more. Also ask if the hotel is renovating; if it is, request a room *away from the renovation work*. Inquire, too, about the location of the restaurants, bars, and discos in the hotel — these could all be a source of irritating noise. And if you aren't happy with your room when you arrive, talk to the front desk. If they have another room, they should be happy to accommodate you, within reason.

Here's some advice to keep in mind when trying to save money on a room:

- ✔ **Ask about corporate discounts** if you'll be staying in one of the chains.

- ✔ A **travel agent** may be able to negotiate a better price at top hotels than you can get yourself. (The hotel gives the agent a discount for steering business its way.)

- ✔ Always ask if the hotel offers any **weekend specials,** which typically require you to stay two nights (either Friday or Saturday, or Saturday or Sunday). In Paris, you can find this kind of deal from September through March at almost all price levels.

- ✔ **Forfaits** (*fohr*–feh) are discounts that require you to stay a certain number of nights — perhaps a minimum of three or five. Sometimes there's something else thrown in — like a bottle of champagne — to sweeten the deal. If you're going to be in Paris for more than three days, always ask if there's a *forfait* and then pick the hotel with the best deal.

- ✔ Visit during the **summer low season** (see also Chapter 2). That's no typo. Room rates tend to be lower in July and August, which, though big tourist months, are considered low season by Paris hoteliers. November and December are also low season, while early fall is high season, with October in particular heavy on conventioneers, making it difficult to find a room.

- ✔ Don't forget about **package deals** (see Chapter 5) that include airfare, hotel, and transportation to and from the airport.

- ✔ Look on the Internet for deals (see "Surfing the Web for Hotel Deals" later in this chapter).

- ✔ If you're a risk taker, stop in at the **Office de Tourisme de Paris,** 127 av. des Champs-Elysées, 8e, during July and August or November and December — slow season for Paris hotels. At these times, hotels with unsold rooms often sell to the tourist office at reduced rates, and you can stay in a three-star hotel at a two-star price. During the summer slow season, however, you'll have to wait in a long line, and you aren't necessarily guaranteed a room. The Office de Tourisme also charges a small fee for the service (see "What to Do If You Arrive without a Reservation" later in this chapter).

Surfing the Web for Hotel Deals

Although the major travel booking sites (Travelocity.com, Expedia, Yahoo! Travel, and Cheap Tickets; see Chapter 5 for details) offer hotel booking, it can be best to use a site devoted primarily to lodging, because you may find properties that aren't listed on more general online travel agencies. **The Paris Tourist Office** (www.paris-touristoffice.com) gives detailed information on hotels and other lodging sanctioned by the Paris Convention and Visitor's Bureau and provides links to accommodation reservation centers. Some lodging sites specialize in a particular type of accommodations, such as bed and breakfasts, which you won't find on the more mainstream booking services. Others offer weekend deals on major chain properties, which cater to business travelers and have more empty rooms on weekends. Therefore, it's in your best interest to check out some of the online lodging sites, many of which offer discounts.

Hotel Discounts (www.hoteldiscounts.com), a service of the Hotel Reservations Network (HRN), offers bargain room rates at hotels in more than two dozen U.S. and international cities. HRN pre-books blocks of rooms in advance, so sometimes it has rooms — at discount rates — at hotels that are "sold out." **TravelWeb** (www.travelweb.com) lists more than 16,000 hotels worldwide, focusing on chains such as Hyatt and Hilton, and you can book almost 90 percent of these online. Find weekend deals at many leading hotel chains on TravelWeb's Click-It Weekends. **All Hotels on the Web** (www.all-hotels.com) lists tens of thousands of lodgings throughout the world, and **Hotels and Travel on the Net** (www.hotelstravel.com) offers detailed listings of hotels in more than 150 countries and links to 75,000 travel resources. (The hotels on both these sites pay a fee to list.) **Places to Stay** (www.placestostay.com) lists inns, B&Bs, resorts, hotels, and properties you may not find anywhere else.

What to Do If You Arrive without a Reservation

If you arrive in Paris without a reservation, you have two choices. You can pick up a phone and start dialing (after you've purchased a phone card at the nearest *tabac*, a café or kiosk that sells tobacco products). Or you can let the multilingual staff at one of the branches of the **Office de Tourisme de Paris** (127 av. des Champs-Elysées, 8e, ☎ 08-36-68-31-12 or 01-49-52-53-35; Fax: 01-49-52-53-00; www.paris-touristoffice.com; E-mail: info@paris-touristoffice.com; Métro: Charles-de-Gaulle–Étoile, or George V) do it for you. The office is open daily, 9 a.m. to 8 p.m. (Sunday 11 a.m. to 7 p.m., November through April). For a fee, the staff will make an accommodations reservation for you on the same day you want a room. The charge is 8F ($1.15) for hostels and *foyers* ("homes"), and beyond that depends on the French government's star ratings. This system is based on factors like room size, facilities, plumbing, and dining options, with four stars being the best rating a hotel can receive. The tourism office charges 20F ($2.90) for one-star hotels, 25F ($3.60) for two-star hotels, and 40F ($5.70) for three-star hotels. There are small information offices at the airports; their staffs will help you make a hotel reservation, but they work only with hotels that charge more than 350F ($50) a night.

In slow periods, hotels with unsold rooms often sell to the tourist office at a huge discount, providing you with a good way to stay in a three-star hotel at a two-star price. The office is very busy in summer, with lines sometimes stretching outside.

The Office de Tourisme has an auxiliary office at the Eiffel Tower (May through September only, daily 11a.m. to 6 p.m.) and at the Gare de Lyon (Monday through Saturday, 8 a.m. to 8 p.m.).

A Final Word of Advice

In Paris, as in many major world cities, hotels routinely overbook, so booking by credit card doesn't automatically hold your room if you arrive later than expected, or after 6 p.m. To protect against losing your room, be sure to call your hotel immediately if you find that you're going to arrive later than expected.

Hotels in Paris usually ask at what time you'll arrive, so always pad your expected arrival by a few hours to be safe. If you've made a reservation very far in advance, confirm within 24 hours of your expected arrival. If you're experiencing a major delay, alert the hotel as soon as you can.

Chapter 8

Paris's Best Hotels

● ●

In This Chapter

▶ Locating hotels by price

▶ Reviewing a list of Paris favorites

▶ Finding other neat places to stay

● ●

*P*aris has more than 2,200 hotels, but you find just 40 described here. The reason? You don't need an overwhelming, encyclopedic list of all the hotels, just ones that are right for you, and an equally right backup should your first choice be booked. In compiling this Top 40 list, my first step was to consider the average traveler's wish list. And for most of you, that's location. Thus, the first criterion was simple: If the hotel isn't located in the first eight arrondissements, I don't recommend it in this book. The second concern was price. The most expensive category here, $$$$$, contains hotels that cost more than 2100F ($300) a night, which is expensive by nearly anyone's standards. Only two hotels listed here fall into this category because, seriously, why waste your time? Three quarters of the hotels in this chapter rent doubles for under $150 night and still give you comfort, some nice amenities, and that frisson of Parisian character for which the city's hotels are known. And none of the hotels listed here is a dive.

Finally, I took care to represent a variety of neighborhoods and offer a nice range of styles from conservative to trendy. The aim? To make sure that everyone is accounted for, regardless of budget, taste, or travel style.

Reviews are arranged alphabetically for easy reference. Hotels that are especially good for families are designated with the kid-friendly icon. Listed immediately beneath the name of the hotel is the neighborhood of the hotel and the number of dollar signs corresponding to the hotel's rack rates, from the cheapest double room in low season to the most expensive in high season.

Hotel Index by Location

Louvre (1er)

Hôtel Agora $
Hôtel Louvre Forum $
Hôtel Louvre Richelieu $
Hôtel Meurice $$$$$
Hôtel Montpensier $
Citadines Les Halles Aparthotel $$
Citadines Louvre Aparthotel $$

Opéra (2e)

Citadines Paris Opéra Drouot
 Aparthotel $$
Hôtel Tiquetonne $
Hôtel Vivienne $

Le Marais (3e, 4e)

Castex Hôtel $
Grand Hôtel Jeanne d'Arc $
Hôtel du Vieux Saule $
Hôtel de la place des Vosges $
Hôtel Saint-Merry $$

Latin Quarter (5e)

Familia Hôtel $
Grand Hôtel de Suez $
Hôtel Claude-Bernard $$
Hôtel Esmeralda $

Hôtel Marignan $
Hotel Minerve $
Hôtel St-Jacques $
Port-Royal Hôtel $
Timhôtel Jardin des Plantes $$

St-Germain-des-Prés (6e)

L'Abbaye Saint-Germain $$$–$$$$
Grand Hôtel des Balcons $$
Hôtel de Fleurie $$$
Hôtel du Lys $
Hôtel Stanislas $

Eiffel Tower (7e)

Grand Hôtel Lévêque $
Hôtel Amélie $$
Hôtel du Champs de Mars $
Hôtel le Valadon $
Hôtel Lindbergh $
Hotel de Nevers $
Hôtel Prince $
Hôtel le Tourville $$–$$$

Champs-Elysées–Madeleine (8e)

Citadines Préstige Haussmann
 Aparthotel $$$
Four Seasons–George V $$$$$
Hôtel Alison $$

Hotel Index by Price

$

Castex Hôtel (3e)
Familia Hôtel (5e)
Grand Hôtel Jeanne d'Arc (3e)
Grand Hôtel Lévêque (7e)
Grand Hôtel de Suez (5e)
Hôtel Agora (1er)
Hôtel du Champs de Mars (7e)
Hôtel Esmeralda (5e)
Hôtel Lindbergh (7e)
Hôtel Louvre Forum (1er)
Hôtel Louvre Richelieu (1er)
Hôtel du Lys (6e)

Hôtel Marignan (5e)
Hotel Minerve (5e)
Hôtel Montpensier (1er)
Hotel de Nevers (7e)
Hôtel de la place des Vosges (4e)
Hôtel Prince (7e)
Hôtel Stanislas (6e)
Hôtel St-Jacques (5e)
Hôtel Tiquetonne (2e)
Hôtel le Valadon (7e)
Hôtel du Vieux Saule (4e)
Hôtel Vivienne (1er)
Port-Royal Hôtel (5e)

$$

Citadines Paris Opéra Drouot
  Aparthotel (1er)
Grand Hôtel des Balcons (6e)
Hôtel Alison (8e)
Hôtel Amélie (7e)
Hôtel Claude-Bernard (5e)
Hôtel Saint-Merry (4e)
Hôtel le Tourville (7e)
Citadines Les Halles Aparthotel (1er)

Citadines Louvre Aparthotel (1er)
Timhôtel Jardin des Plantes (5e)

$$$

Citadines Préstige Haussmann
  Aparthotel (8e)
Hôtel de Fleurie (6e)
L'Abbaye Saint-Germain (6e)

$$$$-$$$$$

Four Seasons Georges V (8e)
Hôtel Meurice (1er)

Paris Hotels from A to Z

Castex Hôtel

$ Le Marais (4e)

The Castex is a popular budget classic, near everything in the Marais.
Each large room has a writing table or a desk and chair; some have views
overlooking the courtyard. The staff is friendly and accommodating.
Rooms don't have televisions, but you can veg out in the TV salon.
Reserve at least a month in advance.

5 rue Castex. ☎ *01-42-72-31-52. Fax: 01-42-72-57-91. Métro: Bastille or Sully-
Morland. Rates: 240–290F ($34.30–$41.45) single; 320–360F ($45.70–$51.45) double;
410–460F ($58.60–$65.70) triple; 530F ($75.70) quad. Continental breakfast 35F ($5).
AE, DC, MC, V.*

Citadines Les Halles Aparthotel

$$ Louvre (1er)

Citadines recently bought this aparthotel which was part of the Orion
chain. Like its other properties, studios and one-bedrooms have fully
equipped kitchenettes and services include a 24-hour reception desk,
satellite TV, air-conditioning, housekeeping, baby equipment rental, and
a Laundromat.

4 rue des Innocents (100 yards from the Forum des Halles). ☎ *800-755-8266 or
212-688-9489 from the United States;* ☎ *01-40-39-26-50 in Paris. Fax: 212-688-9467.
Internet:* www.citadines.com. *Métro:Les Halles. Rates: 835–900F ($119.30–
$128.60) 2–person studio, 1260–1360F ($180–$194.30) 4–person apt. AE, MC, V.*

Citadines Louvre Aparthotel

$$ Louvre (1er)

This new aparthotel is in an upscale and pretty neighborhood and offers
several studios and apartments equipped for travelers with disabilities.
Studios and one-bedrooms have fully equipped kitchenettes, and services

include a 24-hour reception desk, satellite TV, air-conditioning, house-keeping, baby equipment rental, and a Laundromat.

8 rue de Richelieu (1 block north of the Louvre). ☎ *800-755-8266 or 212-688-9489, from the United States;* ☎ *01-55-35-28-00 in Paris. Fax: 212-688-9467. Internet:* www.apartmenthotels.com. *Métro: Palais-Royal or Pyramides. Rates: 980–1060F ($140–$151.60) 2-person studio; 1575–1700F ($225–$242.90) 4-person apt. AE, MC, V.*

Citadines Paris Opéra Drouot Aparthotel

$$ Opéra (2e)

This is the most central location of the Citadines Aparthotel chain. Fully-equipped kitchenettes are standard for each studio to duplex apartment; available services include a 24-hour reception desk, satellite TV, air-conditioning, baby equipment rental, dry cleaning, Laundromat, house-keeping, bar, and fitness center. A one-bedroom apartment here is a good alternative to renting two rooms in a cheap hotel.

18 rue Favart. ☎ *800-755-8266 or 212-688-9489, from the United States;* ☎ *01-40-05-14-00 in Paris. Fax: 01-44-50-23-50. Internet:* www.citadines.fr. *Métro: Richelieu-Drouot. Rates: 1064F ($152) 2-person studio; 1750F ($250) 4-person apt; ask about special rates for stays of seven days or more. AE, MC, V.*

Citadines Préstige Haussmann Aparthotel

$$$ Champs-Elysées (8e)

This is one of Citadines's prestige properties, which means that its studios and apartments are more expensive but also more spacious and luxurious — featuring rare wood furnishings and granite bathrooms. Services and amenities include a 24–hour reception desk, satellite TV, air-conditioning, baby equipment rental, dry cleaning, Laundromat, housekeeping, bar, and fitness center.

129 bd. Haussmann. ☎ *800-755-8266 or 212-688-9489, from the United States;* ☎ *01- 53-77-07-07 in Paris. Fax:01-45-63-46-64. Internet:* www.citadines.fr. *Métro: Miromesnil. Rates: 935–1325F ($133.60–$189.50) 2-person studio; 1465–2350F ($209.30–$335.75) 4-person apt. Ask about special rates for stays of seven days or more. AE, MC, V.*

Familia Hôtel

$ Latin Quarter (5e)

Currently in the hands of Eric and Sophie Gaucheron, Familia Hotel has many personal touches to make you feel welcome, like window boxes full of flowers, a fountain and frescoes in the lobby, restored stone walls in some rooms, and balconies with enchanting views of the Latin Quarter in others. From the fifth and sixth floors you can see Notre-Dame. Bathrooms are small but modern and tiled. All rooms have cable TV and hair dryers. Staff understand what it's like to travel with children and will try to provide kid-friendly services (such as bottle heating) and larger rooms for the weary traveler who requests ahead. An added bonus — the Jardin des Plantes is down the street.

11 rue des Écoles. ☎ *01-43-54-55-27. Fax: 01-43-29-61-77. Métro: Jussieu. Rates: 395–535F ($56.45–$76.45) single; 465–595F ($66.45–$85) double; 620–695F ($88.60–$99.30) triple; 695–750F ($99.30–$107.15) quad. Breakfast 30F ($4). AE, DC, MC, V.*

Four Seasons George V

$$$$$ Champs-Elysées (8e)

If palatial splendor is business as usual for you, then you can't do much better than the newly renovated Four Seasons George V. From the elegant light-wood-and-marble lobby opening onto an outside marble courtyard decorated with bright blue awnings and umbrellas, to the cascading displays of fresh flowers (by an American expat florist who changes the color scheme every week), to the friendly welcome of the team of concierges, you feel good about staying here. And that's *before* you reach your room, the size of which starts at 450 square feet. Separated from the public corridors by their own hallways for more peace and quiet, rooms are decorated in Louis XVI–style furniture and enjoy the latest technology, including dual phone lines, a modem line, 51-channel TV, stereo system, and VCR. You may not be able to drag your kids away from the Sony PlayStation console, a room standard. Internet access is also available via a wireless infrared keyboard — on the television. Views from the upper floors are truly remarkable, with some rooms offering a stone's throw view of the Eiffel Tower — from their bathtubs. Other amenities include a spa with its own elevator, a bar, and an inspired gourmet restaurant.

31 av. George V. ☎ *01-49-52-70-00. Fax: 01-49-52-70-10. Métro: George V. Rates: 3734–4389F ($533.45–$627) double; 7860F ($1,122.90) one-bedroom suite. AE, DC, MC, V.*

Grand Hôtel des Balcons

$$ St-Germain-des-Prés (6e)

This gracious and comfortable hotel has balconied rooms with modern light oak furnishings, bright fabrics, and new beds. Although most rooms — and their wrought-iron balconies — are small, clever use of space has allowed for large closets and full-length mirrors. Bathrooms are also small but well-designed and come equipped with a clothesline. The higher-priced doubles, triples, and quads are big and luxurious; some have double-sink bathrooms. Free tea and coffee are available in the lounge.

3 rue Casimir Delavigne. ☎ *01-46-34-78-50. Fax: 01-46-34-06-27. Internet:* www. balcons.com. *Métro: Odéon, RER: Luxembourg. Rates: 425–600F ($60.70–$85.70) single; 505–800F ($72.15 –$114.30) double; 950F ($135.70) triple, quad. Buffet breakfast 60F ($8.60), free on your birthday. AE, DC, MC, V.*

Hotels in the Heart of the Right Bank

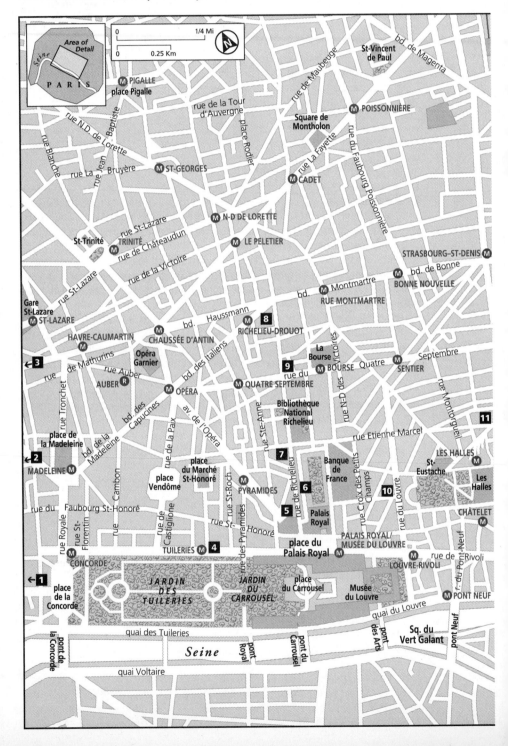

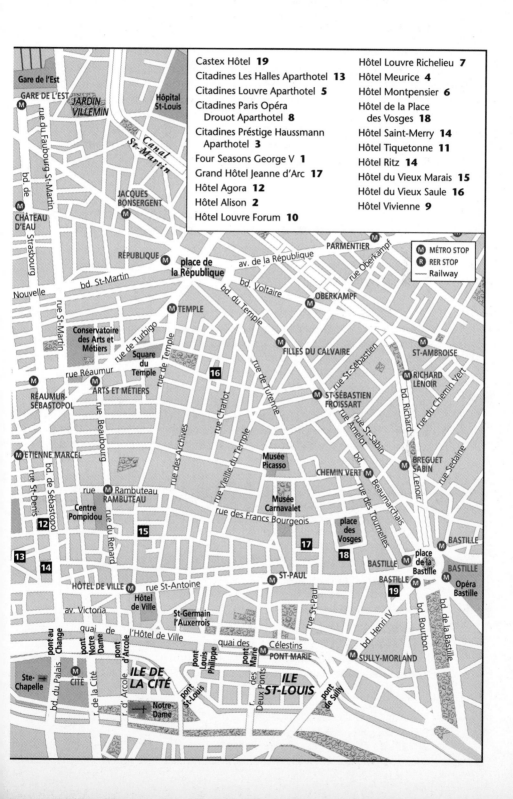

Castex Hôtel **19**
Citadines Les Halles Aparthotel **13**
Citadines Louvre Aparthotel **5**
Citadines Paris Opéra
  Drouot Aparthotel **8**
Citadines Préstige Haussmann
  Aparthotel **3**
Four Seasons George V **1**
Grand Hôtel Jeanne d'Arc **17**
Hôtel Agora **12**
Hôtel Alison **2**
Hôtel Louvre Forum **10**

Hôtel Louvre Richelieu **7**
Hôtel Meurice **4**
Hôtel Montpensier **6**
Hôtel de la Place
  des Vosges **18**
Hôtel Saint-Merry **14**
Hôtel Tiquetonne **11**
Hôtel Ritz **14**
Hôtel du Vieux Marais **15**
Hôtel du Vieux Saule **16**
Hôtel Vivienne **9**

Ⓜ MÉTRO STOP
Ⓡ RER STOP
— Railway

Grand Hôtel Jeanne d'Arc

$ Le Marais (4e)

Reserve well in advance for this great budget hotel that's just off the center of the Marais, near the Musée Picasso, the Bastille, and the Opéra Bastille. The hotel is in an eighteenth-century building, and contemporary artists have hand-painted the walls of the breakfast and sitting rooms. The decent-sized rooms have large windows, card-key access, and large bathrooms, though storage space is a bit cramped. Other room features include direct-dial telephones, satellite TV, and bedside tables. If a view is important, make sure you request one — some rooms don't have views.

3 rue de Jarente. ☎ *01-48-87-62-11. Fax: 01-48-87-37-31. Internet:* www. hotel jeannedarc.com. *Métro: St-Paul or Bastille. Rates: 320–410F ($45.70–$58.60) single; 325–500F ($46.45–$71.45) double; 550F ($78.60) triple; 620F ($88.60) quad. Breakfast 38F ($5.45). MC, V.*

Grand Hôtel Lévêque

$ Eiffel Tower (7e)

Grand Hôtel Lévêque is a large establishment on a colorful pedestrian street with a vivid marketplace full of fresh fruits, cheese, and wine shops. The lobby has a comfortable lounge area with a drink- and ice-dispenser and the daily newspaper. Rooms are a relatively good size and have been renovated with new, if not inspired, decorations, each containing satellite TVs, hair dryers, and ceiling fans. Safes are also available for a fee of 20F ($2.85). The bathrooms are small but in excellent condition. Staff members are very friendly and helpful, and if you ask, they may be able to give you a higher-priced room on the fifth floor with a balcony and partial view of the Eiffel Tower.

29 rue Cler. ☎ *01-47-05-49-15. Fax: 01-45-50-49-36. Internet:* www.interresa. ca/hotel/leveue/. *E-mail:* leveque@hotelleveque.com. *Métro: École-Militaire or Latour-Maubourg. Rates: 400F ($57.15) single or double with bathroom; 420F ($60) twin with bathroom; 580F ($82.85) triple with bathroom. Continental breakfast 40F ($5.70). AE, MC, V.*

Grand Hôtel de Suez

$ Latin Quarter (5e)

Many guests keep returning for the hotel's many good-sized, quiet rooms at a great price. Beds are firm, storage space is ample, and the modern bathrooms have hair dryers. Don't even think of opening the windows to the street side balconies — the Boulevard St-Michel is as noisy as a carnival.

31 bd. St-Michel. ☎ *01-53-10-34-00. Fax: 01-40-51-79-44. Métro: St-Michel. Rates: 395–475F ($56.45–$67.90) single; 420–450F ($60–$64.30) double; 450–535F ($64.30–$76.45) twin; 505–590F ($72.15–$84.30) triple. Continental breakfast 30F ($4.30). AE, DC, MC, V.*

Hôtel Agora

$ Louvre (1er)

This two-star hotel has a traditional French air; the rooms are furnished with antique furniture and decorated with prints of old Paris and old-fashioned wallpapers. The windows are double-glazed, which helps muffle the traffic noise of this busy area. Some rooms have balconies with views of the impressive St-Eustache church, which is a mix of Gothic and Renaissance architecture completed in 1637.

7 rue de la Cossonnerie. ☎ *01-42-33-46-02. Fax: 01-42-33-80-99. Métro: Châtelet. Rates: 365–475F ($52.15–$67.90) single; 550–705F ($78.60–$107.15) double; 720F ($102.90) triple. Breakfast 40F ($6.15). AE, MC, V.*

Hôtel Alison

$$ Madeleine (8e)

This hotel has a sleek, upscale ambience perfectly in tune with the classy neighborhood. The large, well-appointed rooms are furnished in modern style, with black furniture and light walls. Inside the room, you find plenty of storage space, a safe, trouser presses, and double-glazed windows. Hair dryers and Roger & Gallet toiletries grace gleaming, tiled bathrooms with wall-mounted showers. You can relax in the plush lobby or enjoy a drink in the hotel bar.

21 rue de Surène. ☎ *01-42-65-54-00. Fax: 01-42-65-08-17. E-mail:* hotel.alison@ wanadoo.fr. *Métro: Madeleine or Concorde. Rates: 480–880F ($68.60–$125.70) single; 690–880F ($98.60–$125.70) double; 780–880F ($111.40–$125.70) twin; 1,000F ($142.85) triple. Breakfast 45F ($6.40). AE, DC, MC, V.*

Hôtel Amélie

$$ Eiffel Tower (7e)

The pretty Hôtel Amélie has flower pots brimming with bouquets at each window. The interior is more modest, with small renovated rooms and small closets, but the white-tiled bathrooms offer hair dryers and good-quality toiletries. Despite the central location, the atmosphere is peaceful, almost serene.

5 rue Amélie. ☎ *01-45-51-74-75. Fax 01-45-56-93-55. E-mail:* resa@hotel-amelie.com. *Métro: Latour-Maubourg. Rates: 440F ($62.85) single; 550F ($78.60) double; 540F ($77.15) twin beds. Continental breakfast 40F ($5.70). AE, DC, MC, V.*

Hôtel du Champs de Mars

$ Eiffel Tower (7e)

This hotel is a little gem tucked away on a colorful street near the Eiffel Tower. Flowing curtains, fabric covered headboards, throw pillows, and cushioned high-backed seats make each room a delight in comfort.

Bathrooms are in mint condition, with hair dryers, large towels, and good lighting, and those with tubs have wall-mounted showers. A cozy breakfast room is located in the remodeled basement. Reserve at least four months in advance.

7 rue du Champs de Mars. ☎ *01-45-51-52-30. Fax: 01-45-51-64-36. Internet:* www. hotel-du-Champs-de-mars.com. *E-mail:* stg@club-internet.fr. *Métro: École-Militaire. RER: Pont de l'Alma. Rates: 425F ($60.70) single; 430F ($61.40) double, 460F ($65.70) twin beds; 550F ($78.60) triple. Continental breakfast 35F ($5). MC, V.*

Hôtel Claude-Bernard

$$ Latin Quarter (5e)

Evident from the moment you enter the lobby, the three-star Hôtel Claude-Bernard keeps very high standards. Each congenial, spacious room has tasteful wallpaper, a sleek bathroom, and often a charming piece of antique furniture, such as a writing desk. Some particularly attractive suites come with couches and armchairs. A sauna is available for guests' use at 50F ($7.15).

43 rue des Écoles. ☎ *01-43-26-32-52. Fax: 01-43-26-80-56. Internet:* www. hotelcv.com. *Métro: Maubert-Mutualité. Rates: 530–690F ($75.70–$98.60) single; 790–890F ($112.85–$127.15) double; 1,190–1,390F ($170–$198.60) triple; 890–1690F ($127.15–$241.40) suite for 1–4 persons. Continental breakfast 50F ($7.15). AE, DC, MC, V.*

Hôtel Esmeralda

$ Latin Quarter (5e)

This hotel is a favorite of many travelers, and you may have to book months in advance. The Esmeralda is a funky and ramshackle hotel with an old, winding wooden staircase and outstanding views of Notre-Dame and the Seine. Velvet coverings and antique furniture create a homey warmth that almost makes up for the disappointingly dark rear rooms. The front rooms with a view have modern bathrooms with tubs, and some are exceptionally large, making them perfect for travelers with children. The hotel's pet cats are also a hit with kids, and the location — in the center of everything — is a hit with parents accompanying little ones who tend to tire quickly.

4 rue St-Julien-le-Pauvre. ☎ *01-43-54-19-20. Fax: 01-40-51-00-68. Métro St–Michel. 19 units, 16 with bathroom (shower or tub). TEL. 180F ($25.70) single with sink, 350F ($50) single with bathroom; 450–520F ($64.30–$74.30) double with bathroom. Breakfast 40F ($5.70). Shower 10F ($1.65). No credit cards.*

Hôtel de Fleurie

$$$ St-Germain-des-Prés (6e)

This charming Left Bank hotel has all the comforts, including marble bathrooms, quality toiletries, and fresh flowers. Some rooms are furnished in a modern style; others are more classic. A computer is available for guests' use; the charge is 20F ($2.90) for 15 minutes. The staff is friendly, and the hotel is in a superb location.

32–34 rue de Grégoire-de-Tours. ☎ *01-53-73-70-00. Fax: 01-53-73-70-20. Internet:* www.hotel-de-fleurie.tm.fr. *E-mail:* bonjour@hotel-de-fleurie. tm.fr. *Métro: Odéon. 700F ($100) single; Rates: 900–1200F ($128.60–$171.45) double. Breakfast 50F ($7.15). AE, DC, MC, V.*

Hôtel de l'Abbaye Saint-Germain

$$$–$$$$ St-Germain-des-Prés (6e)

Formerly an old abbey, this hotel is a popular destination for travelers who have a taste for chic but cozy air-conditioned surroundings. The lobby has a fireplace and in summer you can have breakfast — included in the price of your room — in the pretty garden. Some of the rooms have their original oak ceiling beams, and all have nineteenth-century-style furnishings and damask upholstery. Rooftop suites have terraces.

10 rue Cassette. ☎ *01-45-44-38-11. Fax: 01-45-48-07-86. Métro: St-Sulpice. Rates: 1030–1650F ($147.15–$235.70) double; 2100–2200F ($300–$314.30) suite.*

Hôtel le Valadon

$ Eiffel Tower (7e)

This hotel is located on a quiet side street near Les Invalides. The rooms are more notable for their spaciousness than for the freshness of their furnishings, which include pink or red bedspreads, white painted mirrors, and a framed rendition of the Last Supper with, instead of the usual suspects, Marilyn Monroe at center, surrounded by James Dean, John Wayne, and Elvis. Still, rooms and bathrooms are tidily maintained and offer conveniences such as hair dryers, full-length mirrors, luggage racks, and large towels.

16 rue Valadon. ☎ *01-47-53-89-85. Fax: 01-44-18-90-56. Métro: École-Militaire. Rates: 380F ($54.28) single; 510–600F ($72.85–85.70) double; 665F ($95) triple. Continental breakfast 36F ($5.15). AE, MC, V.*

Hotels in the Heart of the Left Bank

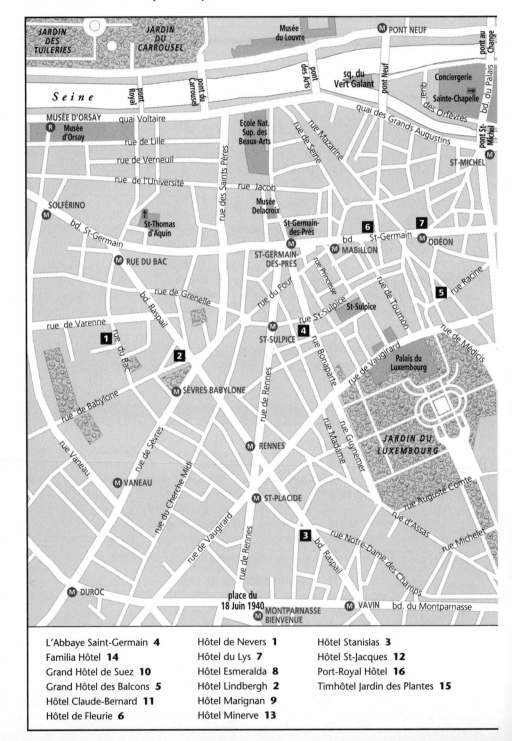

L'Abbaye Saint-Germain **4**
Familia Hôtel **14**
Grand Hôtel de Suez **10**
Grand Hôtel des Balcons **5**
Hôtel Claude-Bernard **11**
Hôtel de Fleurie **6**

Hôtel de Nevers **1**
Hôtel du Lys **7**
Hôtel Esmeralda **8**
Hôtel Lindbergh **2**
Hôtel Marignan **9**
Hôtel Minerve **13**

Hôtel Stanislas **3**
Hôtel St-Jacques **12**
Port-Royal Hôtel **16**
Timhôtel Jardin des Plantes **15**

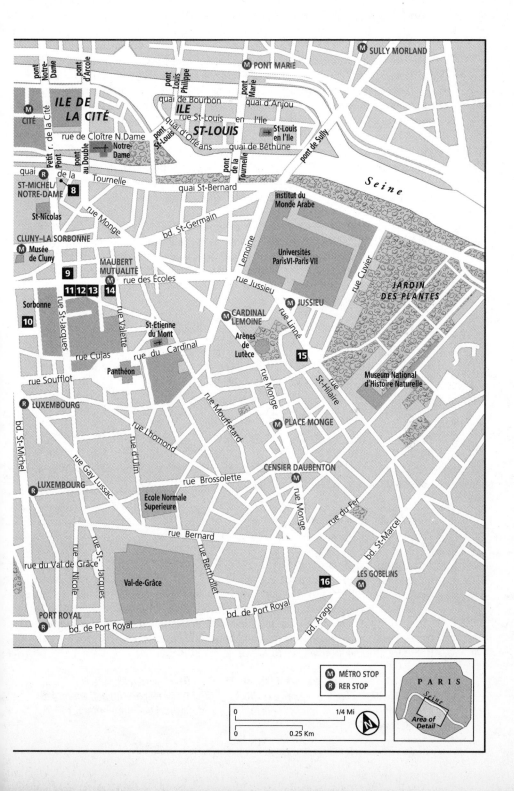

ILE DE LA CITÉ

CITÉ Ⓜ

rue de Cloître N.Dame

Petit r. de la Cité

Pont Notre-Dame

pont d'Arcole

pont Louis Philippe

quai de Bourbon

ILE ST-LOUIS

rue St-Louis en l'Ile

quai d'Anjou

pont Marie

Ⓜ PONT MARIE

Ⓜ SULLY MORLAND

quai de la Tournelle

quai St-Bernard

Seine

Notre-Dame

pont au Double

pont St-Louis

quai d'Orléans

St-Louis en l'Ile

quai de Béthune

pont de Sully

pont de la Tournelle

Ⓡ ST-MICHEL/ NOTRE-DAME

8

rue Monge

St-Nicolas

bd. St-Germain

Institut du Monde Arabe

Universités Paris VI-Paris VII

rue Cuvier

JARDIN DES PLANTES

CLUNY–LA SORBONNE

Ⓜ Musée de Cluny

MAUBERT MUTUALITÉ

9

Ⓜ

rue des Écoles

11 12 13 14

Sorbonne

10

rue St-Jacques

rue de la Valette

rue Cujas

St-Etienne du Mont

rue du Cardinal

Panthéon

rue Souflot

Ⓡ LUXEMBOURG

rue Lhomond

rue d'Ulm

bd. St-Michel

rue Gay Lussac

Ⓡ LUXEMBOURG

Ecole Normale Superieure

rue Brossolette

rue Bernard

rue du Val de Grâce

rue Nicole

rue St-Jacques

Val-de-Grâce

PORT ROYAL

Ⓡ

bd. de Port Royal

rue Berthollet

bd. de Port Royal

rue Lemoine

rue Jussieu

Ⓜ JUSSIEU

Ⓜ CARDINAL LEMOINE

rue Linné

Arènes de Lutèce

15

rue St-Hilaire

rue Mouffetard

rue Monge

Ⓜ PLACE MONGE

CENSIER DAUBENTON

Ⓜ

rue Monge

rue du Fer

bd. St-Marcel

16

LES GOBELINS

Ⓜ

bd. Arago

Museum National d'Histoire Naturelle

Ⓜ MÉTRO STOP

Ⓡ RER STOP

0   1/4 Mi

0   0.25 Km

PARIS

Seine

Area of Detail

Hôtel Lindbergh

$ St-Germain-des-Prés (7e)

This hotel clearly has two themes: aviation and fine accommodations at fair prices. The rooms range from simple and sweet, with colorful bedspreads and matching bathrooms, to refined and elegant, with classic touches such as graceful floor-length curtains, fabric headboards, and color-coordinated cushioned seats.

The owners are friendly and eager to talk about their collections of photographs that include Charles Lindbergh in his plane or standing with Blériot (the first man to fly across the English Channel), and Antoine de Saint-Exupéry, the pilot author of *Le Petite Prince.*

5 rue Chomel. ☎ *01-45-48-35-53. Fax 01-45-49-31-48. Métro: Sévres-Babylone. Rates: 490–510F ($70–$72.85) double with shower, 560F ($80) double (or twin beds) with shower and bath, 670F ($95.70) larger double accommodating 1–4 persons 670–820F ($95.70–$117.15). Continental breakfast 45F ($6.45). AE, MC, V.*

Hôtel Louvre Forum

$ Louvre (1er)

This modern hotel on a quiet street provides comfort at a reasonable price. Best of all, the hotel is steps from the Louvre. The brightly colored rooms are small, but have writing tables, lamps, and chairs. Each room has a small armoire with hanging space and shelves and a modern, tiled bathroom with a hair dryer.

25 rue du Bouloi. ☎ *01-42-36-54-19. Fax 01-42-36-66-31. Métro: Louvre-Rivoli. Rates: 425F ($60.70) single; 490–540F ($70–$77.15) double. Ask about discounts (around 20 percent) available for stays over five nights and in July and August. Continental breakfast 40F ($5.70). AE, DC, MC, V.*

Hôtel Louvre Richelieu

$ Louvre (1er)

The rooms in this hotel are a good size, and you can't beat the location — halfway between the Louvre and the Opéra. Enter through a corridor with restored stone walls; the pleasant reception area and lobby are on the second floor. The two-bed double rooms are dark, but spacious, and have high ceilings. Each room has a writing table, a small closet, and a luggage rack. The lack of an elevator here means you may want to pack light. Reserve at least two weeks in advance for summer.

51 rue de Richelieu. ☎ *01-42-97-46-20. Fax: 01-47-03-94-13. Métro: Palais-Royal–Musée du Louvre, Pyramides. Rates: 345F ($49.30) single with bathroom; 420F ($60) double with bathroom; 490F ($70) triple with bathroom. Continental breakfast 35F ($5). MC, V.*

Hôtel du Lys

$ Latin Quarter (6e)

Housed in a seventeenth-century Renaissance mansion, Hôtel du Lys has homey, yet romantic, rooms decorated in floral wallpaper and exposed-beam ceilings. Rooms feature direct-dial telephones and hair dryers, and nos. 19 and 22 have balconies. People with disabilities should note the lack of an elevator, and the narrow staircase.

23 rue Serpente. ☎ *01-43-26-97-57. Fax: 01-44-07-34-90. Métro: St-Michel or Odéon. Rates: 430–550F ($61.45–$78.60) single; 580F ($82.90) double; 700F ($100) triple. Rates include breakfast. V.*

Hôtel Marignan

$ Latin Quarter (5e)

Owners Paul and Linda Keniger welcome families, and have invested much time and energy in renovating this hotel. They have retained much of the building's architectural detailing, such as the stucco ceiling moldings, while tiling bathrooms, and adding new beds. They don't mind if you bring your own food into the dining room, and during the low season, the kitchen is available, too. You also have a washer-dryer and iron at your disposal.

13 rue du Sommerard. ☎ *01-43-54-63-81. Fax: 01-42-78-14-15. Métro: Maubert-Mutualité or St-Michel. Rates: 270–420F ($38.60–$60) double; 310–560F ($44.30–$80) triple; 360–620F ($51.45–$88.60) quad. Continental breakfast 20F ($2.90). No credit cards.*

Hôtel Meurice

$$$$$ Louvre (1er)

King George VI, Queen Victoria, and the Duke and Duchess of Windsor stayed here and you can see why the newly renovated, recently reopened Hôtel Meurice, came to be known as "the hotel of kings." The hotel is positively awe-inspiring from your first step onto its marble floored (with mosaics, no less), chandelier-lit, eighteenth-century furnished grand lobby, to each of its floors corresponding to a particular period of décor. Rooms are spacious, sound-proofed, air-conditioned, and lack nothing in the way of luxuries, from fresh flowers and antique furnishings to walk-in closets, satellite television, and computer ports. On-site restaurants include the Meurice, for a true French gastronomic experience, and the lighter-fared Winter Garden — go if only to see the splendid, newly restored art-nouveau glass roof. Amenities include an on-site health club and spa with Jacuzzi, Turkish baths, and massage; a laundry and dry cleaner's; office and translation services; and round-the-clock maid service.

228 rue Rivoli. ☎ *01-44-58-10-10. Fax: 01-44-58-10-19. E-mail:* reservations@ meuricehotel.com. *Métro: Tuileries, but if you're going to stay here, you want to arrive by limo or taxi, at the very least. Rates: 3500–15000F ($500–$642.90) double; 4700–15000F ($525–$2,142.90) suite; apartments and royal suite with private terrace available on request. Continental breakfast 175F ($25); American breakfast 250F ($35.70). AE, DC, MC, V.*

Hôtel Minerve

$ Latin Quarter (5e)

Owners Eric and Sylvie Gaucheron have extended beyond their Familia Hotel to purchase and renovate the Hotel Minerve next door. Though it's slightly more upscale than the Familia, the same welcome mat is rolled out for kids. Rooms are also larger and have wood-beamed ceilings, exposed stone walls, carved mahogany wood furnishings, and expensive wallpapers. Delightful handpainted sepia frescos can be found in several of the rooms, and ten have large balconies with a table and chairs over-looking the street.

13 rue des Ecoles. ☎ *01-43-26-26-04. Fax: 01-44-07-01-96. Métro: Cardinal Lemoine or Jussieu. Rates: 460F ($65.70) double with shower; 540–650F ($77.15–$92.85) double with shower and tub. Continental breakfast 37F ($5.30). AE, MC, V.*

Hôtel Montpensier

$ Louvre (1er)

Supposedly the former residence of Mademoiselle de Montpensier, cousin of Louis XIV, this hotel's high ceilings and windows and the stained-glass ceiling in the lounge create a sense of grandeur of which the Sun King would approve. Many rooms on the first two floors, which date from the seventeenth century, have a wonderful faded elegance, while rooms on the fifth floor (an elevator is available) have attractive slanted ceilings and good views. Most rooms are comfortably outfitted with easy chairs, ample closet space, and modern bathrooms with hair dryers — but no shower curtains in rooms with tubs.

12 rue Richelieu. ☎ *01-42-96-28-50. Fax: 01-42-86-02-70. Métro: Palais-Royal–Musée du Louvre. Rates: 500F ($71.40) double; 590F ($84.30) triple. Shower 25F ($3.60). Continental breakfast 40F ($5.70). AE, MC, V.*

Hôtel de Nevers

$ St-Germain-des-Prés (7e)

Tucked away in the St-Germain-des-Pres premier shopping area, this reno-vated seventeenth-century house provides simple rooms at reasonable prices. Enter the charming wood-beamed lobby, thick with North African rugs and amber-toned wall coverings, where friendly staff will check you in. You then are escorted up a quaint, tapestry adorned winding stair-case to a very clean room with wood bureaus and wood-framed mirrors.

Bathrooms are spotless and well maintained, if not brand new. Although you must pay in cash, you can save your credit cards for more shopping in the nearby stores.

83 rue de Bac. ☎ *01-45-44-61-30. Fax: 01-42-22-29-47. Métro: Rue du Bac. Rates: 490F ($70) double with shower; 520F ($74.30) twin beds with bath and shower; 540F ($77.15) double with bath, shower, and terrace. 100F ($14.30) for extra bed. Continental breakfast 35F ($5). MC, V for making reservations, cash or traveler's checks only for payment.*

Hôtel de la Place des Vosges

$ Le Marais (4e)

King Henri IV once kept his horses here, but you'd never know this hotel was a former stable by its plush, antique-filled lobby. Rooms and bathrooms are small but tidy and well maintained. Most beds are firm, but storage space is lacking. All rooms have TVs (suspended from the ceiling), desks, and hair dryers. The entrance to the King's Pavilion on the place des Vosges is only steps away.

12 rue de Birague. ☎ *01-42-72-60-46. Fax: 01-42-72-02-64. Métro: Bastille. Rates: 555–620F ($79.30–$88.60) double. Continental breakfast 35F ($5). MC, V.*

Hôtel Prince

$ Eiffel Tower (7e)

The Hôtel Prince has modern, soundproofed accommodations with pleasant rooms and big bathrooms in which you can warm yourself with fluffy towels. Rooms vary in size but are all pleasant, comfortable, and well kept with double-glazed windows, luggage racks, and ample closets; some have hair dryers and safes. The buffet breakfast, with croissants, fresh fruits, and cereals, is a steal at 40F ($5.70). If you're too worn out from sightseeing to stagger out the door, the hotel will arrange for a local restaurant to deliver a meal. A ground-floor room is available with facilities for travelers with disabilities.

66 av. Bosquet. ☎ *01-47-05-40-90. Fax 01-47-53-06-62. Métro: École-Militaire. Rates: 470F ($67.15) double with shower, 520F ($74.30) double with tub; 520F ($74.30) twin with shower, 625F ($89.30) twin with tub; 625F ($89.30) triple. Buffet breakfast 40F ($5.70). AE, DC, MC, V.*

Hôtel Saint-Merry

$$ Le Marais (4e)

Located next to the Church of Saint-Merri — and formerly the church's seventeenth-century presbytery — this hotel retains some of its medieval atmosphere: Beds have wood screens for headboards, and many of the rooms are dark with beamed ceilings, stone walls, and wrought-iron chandeliers and sconces. Fabrics are sumptuous; rugs are Oriental; and bathrooms are pleasantly modern, fully tiled, and come equipped with hair dryers. Higher prices are for larger rooms with views. In keeping with the medieval feeling, you won't find an elevator in the building.

78 rue de la Verrerie. ☎ *01-42-78-14-15. Fax: 01-40-29-06-82. Métro: Hôtel-de-Ville or Châtelet. Rates: 480–1800F ($68.60–$257.15) double; 1100–2050F ($157.15–$292.90) triple; 2300F ($328.60) quad; 1800–2300F ($257.15–$328.60) suite. Breakfast 55F ($7.90). AE, V.*

Hôtel Stanislas

$ Montparnasse/St-Germain-des-Prés (6e)

This family-owned hotel conveniently located between Montparnasse and St-Germain-des-Prés has some of the nicest staff in Paris, as well as a small café where you can get breakfast or a light snack until midnight. The clean rooms are in good condition and generally large. Satellite TV and double-glazed windows are nice extras for the price. The hotel doesn't have an elevator.

5 rue du Montparnasse. ☎ *01-45-48-37-05. Fax: 01-45-44-54-43. Métro: Notre-Dame-des-Champs. Rates: 330F ($47.15) double with shower, 350F ($70) double with tub. Continental breakfast 35F ($5). AE, MC, V.*

Hôtel St-Jacques

$ Latin Quarter (5e)

This hotel could serve as a set for a movie about a nineteenth-century romance. The wall and ceiling murals in the breakfast room and lounge are recent, but several rooms have original nineteenth-century ceiling murals. Most of the high ceilings have elaborate plasterwork, giving the decor an old-Paris feel that is accentuated with traditional furniture. The owners have added their own touches in the hallways, with stenciling on the walls and trompe l'oeil painting (a clever technique in which architectural elements are "added" to a room by painting them in to appear real) around the doors. Modern comforts include generally spacious rooms, an elevator, immaculate tiled bathrooms with hair dryers and toiletries, double-glazed windows, and ample closet space.

35 rue des Écoles (at rue des Carmes). ☎ *01-44-07-45-45. Fax: 01-43-25-65-50. Métro: Maubert-Mutualité. Rates: 470–630F ($67.15–$90) double with bathroom; 700F ($100) triple. Breakfast 40F ($5.70). AE, DC, MC, V.*

Hôtel Tiquetonne

$ Opéra (2e)

If a view is more important than room space, try to get one of the top rooms at this welcoming budget hotel. They boast views of the Eiffel Tower or Sacré-Coeur. Though the Tiquetonne is located just off a busy street containing body piercing establishments, fine food stores, sex shops, and artsy jewelry shops, it manages to be a haven from the outside world. (With 47 large well-maintained rooms, firm beds, and adequate storage space spread over seven floors), the hotel gets a cheerful touch in the well-lit rooms with the owner's friendly service. Each room has a table and comfortable chairs.

6 rue Tiquetonne. ☎ *01-42-36-94-58. Fax: 01-42-36-02-94. Métro: Etienne Marcel or Réamur-Sébastopol. Rates: 246F ($35.15) double with bathroom. Continental breakfast 25F ($3.60). Shower 30F ($4.30). V only.*

Hôtel du Vieux Marais

$ **Le Marais (4e)**

This hotel has undergone a total renovation and now has a sparkling elegant lobby, air-conditioned rooms, a lighted garden, new wardrobes, and tiled bathrooms with a Mexican-inspired design. Rooms are of average size. The Pompidou Center modern art museum is a two-minute walk away.

8 rue du Plâtre. ☎ *01-42-78-47-22. Fax: 01-42-78-34-32. Métro: Hôtel-de-Ville. Rates: 600–690F ($85.70–$98.60) single or double. Continental breakfast 40F ($5.70). MC, V.*

Hôtel le Tourville

$$–$$$ **Eiffel Tower (7e)**

This splendid hotel behind Les Invalides can be addictive. You get almost all the amenities you find in a considerably pricier hotel — Roger & Gallet toiletries, hair dryers, air-conditioning, chic decor with antiques — with prices that are still manageable. Rooms are decorated in pastels or ochres, with crisp white damask upholsteries, antique bureaus and lamps, and fabulously mismatched old mirrors. Four particularly great rooms come with walk-out terraces covered in vines, and junior suites come with whirlpool baths. The staff is wonderfully helpful.

16 av. de Tourville. ☎ *01-47-05-62-62. Fax: 01-47-05-43-90. Métro: École-Militaire. Rates: 890–1,090F ($127.15–$155.70) double; 1,090F ($155.70) twin; 1,990F ($284.30) junior suite. Breakfast 70F ($10). AE, DC.*

Hôtel du Vieux Saule

$ **Le Marais/Bastille (3e)**

This hotel in the north Marais not only offers air-conditioning, but a sauna, too. The cheerful small rooms have tiled bathrooms, hair dryers, safes, double-glazed windows, luggage racks, satellite TV, trouser presses, and even small irons and ironing boards. The rooms on the fifth floor tend to be bigger. Breakfast is a buffet and served in a cozy vaulted cellar.

6 rue Picardie. ☎ *01-42-72-01-14. Fax: 01-40-27-88-21. Métro: République. Rates: 590F ($84.30) double with shower or tub. Buffet breakfast 50F ($7.15). AE, DC, MC, V.*

Hôtel Vivienne

$ Louvre/Opéra (2e)

This hotel, well located between the Louvre and the Opéra, offers comfortable rooms at a good price. Rooms and bathrooms vary in size from adequate to huge, and all are in good shape. Bathrooms have hair dryers and wall-mounted showers in the tubs, and some rooms have views of the Eiffel Tower.

40 rue Vivienne. ☎ 01-42-33-13-26. Fax : 01-40-41-98-19. E-mail: paris@hotel-vivienne.com. *Métro: Bourse, Richelieu-Drouot, Grands Boulevards. Rates: ($42.90) single; 390–530F ($55.70–$75.70) double. Continental breakfast 40F ($5.70). MC, V*

Port-Royal Hôtel

$ Latin Quarter (5e)

The rates of a super-budget motel, but the look of a high-class hotel with a spacious, air-conditioned, antique-filled lobby make this a budget traveler's dream. Halls are freshly painted, the elevator is super-sized, and all the rooms are decorated with flowery pastel wallpaper. The front rooms have double-glazed windows for peace and quiet, and many rooms have decorative fireplaces. (Don't try to light them, though; they don't work.) A breakfast/TV room and a small courtyard for outside dining are located on the premises. The hotel has been run by the same family for over 60 years. Note that the hotel does not accept credit cards, but a Credit Lyonnais bank with an outdoor ATM is a few doors down.

8 bd. Port-Royal. ☎ 01-43-31-70-06. Fax: 01-43-31-33-67. Métro: Gobelins. Rates: 206–260F ($29.30–$37.15) single with sink; 260F ($37.15) double with sink, 387–477F ($55.30–$68.15) double with bathroom. Continental breakfast 27F ($3.90). No credit cards.

Timhôtel Jardin des Plantes

$$ Latin Quarter (5e)

This great two-star hotel owes its name to its location across from the fascinating park, Jardin des Plantes, which kids will absolutely love. The hotel boasts a roof terrace, sauna, a vaulted cellar/lounge area with a fireplace, and a glass-fronted sidewalk cafe adjoining the lobby. All rooms have tiled bathrooms with hair dryers. The color of the rooms on each floor comes from a flower — iris, geranium, mimosa, and others featured in the Jardin des Plantes — and each room has pretty floral decor in that color. The more expensive rooms on the fifth floor open onto a sunny terrace.

5 rue Linné. ☎ 01-47-07-06-20. Fax: 01-47-07-62-74. E-mail: jardin-des-plants@timhotel.fr. *Métro: Jussieu. Rates: 700F ($100) double; 900F ($128.60) triple. Continental breakfast 50F ($7.15). AE, DC, MC, V.*

Seeking Out the Runner-Up Choices

What if you've browsed the list of hotels, chosen the ones you feel would suit you, and everything is booked? Don't despair, the staff at one of the branches of the **Office de Tourisme de Paris** (127 av. des Champs-Elysées, 8e ☎ **08-36-68-31-12** or 01-49-52-53-35; Fax: 01-49-52-53-00; Internet: www.paris-touristoffice.com; E-mail: info@paris-touristoffice.com; Métro: Charles-de-Gaulle–Étoile or George V) can make a hotel reservation for you. Keep in mind, however, that you need to arrive in person at the office or at one of its branches. The main office is open daily 9 a.m. to 8 p.m. (Sunday 11 a.m. to 7 p.m., November through April). For a fee, the staff will make an accommodations reservation for you on the same day you want a room. (See Chapter 7.)

You can also try the following very good hotels — there just wasn't enough space to include a full listing!

Atelier Montparnasse

$$ St-Germain-des-Prés (6e)   Here you'll find art-deco inspired elegance within shouting distance of three cafés favored by 1920s artists—Le Dôme, Le Select, and La Coupole. *49 rue Vavin.* ☎ *01-46-33-60-00. Fax: 01- 40-51-04-21.*

Caron de Beaumarchais

$$ Le Marais (4e)   Nearly every detail in this hotel pays homage to Paris in its heady pre-Revolution days. *12 rue Vieille-du-Temple.* ☎ *01-42-72-34-12. Fax: 01-42-72-34-63.*

Costes

$$$$$ Louvre (1er)   Deluxe services, sumptuous décor, a fabulous restaurant and celebrity clientele make this hotel an icon of style. *239 rue St-Honoré.* ☎ *01-42-44-50-00. Fax: 01-42-44-50-01.*

Deux Iles

$$ Ile St-Louis (4e)   With only 17 rooms, this charming hotel is intimate and superbly located on the Ile St-Louis. *59 rue St-Louis-en-l'Ile.* ☎ *01-43-26-13-35. Fax: 01-43-29-60-25.*

Hyatt Regency Paris Madeleine

$$$$–$$$$$ Champs-Elysées (8e)   This hotel provides good-sized rooms with all the amenities of the Hyatt hotel chain. *24 bd. Malesherbes.* ☎ *800-223-1234 in the U.S., 01-55-27-12-34 in Paris. Fax: 01-55-27-12-10; Internet:* www.hyatt.com.

L'Astor Westin Demeure

$$$$ **Champs-Elysées (8e)** A reliable hotel with large rooms for families who want to stay near the chain-store madness of the Champs. *11 rue d'Astorg.* ☎ *800-WESTIN1 in the U.S., 01-53-05-05-05 in Paris. Fax: 01-53-05-05-30.*

Lord Byron

$$ **Champs-Elysées (8e)** Luxurious, quiet, and understated, this is one of the best-value hotels around the Champs-Elysées. *5 rue de Chateaubriand.* ☎ *01-43-59-89-98. Fax: 01-42-89-46-04.*

Paris Marriott Champs-Elysées

$$$$$ **Champs-Elysées (8e)** Chic nineteenth-century décor, a fabulous location, soundproofing, business services, and all the amenities the Marriott chain provides can be found here. *70 av. des Champs-Elysées.* ☎ *800-MARRIOT in the U.S., 01-53-93-55-00 in Paris. Fax: 01-53-93-55-01; Internet:* www.marriott.com.

Pavillon de la Reine

$$$$ **Le Marais (3e)** Each room is unique here; some even have sleeping lofts above cozy salons. *28 place des Vosges.* ☎ *800-447-7462 in the U.S., 01-40-29-19-19 in Paris. Fax 01-40-29-19-20.*

Saints-Pères

$$–$$$ **St-Germain-des-Prés (6e)** Poet Edna St. Vincent Millay enjoyed breakfasting in the flower-filled garden here; others will appreciate this hotel's proximity to Cafés Deux-Magots, Flore, and Lipp. *65 rue des St-Pères.* ☎ *01-45-44-50-00. Fax: 01-45-44-90-83.*

Chapter 9

Tying Up the Loose Ends

● ●

● ●

*S*ometimes it seems that the planning for a trip abroad lasts longer than the actual trip itself. Though this chapter can't go out and do everything for you, it *does* advise and help you organize those innumerable loose ends and last-minute tasks that can frustrate the most seasoned travelers.

Getting a Passport

The only legal form of identification recognized around the world is a valid passport. You cannot cross an international border without it (well, land borders in Europe are notoriously lax, but authorities definitely need to see it if you arrive by plane or ferry). Besides clothing, a passport is the only item you absolutely *must* have in order to travel. In the United States, you're used to your driver's license being the all-purpose ID card. Abroad, it only proves that some American state lets you drive. Getting a passport is easy, but it takes some time to complete the process.

To apply for a passport for the first time in the United States, you need to go in person to one of 13 passport offices throughout the country, or one of the many federal, state, or probate courts, or major post offices (not all accept applications; call the number listed later in the chapter to find the ones that do). You need to bring proof of citizenship, which means a certified birth certificate. You should bring along a driver's license, state or military ID, and any other identifying documents. Bring along two *identical* passport-sized photos (2 inches x 2 inches) you've had taken within the last six months. Get the photos at almost any corner photo shop, where a special camera is used to make them identical. You *cannot* use the strip photos from one of those photo vending machines.

When you get your passport photos taken, have the photo shop make up six to eight total. You need the extra photos to apply for an International Driving Permit and student or teacher IDs. Take the rest with you. You may need one for random reasons on the road and — heaven forbid — if you ever lose your passport, you can use one as a replacement photo.

For people 16 years old and over, a passport is valid for 10 years and costs $60 ($45 plus a $15 handling fee); for those under 15 years of age, passports are valid for five years and cost $40 total. If you're over the age of 15 and have a passport issued less than 12 years ago, you can renew it by mail by filling out the application, available at the places described earlier or at the State Department Web site (http://travel.state.gov). By mail, you bypass the $15 handling fee, and it costs just $45.

Allow plenty of time — at least two months, preferably longer — before your trip to apply. The processing takes four weeks on average, but can run somewhat longer during busy periods (especially the spring). It helps speed things along if you write on the application a departure date within the next three weeks. To get your passport quicker — in about five business days — visit an agency directly (or go through the court or post office and have them overnight your application), and pay an additional $35 fee. For more information, such as finding your regional passport office, visit the State Department Web site at http://travel.state.gov or call the **National Passport Information Center** (☎900-225-7778; 35¢ a minute for automated service; $1.05 a minute to speak with an operator).

Keep your passport with you at all times — securely in your money belt. The only times to give it up are at the bank for them to photocopy when they change your traveler's checks, at borders for the guards to peruse (or for the conductor on overnight train rides), of course if any police or military personnel ask for it, and *briefly* to the concierge when you check into your hotel.

A valid passport is the only documentation you need as an American to visit France. They stamp your passport when you enter the country with a temporary tourist *visa* that's good for 90 days of travel within France. If you plan to stay longer, contact any French consulate in the United States before you leave to get a specific visa, or any U.S. consulate once you are abroad.

If you are a resident of Canada, you can pick up a passport application at one of 28 regional passport offices or most travel agencies. The passport is valid for 5 years and costs $60. Children under 16 years of age may be included on a parent's passport but need their own to travel unaccompanied. Applications, which must be accompanied by two identical passport-sized photographs and proof of Canadian citizenship, are available at travel agencies throughout Canada or from the central **Passport Office, Department of Foreign Affairs and International Trade,** Ottawa, Canada K1A 0G3 (☎ 800-567-6868; Internet: www.dfait-maeci.gc.ca/passport). Processing takes five to ten days if you apply in person, about three weeks by mail.

Residents of the UK and Ireland only need an identity card, not a passport, to travel to other EU countries. However, if you already have a passport, you can't go wrong by carrying it.

Australian residents can apply for a passport at a post office or passport office, or search the government Web site (www.dfat.gov.au/passports/). Passports for adults are A$128, and for those under 18 years of age, A$64.

New Zealand citizens can pick up a passport application at the Passport Office, any travel agency, or download the form from the site (www.passports.govt.nz). For more info, contact the Passport Office, Boulcott House, 47 Boulcott St., Wellington (☎ 0800-225-050). Passports for adults are NZ$80; for children under 16 years old, NZ$40.

Always keep a photocopy of the inside page of your passport with your picture packed separately from your wallet or purse. In the event your passport is lost or stolen, the photocopy can help speed up the replacement process. When traveling in a group, never let one person carry all the passports. If the passports are stolen, it can be much more difficult to obtain new ones because at least one person in a group needs to be able to prove his or her identity in order to identify the others.

If you're a U.S. citizen and either lose or have your passport stolen in Paris, go to the Consulate of the American Embassy at 2 rue St. Florentin, 1er (☎ 01-43-12-22-22; Métro: Concorde). Canadians in the same circumstances should visit the Consulate of the Canadian Embassy, 35 av. Montaigne, 8e (☎ 01-44-43-29-00; Métro: Franklin-D-Roosevelt or Alma Marceau). Australians should go to the Australian Embassy at 4 rue Jean-Rey, 15e (☎ 01-40-59-33-00; Métro: Bir-Hakeim). New Zealanders should visit the New Zealand Embassy, 7 rue Léonard de Vinci, 16e (☎ 01-45-00-24-11, ext. 280, from 9 a.m. to 1 p.m.; Métro: Victor-Hugo).

Getting through Customs

You *can* take it with you — up to a point. Technically, no limits are placed on how much loot you can bring back into the United States from a trip abroad, but the customs authority *does* put limits on how much you can take in for free (mainly for taxation purposes, to separate tourists with souvenirs from importers).

You're allowed $400 worth of goods duty-free upon reentry to the U.S., provided you've been out of the country at least 48 hours and haven't used the exemption in the past 30 days. Among the allowable goods are one liter of an alcoholic beverage (you must, of course, be over 21), 200 cigarettes, and 100 cigars. Goods you mail home from abroad are exempt from the $400 limit, but other limits are still in place. You may mail up to $200 worth of goods to yourself (marked "for personal use") and up to $100 to others (marked "unsolicited gift") once each day, so long as the package does not include alcohol or tobacco products. Anything over these limits, you must pay an import duty on.

 Note that buying items at a *duty-free shop* before flying home does *not* exempt them from counting toward your U.S. Customs limits (monetary or otherwise). The "duty" you avoid in those shops is the local tax on the item (like state sales tax in the U.S.), not any import duty that may be assessed by the U.S. Customs office.

If you have further questions, or for a list of specific items you cannot bring into the U.S., look in your phone book (under U.S. Government, Department of the Treasury, U.S. Customs Service) to find the nearest Customs office. Or check out the Customs Service Web site (www. customs.ustreas.gov/travel/travel.htm). If you're not a citizen of the U.S., check with your local Customs department before going abroad to determine your country's policy.

Buying Travel and Medical Insurance

You should consider three primary kinds of travel insurance: trip cancellation insurance, medical, and lost luggage.

Trip cancellation insurance is always a good idea if you pay a large portion of your vacation expenses up front, but the other two types of insurance — **medical** and **lost luggage** — really aren't needed by most travelers. Your existing health insurance should cover you if you get sick while on vacation, but be sure to check your policy before leaving home to see exactly what it promises. Homeowner's insurance should cover stolen luggage if you have off-premises theft. Check your existing policies thoroughly or contact your insurance agent before you buy any additional coverage. (If you rent, remember that renter's insurance doesn't typically cover property that has left the premises, but you can buy insurance with one of the recommended companies in the listing that follows.) The airlines are responsible for $2,500 on domestic flights (and $9.07 per pound, up to $640, on international flights) if they lose your luggage; if you plan to carry anything more valuable than that, keep it in your carry-on bag. Some credit cards (American Express and certain gold and platinum Visa and MasterCards, for example) offer automatic flight insurance against death or dismemberment in case of an airplane crash.

If you still feel you need more insurance, try one of the following reputable issuers of travel insurance:

- ✔ **Access America,** 6600 W. Broad St., Richmond, VA 23230 (☎ **800-284-8300;** Fax: 800-346-9265; Internet: www.accessamerica.com)

- ✔ **Travelex Insurance Services,** 11717 Burt St., Ste. 202, Omaha, NE 68154 (☎ **800-228-9792**; Internet: www.travelex-insurance.com)

- ✔ **Travel Guard International,** 1145 Clark St., Stevens Point, WI 54481 (☎ **800-826-1300**; Internet: www.travel-guard.com)

- ✔ **Travel Insured International, Inc.,** P.O. Box 280568, 52-S Oakland Ave., East Hartford, CT 06128-0568 (☎ **800-243-3174**; Internet: www.travelinsured.com)

 Don't pay for more insurance than you need. For example, if you only need trip cancellation insurance, don't purchase coverage for lost or stolen property. Trip cancellation insurance costs approximately six to eight percent of the total value of your vacation.

Getting Sick Away from Home

Apart from how getting sick can ruin your vacation, it can be hard to find a doctor you trust when you're away from home. Bring all your medications with you, as well as a prescription for more if you worry that you may run out. If you wear contact lenses, bring an extra pair in case you lose one. And don't forget the Pepto-Bismol for common travelers' ailments like upset stomach or diarrhea.

If you have health insurance, check with your provider to find out the extent of your coverage outside your home area. Be sure to carry your identification card in your wallet. And if you worry that your existing policy won't be sufficient, purchase medical insurance (see "Buying Travel and Medical Insurance," earlier in this chapter) for more comprehensive coverage.

If you suffer from a chronic illness, talk to your doctor before taking the trip. For such conditions as epilepsy, diabetes, or a heart condition, wearing a *Medic Alert identification tag* immediately alerts any doctor to your condition and gives the doctor access to your medical records through Medic Alert's 24-hour hotline. Membership is $35, with a $15 renewal fee. Contact the Medic Alert Foundation, 2323 Colorado Ave., Turlock, CA 95382 (☎ **800-432-5378**; Internet: www.medicalert.org).

The French government pays 70 percent of the cost of doctor visits, and its national health insurance covers 99 percent of France's population. Visitors needing medical care in France will find that doctors almost always see them the day of the appointment, and patient fees are relatively inexpensive. Patients will almost always have to pay up front, unless they are citizens of European Union countries with reciprocal medical arrangements. Usually, U.S. health insurance companies will reimburse most of the cost of treating illnesses in foreign countries; make sure to keep all receipts.

If you do get sick, ask the concierge at your hotel to recommend a local doctor — even his or her own doctor if necessary. You can also call SOS Help (☎01-47-23-80-80) between 3 p.m. and 11 p.m. for help in English, and ask for an English-speaking doctor. The **Centre Médicale Europe,** 44 rue d'Amsterdam, 9e, (☎01-42-81-93-33) is another good and efficient option. A host of specialists are located here, and foreigners only pay 115F ($16.50) for a consultation.

Renting a Car in Paris (or Why I Strongly Suggest That You Don't)

Driving a car in Paris is not for the faint-hearted. Why? Traffic is dense. Parisian drivers are ruthlessly aggressive. Traffic circles abound where cars hurtle at you from the left — no better example than the circle called Étoile that surrounds the Arc de Triomphe, where cars enter and exit from *12 different locations* at high speeds. Parking is difficult, both in terms of finding a space and the size of the spaces available; most hotels, except luxury ones, won't have garages. If you do drive, however, remember that a ring called the *périphérique* circles Paris, and its exits aren't numbered. Since the Paris Métro is one of the world's best urban transportation systems, it seems highly unnecessary to have a car in Paris. Even the day trips I recommend (see Chapter 21) are all easily accessible by public transportation.

But if you insist on renting a car, and therefore insist on driving in Paris, make sure you have a copilot to navigate the streets. Children are required by law to sit in the back, and backseat passengers must wear seatbelts. And remember that the majority of rentals available in France (and indeed, most of Europe) have manual transmissions. In fact, you probably end up paying more for a car if you request an automatic transmission.

Car rental agencies in Paris include

- ✔ **Avis,** place Madeleine, 8e (☎01-42-66-67-58; Internet: www.avis.com).
- ✔ **Budget,** information on Paris locations: (☎08-00-10-00-01, 1.29F/18¢ per minute; Internet: www.drivebudget.com).
- ✔ **Hertz France,** 123 rue Jeanne d'Arc, 13e (☎01-45-86-53-33; Internet: www.hertz.com).
- ✔ **National,** 23 bd Arago, 13e (☎01-47-07-87-39; Internet: www.nationalcar.com).

Making Reservations and Getting Tickets in Advance

Paris's cultural and entertainment scene is hot, and you need to book early for opera and ballet performances, classical music concerts, and some museum exhibitions. You also need to reserve ahead if you want to dine at sought-after restaurants (see Chapter 13 for those that require early booking). The most popular walking tours (see Chapter 18) also should be booked in advance because waiting until you arrive in the city may mean you get shut out.

For information on major cultural events, begin from home on the Web with the **French Government Tourist Office** (www.france-tourism.com), the **Office de Tourisme et de Congrès de Paris** (www.paris-touristoffice.com), and the **Maison de la France** (www.franceguide.com). You can also try **Culture Kiosque** (www.culturekiosque.com) for excellent magazine-style sites about opera, dance, and major museum exhibits around the world including schedules, reviews and phone numbers for ordering tickets. Culture Kiosque also features an online magazine in English, *JazzNet,* which includes a calendar of upcoming jazz club dates in Paris. A free monthly English-language magazine published in Paris, the *Paris Free Voice* (http://parisvoice.com), features an events calendar and reviews of current opera, dance, and theater.

You can also try these strategies to secure hard-to-get tickets to music, dance, and opera performances:

- ✔ **Call the box office.** Call the venue's box office directly and pay over the phone with your credit card to purchase tickets. Tickets can be sent to your hotel in your name, or held at the box office. See Chapters 22 and 23 for phone numbers to specific venues.

- ✔ **Contact your hotel's concierge.** If you're planning to stay at a hotel with a staff concierge, phone or fax ahead and ask him or her to obtain tickets for the productions you desire as early as possible, specifying your preferred date with a couple of backup dates, and the maximum amount you're willing to spend. Expect to pay handsomely for hard-to-land tickets, and don't forget to tip him for his efforts (50F discreetly slipped into an envelope which you present to him or her upon receipt of your tickets should be appropriate).

- ✔ **Try a ticket broker.** One of the most respected international ticket agencies is **Keith Prowse**, 234 West 44th St., Suite 1000, New York, NY 10036 (☎800-669-8687; Fax: 914-644-8671; E-mail: tickets@.keithprowse.com). Prowse almost always has excellent seats to upcoming musical concerts, ballets, operas, and some sports events. You can also pre-purchase city tours, museum passes, and transportation discounts here.

> ✔ **Check the Web** for what's going on in Paris. You can get box office phone numbers, and in some cases, you may be able to link to sites and buy tickets directly. *Time Out's* Paris Web site (www.timeout.com) lists events in English and updates them weekly. The Web site of the **Office de Tourisme** (www.paris-touristoffice.com) also provides information in English on entertainment.

Once you're in Paris, you can find several local publications providing up-to-the-minute listings of performances and other evening entertainment. Foremost among these is **Pariscope: Une Semaine de Paris** (3F/43¢), a weekly guide with thorough listings of movies, plays, ballet, art exhibits, clubs, and more. It contains an English-language insert written by staff in *Time Out's* Paris office and can be found at any newsstand. **L'Officiel des Spectacles** (2F/30¢), a weekly guide, and **Paris Nuit** (30F/$5.10), a monthly guide, both contain good articles as well as listings, though neither provides information in English. Costs vary depending on who is performing what on which day of the week. Call the theaters for information, or consult *Pariscope* and the other entertainment listings.

Many concert, theater, and dance tickets are sold through **FNAC** stores as well as at the box office. FNAC outlets number over a dozen throughout Paris; the most prominent is 74 av. des Champs-Elysées (Métro: George V). You can also reserve by phone (☎**01-49-87-50-50**) Monday through Friday from 9 a.m. to 8 p.m., Saturday 10 a.m. to 5 p.m. **Virgin Megastore,** 52 av. des Champs-Elysées (☎**01-49-53-50-00;** Métro: Franklin-D-Roosevelt), is another reputable ticket seller. The store is open Monday through Saturday from 10 a.m. to midnight, noon to midnight on Sunday, and their tickets-by-phone number is ☎**01-44-68-44-08.**

Getting Traveler's Checks and Local Currency

If you decide to carry traveler's checks in Paris, buy them before you leave your home country at almost any bank. **American Express** offers denominations of $10, $20, $50, $100, $500, and $1,000. You pay a service charge ranging from 1 to 4 percent. You can also get American Express traveler's checks online (www10.americanexpress.com) and over the phone if you're an American Express cardholder (☎**800-721-9768**). American Automobile Association members can get checks without a fee at most AAA offices.

Visa (☎**800-227-6811**) also offers traveler's checks, available at Citibank locations across the country and at several other banks. The service charge ranges between 1.5 and 2 percent; checks come in denominations of $50, $100, $500, and $1,000. **MasterCard** also offers traveler's checks; call ☎**800-223-9920** for a location near you.

If you opt to carry traveler's checks, be sure to keep a record of their serial numbers, separately from the checks of course, so you're ensured a refund in an emergency.

Before leaving home, buy French currency (see Chapter 12) — about $50 to $100 worth — unless you don't mind waiting at the exchange offices at the Paris airports. Though you will get the best exchange rate at an ATM machine once you arrive in France, those in the Paris airports are often broken or out of cash. Your best bet before you go is to check the foreign exchange rate in the business section of your local paper, call local banks to inquire their rates of exchange, and buy French francs at the U.S. bank with the rate closest to the one listed in your paper.

Packing Tips

Start by taking everything you think you need and laying it out on the bed. Then get rid of half of it — you won't have space, in your suitcase and in your hotel rooms, for that much.

The trick to packing light is bringing items that are versatile — the addition of a jacket, scarf, or jewelry, the removal of a sweater — allowing you more mileage out of your wardrobe. French women, who always seem so fashion conscious, dress in such a way all the time. If you bring separates in neutral colors that can make several outfits, you never need worry about something to wear and you always look smart.

In order to conserve baggage space, you must limit yourself to two pairs of shoes. No exceptions! One pair should be for walking — preferably not sneakers. Paris is a more formal city where sneakers are looked down upon in many places, and you feel much more comfortable if you're not over- or under-dressed (also, nothing screams tourist more than a pair of bright white sneakers). Try for a "casual Fridays at work" look.

The same holds true for evenings. Think a notch dressier than what you would normally wear out to dinner (even more if your normal evening out attire usually consists of sweats and a Cubs hat). Even at casual neighborhood bistros, most men wear sport jackets and women wear skirts or smart pants at dinner.

Don't forget those handy resealable plastic sandwich bags — they make great toiletry cases, solve the problems of leaky items, and if you've got small kids, you can put a damp washcloth in one to clean up little messes. You can also save space by buying travel-sized plastic bottles at the drugstore to fill with shampoo, conditioner, and other liquid beauty essentials.

When packing your suitcase, remember to fill your shoes with small items like socks and underwear which can help to save space. Fit the rest of your small items around your shoes, and pack breakable items between several layers of clothing. Dry cleaners' plastic bags are great for protecting items that wrinkle easy.

In addition to sneakers, leave your cell phone at home — unless you have one of the brand new phones that adapt to the GSM norm on which the European cell phone system works. And as for appliances, not only are they clumsy to carry around, you need an electrical adapter to use them — European current runs on 210– 220V, while American current is 110V, 60 cycles — along with a transformer to bring the voltage down and the cycles up. If you must bring an appliance, be sure it runs on dual voltage.

For more tips on packing, consult **Travelite** (www.travelite.org), which also gives advice on packing light, choosing luggage, and selecting appropriate travel wear. Its printable packing lists are very helpful.

Blending In: How to Look like a Local

Male tourists usually find it easy to look like a local. The staple casual look for Parisian men is a blazer over a button-down shirt, and khakis (or sometimes nicely pressed Levis) with loafers or other casual shoes that don't fall into the sneaker category. The tie is optional. Men with more formal careers wear beautifully tailored suits and often carry small leather briefcases that one Seinfeld episode jokingly referred to as "the male handbag."

For women, obtaining that *Parisienne* look is a bit harder. In the first place, it seems French women are born understanding how to put outfits together with that *je ne sais quoi* that no foreigner can imitate. Funnily enough, accessorizing is the key. For nights out, bring feminine clothes in neutral colors and accessorize with a pretty scarf or piece of jewelry. For the big nights out, you can never go wrong with a little black dress and pearls. For walking during the day, avoid being instantly picked out as a tourist by investing in a pair of comfortable walking shoes that are dressy enough to wear with a casual skirt. Leave the sneakers, fanny pack, shorts, and baseball cap at home. Though Paris is the most visited city in the world, I recently saw an elderly Parisienne stare disapprovingly at two American women wearing shorts on the Métro. (Many American stores carry comfortable, casual skirts that are perfect for travel.) If you bring a small purse with long straps, you can wear it diagonally across your body for a fashionable and safe way to carry your belongings.

Part III
Settling In to Paris

In this part . . .

*S*ometimes travelers are so concerned with the details of trip planning, they're at a loss once they arrive. This section helps you get from point A to point B without wasting time and money. Chapter 10 guides you from the airport to your hotel, describes the most popular neighborhoods, and tells you where to go for information once you're in Paris. Need to know how to get around by subway, taxi, bus, and on foot? Read Chapter 11 and prepare to start zipping around the city in no time. Chapter 12 helps you to make sense of the French Franc, tells you where you can get cash in Paris, and gives you emergency phone numbers if your wallet or purse is lost or stolen.

Chapter 10

Orienting Yourself in Paris

In This Chapter

▶ Navigating passport control and customs

▶ Securing transportation to your hotel

▶ Getting to know Paris by neighborhood

▶ Finding info after you arrive

*T*he Paris experience begins as soon as your plane lands at the airport — all the sights and sounds are unmistakably French. The smell of strong coffee and fresh croissants is wafting out of the airport cafes. Luggage carts are free! Little dogs peek out of bags or prance at the end of leashes. People are dressed more formally than at home. And, yes, that harsh burning scent is the unmistakable odor of black tobacco — people can smoke in the terminal at Charles-de-Gaulle (but not at Orly airport). It all may seem a little astonishing — especially if you arrived at the spaceship-looking Charles-de-Gaulle — and that's because you've probably landed at some ungodly early morning hour. But, the important thing is you've arrived! Now onto the first item of the day — getting from the airport to your hotel.

Navigating Passport Control and Customs

Most visitors to Paris land at Charles-de-Gaulle Airport, the larger, busier, and more modern airport, commonly known as CDG and sometimes called Roissy–Charles-de-Gaulle, 14½ miles northeast of downtown Paris. Nearly all direct flights from North America land at Charles-de-Gaulle. Bilevel Terminal 1 (Aérogare 1), is the older and smaller of the two terminals and is used by foreign airlines; Terminal 2 (Aérogare 2), is used by Air France, domestic and intra-European airlines, and some foreign airlines, including Air Canada. Terminal 2 is divided into halls A through F. A free shuttle bus *(navette)* connects the two terminals.

Many tourists land very early in the morning, making the podlike glass terminals connected by narrow escalators and moving sidewalks seem even more surreal. More than one person has commented how Charles-de-Gaulle Airport has the feel of a giant spaceship. Fortunately, both terminals are well signposted in French and English to direct you to customs, baggage claim, and transportation to the city. Staff at information desks are also on hand to answer questions.

Two lines are set up for passport control; one for European Union nationals, one for all others. These lines can move quite fast or can be horrendously slow; it usually depends on the clerk riffling through your passport. You may not get a stamp on your passport, either. In the past two years, I have made four stops at French passport control in Charles-de-Gaulle and have not once received a stamp.

When passing through Customs, keep in mind that restrictions differ for citizens of the European Union and for citizens of non-EU countries. As a non-EU national, you can bring in duty-free 200 cigarettes or 100 cigarillos or 50 cigars or 250 grams of smoking tobacco. You can also bring in 2 liters of wine and 1 liter of alcohol over 38.80 proof. In addition, you can bring in 50 grams of perfume, one-quarter liter of toilet water, 500 grams of coffee, and 100 grams of tea. Travelers ages 15 years old and over can also bring in 1,200F ($171.45) in other goods; for those 14 years of age and under, the limit is 600F ($85.75) (See Chapter 19 for what you're allowed to bring home.) Since you probably are not going to need to make a claim, you should be waved through by a bored officer pretty quickly. Custom officers do, however, at times pull random travelers over to check luggage. If this happens to you, don't be offended; be polite and as helpful as you can, and if you don't speak French, let them know.

Regardless of the terminal, you need French francs to get from the airport into Paris. You can find ATM machines in the arrivals area of the airports, as well as bureaux de change, but you're better off buying $100 (700F) worth of francs at home. Airport ATMs are notorious for being broken when you most need them, and the airport bureaux de change are notorious for their bad rates of exchange.

Getting from the Airport to Your Hotel — from Charles-De-Gaulle

You can get to and from the airport in several different ways, and they're all easy.

Taking a taxi

Probably the easiest way, but certainly not the cheapest, to your hotel from the airport is by taxi. A cab into town from Charles-de-Gaulle takes 40 to 50 minutes depending on traffic and costs about 220F

($31.45) from 7 a.m. to 8 p.m., about 40 percent more at other times. Taxis are required to turn the meter on and charge the price indicated plus 6F (90¢) for each piece of luggage stowed in the trunk. If your French is poor or nonexistent, a good idea would be to write down the name and full address of your hotel. The five digit postal code is the most important morsel of information; it lets the driver know the arrondissement in which to drive you. Check the meter before you pay — rip-offs of arriving tourists are not uncommon. If you feel that you might have been overcharged, demand a receipt (which drivers are obligated to provide) and contact the Préfecture of Police (☎ 01-55-76-20-00).

Here's where you find the taxi ranks at Charles-de-Gaulle:

✔ **CDG Terminal 1:** Porte 16, arrivals level

✔ **CDG Terminals 2A and 2C:** Hall A, Porte 7

✔ **CDG Terminals 2B and 2D:** Hall D, Porte 7

✔ **CDG Terminal 2F:** Porte 1, arrivals level

Taking a shuttle

Cheaper than a taxi for one or two people, but more expensive than air-port buses and trains, is the **Airport Shuttle,** 2 avenue Général Leclerc 14e (☎ 01-45-38-55-72; Fax: 01-43-21-35-67; Internet: www.paris-anglo. com/clients/ashuttle; E-mail: ashuttle@club-internet.fr; Métro: Denfert-Rochereau). As soon as you arrive, call Airport Shuttle's toll-free number (as you wait for your bags) to confirm pickup: ☎ 0-800-50-56-10. You are picked up in a minivan at Orly or Charles-de-Gaulle and taken to your hotel for 89F ($12.70) per person for parties of two or more, 120F ($17.15) for a single. No extra charge is assessed for luggage.

Paris Airport Service, BP 41, Cedex 94431 Chennevieres (☎ 01-49-62-78-78; Fax: 01-49-62-78-79; E-mail: pas@magic.fr) offers a similar service. It costs 145F ($20.70) for one person, 180F ($25.70) for two or more from Charles-de-Gaulle; 115F ($16.45) for one person, 135F ($19.30) for two or more from Orly. Both companies accept Visa and MasterCard.

Making tracks for the train

A good option if you're not overloaded with baggage and want to keep down your expenses, is the **RER** (*Réseau Express Régional*) **Line B** sub-urban train which stops near Terminals 1 and 2. Easy, cheap, and con-venient, most Parisians use the RER to get home from the airport after their travels abroad. You can ride from 5 a.m. to midnight Monday through Friday, and from 7 a.m. to 9 p.m. on weekends. A free shuttle bus connects the terminal CDG 1 to the RER train station. If you land in terminal **CDG 1,** exit the terminal at Porte 28 on the arrivals level and look for the bus marked "RER."

If you land in terminal **CDG 2,** there is no shuttle bus, but instead the terminal is linked to the RER (RER is pronounced "air–uh–air" in French) by a walkway. Ask an airport employee or look for the round RER logo. Ask for the **"RER plus Métro"** ticket once you reach the RER ticket counter which costs 47F ($6.70), and hang onto your ticket in case of ticket inspection. (You can be fined 100F/$14.30 if you can't produce your ticket to an inspector.) In any case, you need your ticket later to get off the RER system and into the Métro.

From the airport station, trains depart about every 15 minutes for the half-hour trip into town, stopping on the **Right Bank** at Gare du Nord, Châtelet–Les Halles, and on the **Left Bank** at St-Michel, Luxembourg, Port-Royal, and Denfert-Rochereau, before heading south out of the city.

No thanks, I'm taking the bus

A bus is better than the RER if

- ✔ You're heading into Paris during off-peak driving hours.
- ✔ Your hotel is located near one of the drop–off points. Note that this option from the Charles-de-Gaulle airport won't work for most of the accommodations I recommend in this book. I only recommend hotels within the first eight arrondissements; of those, the bus is only convenient to the 2e and 8e arrondissements. Still, if you're staying in those areas, or if you happen to be staying further out from the center of town, the bus might be the right option for you.

Which bus to take?

If your hotel is located on the **Right Bank,** in the **8e, 16e,** or **17e** arrondissements, an **Air France coach** stops at Porte Maillot before ending up at Etoile, the name for the huge traffic roundabout at the Arc de Triomphe. The bus costs 60F ($8.60) one way and runs every 12 minutes from 5:40 a.m. to 11 p.m. You needn't have flown on an Air France flight to use the service, and tickets are available right on the bus. The trip only takes about 40 minutes to get from the airport into the city in light traffic, such as on weekend mornings. During weekday morning rush hour however, the same trip can take twice as long, if not longer. Pick up the coach from:

- ✔ **CDG Terminal 1:** Porte 34, arrivals level
- ✔ **CDG Terminals 2A and 2C:** Porte 5
- ✔ **CDG Terminals 2B and 2D:** Porte 6
- ✔ **CDG Terminal 2F:** Porte 6, arrivals level

If your hotel is located on the **Right Bank** near the **Bastille** (**11e** or **12e**) or on the **Left Bank** in **Montparnasse** (**14e**), a different **Air France** coach stops at Gare de Lyon before ending up near the back of the Gare de Montparnasse. The bus costs 70F ($10) one way and runs every 30 minutes from 7 a.m. to 9 p.m. It takes about 50 minutes to get from the airport into the city in light traffic. Catch this coach from:

- ✔ **CDG Terminal 1:** Porte 34, arrivals level

- ✔ **CDG Terminals 2A and 2C:** Hall C, Porte 2

- ✔ **CDG Terminals 2B and 2D:** Hall D, Porte 1

- ✔ **CDG Terminal 2F:** Porte 7, arrivals level

Take the **Roissybus** if your hotel is on the **Right Bank** near the **Opéra** (2e or 9e). It leaves every 15 minutes between 6 a.m. and 11 p.m. and costs 45F ($6.45). The drop–off point is on rue Scribe, a block from the **Opéra Garnier** near American Express. You can get to your destination in 45 to 50 minutes in regular traffic. Buy your tickets in the small office next to where the bus is parked. Pick up this coach from:

- ✔ **CDG Terminal 1:** Porte 30, arrivals level

- ✔ **CDG Terminals 2A and 2C:** Hall C, Porte 10

- ✔ **CDG Terminals 2B and 2D:** Hall D, Porte 12

- ✔ **CDG Terminal 2F:** Porte H, arrivals level

If You Fly into Orly

Orly airport, 8½ miles south of the city, has two terminals — **Ouest** (West) and **Sud** (South) — and English speakers find the terminals easy to navigate: French domestic flights land at Orly Ouest, and intra-European and intercontinental flights at Orly Sud. Shuttle buses connect these terminals, and other shuttles connect them to Charles-de-Gaulle every 30 minutes or so. A tourist information desk is nearby where you can pick up city maps and other visitor essentials.

Like Charles-de-Gaulle Airport, two lines are set up for passport control; one for European Union nationals, one for visitors carrying passports from all other countries, and you should be waved through Customs. (See the previous section, "Navigating Passport Control and Customs" for information about what you can bring into France.) If an official asks to inspect your luggage, be courteous and helpful and let him or her know if you don't speak French.

Taking a taxi

A cab from Orly into Paris costs about 170F ($24.30) and takes any-where from 25 minutes to an hour, depending on traffic. You can find the taxi stand just outside Porte H. The same advice as when taking a taxi from Charles-de-Gaulle holds true here: Write down the full name and address of your hotel for the driver. And remember that cabs charge 6F (90¢) for each piece of luggage that's put in the trunk.

When the bus is best

Take the **Air France coach** if your hotel is located on the **Left Bank** near Les Invalides (7e). Buses leave Porte F every 12 to 15 minutes. The bus also leaves from Exit D on the arrival level at Orly Ouest and Exit K at Orly Sud. The trip takes 30 minutes and costs 45F ($6.45). You can request that the bus stop at Montparnasse-Duroc.

The cheapest trip into town is on the **Jetbus.** You can take this bus from Orly to the Métro, which you can board to reach your hotel. Jetbus connects Orly with the Métro station Villejuif–Louis Aragon in south Paris (13e), and costs 26.50F ($3.80) for the 15-minute journey. The bus leaves every 12 to 15 minutes from Exit G2 in Orly Sud and from Exit C, arrivals level in Orly Ouest. The **Orly bus** operates from Exit J, arrivals level at Orly Ouest, and from Exit H Platform 4 at Orly Sud to the Left Bank's Denfert-Rochereau for 35F ($5).

Taking the train

You can also take the **RER C line,** which is a bit of a hassle. You can catch a free shuttle bus from Porte H, Platform 1, to the **Rungis** station, where RER C trains leave every 15 minutes. A one–way fare is 32F ($4.60), and the trip into the city takes 30 minutes, making various stops along the Seine on the **Left Bank.**

If you're staying on the **Right Bank,** you can take the **RER B line.** From Orly Sud, it departs from Exit K near the baggage-claim area; from Orly Ouest, it leaves from Exit W or Exit J on the departure level. You connect at the **Antony** RER station where you board the RER B train to Paris. You need the ticket to get you into the Métro/RER system. A trip to the **Châtelet** station on the Right Bank takes about 30 minutes and costs 57F ($8.15). You can avoid the line by buying your tickets from a machine if you have French coins with you. Once in Paris, the train stops at **Denfert-Rochereau, Port-Royal, Luxembourg,** and **St-Michel** on the Left Bank, then crosses to the Right Bank and stops at **Châtelet** and **Gare du Nord.**

Paris by Neighborhood

You've arrived at your hotel, checked in, and maybe unpacked a little. Taking a nap would prolong your jet lag. So go out and act like a Parisian — have a cup of coffee at a café then get ready to explore.

The Seine River divides Paris into two halves: the **Right Bank** *(Rive Droite)* on the north side of the river; and the **Left Bank** *(Rive Gauche)* on the south side of the river. The Right Bank is where you find the city's business sector, stately monuments, and high-fashion industry. The Left Bank is a funkier place where artists, students, and creative types have traditionally congregated.

The city is divided into 20 numbered *arrondissements* (municipal districts). And while visitors tend to think of Paris in terms of neighborhood names, Parisians think of the city in terms of arrondissement numbers. For example, ask a hometowner where he works and he's more likely to say "in the 5th" and not "in the Latin Quarter." The layout of these districts follows a distinct pattern. The first (abbreviated 1er for *premiere*) arrondissement is dead-center Paris, comprising the area around the Louvre. From there, the rest of the districts spiral outward, clockwise, in ascending order. The lower the arrondissement number, the more central the location. To get a better idea of what I'm talking about, consult the "Paris Neighborhoods" map in this chapter.

Arrondissement numbers are key to locating an address in Paris. Addresses there are generally listed as they are in this book, with the arrondissement number following the specific street address (for instance, 29 rue de Rivoli, 4e, would be in the fourth arrondissement). The arrondissement number is also indicated in the last two digits of the postal code; for instance, an address with the postal code 75007 would be located in the seventh arrondissement. Once you know which arrondissement an address is located in, finding that spot is much easier. Numbers on buildings running parallel to the Seine usually follow the course of the river east to west. On north-south streets, numbering begins at the river.

In the following discussion of neighborhoods, I list them first by arrondissement, and then by neighborhood name. Only the best known arrondissements — meaning the ones that you're most likely to stay in or visit — are mentioned.

On the Right Bank

The following are neighborhoods you're likely to visit on the Right Bank.

1er Arr. (Musée du Louvre/Palais-Royal/Les Halles)

One of the world's greatest art museums (some say *the* greatest), the **Louvre** still lures all visitors to Paris to the 1er arrondissement. You can see many of the city's elegant addresses along the rue de Rivoli, as well as arched arcades under which all kinds of touristy junk is sold. Walk through the **Jardin des Tuileries** (English Tuileries Garden), the most formal garden of Paris, take in the classic beauty of the **place Vendôme,** opulent, wealthy, and home of the Ritz Hotel. **Forum des**

Paris Neighborhoods

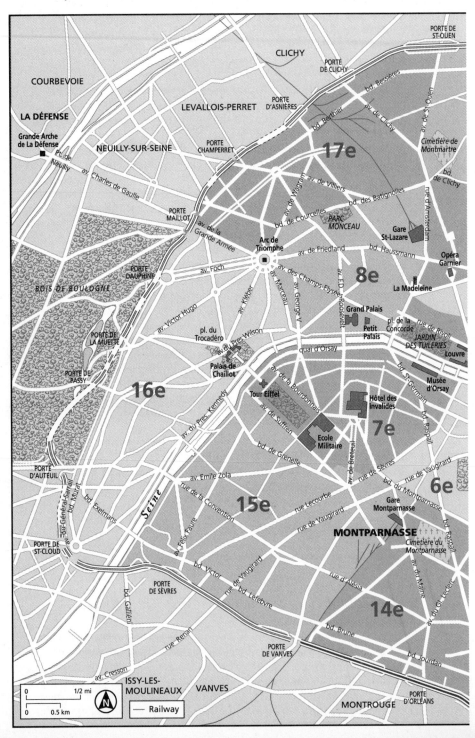

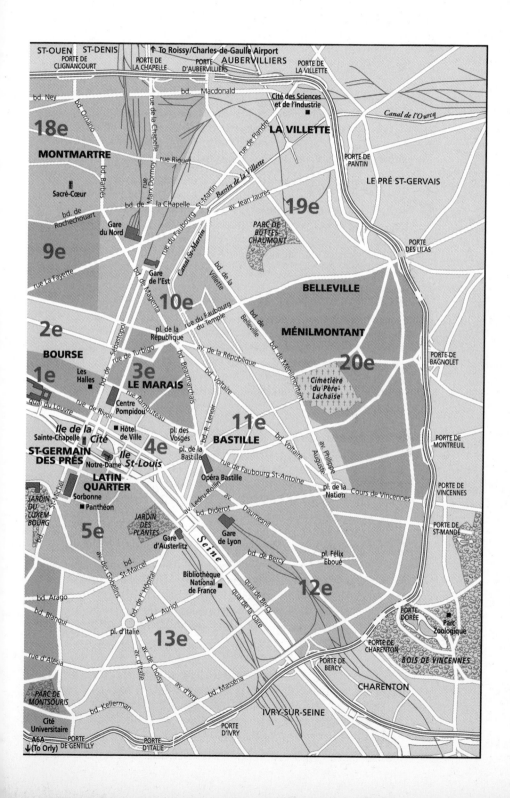

Halles, an above–ground and below–ground shopping and entertainment center, is also here. This arrondissement tends to be crowded, and hotels are higher priced in high tourist season in early fall because the area is so convenient.

2e Arr. (La Bourse)

Often overlooked by tourists, the 2e houses the **Bourse** (stock exchange). The district, lying between the Grands Boulevards and the rue Etienne Marcel, is also home to the garment trade; wholesale fashion outlets abound. Prostitution is not unknown here.

3e Arr. (Le Marais)

Le Marais (the swamp) is one of Paris's hippest neighborhoods, and you find one of the city's most popular attractions, the **Musée Picasso,** here. Paris's old Jewish neighborhood is here around the rue des Rosiers, and the rue Vieille-du-Temple is home to numerous gay bars and boutiques.

4e Arr. (Ile de la Cité/Ile St-Louis/Centre Pompidou)

Aristocratic town houses, courtyards, and antiques shops, flower markets, the **Palais de Justice, Notre-Dame cathedral** and **Sainte-Chapelle,** the **Centre Georges Pompidou museum,** and the **place des Vosges** — they're all here on the two islands of the 4e, the Ile de la Cité and the Ile St-Louis. These islands located in the middle of the Seine compose one of the prettiest, and most crowded, of Paris's arrondissements.

8e Arr. (Champs-Elysées/Madeleine)

The 8e is the heart of the Right Bank, and its showcase is the **Champs-Elysées.** Here you find the fashion houses, the most elegant hotels, expensive restaurants and shops, and the most fashionably attired Parisians. The Champs stretches from the **Arc de Triomphe** to the city's oldest monument, the Egyptian obelisk on **place de la Concorde.**

9e Arr. (Opéra Garnier/Pigalle)

Everything from the **Quartier de l'Opéra** to the strip joints of **Pigalle** falls within the 9e, which was radically altered by Baron Haussmann's nineteenth-century redevelopment projects like his Grands Boulevards that radiate through the district. Try to visit the **Opéra Garnier** (Paris Opera House), which recently reopened after an expensive restoration.

10e Arr. (Gare du Nord/Gare de l'Est)

Though most of this arrondissement is dreary (**Gare du Nord** and **Gare de l'Est** are two of the city's four main train stations), a few bright spots exist along the Canal St-Martin in the east. The **quai de Valmy** and **quai de Jemmapes** are scenic, tree-lined promenades on the canal, where the movie *Hotel du Nord* was filmed.

11e Arr. (Opéra Bastille)

The 11e has few landmarks or famous museums, but the area has become a mecca for hordes of young Parisians looking for casual, inexpensive nightlife. Always crowded on weekends and in summer, the overflow retires to the steps of the **Opéra Bastille,** which opened in 1989.

16e Arr. (Trocadéro/Bois de Boulogne)

Come here to see where the moneyed live. Highlights include the **Bois de Boulogne,** the **Jardin du Trocadéro,** the **Musée de Balzac,** the **Musée Guimet** (famous for its Asian collections), and the **Cimetière de Passy,** resting place of Manet, Talleyrand, Giraudoux, and Debussy. One of the largest arrondissements, the 16e is known today for its exclusivity, its BCBG residents *(bon chic bon genre),* its upscale rents, and some rather posh (and, according to its critics, rather smug) residential boulevards. Prosperous and suitably conservative addresses include the avenue d'Iéna and the avenue Victor Hugo. Also prestigious is the avenue Foch, the widest boulevard in Paris, and home at various times to the late Greek shipping magnate Aristotle Onassis, Shah Mohammad Reza Pahlavi of Iran, and opera star Maria Callas, as well as the current Prince Rainier of Monaco. The arrondissement also includes what some visitors consider the best place in Paris from which to view the Eiffel Tower, the **place du Trocadéro.**

18e Arr. (Montmartre)

Montmartre, the **Moulin Rouge,** the **Basilica of Sacré-Coeur,** and the **place du Tertre** are only some of the attractions in this outer arrondissement. Take a walk through the winding old streets here, and you feel transported into another era. The city's most famous flea market, **Marché aux Puces de la Porte de St-Ouen,** is another landmark.

On the Left Bank

The following are neighborhoods you're likely to visit on the Left Bank.

5e Arr. (Latin Quarter)

Bookstores, schools, churches, night clubs, student dives, Roman ruins, publishing houses, and expensive boutiques characterize the district, called "Latin" because students and professors at the Sorbonne, located here, spoke Latin. Stroll along **quai de Montebello,** inspecting the inventories of the *bouquinistes* and wander the shops in the old streets of rue de la Huchette and rue de la Harpe — but don't eat here. The restaurants have people who will try to pull you in by promising cheap food. They hit your wallet, however, with their overpriced drinks and extras. The 5e also stretches down to the **Panthéon,** and to the fun rue Mouffetard behind it, where you can visit one of the city's best produce markets or eat at a variety of ethnic restaurants.

6e Arr. (St-Germain and the Luxembourg Gardens)

The art school that turned away Rodin, the **École des Beaux-Arts,** is here, as well as some of the chicest designers around. But the secret of the district lies in discovering its narrow streets and hidden squares. Everywhere you turn in the district, you encounter famous historical and literary associations. For instance, the restaurant **Brasserie Lipp,** located here, is where Hemingway lovingly recalls eating potato salad in *A Moveable Feast,* and the **Café aux Deux Magots** is depicted in *The Sun Also Rises.* The 6e takes in the **Luxembourg Gardens,** probably residents' most loved park.

7e Arr. (Near the Eiffel Tower and Musée d'Orsay)

The city's most famous symbol, the **Eiffel Tower,** dominates the 7e, and part of the **St-Germain** neighborhood is here, too. The **Hôtel des Invalides,** which contains both **Napoléon's Tomb** and the **Musée de l'Armée** is also in the 7e, in addition to the **Musée Rodin** and the **Musée d'Orsay,** the world's premier showcase of nineteenth-century French art and culture.

14e Arr. (Montparnasse)

Montparnasse is the former stomping ground of the "lost generation": writers Gertrude Stein, Alice B. Toklas, Ernest Hemingway, and other American expatriates who gathered here in the 1920s. After World War II, it ceased to be the center of intellectual life in Paris, but the memory lingers in its cafés. Some of the world's most famous literary cafés, including **La Rotonde, Le Select, La Dôme,** and **La Coupole,** are in the northern end of this large arrondissement, near the Rodin statue of Balzac at the junction of boulevard Montparnasse and boulevard Raspail. At its southern end, the arrondissement contains pleasant residential neighborhoods filled with well-designed apartment buildings, many built between 1910 and 1940.

Street Smarts: Where to Get Information after You Arrive

The prime source of information is the **Office de Tourisme de Paris,** 127 av. des Champs-Elysées, 8e (☎ **08-36-68-31-12** or 01-49-52-53-35; Fax: 01-49-52-53-00; Internet: www.paris-touristoffice.com; E-mail: info@paris-touristoffice.com; Métro: Charles-de-Gaulle–Étoile or George V). The office is open daily from 9 a.m. to 8 p.m. (Sunday 11 a.m. to 7 p.m. November through April).

The Office de Tourisme has an *auxiliary office* at the Eiffel Tower (May through September only, daily from 11 a.m. to 6 p.m.) and at the Gare de Lyon (Monday through Saturday from 8 a.m. to 8 p.m.). At the main and auxiliary offices, you can also reserve concert, theater, or cabaret tickets without an extra fee.

Chapter 11

Getting around Paris

After you arrive safely in Paris, start exploring. How you get around depends on how much ground you need to cover in a given time frame, but you can use several modes of transportation before your trip is over. This chapter gives you pointers on how to master the public transportation system, how to find a cab when you need one most, and what to watch out for while walking.

Probably your best introduction to Paris, and to the way the city is laid out, is from the tower at Notre-Dame. The magnificent cathedral is visible from many parts of the city, and a visit helps you get oriented. You also realize that the river Seine is actually Paris's most important "street."

Getting around by Métro

The best way to get around Paris is to walk, but for longer distances the Métro, or subway, rules.

The **Métro** is fast, safe, and easy to navigate. Pretty spry for a 101 year old. A dozen stations also enjoyed a recent centenary makeover as well; based on themes, the newly designed stations include Bonne Nouvelle, which now resembles a film set and displays film screens showing various old movies. Operated by the RATP (*Régie Autonome des Transports Parisiens*), as are city buses, the Métro has a total of 16 lines and more than 360 stations, making it likely that one is near your destination. The Métro is connected to the **Réseau Express Régional (RER),** which connects downtown Paris with its airports and suburbs. Subway trains run from 5:30 a.m. to 1 a.m., and you often witness people running down streets at about 12:50 a.m. trying to catch the last train. After that, the RATP operates **Noctambuses** that run on the hour from 1:30 a.m.–5:30 a.m. from Châtelet-Hôtel de Ville, but they don't cover every arrondissement. Check the maps at the entrance to Métro stations to determine if a Noctambus services your destination. (If your hotel isn't in a Noctambus zone, consult the sidebar "Top taxi stands" later in this chapter for the one nearest you and queue up with all the others who missed the train.) You recognize the bus by its yellow and black owl symbol. Noctambus tickets cost 30F ($4.30). Métro and the RER tickets cost 8F ($1.15) to any point within the first 20 arrondissements of Paris, and slightly more if you're traveling to an outlying suburb (the exact cost depends on where your particular destination is).

A 10-ticket *carnet* (booklet) good for the Métro and on buses is a good deal for 55F ($7.90) because a single ticket costs 8F ($1.15). *Carnets* are on sale at all Métro stations as well as *tabacs* (cafés and kiosks that sell tobacco products). You also see ads for the **Paris Visite** card, which starts at 55F ($7.90) a day. It does offer free or reduced entry to some attractions in addition to unlimited travel, but make sure the attractions that interest you are included on the list.

At the turnstile entrances to the station, insert your ticket in the turnstile, pass through the entrance, and take your ticket out of the machine. You must keep your ticket until you exit the train platform, at which point an inspector may ask to see your ticket again. If you fail to produce it, you are subject to a steep fine. When you ride the RER, you must keep your ticket because you have to insert it in a turnstile when you exit the station.

Some older Métro stations are marked by elegant art nouveau gateways reading MÉTROPOLITAIN; others are marked by big yellow M signs. Every Métro stop has maps of the system, which are also available at ticket booths. Once you decide which line you need, make sure you are going in the right direction: On Métro line 1, *"Direction: Esplanade de la Defense"* indicates a westbound train, *"Direction: Château de Vincennes"* is eastbound. To change train lines, look for the CORRESPONDANCE signs; blue signs reading *sortie* mark exits.

Near the exits is usually a *plan du quartier,* a very detailed pictorial map of the streets and buildings surrounding the station, with all exits marked. A good idea is to consult the *plan du quartier* before you climb the stairs, especially at very large stations; you may want to use a different exit to reach the other side of a busy street or wind up closer to your destination.

How long do you plan to be in Paris? If you plan to use public transportation frequently, consider buying the **Carte Orange.** The weekly or monthly pass is inexpensive — 80F ($11.45) for a week's unlimited travel *(coupon hebdomadaire)* or 271F ($38.70) for a month's pass *(coupon mensuel)* covering the first 20 arrondissements.

Top Five Songs You'll Hear on the Métro

You're likely to hear at least one of these songs on the Métro during your stay in Paris, either sung, or played on a violin, guitar or accordion:

"La Vie en Rose"

"Non, Je Ne Regrette Rien

"The Sounds of Stillness"

"Mrs. Robinson"

anything by the Gipsy Kings

The only catch is that you must supply a little photo of yourself. Bring one from home, or visit a photo booth at one of the many Monoprix stores, major Métro stations, department stores, or train stations, where you can get four black-and-white pictures for 25F ($3.60). The weekly Carte Orange is on sale Monday through Wednesday morning and is valid through Sunday, but the monthly card is only sold the first two days of the month.

For more information on the city's public transportation, stop in at the **Services Touristiques de la RATP,** at place de la Madeleine, 1er (☎ **01-40-06-71-45;** Internet: www.ratp.fr; Métro: Madeleine), or call ☎ **08-36-68-41-14** for information in English.

Getting around by Bus

The bus system is also convenient and can be an inexpensive way to sight-see without wearing out your feet. Each bus shelter has a route map, which you want to check carefully. Because of the number of one-way streets, the bus is likely to make different stops depending on its direction. Métro tickets are valid for bus travel, or you can buy your ticket from the conductor, but you can't buy *carnets* on board. Tickets must be punched in a machine inside the bus and retained until the end of the ride.

Some bus routes are great for sightseeing because they take a scenic route and pass many attractions. Try these bus routes for easy jump–on, jump–off sightseeing itineraries: **Bus 69:** Eiffel Tower, Invalides, Louvre, Hôtel de Ville, place des Vosges, Bastille, Père Lachaise Cemetery. **Bus 80:** Department stores on bd. Haussmann, Champs-Elysées, Ave. Montaigne haute–couture shopping, Eiffel Tower. Bus 96: St-Germain-des-Prés, Musée de Cluny, Hôtel de Ville, place des Vosges.

Getting around by Taxi

Parisian taxis are expensive, and you need to know a few things before you hail one.

Look for the blue taxi sign denoting a taxi stand; although you can hail taxis in the street (look for a taxi with a white light on; an orange light means the cab is occupied), most drivers refuse to pick you up if you are in the general vicinity of a taxi stand.

For one to three people, the drop rate in Paris proper is 13F ($1.90); the rate per kilometer is 3.45F (49¢) from 7 a.m. to 7 p.m.; otherwise, 5.70F (81¢). You will pay supplements from taxi ranks at train stations and at the Air France shuttle-bus terminals of 5F (75¢), 6F ($.90) for luggage, and, if the driver agrees to do so, 10F ($1.45) for transporting a fourth person. Common practice is to tip your driver 2F to 3F (30¢ to 45¢), except on longer journeys when the fare exceeds 100F ($14.30); in these cases, a 5 to 10 percent tip is appropriate.

Check the meter carefully, especially if you are coming in from an airport; rip-offs are very common. If you feel that you may have been overcharged, demand a receipt (which drivers are obligated to provide) and contact the Préfecture of Police (☎ **01-55-76-20-00**).

Getting around by Car

Streets are narrow, parking is next to impossible and nerve, skill, ruthlessness, and a knowledgeable copilot are required if you insist on driving in Paris. I *strongly* recommend that you do not.

A few tips: Get an excellent street map and ride with another person; traffic moves so lightning-fast you don't have time to think at intersections. For the most part, you must pay to park in Paris. Depending on the neighborhood, expect to pay 5F to 15F (75¢ to $2.15) an hour for a maximum of two hours. Place coins in the nearest meter, which issues you a ticket to place on your windshield. You can also buy parking cards at the nearest *tabac* for meters that accept only cards. Parking is free on Sundays, holidays, and for the entire month of August.

Drivers and all passengers must wear seat belts. Children under 12 must ride in the back seat. Drivers are supposed to yield to the car on the right, except where signs indicate otherwise, as at traffic circles.

Watch for the *gendarmes* (police officers), who lack patience and who consistently contradict the traffic lights. Horn blowing is frowned upon except in emergencies. Flash your headlights instead.

Top taxi stands

Go to the following locations within each arrondissement to find the most convenient taxi stands:

1er Arrondissement

Métro Concorde

Pl. André Malraux

Pl. du Châtelet

2e Arrondissement

Pl. de l'Opéra

3e Arrondissement

Métro Rambuteau

Square du Temple

4e Arrondissement

Métro St-Paul

5e Arrondissement

Pl. des Gobelins

Pl. Maubert

Pl. Monge

Pl. St-Michel

Pont de la Tournelle

6e Arrondissement

Métro Mabillon

Métro Port-Royal

Métro St-Germain

7e Arrondissement

Métro Bac

Métro La Tour-Maurbourg

Métro Solferino

Pl. de l'Ecole Militaire

Tour Eiffel

8e Arrondissement

Av. de Friedland

Pl. de L'Alma

Pl. de la Madeleine

Pl. des Ternes

Rond Point des Champs-Elysées

9e Arrondissement

Métro Richelieu-Drouout

Pl. d'Estienne d'Orves

Square de Montholon

11e Arrondissement

Métro Faidherbe-Chaligny

Métro Goncourt

Pl. de la Bastille

Pl. de la Nation

Pl. de la République

12e Arrondissement

Hôpital Trousseau

Château de Vincennes

Porte Dorée

13e Arrondissement

Métro Glacière

Porte d'Italie

Hôpital Pitié-Salpétrière (bd. de l'Hôpital)

14e Arrondissement

Métro Plaisance

Porte d'Orléans

Pl. Denfert-Rochereau

(continued)

(continued)

15e Arrondissement
Métro Bir-Hakeim

Métro LaMotte-Piquet Grenelle

Métro Convention

Place Balard

16e Arrondissement
Métro Muette

Métro Passy

Maison de la Radio

Pl. d'Iéna

Pl. du Trocadero

17e Arrondissement
Métro Brochant

Métro Villiers

Pl. Charles de Gaulle

Porte de Clichy

Porte de Saint-Ouen

18e Arrondissement
Métro Lamarck-Calaincourt

Pl. Blanche

Pl. de la Clichy

Pl. Jules Joffrin

Pl. du Tertre

19e Arrondissement
Métro Stalingrad

Métro Botzaris

Porte de Lilas

Porte de Pantin

Porte de la Villette

20e Arrondissement
Métro Ménilmontant

Métro Père Lachaise

Métro Porte de Montreuil

Métro Pyrénées

Getting around by Bicycle

City planners have been trying to encourage more cycling by setting aside 62 miles of bicycle lanes throughout Paris. The main routes run north-south from the Bassin de La Villette along the Canal St-Martin through the Left Bank and east-west from Château de Vincennes to the Bois de Boulogne and its miles of bike lanes. For more information and a bike map, pick up the *Plan Vert* from the tourist office. In addition, the banks of the Seine are closed to cars and opened to pedestrians and cyclists each Sunday from March to November 10 a.m. to 5 p.m. It may not make much of a dent in the air quality, but bicycling is a fun and healthy way to spend a Sunday afternoon.

To rent a bicycle, contact **Paris-Vélo,** 2 rue du Fer-à-Moulin, 5e (☎ 01-43-37-59-22; Métro: St-Marcel). The price is 80F ($11.45) a day, 60F ($8.60) a half-day. A steep deposit is required.

You don't need a deposit to take a bike tour of the city (see Chapter 18).

Getting around Paris á Pied (on Foot)

Paris is one of the prettiest cities in the world for strolling, and getting around on foot is probably the best way to really appreciate the city's character. The best walking neighborhoods are **St-Germain-des-Prés** on the Left Bank and the **Marais** on the Right Bank, both of which are filled with romantic little courtyards, wonderful boutiques, and congenial cafés and watering holes. The quais of the Seine, as well as its bridges, are also lovely, especially at sunset when the sun fills the sky with a pink glow that's reflected on the water.

 A word to the wise: Take special care when crossing streets, even when you have the right of way. The number one rule of the road in France is that whoever is coming from the right side has the right of way. Drivers often make right turns without looking, even when faced with pedestrians at crosswalks. And don't *ever* attempt to cross a traffic circle if you're not on a crosswalk. The larger roundabouts, such as the one at the Arc de Triomphe, have pedestrian tunnels.

Chapter 12

Money Matters

● ●

In This Chapter

▶ Understanding the franc

▶ Finding out where to get cash in Paris

▶ Getting the last word on tax

● ●

*H*istoric monuments commemorating the events that created Paris
are free. Many museums offer reduced entrance fees at certain
times, and are free the first Sunday of every month. The parks are free,
and you can linger over a glass of wine in a café, or walk to your heart's
content among floodlit monuments, or stroll the quays *(quais)* and
bridges of the Seine. So how expensive, really, is Paris? At press time, a
surging dollar made it about on par with New York and San Francisco. If
you're not from those cities, however, Paris can still seem expensive
because merchants need to cover the 20.6 *détaxe* (abbreviated TVA),
which is also called a value added tax (VAT).

Fortunately, you have plenty of ways to keep your travel costs down.
Consider this chapter a toolkit to help you do just that.

French Currency: The Franc and the Euro

The unit of French currency is the *franc* (written F or FF), divided into
100 centimes. Bills come in denominations of 500F, 100F, 50F, and 20F;
you also must deal with 20F, 10F, 5F, 1F, 1/2F and 20, 10, and 5 centime
coins. Franc coins are silver and heavier, while centime coins are
copper and lighter. Franc coins add up quickly, so think twice about
emptying out your pockets to panhandlers; you may have a dinner's
worth of change on you. Remember, too, in preparation for the end of
your trip, that exchange bureaus do not change coins, so if you're
weighted down with change on your way out of the country, you're
going to be stuck with it.

At this writing, the rate of exchange was at a pleasantly favorable 7F to
the dollar. For a look at the most recent rates of exchange (updated

each minute), check out www.xe.net/currency or the exchange rate in the financial pages of your local newspaper.

Note that when writing sums of money, the French use commas where we use decimal points, and vice versa. For example, 1,200.58 francs is written as 1.200,58F.

The year 2001 is the last in which local commerce in France is conducted in the *franc.* After January 2002, 11 countries in the European Union will begin using the banknotes and coins of the *euro,* the single monetary unit that will eventually make it possible to travel in Europe without changing currency. Today the euro is used in financial transactions at the fixed rate of 6.55 francs to 1 euro. Many of your sales receipts will show totals in both euros and francs in preparation for the switch.

Here's a tip: The euro is very close in value to the dollar. As long as this balance lasts, you'll have a much easier time of estimating costs throughout France in terms of dollars.

Where to Get Cash

You can find a bank on nearly every corner in Paris, but if you're nervous about finding one, pay a visit to the Visa (www.visa.com/pd/atm) and MasterCard (www.mastercard.com/atm) Web sites, which identify the locations of cash machines all over Paris. Most of the major banks in Paris, such as Credit Lyonnais, Credit Agricole, Banque Nationale de Paris (BNP), Banque Populaire, Credit Commercial de France (CCF), Credit du Nord, and even some branches of the post office have automatic cash distribution machines. But you won't be able to check your balance or transfer funds, so keep track of your withdrawals while you travel. For more on using your ATM card in France, see Chapter 3.

You can exchange traveler's checks for francs at any of the following banks:

- ✔ **American Express,** 11 rue Scribe, 9e (☎ **01-47-14-50-00;** Métro: Opéra Chaussée-d'Antin or Havre-Caumartin; RER: Auber).

- ✔ **Barclay's,** 24 av. de l'Opéra, 1er (☎ **01-44-86-00-00;** Métro: Pyramides), or 96 rue Turenne, 3e (☎ **01-42-77-24-70;** Métro: St-Paul).

- ✔ **Citibank,** 125 av. Champs-Elysées, 8e (☎ **01-53-23-33-60;** Métro: Charles de Gaulle Étoile).

- ✔ **Lloyd's Bank,** 15 av. d'Iéna, 16e (☎ **01-44-43-42-41;** Métro: Iéna).

- ✔ **Thomas Cook,** 194 rue de Rivoli, 1er (☎ **01-42-60-37-61;** Metro: Tuileries), or 25 bd. des Capucines, 2e (☎ **01-42-96-26-78;** Metro: place de l' Opéra), and 18 other locations around Paris.

What to Do if Your Credit Card Is Lost or Stolen

Almost every credit card company has an emergency 800 number or toll-free international number that you can call if your wallet or purse is stolen. The company may be able to wire you a cash advance off your credit card immediately, and, in many places, can deliver an emergency credit card in a day or two. Call ☎ **08-36-69-08-80** if you've lost or had your **Visa** card stolen.

American Express card and traveler's check holders in France can call international collect (☎ **0800-99-00-11** for an AT&T operator; ☎ **0800-99-00-19** for MCI; ☎ **0800-99-00-87** for Sprint) ☎ **336-393-1111** for money emergencies; to report lost cards, call ☎ **01-47-77-72-00.**

For **MasterCard**, call ☎ **01-45-67-53-53** or 08-00-90-1387.

Taxing Matters

As noted earlier in the chapter, the price of all goods in Paris includes a 20.6-percent sales tax called the *détaxe*, abbreviated *TVA*. (Also sometimes referred to as value-added tax.) If you live outside the European Union, you can be reimbursed for part of the TVA you paid, but as always, a catch is involved: you have to spend at least 1200F ($171.45) in the same store *in the same day*. The amount of the refund varies from store to store, but generally comes out to about 13 percent of the tax you paid on the item. The department stores **Au Printemps** and **Galeries Lafayette** have special *détaxe* desks where clerks prepare your sales invoices, but small shops don't always have the necessary paperwork. (For information on how to get a TVA refund, see Chapter 19.)

Part IV
Dining in Paris

"Now THAT was a great meal! Beautiful
presentation, an imaginative use of
ingredients, and a sauce with nuance
and depth. The French really know
how to make a 'Happy Meal'."

In this part . . .

With many of the world's best chefs — and best restaurants — dining in Paris can be a wonderful experience that travelers greatly look forward to. Though dining out can be the highlight of your trip, it can also cause a lot of confusion if you're not familiar with the language, the regional specialties, the order in which the food is served, and tipping. Forget your worries — this section tells you all you need to know about French dining so that you can soon be chorusing *Bon appetit* as though you were born eating this way.

Chapter 13 presents an overview of French dining — what's hot now in Paris, where locals eat, how to dress to dine — and gives you tips for saving money, as well as a glossary that covers everything from cuts of meat to how dishes are prepared. Chapter 14 contains an alphabetical list of some of my favorite places to eat in Paris, with lots of low-to moderate-priced restaurants and only two true *haute cuisine* establishments. The restaurants are indexed by type of cuisine, price, and location for reader-friendliness. Chapter 15 provides options for when you just don't want to sit down to a full-course meal; everything's covered, from street food and sandwich shops to tea salons, cafés, wine bars, and ice cream places.

Chapter 13

The Lowdown on Paris Dining

*P*aris is restaurant heaven — but unless you grew up in France, it can be difficult to translate the different dishes on the menu or, sometimes, to make sense of the dining customs. (Salad before the meal and cheese after? Cheese before dessert or instead of it?) I designed this chapter to make you feel comfortable about dining in Parisian restaurants so that you can enjoy your dining experiences. I explain the differences between bistros, brasseries, cafés, and restaurants; offer money saving tips and suggestions on how to dress; and help you to become fluent in the whole business of dining *á la française*. And, oh, yes, let me get the matter of tipping out of the way now — don't worry about tipping in France because a 15-percent service charge is added to the bill. Etiquette dictates leaving a small token sum — 10F for a moderately priced meal — to let the waiter know you enjoyed your meal.

This is also probably a good time to mention that in France, as anywhere, you should never underestimate the importance of good manners. Your meal will be much smoother if you remember essential but basic phrases such as *"Bonjour, monsieur"* (hello, sir) and *"Merci, madame"* (thank you, madam). Keep in mind, too, that French table manners require that all food, even fruit, be eaten with a knife and fork.

Contrary to what you may have seen in the movies, never refer to the waiter as *"garcon,"* (man) and don't snap your fingers at him or her. Instead, say, *"Monsieur, s'il vous plaît!"* or *"Madame/Mademoiselle, s'il vous plaît!"* (Sir/Madam/Miss, if you please!).

Discussing the Latest Trends

Parisians take dining very seriously. They expect the same freshness and quality in their meals that their ancestors had, and newspapers are full of outrage that American fast food chains have made inroads into their country. They worry about the consequences of genetically altered fruits and vegetables, and though mad cow disease has not been as prevalent in France as it has been in England, each new case merits mention on the national news. But all this turmoil doesn't stop Parisians from dining out. They are on an eternal quest for the perfect meal, and make a pastime of sharing *les bonnes addresses* (the right addresses) with their friends.

And how many *bonnes addresses* are out there these days! In the last decade, the city has seen celebrity chefs open *baby bistros* — restaurants offering simpler and less expensive meals than served at their deluxe establishments — and the gifted young apprentices of these celebrity chefs, the *young upstarts,* open their own restaurants. The best baby bistros, like Spoon, Food & Wine from the seasoned chef Alain Ducasse, are still going strong, and the well prepared, home-style food of the young upstarts, such as that served by La Bastide Odéon, has become a trend everyone appreciates. Check out Chapter 14 for more on these restaurants and other great baby bistros and young upstarts in Paris.

In addition, the reopenings of two palace hotels that had been closed for renovations — the Hôtel Meurice and the George V (now called the Four Seasons Hotel George V) — have given Paris two new gastronomically sophisticated restaurants that are drawing raves and are almost certain to draw Michelin stars. (See Chapter 14 for a review of Le Cinq, the restaurant in the Four Seasons Hotel George V.)

Figuring Out Where the Locals Eat

Eateries go by various names in France, and in theory at least, these labels give you some clue to how much a meal costs. From most expensive to least expensive, the lineup generally goes like this: restaurant, bistro, brasserie, café. The key word is *generally*. Never rely on the name of an establishment as the sole price indicator; some of the city's most expensive eateries call themselves cafés. Furthermore, the awnings above quintessential cafés often claim the labels of restaurant, café, brasserie or some other combination. The only way to be sure of the price is to read the menu, which by law must be posted outside the eatery. Here's how the various eateries break out:

> ✔ **Restaurants** are where you go to savor French cuisine in all its glory. At their best, classic dishes are excellent, and new dishes

are invented. Dining is usually more formal than in bistros or brasseries, and service is slower. You may also have more than one server. Like bistros, restaurants serve lunch between noon and 2:30 p.m. and dinner between 7 and 10 p.m. Generally, you must be seated for lunch no later than 2 p.m. if you want a full meal. Between 3 p.m. and 7 p.m., you may find it nearly impossible to have a sit-down meal in a Paris restaurant or bistro. During the swing shift, your best bet is to head to a café, tea room, or wine bar. Dining at 7 p.m. is considered very early dinner in Paris; most Parisians wouldn't think about sitting down before 8 p.m. But starting too late — 10 p.m. is getting dangerous — can also leave you without too many options.

Given the opportunity, check out the *ménu dégustation* (sampler, or tasting, menu; meh–noo day–goo–stah–sion), featured in many of the city's top restaurants. Made up of small portions of the chef's signature dishes, it offers tremendous value because you have the opportunity to try more dishes.

✔ The typical **bistro** used to be a mom-and-pop operation with a menu confined to Parisian standbys like *boeuf bourguignon* (braised beef in red wine sauce*),* and *tarte Tatin* (caramelized upside-down apple pie). Today many bistros have expanded upon the old classics but retained the tradition of offering hearty, relatively low-priced dishes in a convivial, intimate atmosphere. Think crush of elbows and the sounds of corks popping, glasses clinking, and people having a good time. Bistros are where Parisians come to dine the most often.

✔ Literally, the word **brasserie** means "brewery" and refers to the Alsatian menu specialties that include such staples as beer, Riesling wine, and *choucroute* (sauerkraut, usually topped by cuts of ham). Most brasseries are large, cheerful, brightly lit places that open early and close late (some are open 24 hours a day), and have an immense selection of dishes on the menu, although many no longer specialize in Alsatian fare. At brasseries, you can usually get a meal at any time of day, even in hours when restaurants and bistros are closed, and the food is relatively inexpensive.

Sadly, brasseries began to fall to corporate acquisition in the 1970s, and today are part of one all-encompassing chain (with the exception of Brasserie Ile St-Louis in the 1er; see Chapter 14). Although this fact shouldn't stop you from visiting some of Paris's legendary eateries, be on the lookout for places with mundane and repetitive food — they're more numerous than you think. Your best bet is to get a look at the menus of brasseries that interest you (Parisian law states that eateries must post their menus) and compare costs, as well as listings. If *poulet rôti* (rotisserie chicken), *steak frites* (steak and fries), and omelettes seem to be highlights, you may want to try eating somewhere else.

✔ **Cafés** typically open from about 8 a.m. to 1 a.m. They serve drinks and food all day from a short menu that often includes salads, sandwiches, mussels, and french fries. At meal times, selections also include rib-sticking dishes such as steak and fries or *pot-au feu* (beef boiled with vegetables). Cafés are best for light fare in between and after standard meal times. Parisians use cafés the way the British use pubs — as extensions of their living rooms. They're places you meet friends before heading to the movies or a party, read your newspaper, write in your journal, or just hang out and people watch. Regardless of whether you order a cup of coffee or the most expensive cognac in the house, no one will ask you to leave.

Coffee, of course, is the chief drink. It comes black in a small cup, unless you order a *café crème* or *café au lait* (coffee with steamed milk). Tea (*thé*, pronounced tay) is also fairly popular, but is generally not of a high quality. Hot chocolate (*chocolat chaud,* shock-o-lah-shoh), on the other hand, is absolutely superb and made from real ground chocolate.

✔ **Tea rooms,** or *salons de thé,* usually open mid-morning and close by early evening. Some serve light lunches, but most are at their best in the afternoon for desserts with coffee or tea.

✔ From mid-morning to late evening you can order wine by the glass and munch on snacks such as *tartines* (open-face sandwiches), olives, and cheese at **wine bars.** Some offer simple lunch menus, but like cafés and tearooms, they are generally better for light bites. Some of the city's best cafés, tearooms, and wine bars are recommended in Chapter 15.

Understanding the Order of a Meal

Be aware of the traditional way that French restaurants serve food:

✔ An *apéritif* is a drink that precedes the meal, but the French don't like to start a meal by numbing the palate with strong liquor. Try a *kir,* a mixture of white wine and crème de cassis (black currant), which is light and the most common pre-meal drink.

✔ You are always served bread with your meal, but you must request butter.

✔ Water is not placed on the table automatically — you must ask for it. To get regular water, as opposed to the pricey equivalent in a bottle, simply ask for *une carafe d'eau.*

✔ Many times, salads are served after meals, though salad as an appetizer is becoming more common.

✔ Cheese comes after the main course and is usually accompanied by red wine.

✔ Dessert comes after the cheese course, but dessert and cheese can be served at the same time if diners at the same table wish it.

✔ Coffee is not traditionally drunk with dessert but follows it, and is served black in a demitasse cup with sugar cubes on the side. If you want milk with your coffee, you must ask for a *café au lait* or *café crème.*

✔ Although a proper meal consists of three or sometimes four courses, portions are usually moderate.

✔ If you have food left on your plate, you should not ask for a doggie bag.

✔ The *menu du jour* at many establishments includes wine, red or white. The standard measure is *un quart* (a quarter-liter carafe), sometimes served in *un pot or un pichet* (a pitcher). If wine is not included, you can order *vin ordinaire* (house wine) or a Beaujolais (a light, fruity red wine) or Côtes du Rhône (a dry red wine), which are very reasonably priced. Of course, you can always opt for soda, juice, or water instead (*l'eau plat* [low plah] is still water); *l'eau gazeuse* [low gaz–ooz] is carbonated water). Cocktails are available but discouraged, as they are thought to numb the palate.

✔ Coffee is never drunk during a meal.

Finding Ethnic Eateries

Even the French need a break from French food every once in a while, and you may find your taste buds craving something different and perhaps highly spiced. If this is the case, take advantage of the Chinese, Thai, Vietnamese, Indian, Tex-Mex, and Russian restaurants that are popular with residents, although not necessarily cheaper than French restaurants. Try the 10e or 18e for North African, Turkish, Vietnamese, and Thai. Probably the most popular ethnic dish in France is couscous from North Africa — steamed semolina garnished with broth, stewed vegetables, and meat; you can find at least one restaurant or *couscouserie* on nearly every street in the capital.

Dressing to Dine

Only the most expensive restaurants enforce dress codes (suit and tie), and in theory you can dress up or down as you like. Realize, however, that Parisians are a pretty stylish lot, even when dressing informally. Relaxed dressing doesn't mean sloppy jeans and sneakers — *especially* sneakers. The look to aim for is casual Fridays at work. You won't go wrong if you dress in neutral colors — think black, beige, cream, navy, and chocolate. Go a notch dressier than what you'd wear at home. Even at neighborhood bistros, most men wear sports jackets and women wear skirts or smart pants suits and the ever-present scarf.

What's that? A few traditional (and a few adventurous) French dishes

Even with English translations, confronting a French menu can be a daunting experience. Dishes that have been familiar to French people since childhood are often unknown to outsiders. Following is a user's guide to typically French dishes that you are likely to encounter.

Andouillette. A sausage of pork organs encased in intestines. Andouillette has a strong flavor with a distinct aftertaste and is usually grilled and served with mustard and French fries. Look for the A.A.A.A.A. label — the Association Amicale des Authentiques Amateurs d'Andouillettes (association of real andouillette lovers) stamps it on the best andouillettes.

Blanquette de veau. Veal cooked in a "white" stew that includes eggs and cream.

Boeuf Bourguignon. Beef cooked with red burgundy wine, mushrooms, and onions.

Boudin. A rich sausage made from pig's blood, usually combined with _crème fraîche,_ onions, and eggs. More elaborate versions may feature a touch of garlic or chestnuts. The dish is often served with sautéed apples or mashed potatoes, which enhance the slightly sweet taste of the sausage.

Boudin blanc. A "white sausage" made from veal, chicken, or pork.

Bouillabaisse. A fish stew from the Mediterranean that includes assorted shellfish and white fish accompanied by croutons, grated cheese, and _rouille,_ a mayonnaise made with garlic.

Brandade. Salt cod _(morue)_ soaked in cold water, shredded, and cooked with garlic, olive oil, milk, and potato. It has the look and consistency of mashed potatoes but tastes like salted fish. A green salad makes a good accompaniment.

Carpaccio. Thinly sliced, cured raw beef or tuna.

Cassoulet. A rich stew made of white beans, dry sausage, onion, duck meat, prosciutto, herbs, carrots, and tomatoes which is cooked slowly and usually served in a ceramic bowl or pot. Absolutely delicious, but heavy; don't plan any serious physical exertions after eating, digestion will be enough.

Cervelles. Pork or sheep brains.

Cheval. Horse meat.

Choucroute. Sauerkraut cooked with juniper berries and wine, served with an assortment of pork cuts, usually including brisket, pork shoulder, ham, frankfurters, or spicy sausage. It goes well with boiled potatoes and is served with mustard.

Confit de Canard. A duck leg cooked and preserved in its own fat. The fatty skin is usually salty, but the meat underneath is tender and juicy. Mashed potatoes make a good side dish.

Cuisses de grenouilles. Frogs' legs.

Escargots. Snails.

Foie. Liver.

Gesiers. Gizzards, very good in *salade landaise* or *salade gesiers*.

Lapin à la Moutarde. Rabbit cooked with mustard, créme fraîche, and sometimes white wine. The mustard perks up the rabbit meat, which has a mild flavor.

Lièvre. Hare.

Magret de Canard. The sliced breast of a fattened duck, sautéed and sometimes served with a green peppercorn sauce. The result more closely resembles red meat than poultry. As with any meat, specify how you would like it cooked — *bleu* (very rare), *saignant* (rare), *à point* (medium), or *bien cuit* (well done).

Pieds de cochon. Pig's feet.

Plateau de Fruits de Mer. A variety of raw and cooked seafood served on ice. You usually find two kinds of oysters— flat, round *belon,* and larger, crinkly *creuse.* Both types are cultivated, not harvested. The oysters are eaten with lemon or red-wine vinegar accompanied by thin slices of buttered rye bread. In addition to various kinds of shrimp, clams, and mussels, you also see periwinkles *(bulots),* which are eaten with mayonnaise.

Pot-au-Feu. A hearty dish of boiled vegetables and beef that sometimes includes the marrow bone. Scrape out the marrow, spread it on toast, and sprinkle it with salt. Sometimes the broth is served first, followed by the vegetables and beef. Mustard is the preferred condiment.

Ris de Veau. The thymus gland of a calf (a white meat) sautéed in a butter and cream sauce. It has a delicate, pleasant taste but is high in cholesterol.

Rognons. Kidneys.

Tête de veau. Calf's head.

Benefiting from Some Money-Saving Advice

If you're watching your pocketbook when it comes to dining out, following a few of these simple tips can go a long way toward making the bill as appealing as the food you are served.

✔ **Order prix-fixe (set-price) meals.** These set-price meals are up to 30 percent cheaper than ordering the same dishes *a la carte.* What's the trade-off? Your options are more limited than if you order from the main menu. Review the prix-fixe option carefully to determine what you're getting at that price. Does it come with wine, and, if so, how much — a glass or a half bottle? Is dessert or coffee included?

✔ **Make lunch your main meal.** Many restaurants offer great deals on a fixed-price lunch. You probably won't be hungry for a full meal after two or three courses at lunch.

✔ **Try the crêperies.** Crêperies (you can find many off the bd. du Montparnasse around the Square Delambre) offer a great value — you can enjoy meat- or vegetable-filled *galettes* and dessert crêpes with a bowl of cider in Brittany-inspired surroundings.

✔ **Eat at chain restaurants.** Chain restaurants such as Batifol, Hippopotamus, Léon de Bruxelles, and l'Écluse offer some good-value meals, as well as sandwich shops such as Pommes des Pains and Lina's.

✔ **Pay attention to the details of the menu.** On most menus the cheaper dishes are made of cheaper cuts of meat or the organs of animals, like brains, tripe, and the like.

✔ **Don't eat breakfast at your hotel** unless you want to add at least $5 more per person to your hotel bill. Grab a croissant or a *pain au chocolat* (chocolate pastry) from a *boulangerie* (bakery).

✔ **Know the tipping rules.** Service is usually included at restaurants; don't double-tip by mistake. If service is excellent, however, you may want to round up the price with a few francs.

Making Reservations

The vast majority of French restaurants are very small establishments with limited seating, and tables are scrupulously saved for folks who book. Always try to make at least a same-day reservation, even for a modest neighborhood bistro. Some top restaurants require several weeks' notice. Remember to call if you're going to be more than 20 minutes late. Showing up late is considered bad form.

If you're staying at a hotel with a staff concierge, phone or fax ahead and ask the concierge to make a reservation at the sought-after restaurant where you'd like to eat. Do this as early as possible, specifying your preferred date with a back-up date or two. Don't forget to tip him for his efforts (slip 50F discreetly into an envelope which you present to him when checking out).

A Glossary That's Good Enough to Eat

Use this helpful guide when you're trying to decide what to order and how you want it cooked.

General terms

Compris (comb–*pree*)   included
Déjeuner (*day*–zhu–nay)   lunch
Dîner (*dee*–nay)   dinner

Petit Déjeuner (pet–*tee day*–zhu–nay)   breakfast
Supplément (sup–play–*mahn*)   extra charge

Les Entrées (Appetizers)

Charcuterie (shar–koot–*ree*)   assorted cold cuts

Crudités (kroo–dee–*tay*)   assorted raw vegetables

Foie gras (fwah grah)   goose liver paté

Saumon fumé   (soh–*moh foo*–may)   smoked salmon

Soupe à l'oignon (soop–ah–lowh–*yon*)   onion soup

Soupe à pistou (soop–ah–pees–*too*)   vegetable soup with pesto

Velouté (vay–loot–*ay*)   cream-based soup

Vichyssoise (vee–shee–*swahz*)   cold leek and potato soup

Salade composée (sa–*lad com*–poh–zay)   mixed salad

Salade de chèvre chaud (sa–*lad* deh–shev–rah–*sho*)   salad with warm goat cheese on croutons

Salade gesiers (sa–*lad* zheh–shee–*air*)   salad with sauteed chicken gizzards

Salade landaise (sa–*lad* lahn–*dehs*)   salad containing duck breast, duck liver, and duck gizzards

Salade de Niçoise (sa–*lad* nee–*shwahz*)   salad with tuna, canned corn, anchovies, and potato

Boeuf (Beef)

à point (a pwahn)   medium

Bavette (bah–*vet*)   flank steak

Bien cuit (byen kwee)   well done

Bleu (bluh)   very rare

Chateaubriand (cha–tow–bree–*ahn*)   Porterhouse

Contre-filet (*kahn*–trah–fee–lay)   Filet steak

Côte de boeuf (cote dah boof)   T-bone

Entrecôte (ahn–trah–*cote*)   rib-eye

Faux-filet (foe–fee–*lay*)   sirloin

Filet mignon (fee–*lay* mee–*nyahn*)   tenderloin

Langue de boeuf (lahng dah boof)   tongue

Onglet (ahn–*glay*)   hanger steak

Pavé   (pah–*vay*)   thick steak (translates literally as "paving stone")

Queue de boeuf (kyew dah boof)   oxtail

Rôti de boeuf (*roe*–tee dah boof)   roast beef

Saignant (sen–*yahn*)   rare

Steack haché (stake *ha*–shay)   minced meat or hamburger

Steak tartare (stake tar–*tar*)   a lean cut of beef that is minced and served raw (a high quality dish prepared by experts, people rarely get sick from eating this)

Tournedo (*tor*–nay–doe)   small tender filet usually grilled or sautéed

Veau (voe)   veal

Other meats

Agneau (ah–*nyoe*)   lamb

Gigot (*gee*–joe)   leg (usually of lamb)

Jambon (zhahm–*bon*)   ham

Médaillon (meh–dah–ee–*on*)   medallions (beef, veal, lamb)

Merguez (mare–*gay*)   spicy sausage

Porc (pork)   pork

Saucisses/saucisson (soh–*sees*, soh–see–*sohn*)   sausage/little sausage

Volailles (Fowl)

Blanc de volaille (blahn dah voe–*lai*)   chicken breast

Caille (kaih)   quail

Canard (kah–*nahr*)   duck

Dinde (dand)   turkey

Magret de canard (mah–*gret* dah kah–*nahr*)   duck breast

Oie (wah)   goose

Pigéon (pee–jee–*ohn*)   game pigeon

Pintade (pan–*tahd*)   guinea fowl

Poulet (*poo*–lay)   chicken

Fruits de Mer/Poissons (Seafood/Fish)

Bar (bar) bass
Coquilles St-Jacques (*koe*–kee san–*jahk*) scallops
Crevettes (kreh–*vet*) shrimp
Daurade (doe–*rahd*) sea bream
Homard (oe–*mahr*) lobster
Huîtres (wee–*tra*) oysters
Langoustine (lang–oo–*steen*) crayfish

Morue/Cabillaud (moh–roo, ka–bee–*oh*) cod
Moules (mool) mussels
Rascasse (ras–*kass*) scorpion fish
Raie (ray) skate
Rouget (roo–*zhay*) red mullet
Saumon (soh–*moh*) salmon
Thon (than) tuna
Truite (trweet) trout

Les Légumes (Vegetables)

Artichault (ar–tee–*show*) artichoke
Asperge (as–*pearzh*) asparagus
Aubergine (oe–bur–*zheen*) eggplant
Champignons/Cèpes/Truffes/Girolles (sham–pee–*nyahn*, sep, troof, *gee*–roll) mushrooms
Choucroute (shoo–*kroot*) cauliflower
Choux (shoo) cabbage
Choux de Bruxelles (shoo dah broo–*zells*) Brussels sprouts
Courgette (kore–*zhette*) zucchini
Épinard (ay–pee–*nahr*) spinach
Haricots (ahr–ee–*koe*) beans
Haricots verts (*ahr*–ee–koe–vair) string beans

Oignons (wah–*nyoh*) onions
Petits pois (*pet*–tee pwah) peas
Poireaux (pwah–*roe*) leeks
Poivron rouge (pwah–vrah–*roozh*) red pepper
Poivron vert (pwah–vrah–*vair*) green pepper
Pomme de terre (pum–dah–*tair*) potato
Pommes frites (pum freet) French fries
Riz (ree) rice
Tomate (toe–*maht*) tomato

Les Fruits (Fruit)

Abricot (*ah*–bree–koh) apricot
Ananas (a–*na*–nas) pineapple
Banane (bah–*nan*) banana
Cerise (sair–*ees*) cherry
Citron (see–*troh*) lemon
Citron vert (see–troh–*vair*) lime
Fraise (frayz) strawberry
Framboise (frahm–*bwahz*) raspberry
Myrtille (meer–*teel*) blueberry

Pamplemousse (pahm–pull–*moos*) grapefruit
Pêche (pehsh) peach
Poire (pwahr) pear
Pomme (pum) apple
Prune (proon) plum
Pruneau (proo–*noh*) prune
Raisin (rah–*zeen*) grape
Raisin sec (rah–zeen–*sek*) raisin

Les Desserts (Desserts)

Clafoutis (clah–foo–*tee*) thick batter filled with fruit and fried
Charlotte (shar–*lote*) molded cream ringed with a biscuit
Crème brûlée (krem broo–*lay*) creamy custard with caramel topping
Fromage blanc (froe–*mahzh* blahn) smooth cream cheese
Gâteau (gah–*toe*) cake
Glace (glahs) ice cream

Marquise (mar–*keez*) light, mousse-like cake
Mousse au chocolat (moos oh shok–*lah*) chocolate mousse
Tarte aux . . . (tart oh . . .) pie
Tarte tatin (tart ta–*ta*) caramelized upside-down apple pie
Vacherin (*Vahsh*–reh) cake of layered meringue, fruit, and ice cream

How dishes are prepared

À l'ail (ah lai)   with garlic

Au four (oh fore)   baked

Béarnaise (bare–*nayse*)   Hollandaise sauce with tarragon, vinegar, and shallots

Bechamel (beh–sha–*mel*)   white sauce made with onions and nutmeg

Beurre blanc (bur blahn)   white sauce made with butter, white wine, and shallots

Bordelaise (bore–dah–*lays*)   brown meat stock made with red wine, mushrooms, shallots, and beef marrow

Bouilli (bwee–*ee*)   boiled

Bourguignon   (bore–gee–*nyoh*) brown meat stock flavored with red wine, mushrooms, and onions

Confit (kahn–*fee*)   meat (usually duck or goose) cooked in its own fat

Consommé (kahn–soe–*may*)   clear broth

Coulis (koo–*lee*)   any nonflour sauce, purée, or juice

En croûte (ahn *kroot*)   in a pastry crust

Cru (kroo)   raw

Diable (dee–*ah*–blah)   brown sauce flavored with cayenne pepper, white wine, and shallots

Estouffade (ay–too–*fahd*)   meat that has been marinated, fried, and braised

Farci (fahr–*see*)   stuffed

Feuilleté (fwee–eh–*tay*)   in puff pastry

Fumé (*foo*–may)   smoked

Gratiné (*grah*–tee–nay)   topped with browned bread crumbs or cheese

Grillé (*gree*–ay)   grilled

Hollandaise (ahl–lan–*dehs*)   white sauce with butter, egg yolks, and lemon juice

Lyonnais (lee–ohn–*nay*)   with onions

Marinière (mar–ee–*nyair*)   steamed in garlicky wine stock

Meunière (moo–*nyur*)   fish rolled in flour and sautéed

En papillote (ohn pah–pee–*oat*) cooked in parchment and opened at the table (usually fish)

Parmentier (pahr–men–tee–*ay*)   with potato

Provençal (pro–ven–*saw*)   tomato-based sauce, with garlic, olives, and onions

Rôti (*roe*–tee)   roasted

Terrine (tuh–*reen*)   cooked in an earthenware dish

Chapter 14

Paris's Best Restaurants

• •

• •

You're in Paris, home to some of the world's greatest restaurants, and chances are you're going to want to experience a true French meal that stretches blissfully over several courses. You can do just that at most of the establishments listed in this chapter. They have all the ingredients of a great dining spot — fantastic cooking, reasonable prices, and great atmosphere — and create the kind of experience that lingers on in your memory after the last dishes are cleared away. When you're in the mood for just a light bite, turn to Chapter 15 for cafes, tearooms, wine bars, family chains, and sandwich shops.

The list here concentrates on moderately priced establishments from homey neighborhood favorites to chic "in" spots. Also included are some bargain eateries and a few of the city's most sumptuous restaurants where haute cuisine is an art form.

Restaurants are listed alphabetically for easy reference, followed by price range, neighborhood, and type of cuisine. Price ranges reflect the cost of a three-course meal for one person ordered à la carte featuring an appetizer, main dish, dessert, and coffee:

$	Under 125F ($17.90)
$$	125–200F ($17.90–$28.60)
$$$	200–300F ($28.60–$42.90)
$$$$	300–500F ($42.90–$71.45)
$$$$$	Over 500F ($71.45)

The dollars give you a general idea of how much a meal costs at dinner — but don't make price your only criteria for choosing a restaurant. Most establishments offer fixed-price menus (also called *formules* or *prix fixe*) that can bring the cost down one whole price category.

Restaurants on the Right Bank

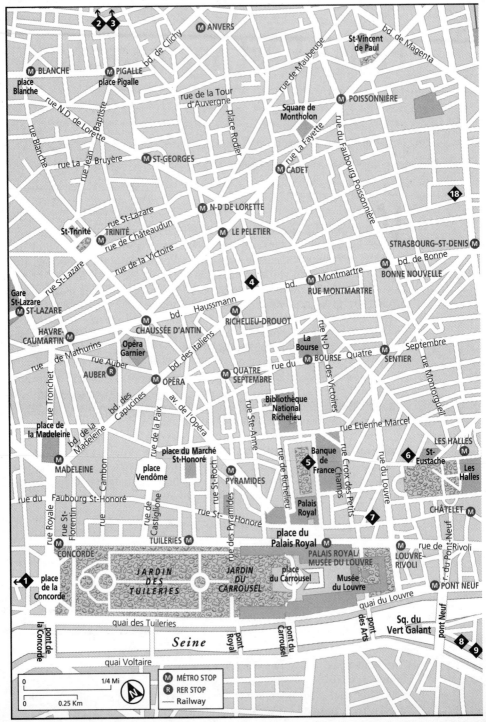

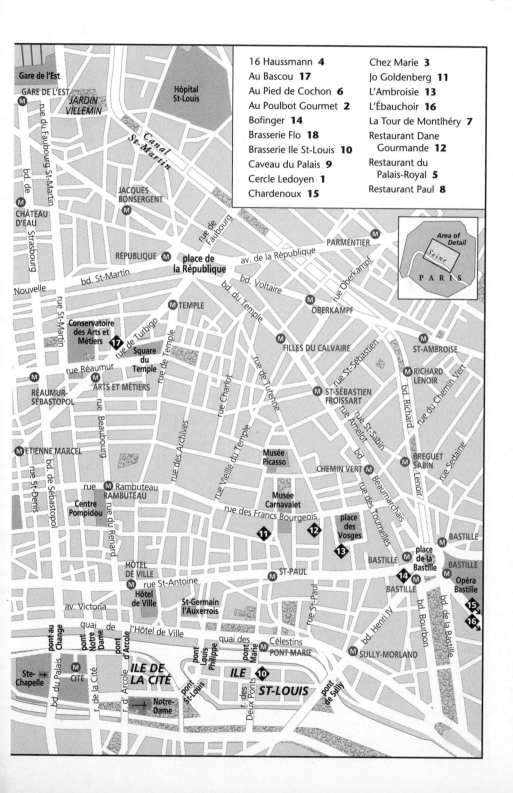

16 Haussmann **4**
Au Bascou **17**
Au Pied de Cochon **6**
Au Poulbot Gourmet **2**
Bofinger **14**
Brasserie Flo **18**
Brasserie Ile St-Louis **10**
Caveau du Palais **9**
Cercle Ledoyen **1**
Chardenoux **15**

Chez Marie **3**
Jo Goldenberg **11**
L'Ambroisie **13**
L'Ébauchoir **16**
La Tour de Montlhéry **7**
Restaurant Dane
  Gourmande **12**
Restaurant du
  Palais-Royal **5**
Restaurant Paul **8**

Also, if you're dying to try a place that's above your budget, visit it at lunch — when meals are cheaper.

Paris Restaurants at a Glance

Use these handy indexes to choose a restaurant according to location, budget, and/or type of cuisine. Then read their individual reviews.

Restaurant index by location: Right Bank

The following lists restaurants by neighborhood on the Right Bank of the Seine:

Louvre, Ile de la Cité (1er)
Caveau du Palais $$
Restaurant du Palais-Royal $$
Restaurant Paul $$

Les Halles (1er)
Au Pied de Cochon $–$$
La Tour de Montlhéry $$
Les Halles $–$$

Opéra (2e, 9e)
16 Haussmann $$–$$$
Chartier $

Le Marais, Ile St-Louis (3e, 4e)
Au Bascou $
Bofinger $$
Brasserie Ile St-Louis $–$$

Jo Goldenberg $
L'Ambroisie $$$$$
Restaurant Dane Gourmande $$

Champs-Elysées (8e and 17e)
Cercle Ledoyen $$$
Le Cinq $$$$$
Rotisserie Armaillé $$–$$$
Spoon, Food and Wine $$–$$$

Gare du Nord, Edge of Belleville (10e)
Brasserie Flo $$ (Gare du Nord)
Chez Casimir $
Chez Michel $$
Le Galopin $ (Belleville)

Bastille (11e)
Chardenoux $–$$
Dame Jeanne $$
L'Ebauchoir $–$$

Montmartre (18e)
Au Poulbot Gourmet $–$$
Chez Marie $–$$

Restaurant index by location: Left Bank

The following lists restaurants by neighborhood on the Left Bank of the Seine:

Latin Quarter (5e)
Brasserie Balzar $–$$
Chantairelle $–$$

Le Grenier de Notre-Dame $
Restaurant Perraudin $–$$
Vivario $$

St-Germain-des-Prés (6e)
À la Bonne Crêpe $
Alcazar $$$$
Chez Maître Paul $$
La Bastide Odéon $$
La Petite Chaise $$
Le Polidor $–$$
Vagenende $$

Eiffel Tower and Invalides (7e and 15e)

Au Bon Accueil $$–$$$
La Cigale $–$$
La Petite Chaise $$
Le Père Claude $$

Montparnasse (6e and 14e)

Closerie des Lilas $$–$$$$

Restaurant index by price category

$

À La Bonne Crêpe (St-Germain-des-Prés)
Au Bascou (Le Marais)
Chartier (Opéra)
Jo Goldenberg (Le Marais)
Le Galopin (Belleville)
Le Grenier de Notre-Dame
     (Latin Quarter)

$$

Au Pied de Cochon (Les Halles)
Au Poulbot Gourmet (Montmartre)
Bofinger (Le Marais)
Brasserie Balzar (Latin Quarter)
Brasserie Flo (Gare du Nord)
Brasserie Ile St-Louis. (Ile-St-Louis)
Caveau du Palais (Louvre)
Chantairelle (Latin Quarter)
Chardenoux (Bastille)
Chez Maître Paul (St-Germain-des-Prés)
Chez Marie (Montmartre)
Dame Jeanne (Bastille)
La Bastide Odéon (St-Germain-des-Prés)

La Cigale (Eiffel Tower)
La Petite Chaise (Eiffel Tower)
La Tour de Montlhéry (Les Halles)
Le Père Claude (Eiffel Tower)
Le Polidor (St-Germain-des-Prés)
Les Halles (Les Halles)
Restaurant Dane Gourmande
     (Le Marais)
Restaurant du Palais-Royal (Louvre)
Restaurant Paul (Ile de la Cité)
Restaurant Perraudin (Latin Quarter)
Vagenende(St-Germain-des-Prés)
Vivario (Latin Quarter)

$$$

16 Haussmann (Opéra)
Au Bon Accueil (Eiffel Tower)
Cercle Ledoyen (Champs-Elysées)
Closerie des Lilas (Montparnasse)
Rotisserie Armaillé (Champs-Elysées)
Spoon, Food and Wine (Champs-
     Elysées)

$$$$–$$$$$

Alcazar (St-Germain-des-Prés)
L'Ambroisie (Le Marais)
Le Cinq (Champs-Elysées)

Restaurant index by cuisine

Alsatian/Brasserie

Alcazar ($$$$, St-Germain-des-Prés)
Bofinger ($$–$$$, Le Marais)
Brasserie Balzar ($–$$, Latin Quarter)
Brasserie Flo ($$, Gare du Nord)

Brasserie Ile St-Louis ($–$$, Ile St-Louis)
Closerie des Lilas ($$–$$$$,
     Montparnasse)
Le Galopin ($, Belleville)
Vagenende ($$, St-Germain-des-Prés)

Auvergne

Chantairelle ($–$$, Latin Quarter)
Basque/Southwest
Au Bascou ($, Le Marais)

Restaurants on the Left Bank

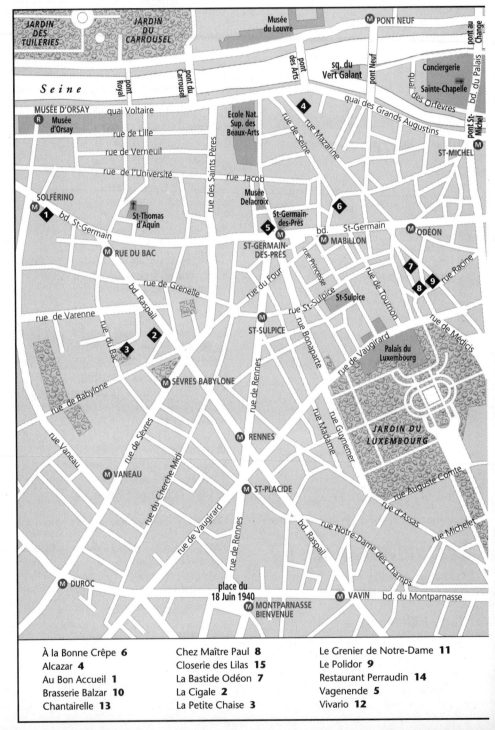

À la Bonne Crêpe **6**	Chez Maître Paul **8**	Le Grenier de Notre-Dame **11**
Alcazar **4**	Closerie des Lilas **15**	Le Polidor **9**
Au Bon Accueil **1**	La Bastide Odéon **7**	Restaurant Perraudin **14**
Brasserie Balzar **10**	La Cigale **2**	Vagenende **5**
Chantairelle **13**	La Petite Chaise **3**	Vivario **12**

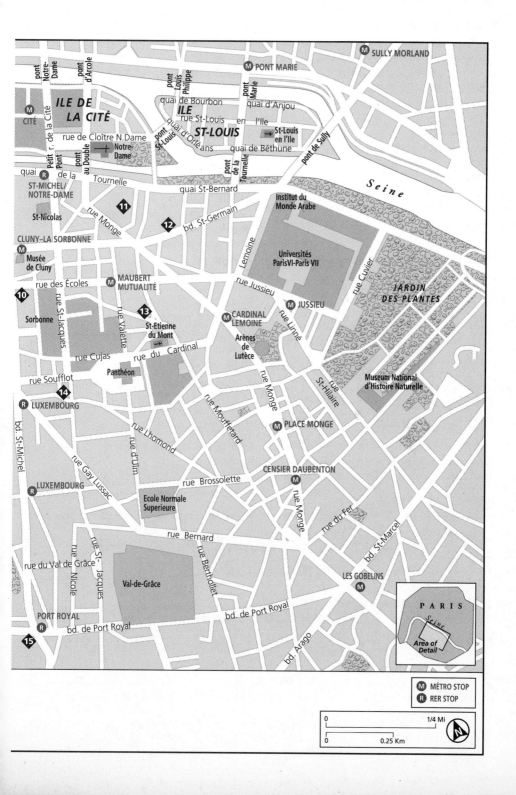

SULLY MORLAND

PONT MARIE

pont Notre-Dame

pont d'Arcole

pont Louis Philippe

pont Marie

quai de Bourbon

quai d'Anjou

ILE DE LA CITÉ

ILE ST-LOUIS

rue St-Louis en l'Ile

CITÉ

rue de Cloître N.Dame

Petit r. de la Cité

quai d'Orléans

rue St-Louis

quai de Béthune

St-Louis en l'Ile

Notre-Dame

Pont au Double

pont de la Tournelle

pont de Sully

quai de la Tournelle

ST-MICHEL/ NOTRE-DAME

quai St-Bernard

Seine

Institut du Monde Arabe

St-Nicolas

rue Monge

bd. St-Germain

11

12

CLUNY–LA SORBONNE

Musée de Cluny

Universités ParisVI-Paris VII

rue Lemoine

rue Cuvier

JARDIN DES PLANTES

rue des Écoles

MAUBERT MUTUALITÉ

rue Jussieu

rue St-Jacques

10

Sorbonne

rue Valette

13

St-Etienne du Mont

CARDINAL LEMOINE

JUSSIEU

rue Linné

rue Cujas

rue du Cardinal

Arènes de Lutèce

rue St-Hilaire

Museum National d'Histoire Naturelle

rue Soufflot

Panthéon

14

LUXEMBOURG

rue Mouffetard

rue Monge

PLACE MONGE

bd. St-Michel

rue Lhomond

rue d'Ulm

CENSIER DAUBENTON

rue Monge

rue du Fer

LUXEMBOURG

rue Gay Lussac

rue Brossolette

Ecole Normale Superieure

bd. St-Marcel

rue Bernard

rue du Val de Grâce

rue Nicole

rue St- Jacques

rue Berthollet

Val-de-Grâce

LES GOBELINS

PORT ROYAL

bd. de Port Royal

bd. de Port Royal

bd. Arago

15

P A R I S

Seine

Area of Detail

M MÉTRO STOP

R RER STOP

0   1/4 Mi

0   0.25 Km

Breton/Crêpes

À la Bonne Crêpe ($, St-Germain-des-Prés)
Chez Michel ($$, Gare du Nord)
Central European
Jo Goldenberg ($, Marais)

Classic Bistro

Chardenoux ($–$$, Bastille)
La Cigale ($–$$, Eiffel Tower)
L'Ébauchoir ($–$$, Bastille)
Le Père Claude ($$, Eiffel Tower)
Le Polidor ($–$$, St-Germain-des-Prés)
Restaurant Perraudin ($–$$, Latin Quarter)

Classic French

16 Haussmann ($$–$$$, Opéra)
Au Pied de Cochon ($–$$, Les Halles)
Au Poulbot Gourmet ($–$$, Montmartre)
Caveau du Palais ($$, Ile de la Cité)
Cercle Ledoyen ($$$, Champs-Elysées)
Chez Casimir ($, Gare du Nord)
Chez Maître Paul, ($$, St-Germain-des-Prés)
Chez Marie ($–$$, Montmartre)
La Petite Chaise ($$, St-Germain-des-Prés)
La Tour de Montlhéry ($$, Les Halles)
Restaurant du Palais-Royal ($$, Louvre)
Restaurant Paul ($$, Ile de la Cité)

Corsican

Vivario ($$, Latin Quarter)

Haute Cuisine

L'Ambroisie ($$$$$, Le Marais)
Le Cinq ($$$$$, Champs-Elysées)

Lyonnaise

Restaurant Dane Gourmande ($$, Le Marais)

Modern Bistro

Au Bon Accueil ($$–$$$, Eiffel Tower)
Dame Jeanne ($$, Bastille)
Rotisserie Armaillé ($$–$$$, Champs-Elysées)
Spoon, Food and Wine ($$–$$$, Champs-Elysées)

Modern Brasserie

Alcazar ($$$$, St-Germain-des-Prés)

Provençal

La Bastide Odéon ($$, St-Germain-des-Prés)

Vegetarian

Le Grenier de Notre-Dame ($, Latin Quarter)

Ooh! La! La! Sampling the regional French cuisines

Alsatian/Brasserie

Alsatian refers to the specialties from the Alsace region of France, which lies close to Germany. Most notable among these specialties are beer, Riesling wine, and *choucroute* (sauerkraut cooked in wine, topped with tender morsels of beef or pork, and accompanied by potatoes). Most Alsatian restaurants in Paris are brasseries.

Auvergne

This rugged region in the center of southern France is known for hearty peasant cooking with generous portions. *Potée*, a thick soup from this region, filled with cabbage, turnips, potatoes, leeks, and morsels of pork, is especially rich.

Breton/Crêpes

You'll know a place is Breton if the menu consists of oysters, crêpes, and cider. Breton refers to the Brittany region on France's west coast, and Breton restaurants often boast low-beamed ceilings, checkered tablecloths, wildflowers in jugs, and an open stove.

Classic French

The meals of traditional French cooking have been enjoyed in France for centuries. French cooking is rich, however — dishes are made with butter, cream, and eggs, and organ meats are used often. Menus may include *cuisses de grenouilles* (frog's legs), *confit de canard* (duck leg preserved and cooked in its own fat), *blanquette de veau* (veal cooked in a whitish stew that includes eggs and cream), *pot-au-feu* (a hearty dish of boiled vegetables and beef that may include bone marrow), and *tarte tatin* (carmelized upside down apple pie).

Corsican

The earthy regional specialties from this island off the southern coast of France are not to be missed. Corsican livestock eat the herb-filled underbrush known as *maquis* that spicily infuses meats (*sanglier*, or wild boar, is a particular specialty) and cheeses (try the *brébis* in the cheesecake-like *fiadone*, a dessert from the island). Italian-influenced sauces and pasta are also on the menus; Corsica was once part of Italy.

Lyonnaise

Lyon, in central France, is home to celebrated chef Paul Bocuse, and sophisticated gastronomy is one of the city's chief attractions. A restaurant claiming to be Lyonnaise will have classic French dishes cooked to perfection and Lyonnaise specialties that may include *Jésus* (sausage with truffles) and *tablier de sapeur* (tripe).

Provençal

The dishes in this southeastern region of France rely heavily on tomatoes, herbs, garlic, and olive oil, with olives and anchovies also figuring prominently. *Bouillabaisse*, a stew made with three kinds of fresh fish, saffron, onions, tomatoes, and herbs, is the region's most famous dish.

Basque/Southwest

This beautiful area bordering Spain is home to the spiciest cuisine of the French regions. Menus may include *cassoulet basquaise*, made with red beans and duck, and the very spicy *boudin noir* (blood sausages).

Paris Restaurant Favorites from A to Z

16 Haussmann
$$–$$$ Opéra (9e)   CLASSIC FRENCH

A daring color scheme and bold concoctions are the hallmarks of this restaurant. *Oeufs coques à la crème d'épices et caramel de xérès* (soft-boiled eggs in sherry cream sauce with spices) is a good dish to start off your meal, while the *daube de joue de boeuf* (beef stew with carrots and leeks) is a delicious main course. Even with a tureen of salmon spread as an hors d'oeuvre, the two-course menu may not satisfy a large appetite, so plan on sampling one of the luscious desserts. Wines begin at 85F ($12.15) per half bottle, and a good selection of wines is available by the glass.

In the Hôtel Ambassador, 16 bd. Haussmann. ☎ *01-48-00-06-38. Métro: Chausée d'Antin or Richelieu-Drouot. Two-course menu 165F ($23.60); 3-course menu 200F ($28.60). AE, DC, MC, V. Open Mon–Fri noon–2:30 p.m. and 7–10:30 p.m.*

À la Bonne Crêpe
$ St-Germain-des-Prés (6e)   BRETON/CREPES

Sit at picnic like tables covered in checkered cloth, sip some hard cider, Brittany's answer to beer, and watch mouth watering crêpes being made on open stoves just a few feet away. Savory crêpes filled with cheese, meat, seafood, or other hearty ingredients are the main courses here, and sweet crêpes filled with jam, fruit or chocolate are a wonderful dessert.

11 rue Grégoire-de-Tours. ☎ *01-43-54-60-74. Métro: Odéon. Two-course lunch of a crêpe and glass of cider or wine: 50F ($7.15); à la carte: 16–50F ($2.30–$7.15). No credit cards. Open Mon–Sat noon–2 p.m. and 7–11 p.m. Closed last two weeks of August.*

Alcazar
$$$$ St-Germain-des-Prés (6e)   MODERN BRASSERIE

This smart and stylish 200-seat restaurant from England's Sir Terence Conran hit Paris by storm a few years ago; though its reviews have been mixed, Alcazar is still going strong. Chef Guillaume Lutard executes a mixed menu of brasserie fare with platters of shellfish and oysters, Mediterranean-inspired dishes like puff pastry with goat cheese and sun-dried tomatoes and Pan-Asian staples like chicken and duckling infused with soy sauce. The food is good and the service is friendly, but the sheer size of the dining room renders this restaurant deafening. An option is the upstairs piano bar, where you can order wine by the glass and small plates of sushi, oysters, caviar, foie gras, and smoked salmon.

62 rue Mazarine. ☎ 01-53-10-19-99. Reservations required at least two days ahead. Métro: Odéon. Main courses: 140–260F. Open daily noon–3 p.m. and 7:30 p.m. until 1 a.m.

Au Bascou
$ Le Marais (3e)   BASQUE/SOUTHWEST

Specializing in dishes from the Basque country, the corner of south-western France resting on the Spanish border, Au Bascou offers excellent meals. Start with *piperade* (pep–air–ahd), a delicious concoction of sautéed peppers and onions on salad leaves topped with ham; then try superb seasonal fish or *agneau de lait des Pyrénées rôti* (roasted milk-fed lamb). Finish up with *gâteau Basque,* a cake made of ground almonds and jam. A bottle of Basque's Irouleguy, a smooth red wine, makes a nice accompaniment to meals.

38 rue Réaumur. ☎ 01-42-72-69-25. Métro: Arts et Métiers. Main courses: 85F ($12.15). AE, MC, V. Open Tues–Fri noon–2 p.m.; Mon–Sat 8–11 p.m.

Au Bon Accueil
$$–$$$ Eiffel Tower (7e)   MODERN BISTRO

A spectacular view of the Eiffel Tower is offered from any of the outside tables at this restaurant, and the menu, which changes daily according to what the chef finds in the markets, is just as amazing. If you're ordering from the prix-fixe menu, you may start with *filets de sardines mi-cuites à l'huile et romarin méli mélo de legumes provencaux* (sardines lightly grilled in oil with a blend of vegetables from Provence) followed by *steack de thon poêlé et son caviar d'aubergine aux olives* (seared tuna steak with eggplant caviar and olives). Main dishes are divine and can include scallops with asparagus and whole lobster from Brittany roasted in herbs and tomatoes. Fantastic desserts include fig tart and crème brûlée made with walnuts.

14 rue de Monttessuy. ☎ 01-47-05-46-11. Reservations recommended. Métro: Alma Marceau. Main courses: 152–245F ($21.70–$35); three-course prix fixe 165F ($23.60). MC, V. Open Mon–Fri noon–2:30 p.m. and 7:30–10:30 p.m.

Au Pied de Cochon
$–$$ Les Halles (1er)   CLASSIC FRENCH

Au Pied de Cochon, opened in 1946, is a vibrant part of the history of this old market neighborhood. Boasting marble, murals, elaborate sconces, and chandeliers, as well as tourists, the restaurant provides great fun at manageable prices. You can have a plate of half a dozen oysters or onion soup to start. Follow with grilled salmon or an *entrecôte maître d'hôtel* (rib steak in rich red-wine sauce) or their specialty and namesake, *pied de cochon* (pigs feet). Finish with mouth-watering *profiteroles* (cream puffs).

6 rue Coquillière. ☎ *01-40-13-77-00. Métro: Châtelet–Les Halles. Main courses: 86–180F ($12.30–$25.70). AE, DC, V. Open daily 24 hours.*

Au Poulbot Gourmet
$–$$ Montmartre (18e)   CLASSIC FRENCH

Photos of old Montmartre and original drawings by illustrator Francisque Poulbot adorn the walls, and chic burgundy leather banquettes are usually filled with a local crowd savoring moderately priced classic cuisine. Chef Jean-Paul Langevin brings tremendous finesse to the preparation and presentation of dishes such as *noisette d'agneau* (lamb slices) served with delicate splashes of mashed potatoes and spinach, and *marmite de poissons*, assorted fresh fish in a light saffron sauce. As an appetizer, the *oeufs pochés* (poached eggs) with smoked salmon is a standout. For dessert, try the *charlotte glacée,* a ringed concoction made with ladyfingers and ice cream.

39 rue Lamarck. ☎ *01-46-06-86-00. Métro: Lamarck-Caulincourt. Main courses: 92–160F ($13.15–$22.85); three-course prix fixe 190F ($27.15); MC, V. Open Mon–Sat noon–1:30 p.m. and 7:30–10 p.m.; Sun noon–1:30 p.m. only Oct–May.*

Bofinger
$$ Le Marais (4e)   ALSATIAN/BRASSERIE

The 137-year-old Bofinger is one of Paris's best-loved restaurants with its dark wood, gleaming brass, bright lights, curved and painted glass ceiling, and waiters with long white aprons delivering extraordinary food. The menu features many Alsatian specialties, such as *choucroute* (sauerkraut with smoked ham) as well as oysters and foie gras for which the restaurant is renowned. Best of all — the prices are actually quite moderate for Paris.

5–7 rue de la Bastille. ☎ *01-42-72-87-82. Métro: Bastille. Main courses: 75–196F ($10.70–28); lunch and dinner prix fixe including half-bottle of wine 189F ($27). AE, MC, V. Open Mon–Fri noon–3 p.m. and 6:30 p.m.–1 a.m; Sat–Sun noon–1 a.m.*

Brasserie Balzar
$–$$ Latin Quarter (5e)   ALSATIAN/BRASSERIE

Brasserie Balzar has played host to some of France's most famous intellectuals, including Jean-Paul Sartre, and still is always full of rich bohemians, even in the off-hours. People stop here for coffee and pastries between lunch and dinner, and drop in for drinks in the evening. Regulars go for *poulet rôti avec frites* (roast chicken with French fries) or *choucroute garni,* but you can also get *steak au poivre* and a few fresh fish dishes. Portions are copious. For dessert, try the *gâteau au chocolate amère* (bittersweet chocolate cake).

49 rue des Écoles. ☎ *01-43-54-13-67. Métro: Cluny-Sorbonne. Main courses: 75–134F ($10.70–$19.15). AE, MC, V. Open daily noon –midnight. Closed Aug.*

Brasserie Flo
$$ Gare du Nord (10e)   ALSATIAN/BRASSERIE

One of the city's oldest restaurants, built in 1868, Brasserie Flo has a lovely turn-of-the-century ambience. On any given night you can find plenty of tourists and a sprinkling of Parisians, who feast on the renowned *chou-croute* (sauerkraut). Brasserie Flo is also known for its seafood, but that may empty your wallet faster than you can say bouillabaisse.

7 cour des Petites-Ecuries. ☎ *01-47-70-13-59. Métro: Château d'Eau. Main courses: 89–168F ($12.70–$24); three-course prix fixe with wine 189F ($27). AE, DC, MC, V. Open daily noon–3 p.m.; Tues–Sat 7:15 p.m.–1 a.m.; Sun–Mon 7:15 p.m.– 12:30 a.m.*

Brasserie Ile St-Louis
$–$$ Ile St-Louis (1er)   BRASSERIE/ALSATIAN

This is the last remaining independent brasserie in Paris, owned by the same family for over 60 years. Once the favorite haunt of writer James Jones *(The Thin Red Line),* who kept a mug, or *chope,* at the bar, its location is perfect: situated directly off the footbridge from Ile de la Cité to Ile St-Louis with an unparalleled view of the eastern tip of Ile de la Cité (including the back of Notre-Dame). The food is quintessentially Alsatian — *choucroute* with heaps of tender, biting sauerkraut and meaty slices of ham, or the hearty *cassoulet,* laden with rich beans and tender pieces of lamb and pork.

55 quai de Bourbon. 1er. ☎ *01-43-54-02-59. Métro: Pont Marie. Main courses: 60–130F ($8.60– $18.60) lunch and dinner. V. Open Fri–Tues noon–1 a.m.; Thur 6 p.m.–1 a.m.*

Caveau du Palais
$$ Louvre, Ile de la Cité (1er)   CLASSIC FRENCH

This cozy well-kept Parisian secret is located in the heart of the charming, tree-lined place Dauphine, a secluded little park nestled at the tip of Isle de la Cité. Try the house's special *côte de boeuf,* grilled giant ribs, which are prepared for two. The *confit de canard et pommes Sarladaise,* duck served with crispy potato bits sauteed in *foie gras* drippings, is another must.

19 place Dauphine, 1er. ☎ *01-43-26-04-28. Métro: Pont Neuf. Two-course menu 140F ($20); main courses 90-155F ($12.85-$22.15). Open Mon–Sat 12:15 p.m.–2:30 p.m. and 7:15–10:30 p.m. AE, DC, MC, V.*

Cercle Ledoyen

$$$ Champs-Elysées (8e)   CLASSIC FRENCH

The less expensive sister of two-star Ledoyen restaurant, Cercle Ledoyen offers light, classic cooking supervised by Ledoyen's chef, Christian Le Squer. The menu varies but may include *dos de cabillaud aux pousses d'épinards* (cod fillet with baby spinach) or *carré d'agneau roti au romarin* (roasted lamb with rosemary). Desserts, such as pear tart, are wonderful, too. Although a meal for two here with wine runs over $100, this place is well worth the splurge.

1 av. Dutuit. ☎ *01-53-05-10-02. Métro: Champs-Elysées Clemenceau. Main courses: 130F ($18.60). AE, DC, MC, V. Open Mon–Sat noon–2:30 p.m. and 7:30–10:30 p.m.*

Chantairelle

$–$$ Latin Quarter (5e)   AUVERGNE

This charming little place has a backyard garden children will love, while parents will appreciate the atmosphere that literally reeks of the Auvergne, the rugged south-central region of France. (Tiny bottles of essential oils made from native plants give you the smell of the region.) An old church door and a tiny fountain have been incorporated into the decor, and a sound system plays bird songs and church bells. Order an appetizer — maybe some of the famous *charcuterie* or cold sliced meats — only if you're ravenous; the delicious peasant food is presented in enormous portions. Main courses like wonderful stuffed cabbage or *potée* (a tureen filled with pork, cabbage, potatoes, turnips, and leeks in broth) are substantial. Although most dishes use ham or pork, vegetarians enjoy the *Croustade forestière,* of assorted mushrooms and eggs poached with Fourme d'Ambert cheese. The best Auvergne wine is the Chateaugay, a fine fruity red.

17 rue Laplace. ☎ *01-46-33-18-59. Métro: Maubert-Mutualité. Main courses: 72–139F ($10.30–$19.85). MC, V. Open Mon–Fri noon–2 p.m.; daily 7–10:30 p.m.*

Chardenoux

$–$$ Bastille (11e)   CLASSIC BISTRO

This small, charming place is at the top of the list of Parisians' favorite bistros. From the etched plate–glass windows to the swirling stucco decorations on the walls and ceiling, the turn-of-the-century decor is the very essence of old Paris. (It has been appointed a Monument Historique.) Service is friendly and English-speaking, too. A variety of French regional dishes appears on the menu — try the *oeufs en meurette,* a Burgundian dish of poached eggs in a sauce of red wine and bacon, and the *boeuf en daube,* braised beef Provençal style. Desserts are pure comfort food, especially the fruit tarts and the nougat in raspberry sauce.

1 rue Jules-Valles. ☎ *01-43-71-49-52. Métro: Charonne. Main courses: 80–125F ($11.45–$17.85). AE, MC, V. Open Mon–Fri noon–2 p.m.; Mon–Sat 8–11:30 p.m.*

Chez Casimir

$ Gare du Nord (10e) CLASSIC FRENCH

The trip is worth it from almost anywhere to experience this hidden delight next to the Gare du Nord, far from the more touristy sides of Paris. Chef Philippe Tredgeu works magic in his kitchen and his charms emanate out into the captivating dining room of mod style and rustic wood tables. Cooking with ingredients he finds at the market that morning or the night before, he prepares inventive dishes of upscale cuisine. Start with the refreshing *crème de petit pois au parmesan* — cold green bean soup with slices of Parmesan cheese served with toasted bread (take as much as you want from the pot placed on your table), then have *filet de rascasse avec des spaguetti de courgettes* — scorpionfish fillet served with spaghetti-style cooked zucchini, fresh cut tomatoes and a touch of vinegar. For dessert, indulge in homemade pastry topped with raspberries and vanilla cream. The wine list is highly affordable with prices starting at 40F ($5.70) for half a bottle.

6 rue de Belzune. ☎ *01-48-78-28-80. Reservations recommended for dinner. Métro: Gare du Nord. Main courses: 75–80F ($10.70–$11.45). No credit cards. Open Mon–Fri noon–2 p.m. and 7–11:30 p.m.; Sat 7–11:30 p.m.*

Chez Maître Paul

$$ St-Germain-des-Prés CLASSIC FRENCH

The word is out about comfortable Chez Maître Paul, which serves specialties from the Comté region of eastern France. One July night heard nothing but American English in the dining room. Start with a fluffy *rillette de saumon* and follow with *poulet sauté au vin blanc* (chicken sautéed in white wine with mushrooms and tomatoes). Also recommended is *terrine de foie* (liver pâté) and *fricassée de veau* (veal stew). The 195F ($27.85) fixed-price menu offers a choice of cheese or dessert following the main dish. Service is friendly and English speaking.

12 rue Monsieur-le-Prince, 6e. ☎ *01-43-54-74-59. Métro: Odéon. Reservations recommended. Main courses: 82–160F ($11.70–$22.85); 3-course menu 165F ($23.60); three-course menu with a half-bottle of wine 195F ($27.85). AE, DC, MC, V. Open daily noon–2:30 p.m. and 7–10:30 p.m.*

Chez Marie

$–$$ Montmartre (18e) CLASSIC FRENCH

At the base of the steps heading to the Place de Tertre, you can find some of the cheapest eats in this neighborhood not exactly known for bargain dining. Food is hearty, the owners are charming and friendly and they welcome children in their humbly decorated cozy dining room with wood benches, red-and-white picnic tablecloths and wallpaper in the style of Toulouse Lautrec. Stick to the basics like lamb and frites (french fries) or duck *confit* (duck cooked and preserved in its own fat), and you are guaranteed to leave full and content with money in your wallet.

27 rue Gabrielle. ☎ 01-42-62-06-26. Métro: Abbesses. Main courses: 38–136F ($5.45–$19.45); three-course menus (all include an aperitif) at 63F ($9) and 98F ($14) and 120F ($17.15). AE, DC, MC, V. Open daily noon–3:30 p.m. and 6–1:30 a.m. Closed Jan.

Chez Michel
$$ Gare du Nord (10e)   BRETON/CRÊPES

Although it only opened three years ago, this bistro has already added 70 seats to accommodate the crowds of Parisians that come for excellent, unusual food at very fair prices. Chef Thierry Breton, the chef at the Presidential Palace during Mitterand's tenure, puts old-fashioned Breton dishes on his menu — look for succulent scallops, hand picked by scuba divers, that are served with truffles in the winter. For the cheaper menu, sit in the cellar at wooden tables and eat all the shellfish, pâtés, and salads you can fit into your stomach — which is stretched by the end of the night. Choose from over 100 different wines at retail cost, a truly dizzying experience.

10 rue Belzunce. ☎ 01-44-53-06-20. Métro: Gare du Nord. Three-course menu 180F ($25.70), menu "table d'hote" 130F ($18.60). MC, V. Open Tues–Sat noon–2 p.m. and 7–midnight. Closed last week of July and first three weeks of Aug.

Closerie des Lilas
$$–$$$$ Montparnasse (6e)   ALSATIAN/BRASSERIE

This old literary haunt on the border of St-Germain-des-Prés and Montparnasse remains one of the city's most historic and romantic sites for a meal. Literary geniuses Ernest Hemingway, Henry James, and John Dos Passos hung out under the shady lilac bushes, while Russian revolutionaries Lenin and Trotsky debated politics over chess. Note that Closerie is split into two different dining areas — a more expensive, but dark and romantic restaurant and a cheaper, brighter brasserie serving more traditional French fare. A meal may start out with a staple such as *oeufs dur* (eggs with mayonnaise; uhf duhr), oysters in season, a moist and tasty *terrine de fois gras canard avec toasts* (terrine of duck liver with toasted bread), or the classic *steak tartare avec frites maison* (marinated raw steak with house french fries). Dinners may include a tender *selle d'agneau rotie en croute dorée* (roasted lamb flank in a golden crust), a peppery *filet de boeuf au poivre*, or *homard Breton à votre façon* (Brittany lobster cooked the way you choose). Finish up with *café* and *patisseries du jour* or *crêpes Suzette*. Reservations are essential, even though the brasserie is open until 1 a.m.; Closerie has never been more popular.

171 bd. Du Montparnasse. ☎ 01-40-51-34-50. Reservations required. Métro: Port-Royal. Main courses: 120F–450F ($17.15–$64.30). AE, DC, MC, V. Open daily noon–1 a.m.

Dame Jeanne
$$ Bastille (11e) MODERN BISTRO

Chef Francis Lévêque creates memorable dishes at fair prices at this restaurant decorated in autumnal colors illuminated by soft golden lighting. The seasonal fruit and vegetable menu may have dishes like *fricassée de légumes au lard et à l'estragon* (sauteed vegetables served with cured ham and terragon) and desserts like carmelized brioche topped with sweetened banana. The more expensive menus may offer risotto accented with tapenade and topped with diced steamed salmon. The reasonably priced wine list begins with Dame Jeanne's discoveries — lesser-known wines — for 90F ($12.85) a bottle. Service is friendly.

60 rue de Charonne, 11e. ☎ 01-47-00-37-40. Métro: Lédru-Rollin. Two-course menu 148F ($21.15); 3-course menu 178F ($25.40); seasonal fruit and vegetable menu 120F ($17.15). MC, V. Open Tues–Sat noon–2:15 p.m.; Tues–Thurs 7:30–11 p.m.; Fri–Sat 7:30–11:30 p.m.

Jo Goldenberg
$ Marais (4e) CENTRAL EUROPEAN

A Parisian institution in the Marais, the atmosphere at Jo Goldenberg is convivial. The restaurant is adorned with long red banquettes surrounded by photographs of famous patrons, including former French President Mitterand, and original paintings of up-and-coming artists. Eastern specialties abound, such as poulet paprika, goulash, moussaka, and Wienerschnitzel, as well as typical deli offerings like pastrami and corned beef — allegedly invented right here by Goldenberg senior in the 1920s. Adding to the festive air are the Gypsy musicians who begin playing around 9 p.m. For a final touch, Goldenberg, himself, hands departing patrons a gift. You may receive a calendar of Jewish holidays, a neighborhood map, or a drawing of the Hebrew alphabet for kids.

7 rue des Rosiers. ☎ 01-48-87-20-16. Métro: St-Paul. Main courses: 70–89F ($10–$12.70). AE, DC, MC, V. Daily 9 a.m.–midnight.

L'Ambroisie
$$$$$ Le Marais (4e) HAUTE CUISINE

Chef Bernard Pacaud has made a name for himself in this gorgeous seventeeth-century mansion on the place des Vosges, and French President Jacques Chirac and his wife, Bernadette, took Bill and Hillary Clinton here when they wanted to impress the former U.S. first couple. Three-star specialties include fricasée of lobster in wine sauce, roasted free-range chicken with black truffles, and an award-winning *tarte fine,* a chocolate pie served with bitter chocolate and mocha ice cream. The décor in the two high-ceilinged salons evokes an Italian palazzo, with terrace dining in the summer. The restaurant calls out for marriage proposals, anniversaries, and other special and romantic events.

9 place des Vosges. ☎ *01-42-78-51-45. Métro: St. Paul. Reserve at least four weeks ahead. Jacket and tie advised. No prix fixe; expect to spend at least 1100 F ($157.15) per person per meal. AE, MC, V. Open Tues–Sat noon–1:30 p.m. and 8–9:30 p.m. Closed two weeks in Feb and three weeks in Aug.*

La Bastide Odéon
$$ St-Germain-des-Près (6e) PROVENÇAL

Chef Gilles Ajuelos serves delicious Provençal cooking in a lovely dining room strikingly set across the street from the Luxembourg Gardens. The menu changes regularly, but the chef's dynamic creations include rabbit stuffed with eggplant as a starter, then gnocchi with snails and garlic, and as dessert, roasted pear *en brousse* (in a bush) with rosemary, honey, and citrus syrup alongside yogurt sorbet. You can also savor an iced tomato soup with grappa (a dry, colorless brandy) or olives from the chef's *cuisine du marché* (from the market).

7 rue Corneille, 6e. ☎ *01-43-26-03-65. Métro: Odéon. Two-course menu 154F ($22); 3-course menu 194F ($27.70). AE, MC, V. Open Tues–Sat noon–3 p.m. and 7:30–11 p.m. Closed Aug.*

La Cigale
$–$$ Eiffel Tower CLASSIC BISTRO

Stylish yet discreet, Le Cigale serves delicious soufflés (among other specialties) to a sophisticated and high-spirited clientele in an intimate space of soft lighting and cozy tables. The food is simply some of the best you can get in Paris for these prices. The delicate soufflés are beaten high, brim with camembert, sauteed spinach, or a tarragon cream and melt in your mouth. And that's before dessert, which offers — you got it — soufflés of heavenly citron and sinful chocolate. If you're not in the mood for a soufflé, other tempting entrées include a rump roast and succulent lamb chops.

11 rue Chomel, 7e. ☎ *01-45-48-87-87. Reservations recommended. Métro: Sèvres-Babylone. Main dishes: 58–112F ($8.30–$16). MC, DC, V. Open Mon–Fri noon–2:00 p.m.; Mon–Sat 7:30–11 p.m.*

La Petite Chaise
$$ St-Germain-des-Prés (7e) CLASSIC FRENCH

Originally built in the mid–seventeenth century, this small gem is allegedly the oldest restaurant in Paris. The entranceway, adorned with a smoky antique mirror from the early eighteenth-century, leads to a softly illuminated, cozy dining room reminiscent of an old country inn. Start with *escargots bourguignon* or the homemade *foie gras de canard maison.* As a main dish, the *magret de canard pomme et miel* melts away your appetite — the robust duck tastes supple and sweet under honey and lightly salted potatoes gratinée. A piece of chocolate cake with English cream tops off your meal with the elegance the nobility used to enjoy in their visits to the restaurant 300 years ago. The old maxim does hold true: The best things in life never change.

36 rue de Grenelle. ☎ *01-42-22-13-35. Métro: Sèvres-Babylone. Main courses (with a half bottle of wine): 125F ($17.85); two-course menu with a half-bottle of wine 160F ($22.85); three-course menu with a half-bottle of wine 195F ($27.85). AE, MC, V. Open daily noon–2 p.m. and 7–10:45 p.m.*

La Tour de Montlhéry
$$ Les Halles (1er)   CLASSIC FRENCH

This is Old Paris par excellence, including the somewhat brusque service. Beyond the zinc bar lies an attractive dining room with hams and sausages dangling from the beams. The less expensive items on the menu tend to be dishes like tripe Calvados and stuffed cabbage. Other typical dishes are grilled lamb chops and, for those who want to try truly authentic, reputably delicious, French fare, *cervelles d'agneau* (sauteed lamb's brain). *Bon courage!*

5 rue des Prouvaires. ☎ *01-42-36-21-82. Reservations required. Métro: Châtelet–Les Halles. Main courses 95–130F ($13.60–$18.60). V. Open Mon–Fri 24 hours. Closed July 10–Aug 15.*

L'Ébauchoir
$–$$ Bastille (12e)   BISTRO

Tucked into a part of the Bastille often overlooked by tourists, this restaurant is well worth the visit. A mural pays homage to the working class roots of the neighborhood, and the space is just large enough to render dining here a bit noisy. Friendly waiters rush to show diners seated at the first-come, first-served tables the day's offerings written on a tall chalkboard; and once you've sampled lunch or dinner, you find the decibel level is more than made up for — the food is superb. Diners may be offered appetizers of warm *foie gras* or stuffed ravioli followed by mouthwatering smoked tuna with fennel or steak in a red-wine Bordelaise sauce. For dessert, the *mille feuille* (meel fuh–yee) a flaky multi-layered pastry) is divine.

45 rue de Citeaux, 12e. ☎ *01-43-42-49-31. No reservations accepted. Métro: Faidherbe-Chaligny. Main courses: 75F–125F ($10.70–$17.90). MC, V. Open Mon–Thu noon–2:30 p.m. and 8–10:30 p.m.; Fri–Sat noon–2:30 p.m., 8:00–11 p.m.*

Dining zones

If you're short on time or money, the following streets have many restaurants with fast service at low prices.

Avenue d'Ivry and **Avenue de Choisy,** 13e. Far off the tourist track, the Vietnamese, Chinese, and Thai restaurants along these wide avenues cater to the local southeast Asian population. Prices are low and quality is high, and you can eat like the locals.

Bd. de Belleville, 11e. You find many, many couscous places, which are reasonably priced and satisfactory, if not outstanding. Middle Eastern snacks, pastries, and a glass of mint tea make an exotic and inexpensive meal.

Bd. du Montparnasse, 14e. In one block (between rue Vavin and Bd. Raspail), you find four cafes that have literary associations: La Coupoule, Le Dôme, Le Select, and La Rotonde, as well as high and moderately priced seafood restaurants, crêperies, sandwich shops, and ethnic specialties.

Métro Belleville, 11e. The streets radiating out from this station are the northern headquarters for Asian cuisine. You can usually slurp down noodle soup at any hour of the day and into the night.

Rue des Rosiers, in the Marais (3e). People have been known to trudge across town for the huge pita-bread sandwiches sold on this street. Stuffed with falafel, eggplant, and salad, and then topped with your choice of sauce, this must be the best 25F ($3.60) meal in town.

Rue du Montparnasse, 14e. The street between boulevard Edgar Quinet and boulevard du Montparnasse is a Crêperie Row of inexpensive Breton eateries. Whether the *crêpes* are sugared up with syrups and jam or stuffed with vegetables and meat (these are often called *galettes*), they make a tasty light meal for less than 60F ($8.60).

Rue Sainte-Anne, 9e. Sushi is expensive in Paris, but because this street lies in the same neighborhood as many Japanese businesses, you find the freshest fish and most authentic Japanese dishes at moderate prices.

Le Cinq

$$$$$ Champs-Elysées (8e)   HAUTE CUISINE

The celebrated chef Phillippe Legendre is winning raves for his new restaurant, Le Cinq, in the newly renovated Four Seasons George V. Every element is in place, from the stately, yet serene dining room with its high ceilings and overstuffed chairs, to the Limoges porcelain and Riedel stemware and the perfect waitstaff. The sumptuous and inventive cuisine includes *crème de cresson de source glacée au caviar Sevruga* (chilled watercress cream with Sevruga caviar), *ris de veau fermier poêlé aux girolles* (seared sweetbreads with chanterelles), and for dessert, the delightful *autour de la fraise,* a whimsical assortment of strawberry confections ranging from strawberry tiramisu to sorbet of strawberry and green tomato. Dining here is truly a special experience.

31 av. George V. ☎ *01-49-52-71-54. Métro: George V. Reservations required. Gourmet tasting menu 984F ($140.60); main courses 249–394F ($35.60–$56.30) AE, MC, V. Open daily 5:30 p.m.–10:30 p.m.*

Le Galopin
$ Belleville (10e)   ALSATIAN/BRASSERIE

You may have to look for this great find nestled in an unassuming neighborhood on the edge of Belleville. Tasty inexpensive traditional French food in a homey, casual atmosphere is quickly served by a friendly staff, some of whom speak English. Appetizers may include a moist and delicate *terrine campagne* or fresh mushrooms in a light cream sauce, followed by entrees of tuna steak in an herb-sprinkled sauce Provençal, and a delicious *rôti de veau* (roast veal). Fresh ratatouille and a tasty carrot salad garnish many of the dishes. Traditional French music is performed on weekends, and patrons are encouraged to sing along (dinner costs 10 percent more at these times to cover the costs of the musicians).

34 rue Sainte Marthe. ☎ *01-53-19-19-55. Métro: Belleville. Two-and three-course dinner menu: 65F–95F ($9.30–$13.60). AE, DC, MC, V. Open Tues–Sat noon–2:30 p.m. and 8–11 p.m., midnight Sat. Brunch Sun noon–2:30 except summer, dinner 8–11 p.m.*

Le Grenier de Notre-Dame
$ Latin Quarter (5e)   VEGETARIAN

If you're not sure you've reached the right place, take a look around. Le Grenier is enveloped in green, from the walls and tablecloths to the outdoor patio under a balcony of hanging plants, as if to prove that, yes, this is a vegetarian restaurant. Nevertheless, the food is good; especially recommended is the *cassoulet végétarien,* with white beans, onions, tomatoes, and soy sausage. The couscous and the cauliflower *au gratin* are also delicious. Le Grenier has a well-deserved reputation for desserts, such as *tarte de tofu.* The wine list includes a variety of organic offerings.

18 rue de la Bûcherie. ☎ *01-43-29-98-29. Métro: Maubert-Mutualité. Main courses: 64–89F ($9.15–$12.70). MC, V. Open Mon–Thurs 12:30–3 p.m. and 7–10:30 p.m.; Fri–Sat noon–2:30 p.m. and 7:00–11:00 p.m.; Sun noon–3:00 p.m. and 7:00–10:30 p.m.*

Le Père Claude
$$ Eiffel Tower (15e)   CLASSIC BISTRO

French President Jacques Chirac and Don King (how's that for a combo?) have been spotted dining on some of this bistro's extremely well-prepared, hearty dishes. Starters include warm sausage with pistachio and apples, or mussel soup with saffron. The rotisserie behind the bar signals that the house specialty is roasted meat, but seafood lovers won't be disappointed in the *assiette de pecheur aux pates fraiches* (fisherman's plate with fresh terrine). The *panaché de viandes* is an assortment of perfectly roasted meat served with a comforting heap of mashed potatoes. Make sure you specify how you want the beef cooked, or it will be served the way the French like it — *bleue* — very, very rare. The large tables and relaxed atmosphere make this a family-friendly establishment. After dinner, you can stroll up the avenue de La-Motte-Picquet and take in a view of the dazzlingly illuminated Eiffel Tower.

51 av. de la Motte-Picquet. ☎ *01-47-34-03-05. Métro: La-Motte-Picquet–Grenelle. Main courses: 95–160F ($13.60–$22.85). AE, MC, V. Daily 11:30am–2:30 p.m. and 7–midnight.*

Le Polidor

$–$$ St-Germain-des-Prés (6e)   CLASSIC BISTRO

This has been the quintessential Left Bank bistro for about 150 years. Perpetually crowded with people sitting elbow to elbow in a vivid atmosphere surrounded by wood, mirrors, and lace curtains, the cooking is earthy and homemade, with all desserts and ice creams made on the premises. Begin with a spinach salad with nut oil, followed by solid plates of *rognons en madere* (veal kidneys in madeira), *blanquette de veau, boeuf bourguignon,* or *ragoût of pork.* Save room for one of the array of fresh tartes and pies. At lunch on weekdays you can get a quarter-liter of wine for 7F ($1).

41 rue Monsieur-le-Prince. ☎ *01-43-26-95-34. Métro: Odéon. Main courses: 49–76F ($7–$10.85). No credit cards. Open Mon–Sat noon–2:30 p.m. and 7–12:30am; Sun 7–11 p.m.*

Restaurant Dane Gourmande

$$ Le Marais (4e) LYONNAISE

Regulars rave about this tiny bargain at the edge of the Marais run by Dane, a septuagenarian chef who hails from Lyon. With only 16 seats, the plain, brightly lit restaurant fills up quickly each night as guests feast on such starters as a buttery *terrine maison au canard* or a salad with country ham or anchovies. Main courses may include *canard croustillant de miel* (crispy duck cooked in honey) or a delicious *steak au poivre* cooked to your taste and crunchy with green and black peppercorns. Try a homemade tartelette for dessert with ice cream. Dane does all the cooking and most of the serving herself; it would be just like a visit to your grandmother's house — if your grandmother were French and a fabulous cook!

9 rue du Turenne. ☎ *01-42-77-62-54. Métro: Bastille or St. Paul. Prix-fixe lunch with a half-pitcher of wine: 140F ($20), prix-fixe dinner with bottle of wine: 183F ($26.15). Open noon–2:30 and 7:20–10 p.m. Closed Mon lunch.*

Restaurant du Palais-Royal
$$ Louvre (1er) CLASSIC FRENCH

The elegant arcade that encircles the gardens inside the Palais-Royal also surrounds this restaurant, making it one of the most romantic locations in Paris. Sit at the terrace on warm, sun-filled days and begin your meal with starters such as marinated leeks in a beet-juice vinaigrette, or scallop salad. Main dishes vary with the season but may include grilled tuna steak with a Basque relish or roast baby lamb. The desserts are delicious, and the house red wine, served Lyonnaise style in thick-bottomed bottles, is inexpensive — 80F ($11.40) — and very good.

43 rue Valois. ☎ *01-40-20-00-27. Métro: Palais-Royal–Musée du Louvre. Main courses: 112–195F ($16–$27.85). AE, DC, MC, V. Open Mon–Fri 12:30–2:30 p.m. and Mon–Sat 7:30–10:30 p.m.*

Restaurant Paul
$$ Louvre/Île de la Cité (1er) CLASSIC FRENCH

This intimate and relaxed restaurant, nestled on the first floor of an eighteenth-century town house, is overshadowed by its charismatic young owners, Thierry and Chantal, who make visitors feel at home. The couple's affection for their restaurant, which they remodeled with wood banquettes and walls hand painted with discreet, artistic Parisian scenes, is palpable; and they extend that same enthusiasm to their clients, many of whom have become neighborhood regulars. Start with an invigorating lentil salad, tossed with marinated *lardons* (bits of cured ham), or a cool terrine of salmon, asparagus, and dill. Main dishes include a sumptuous haddock covered with a butter-tarragon cream sauce and a surprisingly delicate casserole of tender veal and mushrooms served with rice. As you end a lovely evening with warm *tarte de pomme* (apple tart), look around the room full of jovial people, and empty plates, and you can understand why Chantal and Thierry have been featured in Paris newspapers as innovative restaurateurs.

Two entrances at 15 place Dauphine and 52 Quai des Orfévres, 1er. ☎ *01-43-54-21-48. Métro: Pont Neuf or Cité. Main courses: 85–110F ($12.15–$15.70). AE, MC, V. Open Tue–Sun noon–2:30 p.m. and 7–10:30 p.m.*

Restaurant Perraudin
$-$$ Latin Quarter (5e) CLASSIC BISTRO

People say that Hemingway went to the Closerie des Lilas when rich, and Perraudin was his favorite spot when broke. Everyone else enjoys this historic bistro, too, from its red-checked tablecloths and lace lampshades, to its jolly atmosphere, and staff that welcomes kids. A bargain lunch menu offers a choice of three appetizers, two main courses, and cheese or dessert. You may start with tomatoes and mozzarella, then have ham with endive or roast beef, followed by baba au rhum. Classic dishes like duck confit and *gigot d'agneau* (leg of lamb) with *gratin Dauphinois* (cheese-topped potatoes) are on the à la carte menu. At lunch, Mme Perraudin offers a quarter-liter of red wine for 10F ($1.45). Arrive early for a table, since reservations aren't accepted here.

157 rue St-Jacques. ☎ *01-46-33-15-75. Métro: Luxembourg. Main courses: 59F ($8.45); 3-course gastronomic menu 150F ($21.45). No credit cards. Tues–Fri noon–2:15 p.m.; Mon–Sat 7:30–10:15 p.m.*

Rotisserie Armaillé
$$–$$$ Champs-Elysées (17e)   MODERN BISTRO

Though it may be out of the way, Jacques Cagna is a celebrity chef, and this "baby bistro" is his nod to the current mood for fine dining at a fixed price. Although the decor is pleasant, with light wood paneling and plaid upholstery, his modern approach to hearty bistro dishes is what draws crowds of business people for lunch and the local chic set for dinner. Freshly baked warm bread accompanies starters like the *terrine de laperau aux parfums d'agrumes* (terrine of baby rabbits with citrus zest), and main courses of *squab aux raisins de Smyrnes* (squab in raisins from Smyrnes) or tuna carpaccio. Service is fast and friendly.

6 rue d'Armaillé, 17e. ☎ *01-42-27-19-20. Métro: Charles-de-Gaulle-Étoile or Argentine. Exit from Charles-de-Gaulle-Étoile at av. Carnot; the Arc de Triomphe is behind you. Carnot turns into rue d'Armaillé after rue des Acacias. From Argentine walk up rue des Acacias and turn left onto rue d'Armaillé. Two-course lunch menu: 165F ($23.55); two-course dinner menu 230F ($32.85). AE, DC, MC, V. Open Mon–Fri noon–2:30 p.m.; Mon–Sat 7:30–11 p.m.*

Spoon, Food and Wine
$$–$$$ Champs-Elysées (8e)   MODERN BISTRO

Celebrated chef Alain Ducasse has reinvented the joy of dining out, offering world class food, reasonable prices, and service that borders on indulgent. The wide variety of international dishes are presented through a menu of mixing and matching — the customer gets to choose (from a list of very enticing choices) the condiment, side dishes, and vegetables to complement the main dish. Take, for example, spare ribs — try a marmalade of stewed meat, red wine, tomato, and olives to lavish on the meat beside a heaping portion of potatoes. Spoon also boasts the most international wine list in Paris, with 120 from South Africa, Argentina, and New Zealand. Although bubble gum ice cream and Ben & Jerry's are available for dessert, opt for the oozing warm chocolate "pizza." This affordable splurge organized by a world master chef ends with a Parisian coffee, the second cup is on the house.

14 rue de Marignan. ☎ *01-40-76-34-44. Reservations recommended one month in advance. Métro: Franklin-D-Roosevelt. Main courses: 85–225F ($12.15–$32.15); 3-course Bento Box menu 135F ($19.30). AE, MC, V. Open Mon–Fri 11:45 a.m.– 2:30 p.m. and 6:30–11:30 p.m.*

Vagenende
$$ St-Germain-des-Prés (6e)   ALSATIAN/BRASSERIE

Founded in 1904 as a *bouillon* (canteen or soup kitchen) by M. Chartier — of the 9e arrondissement restaurant of the same name — Vagenende evolved into a brasserie that is now classified as a Monument Historique. The art-nouveau decor is authentic — mirrors, frescoes, and swirling floral patterns abound within walls of dark wood, making this the place to live out your belle époque fantasy. Lace curtains, globe lights, and spacious booths enhance the classic atmosphere. The dishes are equally classic — *confit de canard* (duck confit), *sole meunière,* and *pavé de morue sauce vierge* (cod with lemon-flavored sauce).

142 bd. St-Germain, 6e. ☎ *01-43-26-68-18. Métro: Odéon. Main courses: 68–152F ($9.70–$21.70). AE, DC, MC, V. Open daily noon–1 a.m.*

Vivario
$$ Latin Quarter (5e)   CORSICAN

This is an excellent spot to sample the hearty flavors of the Belle Isle, Napoléon's birthplace. Many of the products used in Vivario's dishes come straight from sunny Corsica to the dim, cavelike restaurant, with ceiling beams and stone walls. To start, opt for the rich traditional Corsican soup, teeming with beans, vegetables, and generous pieces of dried prosciutto, or try the *charcuterie* plate served with a Mason jar of spicy cornichons. Follow with *cabri rôti à la Corse* (roast goat) or eggplant with cheese and spicy tomato sauce. Chewy whole-wheat baguettes accompany the meal, which may end with a selection of Corsican cheeses or the Corsican dessert — *fiadone,* a cheesecake made with mild *bruccio,* the island's famous, pungent cheese.

6 rue Cochin, 5e. ☎ *01-43-25-08-19. Métro: Maubert-Mutualité. Main courses: 55–120F ($7.85–$17.15). AE, MC, V. Open Tues–Fri noon–2 p.m.; Mon–Sat 7:30–10 p.m.*

Chapter 15

On the Lighter Side: Top Picks for Snacks and Meals on the Go

. . . .

In This Chapter

▶ Tracking down the best street food

▶ Ordering up a sandwich

▶ Finding the fixings for a great picnic

▶ Lounging in the hippest cafés

▶ Screaming for ice cream

. . . .

*T*his chapter is essential in helping you find the quick bites for those times when you just won't want to sit down to a full three-course meal or devote hours to doing it. You have your choice from street food and sandwiches to cafeterias and chain restaurants. Some tea salons are included for those longing for "a cuppa" as well as delicious pastries in elegant settings. Armed with this knowledge, you may feel like an insider on the go. If your stay is blessed with fabulous weather, you definitely want to learn the best places to get picnic fare, and they're listed here. (Then check out Chapter 25 for the top ten places to take that picnic grub.)

And we haven't forgotten that Parisian institution, the café. This chapter lets you in on some of the best cafés and their more sophisticated sisters, the wine bars — both are great places to join in the French art of people watching.

Paris Street Food

Some street vendors sell Belgian waffles, called *gaufres,* served warm with powdered sugar, or chocolate sauce, but the quintessential Parisian street food is the *crêpe* — a thin wheat pancake stuffed with a filling, either salty or sweet. When served with savory fillings, like

Light Meals in the Heart of the Right Bank

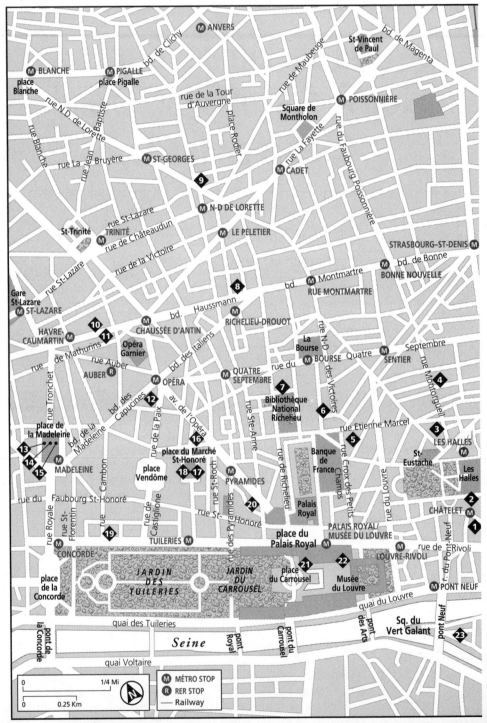

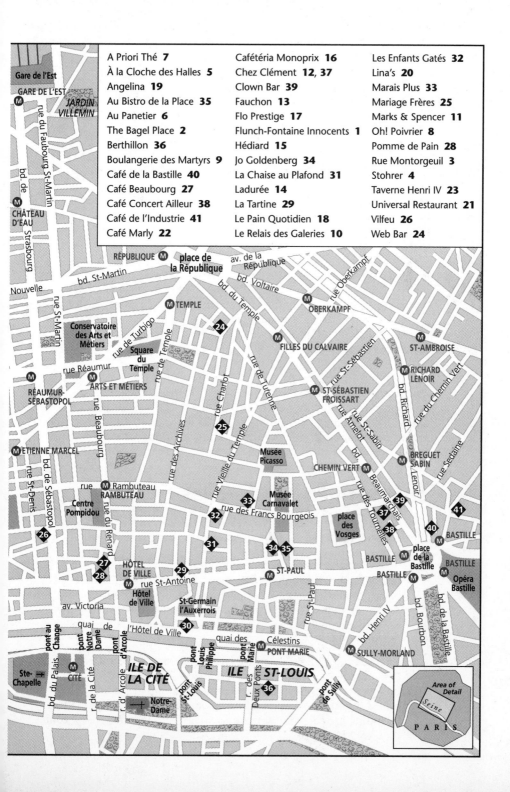

A Priori Thé **7**
À la Cloche des Halles **5**
Angelina **19**
Au Bistro de la Place **35**
Au Panetier **6**
The Bagel Place **2**
Berthillon **36**
Boulangerie des Martyrs **9**
Café de la Bastille **40**
Café Beaubourg **27**
Café Concert Ailleur **38**
Café de l'Industrie **41**
Café Marly **22**

Cafétéria Monoprix **16**
Chez Clément **12, 37**
Clown Bar **39**
Fauchon **13**
Flo Prestige **17**
Flunch-Fontaine Innocents **1**
Hédiard **15**
Jo Goldenberg **34**
La Chaise au Plafond **31**
Ladurée **14**
La Tartine **29**
Le Pain Quotidien **18**
Le Relais des Galeries **10**

Les Enfants Gatés **32**
Lina's **20**
Marais Plus **33**
Mariage Frères **25**
Marks & Spencer **11**
Oh! Poivrier **8**
Pomme de Pain **28**
Rue Montorgeuil **3**
Stohrer **4**
Taverne Henri IV **23**
Universal Restaurant **21**
Vilfeu **26**
Web Bar **24**

cheese or mushrooms, the crêpe becomes a *galette*. Sweet crêpe fillings include the chocolate-hazelnut spread Nutella, ice cream, jam, or just plain powdered sugar.

You can find street carts selling sweet crêpes near most of the major attractions, in the parks and bigger gardens, and along the rue de Rivoli between the Marais and the place de la Concorde. If you buy a crêpe from a street vendor, you won't have much of a choice of sweet fillings; for a more extensive menu visit a crêperie.

Avoid the tourist trap crêperies in the Latin Quarter. (In fact, try to avoid most of the restaurants in the area around rue de la Huchette and rue de la Harpe. These restaurants make a big show of luring you in for a cheap meal with actual "barkers" shouting about the great food, only to hit your wallet with overpriced drinks and other hidden extras.)

Instead of crêpes in the Latin Quarter, make a meal at one of the many good establishments on rue du Montparnasse where you can settle down in a more peaceful atmosphere with a bowl of cider (a Breton specialty), a galette for a main course, and a crêpe for dessert — usually under 70F ($10) a person. (Métro: Edgar Quinet or Montparnasse-Bienvenuë.)

You can find the other typical Parisian street food, the *panini,* just about anywhere. Named for the Italian-style bread they're made with, panini can be almost any filling stuck between two slices of bread, then flattened and grilled between two hot plates. The most common fillings are mozzarella, basil, and sun-dried tomatoes. Panini are cheap and tasty and easy to chow down on the run.

Snacking on sandwiches

Heartier than a crepe, easier to eat, and probably more healthy, too, is the sandwich, and the establishments that follow have elevated it from your average bologna and cheese.

✓ **Lina's** (30 bd. des Italiens, 9e, ☎ **01-42-46-02-06**; Métro: Opéra) packs an assortment of fillings onto whole-meal bread and rolls in American deli-style. Add a soup or salad and finish with a brownie for a quick meal. Another location is at 7 av. de l'Opéra, 1er (☎ **01-47-03-30-29**).

✓ **Cosi** (54 rue de Seine, 6e, ☎ **01-46-33-35-36**; Métro: St-Germain-des-Prés) serves its sandwiches on delicious focaccia-style bread and fillings are plentiful and delicious. To accompany the freshly baked bread, you can choose from an assortment of specialties, including arugula, mozzarella, Parmesan, Italian ham, roast tomatoes, and tapenade.

✔ **Le Pain Quotidien** (18 Marché-St-Honoré, 1er, ☎ 01-42-96-31-70; Métro: Tuileries) is one of the best bakeries in Paris, and you can order one of the delicious tartines (open-faced sandwiches) made with combinations like country ham and Gruyère cheese, or goat cheese and honey; or beef, basil, and Parmesan.

✔ The staff at **Pomme de Pain** (76 rue de Rivoli, 4e ☎ 01-42-74-64-93; Métro: Châtelet) a fast-food style counter, slice baguettes in half and put in the topping of your choice. You can try the Lyonnaise, with slices of *saucisson sec* (dry sausage) and cornichon pickles or a hot mozzarella and tomato special. The drink and sandwich combinations are usually good buys.

✔ About six blocks west of the Louvre is **The Bagel Place** (6 place St-Opportune, 1er, ☎ 01-40-28-96-40; Métro: Châtelet), a mecca for homesick Yanks, offering a baker's dozen of New York-style bagels and a blackboard full of bagel sandwich specials.

Restaurant chains

You see them everywhere, and with good reason. Paris restaurant chains serve attractively priced food with some regional specialties to diners who value their time and money. They're great places to take young children since they have kids' menus, and the staff is used to serving clients who aren't in the mood to linger.

✔ **Batifol** serves generally good food at very fair prices — the standard fixed-price menu is only 75F ($10.70). Included on the menu are basics such as *steak frites* (steak and fries), *hamburger frites* (hamburger and fries), *poulet roti* (rotisserie chicken), salads, and *crème brulee* (creamy custard with caramel topping). A dozen or so locations can be found around the city, including one on the Right Bank at 78 av. des Champs-Elysées, 8e (☎ 01-45-62-64-93), and one on the Left Bank at 1 bd. St-Germain, 5e (☎ 01-43-54-49-05).

✔ **Chez Clément** is probably the best of Paris's chain restaurants. The specialties are spit-roasted meat, imaginatively combined with sweet spices, honey, or dried fruit. The *Grand Rotisserie* — salad, beef, pork, chicken, and mashed potatoes for 85F ($14.15) — is a particularly good deal. Eight branches are located throughout the city, including 123 av. des Champs-Elysées, 8e (☎ 01-40-73-87-00); 17 bd. des Capucines, 2e (☎ 01-53-43-82-00); and 21 bd. Beaumarchais, 11e (☎ 01-40-29-17-00). All are open daily until 1 a.m.

✔ **Hippopotamus** has its red awnings all over town. These places prepare decent red-meat dishes accompanied by fries and salad, and served in a pleasant atmosphere. The extended hours are a convenience as well — you can get a hot meal here when most other places are closed. Try the one at 9 rue Lagrange, 5e

Light Meals in the Heart of the Left Bank

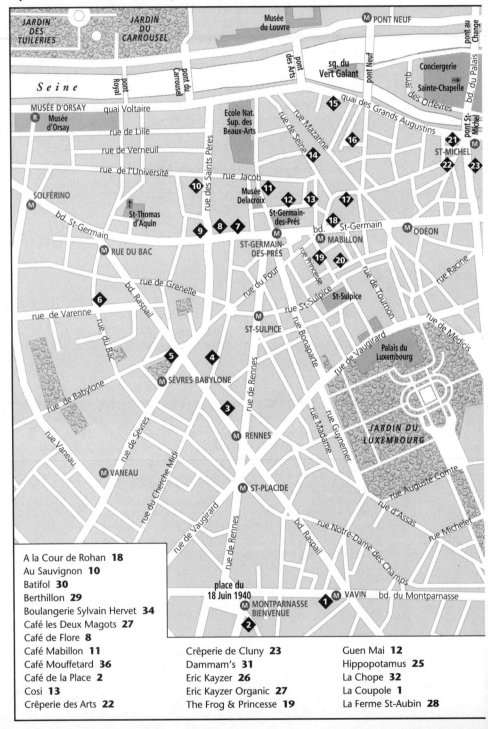

A la Cour de Rohan **18**
Au Sauvignon **10**
Batifol **30**
Berthillon **29**
Boulangerie Sylvain Hervet **34**
Café les Deux Magots **27**
Café de Flore **8**
Café Mabillon **11**
Café Mouffetard **36**
Café de la Place **2**
Cosi **13**
Crêperie des Arts **22**

Crêperie de Cluny **23**
Dammam's **31**
Eric Kayzer **26**
Eric Kayzer Organic **27**
The Frog & Princesse **19**

Guen Mai **12**
Hippopotamus **25**
La Chope **32**
La Coupole **1**
La Ferme St-Aubin **28**

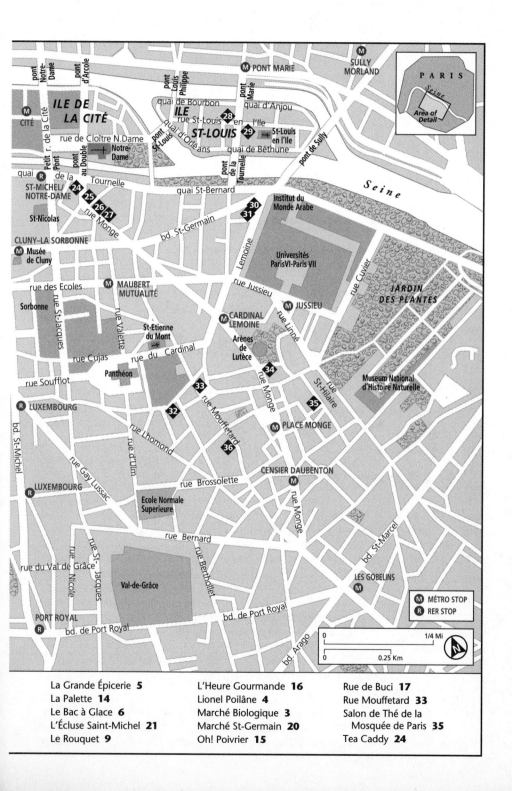

La Grande Épicerie **5**
La Palette **14**
Le Bac à Glace **6**
L'Écluse Saint-Michel **21**
Le Rouquet **9**

L'Heure Gourmande **16**
Lionel Poilâne **4**
Marché Biologique **3**
Marché St-Germain **20**
Oh! Poivrier **15**

Rue de Buci **17**
Rue Mouffetard **33**
Salon de Thé de la
   Mosquée de Paris **35**
Tea Caddy **24**

(☎ **01-43-54-13-99;** Métro: Maubert); The restaurant is open Sunday through Thursday from 11:30 a.m. to 1 a.m., Friday and Saturday 11:30 a.m. to 1:30 a.m.

✔ My particular favorite is **Oh! Poivrier!** with its light fare, moderate prices, and long hours. A salad or open-faced sandwich (known as a *tartine* in French) with duck, prosciutto, or cheese makes a pleasant lunch or supper; you can find a branch at 60 rue Pierre Charron, 15e (☎ **01-42-25-28-65;** Métro: Franklin-D-Roosevelt), one on the Left Bank of the Seine at 25 quai des Grands Augustins, 6e (☎ **01-43-29-41-77;** Métro: St-Michel); and another at 2 bd. Haussmann , 9e (☎ **01-42-46-22-24;** Métro: Richelieu-Drouout).

Joining the cafétéria line

Don't scoff at the idea of eating at a cafeteria — you can fill up cheaply, and the offerings can be quite tasty. My personal favorite is the one at the department store Galeries Lafayette — the food is fresh and the surroundings sleek and modern — the perfect pick-me-up after a morning spent shopping for gifts. Cafeterias include:

✔ **Cafétéria Monoprix,** 23 av. Opéra, 1er, ☎ **01-42-96-34-96.** Métro: Palais Royal-Musée du Louvre.

✔ **Flunch-Fontaine Innocents,** 5 rue Pierre Lescot, 1er, ☎ **01-42-33-54-00.** Métro: Etienne-Marcel.

✔ **Le Relais des Galeries** (6th floor, Galeries Lafayette), 40 bd. Haussmann, 9e, ☎**01-42-82-30-37.** Métro: Havre-Caumartin.

✔ **Universal Restaurant** (in the Carrousel du Louvre), 99 rue de Rivoli, 1er, ☎ **01-47-03-96-58.** Métro: Palais Royal-Musée du Louvre.

Tea Salons (Salons de Thé)

If you're tired of all those short blasts of French coffee, you have an alternative. The French are finally appreciating tea, and tea lovers need look no further than a tea salon for a wide range of blends, steeped to perfection in refined and, often, elegant settings. The pastry selections in these places are usually excellent, but save your full meals for a restaurant — tea salons tend to be expensive.

✔ **Angelina,** 226 rue de Rivoli, 1er, ☎ **01-42-60-82-00.** Open daily 9a.m.–5:45 p.m. (lunch served 11:45a.m.–3p.m.). Métro: Concorde or Tuileries.

✔ **À la Cour de Rohan,** 59–61 rue St-André-des-Arts (actually a passageway off of rue St-André-des-Arts), 6e, ☎ **01-43-25-79-67.** Open Sun–Thurs noon–7:30 p.m.; Fri–Sat noon–11:30 p.m. Métro: Odéon or St-Michel.

✔ **A Priori Thé,** 35–37 Galerie Vivienne (enter at 6 rue Vivienne, 4 rue des Petits-Champs, or 5 rue de la Banque), 2e, ☎ 01-42-97-48-75. Open Mon–Fri 9 a.m.–6 p.m.; Sat 9 a.m.–6:30 p.m.; Sun 12:30–6:30 p.m. Métro: Bourse, Palais-Royal–Musée du Louvre, or Pyramides.

✔ **Ladurée,** 16 rue Royale, 8e, ☎ 01-42-60-21-79. Open Mon–Sat 8:30 a.m.–7 p.m. Métro: Concorde or the Champs-Elysées at no. 75. ☎ 01-40-75-08-75. Métro: Franklin-D-Roosevelt.

✔ **La Formi Ailée,** 8 rue du Fouarre, 5e, ☎ 01-43-29-40-99. Open daily noon–1 a.m. Métro: Maubert-Mutualité.

✔ **Les Enfants Gatés,** 43 rue des Francs-Bourgeois, 4e, ☎ 01-42-77-07-63. Open Sat–Mon 11 a.m.–8 p.m., closed Tues. Métro: St-Paul.

✔ **Marais Plus,** 20 rue des Francs-Bourgeois, 3e, ☎ 01-48-87-01-40. Open daily 11 a.m.–7:00 p.m. Métro: St-Paul.

✔ **Mariage Frères,** 30–32 rue de Bourg-Tibourg, 4e, ☎ 01-42-72-28-11. Open daily noon–7 p.m. Métro: Hôtel-de-Ville.

✔ **Salon de Thé de la Mosquée de Paris,** 39 rue Geoffroy-St-Hilaire, 5e, ☎ 01-43-31-18-14. Open daily 10 a.m.–10 p.m. Métro: Monge.

✔ **Tea Caddy,** 14 rue St-Julien-le-Pauvre, 5e, ☎ 01-43-54-15-56. Open daily noon–7 p.m. Métro: St-Michel.

Assembling a Picnic, Parisian style

Grab a crusty baguette or two, dried sausage, a wedge of cheese, and some fruit and head to the nearest park or garden that takes your fancy. Picnicking in Paris can be as fun and as unforgettable as a meal in a three-star restaurant and is just a fraction of the cost. In this section, I show you where to stock up on provisions.

The traiteurs (gourmet food shops)

Look for the word *traiteur,* which designates a food shop selling ready-made meat, pasta, and salad dishes. The most famous, **Fauchon** and **Hédiard,** are at place de la Madeleine, 8e (Métro: Madeleine), but many grocery stores sell Fauchon products, and the Hédiard has branches all over Paris. Every neighborhood has several good *traiteurs,* so be on the lookout and don't hesitate to ask your hotel staff for recommendations. The following lists the places that I recommend:

✔ **Flo Prestige,** 42 place du Marché-St-Honoré, 1er, Métro: Pyramides (☎ 01-42-61-45-46), is a well respected food shop and caterer with everything from *foie gras* and Norwegian smoked salmon, to fancy breads and cheeses. Open daily with branches around the city.

✔ **La Grande Épicerie,** Bon Marché, 38 rue de Sèvres, 7e, Métro: Sèvres-Babylone (☎ 01-44-39-81-00), is simply the most wonderful grocery store in Paris. It has a large *traiteur* department, a large wine department; and sells everything from cleaning supplies to gourmet chocolate to fresh fish. Open Mon–Sat 10 a.m.–8:30 p.m.

✔ **Lafayette Gourmet,** 52 bd. Haussmann, 9e, Métro: Havre-Caumartin (☎ 01-48-74-46-06) another wonderful grocery store that has everything you need for a picnic, is smack in the middle of the Galeries Lafayette complex (in the basement of the men's store). Open Mon–Sat 9:30 a.m.–7 p.m., Thurs until 9 p.m.

The street markets

Every neighborhood in Paris has its street market — probably the best place to find the freshest produce, cheeses of excellent quality, and other picnic supplies. Even if you don't buy anything, visit one or two for the authentic reflection of Parisian society. Markets are generally open from Tuesday through Saturday, from 8 a.m. to 1 p.m. Some of the more well known:

✔ **Rue Montorgueil,** 1er (Métro: Les Halles/Châtelet): Have breakfast at one of the many sidewalk cafés before you choose your produce.

✔ **Rue Mouffetard,** 5e (Métro: Monge): One of the oldest markets in Paris on one of the city's more interesting streets. Sing along with accordion players on Sunday mornings.

✔ **Rue de Buci,** 6e (Métro: Odéon): This lively market is close to all the Latin Quarter action.

✔ **Rue Poncelet,** 7e (Métro: Ternes): The Poncelet market is especially renowned for its fresh fruit stalls.

✔ **Marché Biologique,** 6e, boulevard Raspail between rue du Cherche-Midi and rue de Rennes (Métro: Rennes): This all-organic market features green grocers, wine makers, butchers, and bakers.

✔ **Rue Cler,** 7e (Métro: Ecole-Militaire): See how the spouses of diplomats shop for their kitchens in this "chic" market.

✔ **Rue Lepic,** 18e (Métro: Abbesses): This winding Montmartre street is filled with food shops, rather than stalls.

The best bakeries

You want a fresh baguette for your picnic, and you can find bakeries *(boulangeries)* on nearly every corner in residential neighborhoods. Keep in mind that quality of the bread varies considerably.

Long lines of locals on weekend mornings or evenings before dinner give away the best bakeries. You can get a quiche to go or a sandwich, but be forewarned that most bakeries make very plain sandwiches — often just a slice of bread or cheese on a baguette with no condiment or other accoutrement.

- ✔ **Au Panetier,** 10 place des petits pères, 2e, ☎ **01-42-60-90-23.** Mon–Fri 8 a.m.–7:15 p.m. Métro: Bourse.

- ✔ **Bonneau,** 75 rue d'Auteuil, 16e, ☎ **01-46-51-12-25.** Tues–Sun 6:30 a.m.–8:30 p.m. Métro Michel–Ange–Auteuil.

- ✔ **Boulangerie des Martyrs,** 10 rue des martyrs, 9e, ☎ **01-48-78-20-17.** Wed–Mon 6:45 a.m.–8:30 p.m. Métro: Notre-Dame-de-Lorette.

- ✔ **Eric Kayzer,** 8 rue Monge, 5e, ☎ **01-44-07-17-81.** Wed–Mon 6:30 a.m.–8:30 p.m. Métro: Maubert Mutualité.

- ✔ **Eric Kayzer Organic,** 14 rue Monge, 5e, ☎ **01-44-07-17-81.** Tues–Sun 8 a.m.–8 p.m. Métro: Maubert Mutualité.

- ✔ **Poilâne,** 8 rue du Cherche-midi, 6e, ☎ **01-45-48-42-59.** Mon–Sat 7:15 a.m.–8:15 p.m. Métro: St-Sulpice or Sèvres Babylone.

- ✔ **Max Poilane,** 87 rue Brancion, 15e, ☎ **01-48-28-45-90.** Mon–Sat 7:30 a.m.–8 p.m. Métro: Porte de Vanves.

- ✔ **Boulangeries Poilâne,** 49 boulevard de Grenelle, 15e, ☎ **01-45-79-11-49.** Tues–Mon 7:15 a.m.–8 p.m. Métro: Dupleix.

- ✔ **Poujauran,** 20 rue Jean Nicot, 7e, ☎ **01-47-05-80-88.** Mon–Sat 8 a.m.–8:30 p.m. Métro Latour Maubourg.

- ✔ **Stohrer,** 51 rue Montorgeuil, 2e, ☎ **01-42-33-38-20.** Open daily 7 a.m.–7 p.m. Métro: Châtelet.

Watching the World Go By at a Café

For many, this section is the most essential section of the book: the best places to read the paper, write postcards, people-watch, soak up the city's atmosphere, and relax with a cup of coffee, glass of wine, or beer — and, if you're hungry, fill up on delicious sandwiches, salads, and sometimes even traditional French specialties like *cassoulet* (a rich bean dish with lamb and pork) or *pot-au-feu* (beef boiled with vegetables). For this reason, I give full listings for the cafés. Cafés are generally open from about 8 a.m. until 1 a.m.

Au Bistro de la Place

This square on the place du Marché Sainte-Catherine is a pedestrian zone on the site of an eighteenth-century market. Although a number of bistros occupy the outdoor terraces on the square, the food is best here. Even if you don't opt for one of the pricey bistro dishes, come here during off-peak hours to enjoy a leisurely drink or pastry on the terrace.

2 place du Marché Sainte-Catherine, 4e. ☎ *01-42-78-21-32. Métro: St-Paul.*

Café Beaubourg

Designed by renowned architect Christian de Portzamparc, this hip bi-level café is cool and elegant with large circular columns that soar to an illuminated ceiling. The walls are filled with books, and a small wooden bridge spans the upper part of the café and leads to quieter, artistically designed tables. In the summer, sit in a wicker chair on the outside terrace and become a main attraction yourself as passersby cast curious glances at the people chic enough to eat here.

100 rue St-Merri, 4e. ☎ *01-48-87-63-96. Métro: Rambuteau or Hôtel-de-Ville.*

Café Concert Ailleur

Listen to what a new generation of musicians is singing about. This relaxed space, run by an artists' collective, attracts bohemians of all ages who are interested in up-and-coming artists.

13 rue Jean de Beausire, 4e. ☎ *01-44-59-82-82. Métro: Bastille.*

Café de Flore

In the heart of St-Germain-des-Prés, this café is still going strong, even though the famous writers have moved on and you now pay high prices for the opportunity to indulge in nostalgia. Sartre is said to have written *Les Chemins de la Liberté (The Roads to Freedom)* at his table here, and other regulars included André Malraux and Guillaume Apollinaire.

172 bd. St-Germain, 6e. ☎ *01-45-48-55-26. Métro: St-Germain-des-Prés.*

Café de la Place

This old-fashioned café overlooking a small, tree-lined square has become a popular spot for young neighborhood residents. Browse the menu of inexpensive bistro specialties, or opt for a simple sandwich and a glass of wine.

23 rue d'Odessa, 14e. ☎ *01-42-18-01-55. Métro: Edgar-Quinet.*

Café de L'Industrie

This popular bar and café is young, friendly, and casual. Plants, wood floors, and wood Venetian blinds lend the two spacious rooms a vaguely colonial flavor. Hip Bastille denizens drift in and out all day, and after 9:30 p.m., the place is mobbed. Closed Saturdays.

16 rue St-Sabin, 11e. ☎ *01-47-00-13-53. Métro: Bastille.*

Light Bites in Montmartre

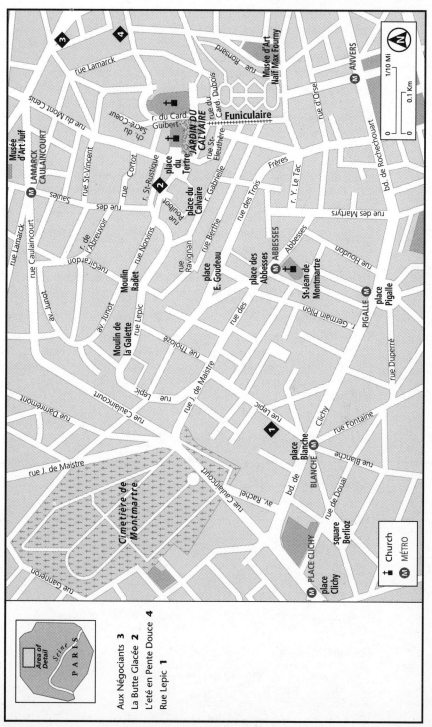

Aux Négociants **3**
La Butte Glacée **2**
L'eté en Pente Douce **4**
Rue Lepic **1**

Café les Deux-Magots

Like its neighbor the Café de Flore, Deux-Magots was a hangout for Sartre and Simone de Beauvoir. The intellectuals met here in the 1950s, and Sartre wrote at his table every morning. With prices that start at 23F ($3.30) for coffee and 12F ($1.75) for a croissant, the café is an expensive place for literary-intellectual pilgrims, but a great spot to watch the nightly promenade on the boulevard St-Germain. Service can be snippy.

6 place St-Germain-des-Prés, 6e. ☎ *01-45-48-55-25. Métro: St-Germain-des-Prés.*

Café Mabillon

Café Mabillon was a simple café until it was renovated about two years ago. Now, during the day, contemporary rock music draws a young, hip crowd to relax on the outdoor terrace or in the ultramodern interior. At night the music changes to techno, and the bordello-red banquettes fill with a wide assortment of night owls. As dawn approaches, the sound drops to a level just loud enough to keep you from dozing off in your seat.

164 bd. St-Germain, 6e. ☎ *01-43-26-62-93. Métro: Mabillon.*

Café Marly

This stunning café at the Louvre has a gorgeous view of the glass pyramid that is the museum's main entrance. With high ceilings, warmly painted pastel walls and luxurious red sofa chairs — the rooms could house the museum's latest art collection. Don't let the elegant ambiance intimidate you — wonderful food at reasonable prices can be found on the menu. Choose from the lovely wine list, sit on the balcony, and enjoy the exquisite lighting on the surrounding eighteenth-century facades. After 8 p.m., seating is for dinner only.

93 rue de Rivoli, cour Napoléon du Louvre, 1er. ☎ *01-49-26-06-60. Métro: Palais-Royal–Musée du Louvre.*

Fouquet's

Not far from the Arc de Triomphe, the turn-of-the-century Fouquet's is a Champs-Elysées institution. Patrons have included James Joyce, Charlie Chaplin, Marlene Dietrich, Winston Churchill, and Franklin D. Roosevelt. You pay dearly for the glitzy associations and nostalgia.

99 av. des Champs-Elysées, 8e. ☎ *01-47-23-70-60. Métro: George V.*

La Chaise au Plafond

Tucked away on a pedestrians-only side street in the heart of the Marais, this friendly, stylish place is a perfect spot for a time-out after visiting the Musée Picasso. It serves enormous salads, imaginative sandwiches, and thick tartes. A weekend brunch (100F/$14.30) is served, but the tiny café tables aren't designed to hold the assortment of dishes, so you may feel squeezed.

10 rue Trésor, 4e. ☎ *01-42-76-03-22. Métro: Hôtel-de-Ville.*

La Chope

This café is worth a stop for its location on top of rue Mouffetard, right on pretty place de la Contrescarpe. The square centers on four lilac trees and a fountain. It can get rowdy at night.

2–4 place de la Contrescarpe, 5e. ☎ *01-43-26-57-26. Métro: Cardinal Lemoine.*

La Coupole

La Coupole has been packing them in since Henry Miller came here for his morning porridge. The cavernous interior is always jammed and bristling with energy. Japanese business people, French yuppies, models, tourists, and neighborhood regulars keep the frenzied waiters running until 2 a.m. You won't know which is more interesting, the scene on the street, or the parade that passes through the revolving doors. The food is good, too.

102 bd. Montparnasse, 14e. ☎ *01-43-20-14-20. Métro: Vavin.*

La Palette

This artists' hangout is a great place to linger and watch the life of the Left Bank flow by. The interior is decorated with colorful murals, and a palette hangs over the bar. The fare is open-faced sandwiches and salads at reasonable prices.

43 rue de Seine, 6e. ☎ *01-43-26-68-15. Métro: Mabillon.*

L'Eté en Pente Douce

To escape the shoulder-to-shoulder tourists on place du Tertre, head down the eastern steps under Sacré-Coeur, where you find yourself on a leafy square, popular with a local crowd. The terrace here faces the stairs and iron lamps painted by Utrillo. The interior is brightly decorated with mosaics, unusual *objets d'art,* and a lovely painted ceiling. Between lunch and dinner, the restaurant serves a tempting array of pastries and sandwiches.

23 rue Muller, 18e. ☎ *01-42-64-02-67. Métro: Chateau-Rouge.*

Les Comptoirs du Charbon

Café Charbon is in the heart of the exploding nightlife scene along rue Oberkampf. This turn-of-the-century dance hall was restored a few years ago and has become the hottest spot in Paris for people who like people and don't mind being crowded. The stunning art nouveau interior has high ceilings, hanging lamps, and walls covered with mirrors, wood, and hand-painted murals — which you can barely perceive through the bustle and haze. During the day or early evening you can relax, hang out, chat, or read a newspaper. After about 9 p.m., the music gets louder, the long wood bar and banquettes fill up, and you are lucky to get in, let alone get a seat.

109 rue Oberkampf, 11e. ☎ *01-43-57-55-13. Métro: Parmentier. MC, V.*

Web Bar

This three-level cybercafé in the Marais exhibits art, plays experimental music, shows short films, and has storytelling, fashion shows, and even an occasional chess tournament. A casual crowd of locals creates a warm mood in contrast to the rather stark decor. Fees for the use of one of the 18 computers are 40F ($5.70) an hour, 25F ($3.60) for a half-hour. Avoid weekdays between 5 and 7 p.m., or you may have to wait to use them.

32 rue de Picardie, 3e. ☎ *01-42-72-66-55. Internet:* www.webbar.fr. *Métro: République.*

A Heady Mix of Wine Bars

À la Cloche des Halles

Look closely at the exterior for the bell that once tolled the opening and closing of the vast food market for which this neighborhood was named. Today the tiny bar and café is crowded at lunchtime with people dining on plates of ham or quiche, accompanied by a bottle of wine. This bar is convivial and fun, but very noisy and crowded. If you can't find a seat, you can usually stand at the bar and eat.

28 rue Coquillière, 1er. ☎ *01-42-36-93-89. Mon–Fri 8 a.m.–10 p.m.; Sat 10 a.m.–5 p.m. Métro: Les Halles or Palais-Royal–Musée du Louvre.*

Aux Négociants

The photographer Robert Doisneau came here often (his picture is on the wall), but today a discerning crowd of regulars keep this tiny, unpretentious wine bar near Montmartre humming. The excellent pâtés and terrines are homemade and served with fresh, chewy bread.

27 rue Lambert, 18e. ☎ *01-46-06-15-11. Mon–Fri noon–3 p.m.; Tues–Thurs 6:30–10:30 p.m. Métro: Château-Rouge or Lamarck-Caulincourt.*

Bistro du Peintre

A collection of Bastille bohemian types — painters, actors, and night crawlers — gathers nightly here. The zinc bar, wood paneling, large terrace, and superb belle-époque style would make this wine bar a highlight even if the wine selection were not as reasonably priced as it is.

116 av. Ledru-Rollin, 11e. ☎ *01-47-00-34-39. Daily 7 a.m.–midnight. Métro: Ledru-Rollin.*

Clown Bar

Located near the Cirque d'Hiver, where many of its patrons work, this bar is decorated with a mélange of circus posters and circus-themed ceramic tiles. The wine list features an extensive selection of French offerings.

114 rue Amelot, 11e. ☎ *01-43-55-87-35. Mon–Sat noon–2:30 p.m. and 7 p.m.–1 a.m. Métro: Filles du Calvaire.*

La Tartine

This is pure prewar Paris, from the nicotine-browned walls and frosted globe chandeliers, to the worn wood furniture. The ambience is funky and working-class, but you find a broad segment of society throwing back little glasses of wine at the bar or lingering over a newspaper in the spacious back room. This is one of the few wine bars in Paris open on Sunday.

24 rue de Rivoli, 4e. ☎ *01-42-72-76-85. Wed–Mon noon–10 p.m. Métro: St-Paul.*

L'Écluse Saint-Michel

A small chain of wine bars bearing the name L'Écluse has grown from this original location. Casually chic and authentic, it offers 20 or so wines by the glass, along with snacks like *carpaccio,* salads, and soups.

15 quai des Grands-Augustins, 6e. ☎ *01-46-33-58-74. Daily 11:30 a.m.–1:30 a.m. Métro: St-Michel.*

Le Griffonnier

Le Griffonnier is noted as much for its first-rate kitchen as for its comprehensive wine cellar. You can sample bistro specialties such as *confit de canard maison,* or try a hearty plate of charcuterie, terrines, and cheese, usually from the Auvergne region of central France. Hot meals are served only at lunchtime and Thursday evenings.

8 rue des Saussaies, 8e. ☎ *01-42-65-17-17. Mon–Fri 7:30 a.m.–9 p.m. Métro: Champs-Elysées–Clemenceau.*

Le Sancerre

Once you settle in at one of the cozy tables here, you find some typically French items on the menu, such as omelettes of all varieties with a side of fried potatoes. The more adventurous can sample the ubiquitous *andouillette*, the sausage that is decidedly an acquired taste. You also have a choice of Loire wines — including, of course, Sancerre.

22 av. Rapp, 7e. ☎ *01-45-51-75-91. Mon–Fri 8 a.m.–10 p.m.; Sat 8 a.m.–4 p.m. Métro: Alma Marceau.*

Mélac

Owner Jacques Mélac has an excellent selection of wine from nearly all the regions of France, which he dispenses to a joyous crowd of regulars. Usually a hot *plat du jour* is available for lunch, but you can feast on a selection of first-rate pâtés, terrines, charcuterie, and cheeses all day.

42 rue Léon Frot, 11e. ☎ *01-43-70-59-27. Mon 9 a.m.–2 p.m.; Tues–Sat 9 a.m.– 10:30 p.m. Métro: Charonne.*

Taverne Henri 1V

A variety of wines by the glass can be accompanied by open-faced sand-wiches (including warm goat cheese), pâtés, and such cheeses as Cantal and Auvergne blue. Although on the expensive side, the wine and food are excellent. An authentic, old-fashioned bar, the regulars are men read-ing the newspaper, discussing the news of the day, and smoking non-stop.

13 place du Pont Neuf, 1er. ☎ *01-43-54-27-90. Mon–Fri noon–10 p.m.; Sat noon– 4 p.m. Métro: Pont-Neuf.*

The Scoop on Paris Ice Cream

A visit to Paris isn't complete without a stop for ice cream; if not for the unusual flavors — rhubarb, plum, cassis, and more — then for the creamy texture. Ask for a *cornet seule* (single scoop cone) or *cornet double* (double scoop) — even the cone is yummy. Prices range from 10F ($1.45) for a single to 20F ($2.90) for a double scoop cone. Most places open daily around 10:30 a.m. and close around 8 p.m. Take note: sitting down to order ice cream is always more expensive; it can be twice as much as ordering your cone to go. You find the best ice cream at **Berthillon** (31 rue St-Louis-en-l'Ile, 4e, ☎ **01-43-54-31-61.** Métro: Cité), but the following also put soft-serve to shame. Berthillon is so popular that it can afford to take a long summer holiday — it's closed from July 15 through the first week in September (the owners post a note on the door directing customers to other nearby shops that sell their ice cream).

- ✔ **Dammam's,** 20 rue Cardinal Lemoine, 5e, ☎ **01-46-33-61-30.** Métro: Cardinal Lemoine.

- ✔ **La Butte Glacée,** 14 rue Norvin, 18e, ☎ **01-42-23-91-58.** Métro: Abbesses.

- ✔ **Le Bac à Glaces,** 109 rue du Bac, 7e, ☎ **01-45-48-87-65.** Métro: Rue du Bac.

- ✔ **Octave,** 138 rue Mouffetard, 5e, ☎ **01-45-35-20-56.** Métro: Monge.

- ✔ **Vilfeu,** 3 rue de la Cossonerie, 1er, ☎ **01-40-26-36-40.** Métro: Les Halles.

Part V
Exploring Paris

The 5th Wave   By Rich Tennant

WHILE IN PARIS, DAVE VISITS THE MUSEÉ d'ORSAY—FAMOUS FOR ITS IMPRESSIONISTS

Now I do for you the actor, James Cagney. You dirty rat...

In this part . . .

So many things to see in Paris . . . where do you even begin? This section tells you a bit about what's worth seeing, and if you still can't decide, I provide you with worksheets at the back of this book to make it easier. Chapter 16 contains an alphabetical list of the city's top sights, described and indexed by neighborhood and attraction type, and Chapter 17 lists some more cool things to see and do for kids, teens, history buffs, and art and literature lovers. You also find some gardens and parks listed here. If you just can't stand the thought of deciding where to go next, Chapter 18 provides you with guided tour options, from buses to bicycles. Die-hard shoppers can appreciate Chapter 19's guide to Parisian shopping. It describes today's shopping scene in Paris, previews four great shopping neighborhoods, covers the outdoor markets, and provides an A to Z of local shops of interest. In Chapter 20, you have the chance to discover Paris in four itineraries and on a walking tour. And just when you were getting used to Paris, Chapter 21 sends you away on one of five great day trips in the Ile de France region.

Chapter 16

Paris's Top Sights

* *

In This Chapter

▶ Paris's top attractions at a glance

▶ Paris's top sights by type

▶ Paris's top sights from A to Z

* *

T his chapter starts off with indexes that list the city's top 20 sights by location and by type, plus its most popular thing to do (a river cruise). Then follows a succinct review of each sight, giving you the lowdown on when to go, how to get there, and why you should visit it in the first place.

Even after whittling down Paris's many attractions to only 20 (actually 21) sights, that's still probably more than you can see in a single trip. At the end of this book is a worksheet where you can plot the top sights according to how much you want to see them. Chapter 20 also outlines very doable itineraries, which take in several top sights.

Index of Attractions by Location

The Right Bank

Louvre (1er)
Jardin du Palais-Royal
Jardin des Tuileries
Musée du Louvre
Vedettes Pont Neuf

Le Marais and the Islands (3e, 4e)
Musée Picasso
Notre-Dame
Place des Vosges

Sainte-Chapelle
Centre Georges Pompidou

Champs-Elysées (8e, 16e)
Arc de Triomphe
Champs-Elysées
Musée Jacquemart-André
Bateaux Mouches

Montmartre (18e) and Beyond
Père-Lachaise Cemetery (20e)
Sacré-Coeur

The Left Bank

Latin Quarter (5e)
Panthéon

St-Germain-des-Prés (6e)
Jardin et Palais du Luxembourg

La Tour Eiffel and Les Invalides (7e)
La Tour Eiffel
Hotel des Invalides (Napoléon's Tomb)
Musée d'Orsay
Musée Rodin
Bateaux Parisiens

Index by Type of Attraction

Museums
Centre Georges Pompidou
Musée Jacquemart-André
Musée du Louvre
Musée d'Orsay
Musée Picasso
Musée Rodin

Churches
Notre-Dame
Sacré-Coeur
Sainte-Chapelle

Parks
Jardin du Palais-Royal
Jardin des Tuileries
Jardin et Palais du Luxembourg
Place des Vosges

Monuments and Architecture
Arc de Triomphe
Champs-Elysées
Eiffel Tower
Hotel des Invalides (Napoléon's Tomb)
Panthéon

Neighborhoods
Montmartre

Cemeteries
Père-Lachaise

Boat cruises
Vedettes Pont Neuf
Bateaux Parisiens
Bateaux Mouches

The Top Attractions from A to Z

Arc de Triomphe
Champs-Elysées (8e)

The Arc de Triomphe is the largest triumphal arch in the world, commissioned by Napoléon in honor of the 128 battles won by his armies. Although it has come to symbolize the thrill of victory, it has also witnessed the agony of defeat, as in 1871 (when Paris was seized by the Prussians during the Franco-Prussian War), and in 1940 (when Nazi armies marched victoriously through the arch and down the Champs-Elysées). Today the Arc houses the Tomb of the Unknown Soldier. The real thrill here, though, is the panoramic view. From the top, 162 feet up, you can see in a straight line the Champs-Elysées, the obelisk in the place de la Concorde, and the Louvre. That big cube at the far end is the Grande Arche de la Défense in St-Denis, built to be the modern equivalent to this arch. (Many think it failed miserably.) Allow an hour to visit.

To reach the stairs and elevators that climb the arch, take the underpass using the white Métro entrances. Please do not try to cross on surface streets; attempting to dodge the warp-speed traffic zooming around the circle will likely get you seriously hurt.

Place Charles-de-Gaulle, 8e. ☎ 01-43-80-31-31. Métro: Charles-de-Gaulle–Étoile. Bus: 22, 30, 31, 52, 73, 92. Open Apr–Sept 9:30 a.m.–11 p.m.; Oct–March 10 a.m.–10:30 p.m. Closed major holidays. Admission 40F ($5.70) adults, 32F ($4.60) ages 12–25, free for children under 12.

Centre Georges Pompidou
Le Marais and the Islands (3e, 4e)

Escalators, elevators, air conditioning and tubular passages resembling a giant gerbil habitat run along the outside of the futuristic, colorful Centre National d'Art et de Culture Georges Pompidou, while the inside is a spacious haven in which to view, touch, or listen to modern art and artists. The newer of Paris's two modern art museums, the Centre Georges Pompidou includes two floors of work from the Musée National d'Art Moderne, France's national collection of modern art. The museum also houses nearly 150 drawings, paintings, and other works by Romanian sculptor Constantin Brancusi in the Brancusi Atelier; a cinema and a huge public library; spaces for modern dance and music; and temporary exhibits that often include video and computer works.

British architect Richard Rogers and Italian architect Renzo Piano designed the building in the late 1960s as part of a redevelopment plan for the Beaubourg neighborhood. Since its opening in 1977, more than 160 million people have visited the Centre Pompidou — and the building began to crumble under the weight of its popularity. It underwent a more than $100 million renovation and reopened January 1, 2000. Even if you miss the museum, you can still take an escalator to the top floor for a breathtaking view of Paris. Don't miss the nearby Igor Stravinsky fountain, either, with its fun sculptures by Tinguely and Niki de Saint Phalle that include red lips spitting water and a twirling grinning skull. Dedicate at least two hours to viewing the works and slipping upstairs for the view. Avoid Georges, the ultrahip restaurant on the top floor which is expensive, plus the portions are tiny, and service is too slow for busy visitors.

Place Georges-Pompidou, 4e. ☎ 01-44-78-12-33. Internet: www.centrepompidou. fr. Métro: Rambuteau, Hôtel-de-Ville, or Châtelet–Les Halles. Bus: 21, 29, 38, 47, 58, 69, 70, 72, 74, 75, 76, 81, 85, 86. Open: Daily 11 a.m.–10 p.m. Admission 30F ($4.30) adults; 20F ($2.85) ages 18–26; free for children under 18. Guided tours 40F ($5.70).

Paris's Top Attractions

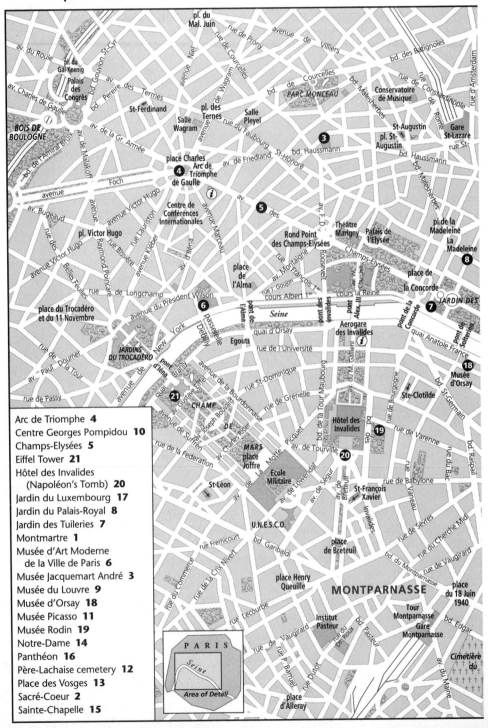

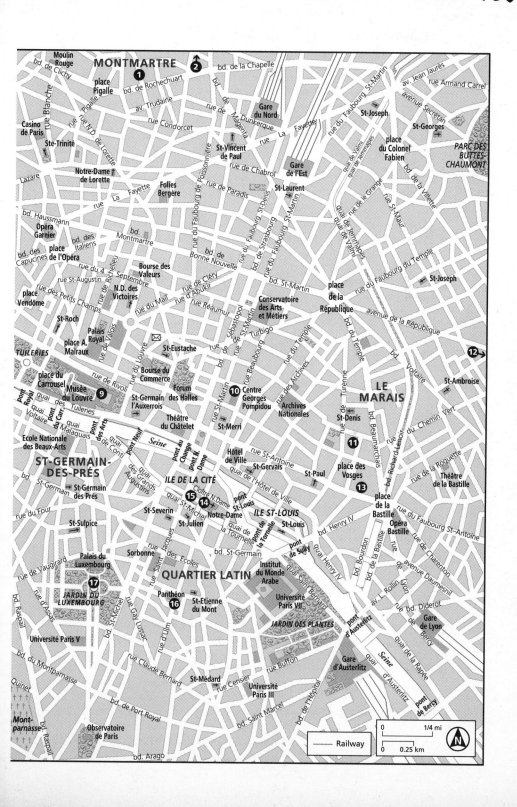

Moulin
Rouge
bd. de Clichy
MONTMARTRE ❶ ❷
place
Pigalle
bd. de Rochechuart
bd. de la Chapelle
av. Jean Jaurès
rue Armand Carrel
avenue Secrétan
av. Trudaine
rue de Magenta
Gare
du Nord
rue de La Fayette
St-Joseph
St-Georges
Casino
de Paris
rue Blanche
rue N.D. de Lorette
Pigalle
rue Condorcet
Gare
de l'Est
St-Vincent
de Paul
rue de Chabrol
place
du Colonel
Fabien
PARC DES
BUTTES-
CHAUMONT
Ste-Trinité
Notre-Dame
de Lorette
Folies
Bergère
rue du Faubourg Poissonnière
St-Laurent
quai de Valmy
quai de Jemmapes
rue de la Villette
Lazare
rue La Fayette
rue de Paradis
rue du Faubourg St-Denis
rue du Faubourg St-Martin
rue de la Grange
rue St-Maur
bd. Haussmann
Opéra
Garnier
bd. des
Italiens
bd.
Montmartre
bd. de
Bonne Nouvelle
bd. St-Martin
place
de la
République
rue du Faubourg du Temple
St-Joseph
place des
Capucines de l'Opéra
rue du 4
Septembre
Bourse des
Valeurs
rue de Cléry
rue d'Abukir
Conservatoire
des Arts
et Métiers
avenue de la République
place
Vendôme
rue St-Augustin
rue de Richelieu
N.D. des
Victoires
rue du Mail
rue Réaumur
bd. du Temple
bd. du Temple
St-Roch
rue des Petits Champs
Palais
Royal
place A.
Malraux
St-Eustache
rue de Sébastopol
Turbigo
rue du Temple
Voltaire
LE
MARAIS
St-Ambroise
TUILERIES
place du
Carrousel
Bourse du
Commerce
Forum
des Halles
Centre
Georges
Pompidou
rue des Archives
rue de Turenne
❿
⓫
⓬
Musée
du Louvre ❾
rue de Rivoli
St-Germain
l'Auxerrois
Archives
Nationales
St-Denis
rue de Beaumarchais
place des
Vosges
St-Ambroise
pont
Royal
quai des
Tuileries
Théâtre
du Châtelet
St-Merri
rue du Chemin Vert
Théâtre
de la Bastille
Ecole Nationale
des Beaux-Arts
pont des Arts
pont du Carr.
pont Neuf
Seine
Hôtel
de Ville
rue St-Antoine
St-Gervais
St-Paul
rue de la Roquette
ST-GERMAIN-
DES-PRÉS
quai de Conti
quai des Grands Augustins
pont au Change
pont N. Dame
ILE DE LA CITÉ
quai de l'Hôtel de Ville
⓭
place de la
Bastille
rue du Faubourg St-Antoine
bd. St-Germain
St-Germain
des Prés
Cloître N.Dame
⓯ ⓮
Notre-Dame
ILE ST-LOUIS
St-Louis
Opéra
Bastille
rue de Charenton
rue du Four
St-Séverin
quai St-Michel
quai de
la Tournelle
pont de
la Tournelle
bd. Henry IV
quai de la Bastille
rue de Lyon
avenue Daumesnil
St-Sulpice
St-Julien
pont de Sully
quai Henry IV
rue bd. Diderot
Palais du
Luxembourg
Sorbonne
rue des Ecoles
bd. St-Germain
quai Saint Bernard
quai de la Rapée
Gare
de Lyon
rue de Vaugirard
QUARTIER LATIN
Institut
du Monde
Arabe
av. L. Rollin
bd. d'Assas
⓱
JARDIN DU
LUXEMBOURG
Panthéon
rue Gay Lussac
rue d'Ulm
St-Etienne
du Mont
⓰
Université
Paris VII
JARDIN DES PLANTES
pont
d'Austerlitz
quai de Bercy
Université Paris V
bd. du Montparnasse
rue Claude Bernard
St-Médard
Université
Paris III
Seine
rue Buffon
Gare
d'Austerlitz
quai d'Austerlitz
Quinet
bd. Raspail
rue Censier
bd. de Port Royal
bd. Saint Marcel
bd. de l'Hôpital
pont
de Bercy
Mont-
parnasse
Observatoire
de Paris
bd. Arago

| | 0 | 1/4 mi |
| Railway | 0 | 0.25 km |

Ⓝ

Champs-Elysées
Champs-Elysées (8e)

If you were in Paris when the Millenium turned, or the nights the French won the World and Euro Cup soccer championships (2000 and 1998, respectively), you understand what the Champs-Elysées means to the French. As close to a million singing, flag-waving Parisians spilled into the avenue, it was said the country hadn't experienced such group euphoria since the days following the Liberation of Paris by the Allies in 1944. The Champs is also the avenue where the military march on Bastille Day; Lance Armstrong won his second Tour de France here in July 2000. The scene here is liveliest at night, with people lining up for the numerous cinemas (see English–language–films here by looking for v.o for *version originale* on schedules and movie posters), and floodlights illuminating the Arc de Triomphe and place de la Concorde. Restaurants consist mainly of standard chain cafes (Chez Clément, Hippo) and American-style fast food (McDonald's, Planet Hollywood, ChiChi's), though good restaurants abound on the streets surrounding the avenue (see Chapter 14). You can shop at reasonably priced stores, such as Zara to the very luxe (Louis Vuitton), to chain stores that you'd see in any American mall (the Disney Store). Many of the stores are open on Sunday. Allow an hour to walk from top to bottom, longer if you want to shop, eat, or dawdle.

Champs-Elysées (8e). Métro: Concorde, Champs-Elysées Clémenceau, Franklin-D-Roosevelt, George V, Charles-de-Gaulle-Étoile. Bus: Many lines cross it, but only the 73 travels its entire length.

Eiffel Tower
La Tour Eiffel and Les Invalides (7e)

You can fill an entire page with fun trivia about Paris's most famous symbol. For starters, it weighs 7000 tons, soars 1,056 feet, and is held together with 2.5 million rivets. Gustave Eiffel beat 699 others in a contest to design what was supposed to be a temporary monument for the Exposition Universelle (World's Fair). His designs for the tower spanned 6,000 square yards of paper. Praised by some and damned by others, the tower created as much controversy in its time as I. M. Pei's pyramid at the Louvre did 100 years later. Upon completion the Eiffel Tower was the tallest human-built structure in the world, and the Prince of Wales (later Edward VII) and his family were invited to ascend it first. People have climbed it, bungee-jumped from it, and cycled down the tower's steps. In 1989, the tower's centennial was celebrated with 89 minutes of music and fireworks, and in the 1990s it counted down the days and then the minutes until the Millenium and another spectacular fireworks show. Six months later, more fireworks took flight when upwards of 500,000 people gathered on the Champs de Mars to hear French superstar Johnny Hallyday give a free concert at the base of the tower. Since the first day of the year 2000, a breathtaking show of twinkling lights has played from the tower for 10 minutes every hour on the hour at night. Allow two hours for your visit: one to line up for the elevator and another to take in the panorama. Lines are shorter first thing in the morning, but the Eiffel Tower at night shouldn't be missed. The lights frame the lacy steelwork in a way that daylight doesn't, while beneath you the city twinkles and the Seine reflects it all.

Parc du Champs de Mars (7e). ☎ *01-44-11-23-45. Internet:* www.tour-eiffel.fr. *Métro: Trocadéro, Bir-Hakeim, or École-Militaire. RER: Champs-de-Mars. Bus: 42, 69, 82, 87. Open: Daily Sept to mid-June 9:30 a.m.–11 p.m.; late June to Aug 9 a.m.–midnight. Fall and winter, stairs close at 6:30 p.m. Closed major holidays. Admission: 22F ($3.15) for elevator to 1st level (188 ft.); 44F ($7.30) to 2nd level (380 ft.); 62F ($8.90) to highest level (1,060 ft.); 18F ($2.60) for stairs to 1st and 2nd levels. Reduced admission for children under 12.*

Hôtel des Invalides (Napoléon's Tomb)
La Tour Eiffel and Les Invalides (7e)

The best way to get the sense of the awe that the Hôtel des Invalides inspires is to walk to it by crossing over the Alexander III bridge. You see the dome of the **Église du Dôme** (gilded with 12 kilograms of real gold), one of the high points of classical art, rising 107 meters from the ground, with 16 green copper cannons pointed outwards in a powerful display. Invalides was built by Louis XIV, who liked war and waged many, as a hospital and home for all veteran officers and soldiers. It still has offices for departments of the French armed forces, and part of it is still a hospital.

You see a row of enemy flags captured during the military campaigns of the nineteenth and twentieth centuries on the **Église de St-Louis,** part of the Invalides known as the Church of the Soldiers, but most visitors come to see the **Tomb of Napoléon,** where the emperor is buried in six coffins, one inside the other under the great dome. The first coffin is iron, the second mahogany, the third and fourth lead, the fifth ebony, and the outermost oak. The emperor's remains were transferred to his final resting place in 1840, almost 20 years after his death on the island of St. Helena, where he was exiled following his defeat at Waterloo.

If you like military lore, you may want to visit the **Musée de l'Armée —** admission is included when you buy your ticket for Napoléon's tomb, one of the greatest army museums in the world. It features thousands of weapons dating from prehistory to World War II.

☎ *01-44-42-37-72. Métro: Latour-Maubourg, Invalides, or Varenne. Bus: 63, 83, 93. Admission: 38F ($6.35) adults; 28F ($4.65) students 12–25; free for children under 12. Open: Daily Oct–Mar 10 a.m.–5 p.m.; Apr–Sept 10 a.m.–6 p.m. Tomb of Napoléon open until 7 p.m. June–Sept. Closed major holidays.*

Jardin and Palais de Luxembourg
St-Germain-des-Prés (6e)

The 6e arrondissement's **Jardin du Luxembourg** was commissioned by King Henri IV's queen, Marie de Medici, and is one of Paris's most beloved parks. Not far from the Sorbonne and just south of the Latin Quarter, the large park is popular with students and children who love it for its playground, toy boat pond, pony rides, and puppet theater. Besides pools, fountains, and statues of queens and poets, you can occupy your time on the tennis and *boules* courts (*boule* means ball; in this game, players compete to see who can roll their small steel ball closest to a larger steel ball that lies further down the court).

Orchards in the park's southwest corner contain 360 varieties of apples, 270 kinds of pears, and various grape vines. Members of the French Senate get to eat the fruit, but leftovers go to a soup kitchen. Walk north and you come across a bevy of beehives behind a low fence. A beekeeping (apiculture) course is taught here weekends.

The **Palais du Luxembourg,** at the northern edge of the park, was also built for Marie de Medici who was homesick for the Palazzo Pitti in Florence, where she had spent her childhood. When the queen was banished in 1630, the palace was abandoned until the Revolution, when it was used as a prison. The palace is now the seat of the French Senate, but is not open to the public.

St-Germain-des-Prés (6e). Main entrance at the corner of bd. St-Michel and rue des Médicis (☎ 01-43-29-12-78) Métro: Odéon. RER: Luxembourg, Port-Royal. Bus: 38, 82, 84, 85, 89. Open: Daily dawn to dusk. Admission: free.

Jardin du Palais-Royal
Louvre (1er)

Cardinal Richelieu ordered the Royal Palace built in 1630 as his personal residence, complete with grounds landscaped by the royal gardener. Today the palace is no longer open to the public, but its statue-filled gardens, including the controversial prison-striped columns built in 1986, remain one of the most restful places in the city. The square is also ringed by restaurants, art galleries, and specialty boutiques, and is also home to the Comédie Française.

Louvre, 1er. Entrances on rue de Rivoli and place de la Concorde, 1er. Métro: Concorde or Tuileries. Bus: 42, 69, 72,73,94. Open: Daily 7:30 a.m.–dusk. Admission: free.

Jardin des Tuileries
Louvre (1er)

Spread out over 63 acres, the city's most formal gardens originally ran between the Louvre and the Tuileries Palace, which was burned down during the 1871 Paris Commune. In keeping with the French style of parks, trees are planted according to orderly design and the sandy paths are arrow straight. You can catch some rays from one of the chairs surrounding the ponds and fountains, and get a light snack at one of the outdoor cafés. During the summer, a carnival features an enormous Ferris wheel (with great views of the city), a log flume, fun house, ice-cream stands, and arcade-style games. Come for a stroll before or after visiting the Louvre.

Louvre, 1er. Entrances on rue de Rivoli and place de la Concorde, 1er. Métro: Concorde or Tuileries. Bus: 42, 69, 72, 73, 94. Open: Daily, 7:30 a.m.–dusk. Admission: free. Free guided visits of the gardens (in French) Sun, Wed, Fri 3 p.m.

Montmartre
Right Bank (18e)

Take the Métro to Abbesses, and admire the splendid art nouveau Métro stop before taking the funicular to the top of the *butte*. After visiting Sacré-Coeur and the touristy, but fun, place du Tertre, wander down the hill where you eventually stumble across Paris from another era — surprisingly unspoiled lanes, quiet squares, ivy-clad shuttered houses with gardens, and even Paris's only vineyard. Together, it all creates a sense of the rustic village still apart from the churning metropolis below.

Musée Jacquemart André
Champs-Elysées (8e)

Edouard André, the heir of a prominent banking family, and Nélie Jacquemart, a well-known portraitist, commissioned architect Henri Parent to build this impressive residence, then set about filling it with French, Flemish, and Italian paintings, furniture, and tapestries. Now a museum, the Musée Jacquemart André is a paradise for Renaissance art fans, worth visiting as much for a glimpse of how filthy rich Parisians lived in the nineteenth century as for its Italian and Flemish masterpieces by Bellini, Botticelli, Carpaccio, Uccello, Rubens, Rembrandt, and Van Eyck. Take advantage of the free audio which guides you through the mansion with fascinating narrative. Allow an hour to visit the museum, then take a break in what was Madame's lofty ceilinged dining room, now a classy tearoom serving light lunches and snacks.

158 bd. Haussmann, 8e. ☎ 01-42-89-04-91. Métro: Miromesnil. Bus: 28, 32, 49, 80. Open: Daily (including Christmas) 10 a.m.–6 p.m. Admission: 49F ($7) adults; 37F ($5.30) students and children under 18.

Musée du Louvre
Louvre (1er)

You can visit the Louvre every day for a month and still see each of its more than 30,000 treasures. So to have an enjoyable, non-exhausting, experience, you need to limit your focus or plan more than one trip. The sheer scale of the Louvre, organized in three wings — Sully, Denon, and Richelieu — makes it easy to get lost, so grab a map on the way in. The Louvre bookstore in the Carrousel de Louvre sells many comprehensive guides and maps in English; you can grab brochures for "visitors in a hurry," or a guidebook, "The Louvre, First Visit." You can also try the 90-minute tour by a museum guide (☎01-40-20-51-77) covering the most popular works which gives you a quick orientation to the museum's layout. Or, you can set your own pace with the 4-hour "audiotour" (30F/$4.30); rent it at the entrance to any of the wings.

If you're in a hurry, but want to do the Louvre on your own, do a quick, "best of the Louvre" tour, starting with Leonardo da Vinci's *Mona Lisa* (Denon wing, first floor). On the same floor nearby, are two of the Louvre's most famous French paintings, Géricault's *The Raft of Medusa* and Delacroix's *Liberty Guiding the People*. Next, visit the *Winged Victory* and Michelangelo's *Slaves* (both Denon wing, ground floor) before seeing *the Venus de Milo* (Sully wing, ground floor). After that, let your own interests guide you. Consider that only Florence's Uffizi Gallery rivals the Denon wing for its Italian Renaissance collection, which includes Raphael's *Portrait of Balthazar Castiglione* and Titian's *Man with a Glove*. And the revamped Egyptian antiquities department is the largest exhibition of Egyptian antiquities outside Cairo. In April 2000, a new exhibit featuring 120 arts and antiquities from the earliest civilizations in Africa, Asia, Oceania, and the Americas opened on the ground floor near the Denon wing. The exhibit will be housed in the Louvre until 2004, when Musée de Quai Branly, to which it belongs, opens. If it all seems never ending, consider that the huge palace evolved over several centuries, first opening as a museum in 1793.

Relatively recent renovations have doubled its gallery space and added architect I. M. Pei's glass pyramid, now the main entrance to the museum. Avoid this entrance and its long lines by using **the rue de Rivoli/ Carrousel du Louvre** entrance, or take the stairs at the **Porte des Lions** near the Arc du Triomphe du Carrousel.

Rue de Rivoli, 1er. ☎ 01-40-20-50-50 for recorded message, 01-40-20-53-17 for information desk. Internet: www.louvre.fr. Métro: Palais-Royal–Musée du Louvre. Admission: 45F ($6.40) adults; 26F ($3.70) after 3 p.m. and on Sun; free first Sun of month and for children under 18. Mon (certain rooms only) and Wed 9 a.m.– 9:45 p.m.; Thurs–Sun 9 a.m.–6 p.m. Closed Tuesday. Tours in English (call 01-40-20-52-09 for hours) 17F ($2.45).

The Louvre

The Pyramid

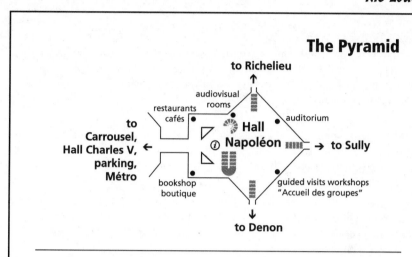

to Richelieu

audiovisual rooms

restaurants cafés

Hall Napoléon

auditorium

to Sully

to Carrousel, Hall Charles V, parking, Métro

bookshop boutique

guided visits workshops "Accueil des groupes"

to Denon

The Levels

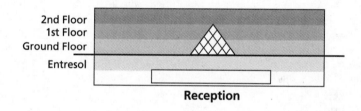

2nd Floor
1st Floor
Ground Floor
Entresol

Reception

The Wings

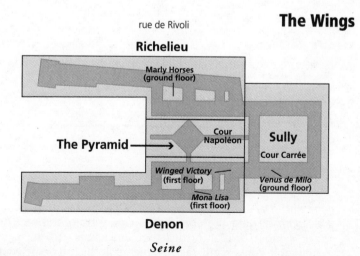

rue de Rivoli

Richelieu

Marly Horses (ground floor)

The Pyramid

Cour Napoléon

Sully

Cour Carrée

Winged Victory (first floor)

Venus de Milo (ground floor)

Mona Lisa (first floor)

Denon

Seine

Taking a Seine River Cruise

One of the most romantic and beautiful ways to see Paris is by one of the sight-seeing boats that cruise up and down the Seine. Don't, however, take one of the overpriced dinner or lunch cruises — they cost between 350–500F ($50–$71) per person. Instead, opt for an evening cruise. With its dramatically lit monuments and romantic bridges, Paris is truly breathtaking at night.

Three companies offer the tours which are all similar and cost about the same price. Perhaps the most well known are the **Bateaux-Mouches** that sail from the pont de l'Alma on the Right Bank and have huge floodlit boats. They offer recorded commentary in up to six languages. You can't miss their huge neon sign at night.

Bateaux-Parisiens sail from the port de la Bourdonnais on the Left Bank, while **Vedettes Pont Neuf** sail from the riverside where the Pont Neuf crosses the Ile de la Cité. Vedettes boats are smaller, more intimate, and not all of them are covered. Commentary is live.

For a boat ride without commentary, take one of the **Bat-o-bus** shuttles that stops at Trocadéro, Musée d'Orsay, Louvre, Notre-Dame and Hôtel de Ville. A ticket costs 65F ($9.30), 35F ($5) for children under 12, and you can jump off and on when you want.

Bateaux-Mouches, pont de l'Alma, Right Bank, 8e. ☎ 01-42-25-96-10 or 01-42-76-99-99 for reservations. Métro: Alma Marceau. Departures: Every 45 minutes until noon, every half hour afterward: March through mid-November, 10 a.m.–11 p.m.; every hour November through March, 11 a.m.–9 p.m. Rates: 40F ($5.70) for adults, 20F ($2.90) for children 5 to 13 and adults over 65, children under 5 ride free.

Bateaux-Parisiens, port de la Bourdonnais, Left Bank, 7e. ☎ 01-44-11-33-44. Métro: Bir-Hakeim. Departures: Every half hour March–October 10 a.m.–10 p.m. and Saturdays and Sundays in winter; every hour October–March 10 a.m.–9 p.m. Rates: 52F ($7.45) adults, 26F ($3.70) ages 12 and under.

Vedettes Pont Neuf, square du Vert-Galant, 1er. ☎ 01-46-33-98-38. Métro: Pont-Neuf, sail from the riverside where the Pont Neuf crosses the Ile de la Cité. Departures: Every half hour March–October 10:30 a.m.–11 p.m.; every 45 minutes November–February 10:30 a.m.–10 p.m., Saturdays and Sundays until 10:30 p.m. Rates: 50F ($7.15) adults, 25F ($3.60)ages 4–12.

Musée d'Orsay

La Tour Eiffel and Les Invalides (7e)

One of the greatest achievements of Jacques Chirac as mayor of Paris has been turning the abandoned Orsay train station into one of the world's most brilliantly designed museums. To get a sense of this remarkable conversion, take a moment at the top of the central staircase to envision where the trains once pulled into the station under the curved roof. Then enjoy the Musée d'Orsay's real claim to fame — its unsurpassed collection of Impressionist masterpieces.

In order to appreciate them, don't visit the museum from bottom to top, because you may get tired. Instead, go directly to the top floor and work your way down after soaking up Monet, Renoir, Degas, Cézanne, Gauguin, van Gogh, and their contemporaries. Allow 90 minutes for the Impressionists, longer to see the whole museum (the art-nouveau rooms are extraordinary). The Café des Hauteurs, which looks out toward the Right Bank through the train station's enormous clock, is a terrific place for a light lunch or snack.

62 rue de Lille/1 rue Bellechasse, 7e. ☎ *01-40-49-48-14,* *or 01-40-49-48-48 for information desk. Internet:* www.musee-orsay.fr. *Métro: Solférino. RER: Musée-d'Orsay. Bus: 24, 68, 69, 73. Open: Tues–Wed and Fri–Sat 10 a.m.–6 p.m.; Thurs 10 a.m.–9:45 p.m.; Sun 9 a.m.–6 p.m. June 20–Sept 20 museum opens at 9 a.m. Admission: 40F ($5.70) adults; 30F ($4.30) ages 18–24 and on Sun; free for children under 18.*

Musée Picasso
Le Marais and the Islands (3e, 4e)

In 1973, following Picasso's death, his heirs donated his personal art collection to the state in lieu of paying outrageous inheritance taxes, and the Musée Picasso was created from these holdings. Because the works here are exhibited in rotation, you can pay a visit to this museum on each trip to Paris and see something different each time. The spectacular collection includes more than 200 paintings, almost 160 sculptures, 88 ceramics, and more than 3,000 prints and drawings — every phase of his prolific 75-year career is represented. Works can be viewed chronologically; budget at least a few hours here, if not more. The museum also displays works by other artists collected by Picasso, including Corot, Cézanne, Braque, Rousseau, Matisse, and Renoir. The seventeenth-century Hôtel Salé housing it all (the name Salé, means salty; the former owner was a salt tax collector) has a gorgeous carved stairway and is worth a visit in its own right.

Hôtel Salé, 5 rue de Thorigny, 3e. ☎ *01-42-71-25-21. Métro: Chemin-Vert, St-Paul, or Filles du Calvaire. Bus: 24, 68, 69, 73. Open: Apr–Sept Wed–Mon 9:30 a.m.–6 p.m.; Oct–Mar Wed–Mon 9:30 a.m.–5:30 p.m., Thursdays until 8 p.m. Admission: 38F ($5.45) adults; 28F ($4) ages 18–25; free for children under 18. Sunday admission 28F ($4). Free the first Sunday of each month.*

Musée Rodin
La Tour Eiffel & Les Invalides (7e)

Auguste Rodin, often regarded as the greatest sculptor of all time, lived and worked here from 1908 until his death in 1917. The museum is in the eighteenth-century Hôtel Biron, which was a convent before it became a residence for artists and writers. Matisse, Jean Cocteau, and the poet Rainer Maria Rilke lived and worked in the mansion before Rodin moved there, at the height of his popularity. If you don't have a lot of time or money, pay the 5F (70¢) admission to visit just the gardens, where some of the artist's most famous works — *The Thinker, The Gates of Hell, Balzac,* and *The Burghers of Calais* — stand among 2,000 rosebushes. The highlight of the indoor exhibits are *The Kiss* and *Eve.* Allow at least an hour to visit, longer if you want to break for coffee in the garden café.

Hôtel Biron, 77 rue de Varenne, 7e. ☎ 01-44-18-61-10. Métro: Varenne. Bus: 69, 83. Open: Apr–Sept Tues–Sun 9:30 a.m.–5:45 p.m.; Oct–Mar Tues–Sun 9:30 a.m.–4:45 p.m. Garden closes at 5:45 p.m. in summer, last admittance one hour before. Admission: 28F ($4) adults; 18F ($2.60) ages 18–24 and on Sun; 5F (70¢) for garden only; free for children under 18.

Cathedral de Notre-Dame
Le Marais and the Islands (3e, 4e)

Crusaders prayed here before leaving for the holy wars. Napoléon crowned himself emperor here, and then crowned his wife, Josephine, empress. When Paris was liberated during World War II, General de Gaulle rushed to this cathedral to give thanks.

Construction of Notre-Dame started in 1163 when Pope Alexander III laid the cornerstone and was completed in the fourteenth century. Built in an age of illiteracy, the cathedral windows tell the stories of the Bible in its portals, paintings, and stained glass. Angry citizens pillaged Notre-Dame during the French Revolution, mistaking religious statues above the portals on the west front for representations of kings and beheading them.

Nearly 100 years later, when Notre-Dame had been turned into a barn, writer Victor Hugo and other artists called attention to the Notre-Dame's dangerous state of disrepair and architect Viollet-le-Duc's began the much-needed restoration. He designed Notre-Dame's spire, a new feature, and Baron Haussmann (Napoléon III's urban planner) evicted the residents of the houses that cluttered the cathedral's vicinity and tore down the houses for better views of the cathedral.

Before entering, walk around to the east end of the church to appreciate the spectacular flying buttresses. Visit on a sunny morning to catch the giant rose windows — which retain some of their thirteenth-century stained glass — in all their glory. The highlight for kids will undoubtedly be climbing the 387 steps to the top of one of the towers for a fabulously Quasimodo view of the gargoyles and of Paris. Allow 30 minutes to visit, longer if you visit the tower.

6 Parvis Notre-Dame, Ile de la Cité, 4e. ☎ 01-42-34-56-10. Métro: Cité or St-Michel. RER: St-Michel. Bus: 21, 38, 85,96. Open: Cathedral daily 8 a.m.–6:45 p.m. (closed Sat 12:30–2 p.m.); treasury Mon–Sat 9:30 a.m.–5:30 p.m. Six masses celebrated on Sun, four on weekdays, one on Sat. Free guided visits in English noon Wed, Thurs.

Notre-Dame

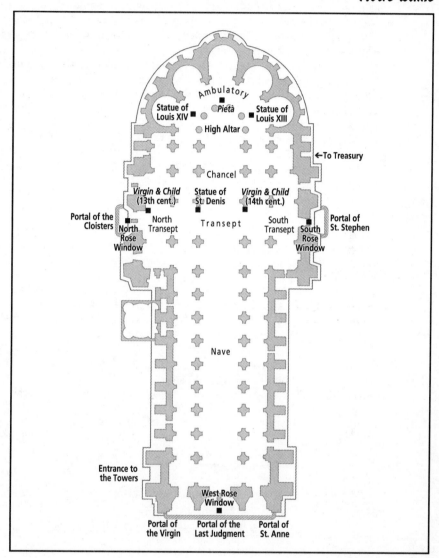

Admission: To church free; to tower: 35F ($5) adults; 25F ($3.60) ages 12–25; under–12 is free.

Panthéon
Latin Quarter (5e)

The Panthéon is to France what Westminster Abbey is to England: a final resting place for many of the nation's great men. Inside the domed church's barrel-vaulted crypt, you find the tombs of Voltaire, Rousseau,

Hugo, Braille, and Zola. André Malraux was the last to be entombed there in 1996. Louis XV originally built the Panthéon as a church in thanksgiving to Ste-Geneviève after his recovery from gout. Construction started in 1755, and it was named the church of Ste-Geneviève. After the French Revolution, the church was renamed the Panthéon — in remembrance of ancient Rome's Pantheon — and rededicated as a burying ground for France's heroes. All Christian elements were removed and windows were blocked. From 1806–1884, officials turned the Pantheon back into a church two more times before finally declaring it what it currently is today. You can't miss the Panthéon at night, lit from the inside with eerie blue lights that give it the appearance of a UFO — or a trendy disco.

Place du Panthéon, 5e. ☎ *01-44-32-18-00. Métro: Cardinal-Lemoine or Maubert-Mutualité. Bus: 84, 85, 89. Open: daily Apr–Sept 9:30 a.m.–6:30 p.m.; Oct–Mar 10 a.m.–6:15 p.m. Admission: 35F ($5) adults; 23F ($3.30) ages 18–25; free for children under 18.*

Père-Lachaise Cemetery
Montmartre and Beyond (18e)

The world's most visited cemetery is more outdoor museum than place of mourning. No wonder Parisians have always come here to stroll and reflect; with its winding, cobbled streets, park benches, and street signs, the 110-acre Père-Lachaise is a mini-city unto itself. Many visitors leave flowers or notes scrawled on Métro tickets for their favorite celebrity residents, who include Isadora Duncan, Edith Piaf, Oscar Wilde, Chopin, Jim Morrison, Modigliani, Molière, Pissarro, Proust, Sarah Bernhardt, and Gertrude Stein. If you're interested in nothing else, go for the striking and often poignant statuary: the boy who seems to sit up in bed as if he'd heard a noise; the young woman who's frozen, mid-dance, as if turned to stone without warning. You can obtain a free map from the gatekeeper at the main entrance, but the better map is one sold outside the entrance for 10F ($1.45). Allow at the very least two hours to visit.

16 rue du Repos, 20e. Main entrance on bd. du Ménilmontant. Métro: Père-Lachaise. Bus: 61, 69. Open: Mar 16–Nov 5 Mon–Fri 8 a.m.–6 p.m., Sat 8:30 a.m.–6 p.m., Sun 9 a.m.–6 p.m.; Nov 6–Mar 15 Mon–Fri 8 a.m.–5:30 p.m., Sat 8:30 a.m.–5:30 p.m., Sun 9 a.m.–5:30 p.m. Admission: free.

Place des Vosges
Le Marais and the Islands (3e, 4e)

The most beautiful square in Paris sits right in the middle of Le Marais — a symmetrical block of 36 rose-colored townhouses, nine on each side, with handsome slate roofs and dormer windows. At ground level is a lovely arcaded walkway that's now home to galleries, cafés, antiques dealers and smart boutiques. In the early seventeenth century, Henri IV transformed this area into the most prestigious neighborhood in France, putting his royal palace here, and the square quickly became the center of courtly parades and festivities. After the Revolution, it became place de l'Indivisibilité and later place des Vosges, in honor of the first *département* in France that completely paid its taxes. Victor Hugo lived at no. 6 for 16 years.

Allow 30 minutes to walk all the way around the square under the arcades and a brief stroll in the park.

Le Marais, 4e. Métro: St-Paul. Bus: 69, 76, 96.

Sacré-Coeur
Montmartre (18e)

The white Byzantine-Romanesque church dominating Paris's highest hill — the one that you can see from all over the city — is Sacré-Coeur. The best reason to come here is for the city-spanning views from its dome — visibility is 30-miles across the rooftops of Paris on a clear day. The climb from church floor to dome, however, is on a flight of nail-bitingly steep corkscrew steps. A better idea, and one that kids will enjoy, is to conserve your pre-Dome climbing energy by taking the elevator up from the Anvers Métro station, walking the short distance from rue Steinkerque and turning left onto rue Tardieu, where a *funiculaire* will whisk you from the base of the Montmartre butte right up to the outside of the church. Built from 1876, after France's defeat in the Franco-Prussian War, to 1919, the church's interior is not as striking as its exterior and is, in fact, vaguely depressing.

On the other side of Sacré-Coeur is the **place du Tertre,** where Vincent van Gogh once lived; he used it as a scene for one of his paintings. The place is usually swamped by tourists and quick-sketch artists in the spring and summer. Following any street downhill from the place du Tertre leads you to the quiet side of Montmartre. The steps in front of the church come alive around dusk, when street musicians entertain the crowd that gathers to watch the city's lights come on.

25 rue du Chevalier-de-la-Barre, 18e. ☎ 01-53-41-89-00. Métro: Abbesses. Take elevator to surface and follow signs to funiculaire, which runs to the church (fare: 1 Métro ticket). Bus: The only bus that goes to the top of the hill is the local Montmartrobus. Open: Basilica daily 6:45 a.m.–11 p.m. Dome and crypt daily Apr–Sept 9 a.m.–7 p.m.; Oct–Mar 9 a.m.–6 p.m. Admission: To basilica free; to dome 15F ($2.15) adults, 8F ($1.15) students 6–24; to crypt 15F ($2.15) adults, 8F ($1.15) students 6–24.

Sainte-Chapelle
Le Marais and the Islands (3e, 4e)

If you save Sainte-Chapelle for a sunny day, its 15 perfect stained-glass windows soaring 50 feet high to a star-studded vaulted ceiling will take your breath away. You may think you've stepped into a kaleidoscope by mistake. Louis IX, the only French king to become a saint, had Sainte-Chapelle,

Père-Lachaise Cemetery

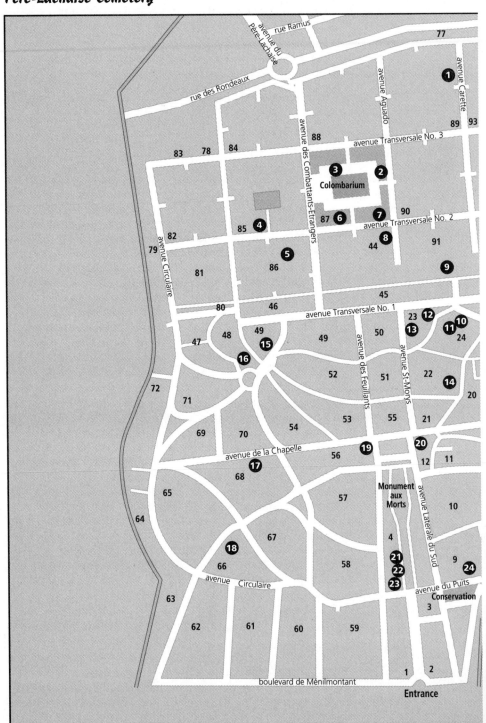

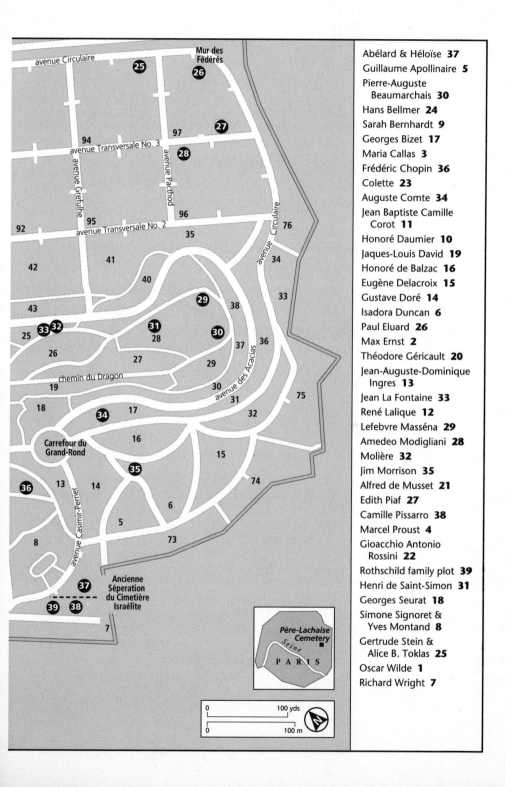

avenue Circulaire

Mur des Fédérés

25
26

27

94
avenue Transversale No. 3
97
28

avenue Pachtod

avenue Greffulhe

92
95
avenue Transversale No. 2
96
76

42
41
35
34

40

43
38
33

29

25
33 **32**
31
30
37
36

26
28
27
29

chemin du Dragon
19
30
31
75

18
17
32

34

Carrefour du
Grand-Rond
16
15

35

36
13
14
74

6

5
73

8

avenue Casimir-Perrier

Ancienne
Séperation
du Cimetière
Israélite

37

39 **38**

7

avenue des Acacias

avenue Circulaire

Père-Lachaise
Cemetery
Seine
P A R I S

0   100 yds
0   100 m

the "Holy Chapel," built as a shrine to house relics of the crucifixion, including the Crown of Thorns that Louis bought from the Emperor of Constantinople. Building Sainte-Chapelle certainly cost less than the outrageously expensive Crown of Thorns, which was said to have been acquired at the crucifixion and now resides in the vault at Notre-Dame.

Built between 1246 and 1248, Sainte-Chapelle consists of two chapels, one on top of the other. Palace servants used the *chapelle basse* (lower chapel), ornamented with fleur-de-lis designs. The *chapelle haute* (upper chapel) is one of the highest achievements of Gothic art. If you spend the time (which can take hours or even a day!), you would see that the 1,134 scenes in the stained glass of the 15 windows trace the Biblical story from the Garden of Eden to the Apocalypse. The first window to the right represents the story of the Crown of Thorns; St. Louis is shown several times. Some evenings, when the upper chapel becomes a venue for classical-music concerts, the effect of its chandelier lights dancing off the windows is magical.

4 bd. du Palais, Palais de Justice, Ile de la Cité, 4e. ☎ 01-53-73-78-50. Métro: Cité or St-Michel. RER: St-Michel. Bus: 21, 38, 85, 96. Open: Daily Apr–Sept 9:30 a.m.– 6:30 p.m.; Oct–Mar 10 a.m.–5 p.m. Closed major holidays. Admission: 26F ($3.70) adults; 7F ($1) ages 12–25; free for children under 12.

Chapter 17

More Cool Things to See and Do

⊙ ⊙

In This Chapter

▶ Especially for kids

▶ Especially for teens

▶ Especially for history buffs

▶ Especially for art lovers

▶ Literary landmarks

▶ Parks and gardens

⊙ ⊙

*V*isiting Paris is more than seeing the Eiffel Tower or Da Vinci's *Mona Lisa* at the Louvre (but if that's what you're after, see Chapter 16). After you hit all of the city's top attractions, you may want to search out some of its lesser known but still captivating sights. This chapter introduces you to some of those spots; organized with specific interests in mind, it gives you ideas about how to make Paris truly your own.

Sights Sure to Please the Kids

Both you and your kids can have a great time in Paris climbing to the top of the Eiffel Tower, Notre-Dame, or the Arc de Triomphe (all covered in Chapter 16). Another great outing is to attend puppet shows, a great Paris tradition, in the Jardin du Luxembourg, the Champs de Mars, and the Jardin des Tuileries. All Parisian parks, in fact, are wonderful for children, even without puppet shows; one of the best is **Parc Monceau,** with its assorted ruins and other eccentric features around which children love to play. You can find a wonderful labyrinth at the **Jardin des Enfants aux Halles,** 105 rue Rambureau (☎ **01-45-08-07-18;** Métro: Chatelet).

Children also have fun sailing along the Seine (See Chapters 16 and 18) and seeing art and history made real before their eyes in museums.

More Fun Things to Do in Paris

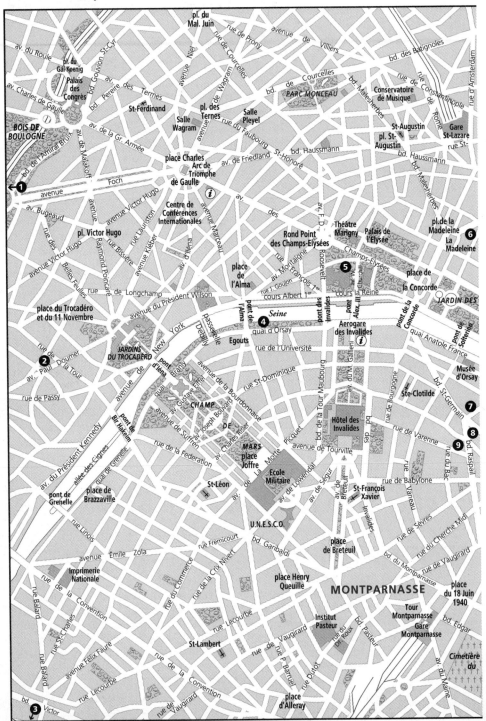

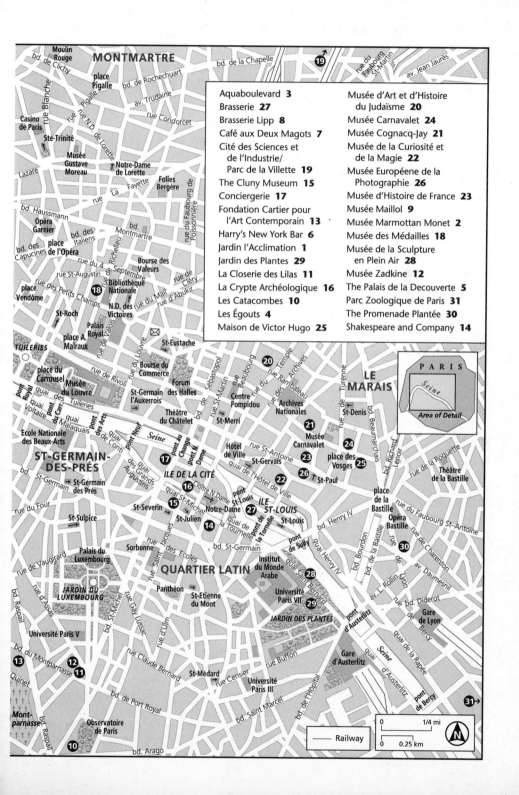

Moulin Rouge
bd. de Clichy
MONTMARTRE
bd. de la Chapelle
place Pigalle
bd. de Rochechuart
rue Blanche
rue Pigalle
rue N.D. de Lorette
av. Trudaine
rue Condorcet
Casino de Paris
Ste-Trinité
Lazare
Musée Gustave Moreau
Notre-Dame de Lorette
La Fayette
Folies Bergère
rue du Faubourg de Poissonnière
bd. Haussmann
Opéra Garnier
bd. des Italiens
bd. Montmartre
bd. des Capucines
place de l'Opéra
rue du 4 Septembre
rue de Richelieu
Bourse des Valeurs
rue de Cléry
rue St-Augustin
place Vendôme
Bibliothèque Nationale
rue des Petits Champs
rue du Mail
rue d'Abukir
St-Roch
N.D. des Victoires
Palais Royal
place A. Malraux
TUILERIES
St-Eustache
Bourse du Commerce
rue du Louvre
place du Carrousel
rue de Rivoli
Musée du Louvre
Forum des Halles
Tuileries
St-Germain l'Auxerrois
Théâtre du Châtelet
St-Merri
LE MARAIS
Centre Pompidou
Archives Nationales
St-Denis
Musée Carnavalet
Ecole Nationale des Beaux-Arts
ST-GERMAIN-DES-PRÉS
Seine
Hôtel de Ville
rue St-Antoine
place des Vosges
St-Paul
Théâtre de la Bastille
St-Germain des Prés
ILE DE LA CITÉ
Cloître N.Dame
St-Gervais
rue de la Roquette
rue du Four
St-Séverin
Notre-Dame
ILE ST-LOUIS
St-Louis
place de la Bastille
Opéra Bastille
St-Sulpice
St-Julien
bd. Henry IV
Palais du Luxembourg
Sorbonne
QUARTIER LATIN
Institut du Monde Arabe
rue de Vaugirard
JARDIN DU LUXEMBOURG
Panthéon
St-Etienne du Mont
Université Paris VII
Université Paris V
JARDIN DES PLANTES
Gare de Lyon
Université Paris III
Gare d'Austerlitz
St-Médard
Mont-parnasse
Observatoire de Paris
bd. Arago

PARIS
Seine
Area of Detail

Aquaboulevard **3**
Brasserie **27**
Brasserie Lipp **8**
Café aux Deux Magots **7**
Cité des Sciences et de l'Industrie/ Parc de la Villette **19**
The Cluny Museum **15**
Conciergerie **17**
Fondation Cartier pour l'Art Contemporain **13**
Harry's New York Bar **6**
Jardin l'Acclimation **1**
Jardin des Plantes **29**
La Closerie des Lilas **11**
La Crypte Archéologique **16**
Les Catacombes **10**
Les Égouts **4**
Maison de Victor Hugo **25**

Musée d'Art et d'Histoire du Judaïsme **20**
Musée Carnavalet **24**
Musée Cognacq-Jay **21**
Musée de la Curiosité et de la Magie **22**
Musée Européene de la Photographie **26**
Musée d'Histoire de France **23**
Musée Maillol **9**
Musée Marmottan Monet **2**
Musée des Médailles **18**
Musée de la Sculpture en Plein Air **28**
Musée Zadkine **12**
The Palais de la Decouverte **5**
Parc Zoologique de Paris **31**
The Promenade Plantée **30**
Shakespeare and Company **14**

0   1/4 mi
0   0.25 km
Railway
N

Cité des Sciences et de l'Industrie

If your kids are 5 and older, head to this enormous, modern science complex with interactive exhibits on everything from outer space to genetically manipulated plants. You'll find a planetarium as well as an adventure playground designed specifically for 3- to 12-year-olds. At Explora, exhibits, models, and interactive games demonstrate scientific techniques and present subjects including the universe, the earth, the environment, space, computer science, and health. The gigantic Géode sphere is a wonder, with a huge hemispheric screen that seems to immerse the audience in the spectacle of action provided by the six or so films shown daily. Your kids can climb aboard an actual submarine in the l'Argonaute exhibit and participate in interactive demonstrations at the Technocité. After the visit, let them run wild in the expansive, green Parc de la Villette. You can cross over the canal and also visit the Musée de la Musique.

30 av. Corentin-Cariou, 19e. ☎ *01-40-05-81-00; Internet:* www.cite-sciences. fr. *Métro: Porte-de-la-Villette. Admission: to exhibitions, including Argonaut, 50F ($7.15), free for children under 7; to the Géode, 57F ($8.15); to Cinaxe theater, 34F ($4.90), to Explora 50F ($7.15). Admission to Cité des Enfants 25F ($3.60). Open: Tues–Sat 10 a.m.–6 p.m.; Sun 10 a.m.–7 p.m.*

Jardin l'Acclimation Bois de Boulogne

Follow the circular road to this 25-acre amusement park on the north side of the former royal hunting ground. Attractions include a house of mirrors, an archery range, a miniature golf course, zoo animals, an American-style bowling alley, a playground, pony rides, paddleboats and junior-scale rides, shooting galleries, and ice-cream and waffle stands.

16e. ☎ *01-40-67-90-82. Take Métro Line 1 to Les Sablons, or from the Champs-Elysées, catch bus no. 73 heading west. Admission: 12F ($1.70); free for kids under 3 years old. Daily 10 a.m.–6 p.m.*

Jardin des Plantes

The rows of trees, beds of herbs and flowers, seventeeenth-century maze, greenhouses, and specialized gardens are only some of the sights to marvel at within these immense former royal medicine gardens. Your kids can stare in awe at the bugs, bones, minerals, meteorites, dinosaurs, fossils, and endangered species in the galleries of the Jardin's Musée National d'Histoire Naturelle. Here, the Grand Gallery of Evolution traces life and humankind's relationship to nature. Don't miss the endangered and extinct species room, which displays Gabonese monkeys, Sumatran tigers, lemurs of Madagascar, and a mock-up of the dodo bird. English explanations of some exhibits are available. Also part of the natural history museum are the Mineralogical Gallery (1,800 minerals, meteorites, and precious stones), the Entomological Gallery (1,500 insect specimens for bug-loving kids), and the Paleobotanical Gallery (plant evolution and specimens of fossil plants). Save for last the medium-sized menagerie, one of the oldest zoos in the world, containing bears, buffalo, big cats, apes, antelope, reptiles (including an alligator found in a room at the Hôtel de Paris), tortoises, and birds. Don't overlook the Vivarium — the spiders and insects are remarkable, especially the bugs that look like living tree branches! — or the Microzoo, where your kids use micro-scopes to get a look at the life of the tiniest animals. A small restaurant on the zoo's premises offers pick-me-ups for the tired and cranky, and their parents.

Take the Métro to Gare d'Austerlitz and exit from the rue Buffon side; you are right next to the Gallery of Anatomy and Paleontology. You can also take the Métro to Jussieu and walk up rue Geoffroy St-Hilaire to the Grand Gallery of Evolution. Admission: Grande Galerie — 40F ($5.70) adults, 30F ($4.30) students, free over-60s and under-5s; other galleries 30F ($4.30) adults, 20F ($2.90) students, free for adults over 60 and children under 5. Menagerie — 30F ($4.30) adults, 20F ($2.90) students, free for adults over 60 and children under 5. The park is open during the summer from 7:30 a.m.–8 p.m. and winter until 5:30 p.m.; galleries open 10–6 p.m. April–Oct, 10–5 p.m. Oct–Apr. Closed Tues. Menagerie open every day 9–6:30 summer, 9–5:30 winter.

The Palais de la Decouverte

This is a full funhouse of things for kids to do. Their hair stands on end in the electrostatics room; they can light up displays, test their muscle reactions on special machines, and watch live experiments.

Grand Palais Av. Franklin-D-Roosevelt, 8e. ☎ 01-56-43-20-21. Métro to Franklin-D-Roosevelt, the museum is just up the street on the left. Admission 30F ($4.30) adults; 20F ($2.90) students and children 8–17. Planetarium supplement 15F ($2.15). Tues–Sat 9:30 a.m.–6 p.m.; Sun 10 a.m.–7 p.m.

Parc Zoologique de Paris

The zoo is big enough to keep your kids occupied for an afternoon, with lions, tigers, bears, and a cool climbing tower with a great view of the animals. Most animals live in settings that closely resemble their natural habitats; you can even watch while some are fed lunch (bears at 11:30 a.m., pelicans 2:15 p.m., seals and sea lions 4 p.m.).

Bois de Vincennes, 12e. ☎ 01-44-75-20-10. Fax: 01-43-43-54-73. Take the Métro to Porte Dorée. Admission 40F ($5.70), 30F ($4.30) ages 4–25; free for children under 4. Daily in summer 9 a.m.–6 or 6:30 p.m., in winter 9–5 or 5:30.

Musée de la Curiosité et de la Magie

Bona fide magicians escort you through a collection of trick mirrors, ani-mated paintings, talking genies, and the history of illusion in general. You and your kids can play with the many interactive displays — who is brave enough to stick his hand in the open mouth of a lion and see if it really is an illusion? Live magic shows performed throughout the afternoon are also highly entertaining. The museum shop sells all the tools your kids need to cast spells back home.

11 rue St-Paul, 4e. ☎ 01-42-72-13-26. Métro: St-Paul. Admission 45F ($6.40) adults; 30F ($4.30) children under 13. Wed, Sat–Sun 2–7 p.m.

Fun for the Teenage Set

The kid-friendly sights previously mentioned are appropriate for teenagers as well. But here are a few more suggestions for kids who are a bit older. You may consider seeing the city on a bike tour, especially if the weather is favorable during your visit (see Chapter 18).

Aquaboulevard

If your teens are griping about the heat, send them here. It may not be the beach, but its water slides, indoor and outdoor pools, and wave machines make it a fun substitute, and it's safer than swimming in the Seine. A McDonald's, an Oh! Poivrier, and a pizza place are located on the premises.

4 rue Louis-Armand, 15e ☎ 01-40-60-10-00. Take the Métro to Balard, head down avenue de la Porte de Sèvres. Just after you walk under the overpass, you find Aquaboulevard straight ahead. Admission: 70F ($10) on weekdays, 75F ($10.70) weekends for three hours; 120F ($17.15) weekdays, 140F ($20) weekends full-day pass. Daily 9 a.m.–11 p.m.

Les Catacombes

Older kids and teens usually love all things dark and spooky, and the Catacombes are perfect for hardy kids over 10. About 6 million skulls and skeletons are stacked in thousands of yards of tunnels, and a visit is bound to provoke at least a little bit of fear. Les Catacombes, a former quarry, began housing bones in 1785 from the Cimetière des Innocents and an assortment of other overstocked Parisian cemeteries.

Those prone to claustrophobia should think twice about entering — the deep, dark tunnels close in rapidly and tightly. Equip yourself with flashlights, to navigate the poorly illuminated corridors and read the inscriptions, and wear proper shoes (sneakers or hiking boots) to avoid a misstep on the rocky, often slick passageways. A hood of sorts protects you from the water dripping overhead. Les Catacombes earned the nickname *place d'Enfer* ("Hell Square"), which later became *place Denfert-Rochereau,* and you can take Métro line 4 or 6, or RER B to the stop of the same name.

1 place Denfert-Rochereau, 14e. ☎ 01-43-22-47-63. Admission: 33F ($4.70) adults; 17F ($2.45) ages 8–26; free for children under 8. Tues–Fri 2–4 p.m.; weekends 9–11 a.m. and 2–4 p.m.

Champs-Elysées

On this famous street your teens can shop to their hearts' content at clothing stores such as O'Neill, Quiksilver, Zara, Naf Naf, and Kookai, and music stores Virgin and FNAC. They can catch movies in French or English (look for "V.O." for *version originale* on the marquee and in listings for U.S. releases that have not been dubbed into French) in one of the many movie theaters; and eat familiar fast food at McDonald's or KFC. Many of the stores on this street are open Sunday and plenty of teens — both residents and tourists — hang out here.

Métro: Concorde, Champs-Elysées, Clémenceau, Franklin-D-Roosevelt, George V, Charles de Gaulle-Etoile. Many bus lines cross the Champs but only the 73 travels its entire length.

Les Égouts

Believe it or not, this tour of the city's sewers is so popular that you sometimes have to wait as long as a half hour in line. The tours starts with a short film about the history of sewers, followed by a visit to a small museum, and finally a short trip through the maze. Paris's sewers are laid out like an underground city, with streets clearly labeled and each branch pipe bearing the name of the building to which it's connected. Don't worry; you won't trudge through anything *dégoutant* (disgusting), but the visit may leave your clothes smelling a bit ripe. Visit at the end of the day, and wear something you don't plan to wear again until after the next wash day.

☎ 01-53-68-27-82. Fax: 01-53-68-27-89. Get off Métro line 9 at Alma-Marceau, then walk across the bridge to the Left Bank. Or take RER C to Pont de l'Alma. The entrance is a stairway on the Seine side of the Quai d'Orsay, facing No. 93. Admission 25F ($3.60) adults; 20F ($2.85) students and adults over 60; 15F ($2.15) children 5–12, free for under-5's. May–Sept, Sat–Wed, 11 a.m.–5 p.m.; Oct–Apr 11 a.m.–4 p.m. Closed three weeks in Jan.

Digging into the City's History

Paris resounds with history. Blue plaques on buildings tell you the names and dates that famous people lived there. Brown and orange signs in French give you an overview of an area's particular story. The city is filled with wonderful museums to satisfy even the pickiest buff's thirst for knowledge. In this section, I list a few of the particularly good ones.

The Cluny Museum

This museum (officially the Musée National du Moyen Age/Thermes de Cluny) is one of Paris's treasures, and at press time its renovated gardens were scheduled to open to the public. This is the city's foremost example of civil architecture from the Middle Ages and before. Here you see ancient Roman baths and the statues that furious revolutionaries tore from Notre-Dame, thinking they represented royalty.

In the nineteenth century, the Hôtel de Cluny belonged to a collector of medieval art; upon his death in the 1840s, the government acquired the house and its contents. The exhibits are absolutely fascinating and include wood and stone sculpture, brilliant stained glass and metalwork, and rich tapestries. The famous fifteenth-century tapestry series of *The Lady and the Unicorn* is an allegory representing the five senses; the meaning of the sixth tapestry remains a mystery. The gift shop here is a wonderful place for souvenirs.

6 place Paul-Painlevé, 5e. ☎ *01-53-73-78-00. Métro: Cluny-Sorbonne. Admission 27F ($3.90) adults; 18F ($2.60) ages 18–25 and on Sun; free for children under 18. Wed–Mon 9:15am–5:45 p.m.*

Conciergerie

The Conciergerie dates from the Middle Ages, when it was an administrative office of the Crown. The far western tower, the Tour Bonbec, came to be known facetiously as the Tower of Babel because of the frequent screams from the many prisoners tortured there. But the Conciergerie is most famous for its days as a prison during "The Terror" years of the French Revolution, when 4,164 "enemies of the people" passed through here. More than half of them headed for the guillotine on the place de la Révolution, now called the place de la Concorde. Besides revolutionary ringleaders Danton and Robespierre, assassin Charlotte Corday and the poet André Chenier were imprisoned here. Marie Antoinette was kept here in a fetid 11-foot-square cell to await her fate. When she was taken to her execution, the despised queen was forced to ride backward in the cart so she would have to face a jeering, taunting crowd. Her cell is now a chapel, and the other cells have been transformed with exhibits and mementos designed to convey a sense of prison life in a brutal era.

Palais de Justice, Ile de la Cité, 1er. ☎ *01-53-73-78-50. Métro: Cité, Châtelet–Les Halles, or St-Michel. RER: St-Michel. Admission 35F ($5) adults; 23F ($3.30) ages 12–25; free for children under 12. Combined Sainte-Chapelle and Conciergerie ticket 50F ($7.15). Daily Apr–Sept 9:30 a.m.–6:30 p.m.; Oct–Mar 10 a.m.–5 p.m.*

La Crypte Archéologique

In 1965, excavations for a new parking lot under the parvis (a portico in front of the church) of Notre-Dame revealed Gallo-Roman ramparts, third-century Gallo-Roman rooms heated by an underground furnace system called a hypocaust, and cellars of medieval houses. The parking lot project was abandoned, and the excavations were turned into this neat archaeological museum. When you go down to the crypt, you are at the Ile de la Cité's original level. Over the centuries, builders erected new structures over the ruins of previous settlements, raising the island about 23 feet. To help you visualize the buildings that once stood here, scale models show how Paris grew from a small settlement to a Roman city, and photographs show the pre-Haussmann parvis.

Place du Parvis Notre-Dame, 4e. ☎ *01-43-29-83-51. Métro: Cité, RER: St-Michel-Notre-Dame. Admission 35F ($5) adults; free under 25. Daily 10 a.m.–6 p.m.*

Musée Carnavalet

If you like history but not the pesky reading of textbooks, this is the museum for you. Housed inside two beautiful Renaissance mansions (one is the former home of Madame de Sévigné, one of France's greatest letter writers, and her daughter), an incredible selection of paintings and other items help Parisian history come alive. The chess pieces that Louis XVI played with while awaiting his beheading are here, as are Napoléon's cradle and a replica of Marcel Proust's cork-lined bedroom. Many salons depict events related to the revolution, and the paintings of what Paris used to look like are fascinating. In December 2000, the museum opened a $1.6 million dollar wing devoted to the archaeology of Paris's earliest settlements (some artifacts, such as the fishing boats used by settlers, date back to between 2200 and 4400 B.C.). Visitors can even touch some of the exhibits here.

23 rue de Sévigné, 3e. ☎ *01-42-72-21-13. Métro: St-Paul. Turn left on rue de Sévigné. Admission: 35F ($5) adults; 25F ($3.60) students; Sun admission 20F ($2.85). Tues–Sun 10 a.m.–5:40 p.m.*

Musée d'Histoire de France

This extraordinary palace was purchased in 1700 by François de Rohan, prince de Soubise. As heir of one of the most powerful families in eighteenth century, the prince received many gifts from Louis XIV — not only due to his stately position but also for the many "favors" imparted by his wife, Anne Chabot de Rohan, onto the King. In 1808, Napoléon ordered the acquisition of the Rohan-Soubise estate to house Empire archives; the palace also contains the National Archives. The interior includes works by Boucher, whose delicate rococo paintings of landscapes and shepherdesses won him the favor of Madame de Pompadour, Louis XV's influential mistress; Natoire, a contemporary painter of Boucher's and director of Rome's French Academy; and Van Loo, first painter to Louis XV. The first floor is devoted to the *Musée de l'Histoire de France* (the Museum of the History of France), which contains some of the most important documents pertaining to the country's history, as well as personal papers related to famous French citizens. Exhibits include Henry IV's Edict of Nantes (a document which guaranteed religious liberty),

Louis XIV's will, Louis XVI's diary and will, the Declaration of Human Rights, Marie Antoinette's last letter, Napoléon's will, and the French constitution. Rooms are devoted to the Middle Ages, the French Revolution, and other themes.

Hôtel de Soubise, 60 rue des Francs-Bourgeois, 3e. ☎ *01-40-27-60-96. Métro: Rambuteau. Admission to museum 20F ($2.85) adults; 15F ($2.15) ages 18–24 and over 60; free for children under 18. Mon, Wed–Fri 10:00–5:45 p.m., Sat–Sun 1:45–5:45 p.m.; courtyard Mon–Fri 9 a.m.–7 p.m., Sat–Sun 1:45–5:45 p.m.*

Musée d'Art et d'Histoire du Judaïsme

This enormous collection displayed in a beautiful seventeenth-century mansion traces the development of Jewish culture in France and Europe, from life in the Middle Ages to the twentieth century. In addition to beautifully crafted religious objects including torahs, rams horns, Menorahs, and spectacular velvet cloaks reflecting both the Sephardic and Ashkenazi traditions throughout Europe and North Africa, the museum presents newly available documents relating to the Dreyfus affair, the notorious scandal that falsely accused a Jewish army captain of providing secret military information to the German government in 1894. The free audio tour is very informative. The exhibits end with a collection of works by Jewish artists, including paintings by Modigliani, Soutine, Zadkine, and Chagall.

71 rue du Temple, 3e. ☎ *01-53-01-86-53. Métro: Rambuteau. Admission 40F ($5.70) adults; 25F ($3.60) ages 18–26; free for children under 18. Mon–Fri 11 a.m.–6 p.m.; Sun 10 a.m.–6 p.m.*

Musée des Médailles

This is the site of France's original national library, the cavernous Bibliothéque Nationale de France (still referred to as the Bibliothéque Nationale de France Richelieu) and home of the Musée des Médailles. Ten million books were removed in 1998 to the new Bibliothéque Francois Mitterand in the 13e, but the impressive display of archaeological objects, cameos, bronzes, medals, and money that was originally assembled by French kings remains. Among the more exceptional objects are the Treasure of Berthouville, a collection of Gallo-Roman money; the Cameo of Sainte-Chapelle, a huge multicolored cameo dating from the first century; and the Treasure of Childéric, one of the oldest remnants of the French monarchy. Take a peek into the Salle Labrouste, a lovely reading room built in 1868, which now sadly echoes without its book collection. The garden, a virtual mini-Versailles, also merits a stop.

Bibliothèque Nationale de France, 58 rue de Richelieu, 2e. ☎ *01-47-03-83-30. Métro: Palais-Royal–Musée du Louvre or Bourse. Admission 22F ($3.15) adults (25F [$3.60] special exhibits); 15F ($2.15) students (24F [$3.45] special exhibits). Mon–Fri 1 p.m.–5:45 p.m.; Sat 1–4:45 p.m.; Sun noon to 6 p.m.*

Place de la Bastille

Ignore the traffic and try to imagine the place de la Bastille just over 200 years ago, when it contained eight towers rising 100 feet. It was here, on July 14, 1789 (now commemorated in France as Bastille Day), that a mob attacked the old prison, launching the French Revolution. Although the Bastille had long since fallen into disuse, it symbolized the arbitrary power of a king who could imprison anyone for any reason. Prisoners of means could buy a spacious cell and even host dinner parties, but the poor disappeared within the prison's recesses and sometimes drowned when the Seine overflowed its banks. The attack on the prison was therefore a direct assault on royal power. The Bastille was razed in 1792. In its place stands the Colonne de Juillet, a 171-foot bronze column built between 1830 and 1849 to commemorate Parisians killed in uprisings in 1830 and 1848.

11e. Métro: Bastille.

More Museums for Art Lovers

Paris and art go together like a baguette and *jambon* (ham). Okay, that's a dumb analogy, but the art museums of Paris are far from clichéd. In fact, art in Paris is not merely French art. Many French movements began or developed here, but generations of artists from all parts of the world have thrived in Paris, and the city's museums and galleries hold enough art for several lifetimes of daily viewing. From galleries in the Marais, Bastille, St-Germain-de-Prés, and near the Champs-Elysées, to the Egyptian, Assyrian, and Greco-Roman art at the Louvre, through realism, impressionism, and art nouveau at the Musée d'Orsay, to the modern international masters at the Centre Pompidou and the Musée de l'Art Moderne, Paris offers a vast wealth of art. Each October, Paris also presents the *Foire Internationale d'Art Contemporain,* one of the largest contemporary art fairs in the world, and has stands from more than 150 galleries, half of them foreign (see Chapter 2). You may find the following museums often less crowded than their larger and more famous counterparts, but still capable of awing you.

Fondation Cartier pour l'Art Contemporain

Resembling a futuristic greenhouse, this almost completely transparent structure, designed by architect Jean Nouvel, is one of the most striking modern buildings in Paris. It has a glass and metal screen that stands between the street and the glass and metal building, creating an optical illusion that makes courtyard greenery appear as if the plants are growing indoors. Oh — and the art is good, too! The offices for the Cartier jewelry empire are upstairs, and most of the first-rate contemporary art exhibits that the foundation hosts are in the basement. Visit Thursday nights (except July and August) for the performance art and music of *Les Soirees Nomades* (Nomadic Evenings).

261 bd. Raspail, 14e. ☎ *01-42-18-56-51. Internet:* www.fondation.cartier.fr. *Métro: Raspail. Admission 30F ($4.30) adults; 20F ($2.85) students under 25; free for children under 10. Tues–Sun noon to 8 p.m.*

Musée Cognacq-Jay

This collection, housed in the sixteenth-century Hôtel Donon, was collected by La Samaritaine department store founder Ernest Cognacq and his wife, and is a window into the aristocratic lifestyle that flourished before the Revolution. The eighteenth-century rococo art, with works by Boucher, Fragonard, Rubens, Van Loo, Watteau, and Tiepolo, grace Louis XV and Louis XVI paneled rooms. Shelves of porcelain and porcelain figures, rich cabinets, and furniture are also on display. You can walk through a little manicured garden, open May to September, to enjoy sunny days. Temporary exhibits are presented two to three times a year.

8 rue Elzévir, 3e. ☎ *01-40-27-07-21. Métro: St-Paul. Admission 22F ($3.15) adults; free ages 7–26 and over 60; admission for expositions 30F ($4.30) adults; 15F ($2.15) ages 7–26; 20F ($2.85) over 60. Tues–Sun 10 a.m.–5:40 p.m.*

Maison Européenne de la Photographie

In addition to the ever-changing displays of photographs in this sleek museum (created from two magnificent eighteenth-century townhouses), you find a projection room, permanent collections of Polaroid art, and an excellent video library that allows you to look up thousands of photographs. Exhibits in 2001 include works by Irving Penn.

5–7 rue de Fourcy, 4e. ☎ *01-44-78-75-00. Internet:* www.mep-fr.org. *Métro: St-Paul or Pont-Marie. Admission 30F ($4.30) adults; 15F ($2.15) ages 8–26 and over 60, free admission for all visitors on Wednesday between 5 p.m.–8 p.m.; free for children under 8. Wed–Sun 11 a.m.–8 p.m.*

Musée Gustave Moreau

This house and studio displays the works of the teacher of Henri Matisse, Gustave Moreau (1826–98). A symbolist painter, Moreau embraced the bizarre, and painted mythological subjects and scenes in a sensuous, romantic style. Among the works displayed are *Orpheus by the Tomb of Eurydice* and *Jupiter and Semele.* Moreau taught at the École des Beaux-Arts; his museum's first curator, Rouault, was once his student. Moreau's modest apartment is also here.

14 rue de la Rochefoucault, 9e. ☎ *01-48-74-38-50. Métro: St-Georges. Admission 22F ($3.15) adults; 15F ($2.15) students ages 18–25 and on Sun; free for children under 18. Mon, Wed 11 a.m.–5:15 p.m.; Thurs–Sun 10 a.m.–12:45 p.m. and 2–5:15 p.m.*

Musée Maillol

Curvaceous and graceful bronze statues of Aristide Maillol's (1861–1944) favorite model, Dina Vierny, as well as the works of impressionist and post-impressionist artists, are on display in this contemporary-style museum occupying an eighteenth-century renovated convent. The elegant upper floors of the museum display crayon and pastel sketches of Vierny. Maillol's personal collection includes the work of his friends, Matisse and Bonnard, as well as two sculptures by Rodin, works by Gauguin, Dégas, Rousseau, Kandinsky, and Renoir. The museum features splendid temporary exhibits; a recent exhibit displayed works by Raymond Mason and a collection from Bonnard.

59–61 rue de Grenelle, 7e. ☎ *01-42-22-59-58. Métro: Rue du Bac. Admission 40F ($5.70); 30F ($4.30); free for children under 18. Wed–Mon 11 a.m.–6 p.m. (last ticket sold 5:15 p.m.).*

Musée Marmottan Monet

The Musée Marmottan Monet celebrates the painter Claude Monet and contains an outstanding collection of his water lily paintings, as well as his more abstract representations of the Japanese Bridge at Giverny. Here you find the painting *Impression: Sunrise,* from which the term "impressionism" was coined to describe the painting style and subsequent artistic movement. Also on hand, is Monet's personal collection that includes works by his contemporaries Pissarro, Manet, Morisot, and Renoir.

The museum, located between the Ranelagh garden and the Bois de Boulogne, is in a nineteenth-century mansion that belonged to the art historian Paul Marmottan. When Marmottan died in 1932, he donated the mansion and his collection of Empire furniture and Napoleonic art to the Académie des Beaux-Arts. When Claude Monet's son and heir bequeathed his father's collection to the Marmottan, the museum paid permanent homage to the artist's unique vision. Subsequent donations have expanded the collection to include more impressionist paintings and the stunning Wildenstein collection of late medieval illuminated manuscripts.

2 rue Louis-Boilly, 16e. ☎ *01-42-24-07-02. Internet:* http://www.marmottan. com/uk/sommaire/index.html. *Métro: La-Muette. Admission 40F ($5.70) adults; 25F ($3.60) ages 9–25; free for children under 8. Tues–Sun 10 a.m.–5 p.m.*

Musée de la Sculpture en Plein Air

Displayed here are the sculptures of 29 artists including César, Zadkine, and Stahly. Located on the banks of the Seine, you may have passed it on one of your strolls without realizing this graceful waterside park is really a museum.

Quai St-Bernard, 5e. Métro: Sully-Morland or Gare d'Austerlitz. Free admission.

Musée Zadkine

The beautiful sculpture garden of Ukrainian sculptor Ossip Zadkine (1890–1967) is free and the museum not too much more. It's worth a visit if you like contemporary sculpture or are familiar with the artist's work. Zadkine lived and worked in this house and studio until his death. His art, books, tools, and furniture are all on display, as well as many of his works in brass, wood, and stone.

100 bis rue d'Assas, 6e. ☎ 01-43-26-91-90. Métro: Notre-Dame-des-Champs or Vavin. Admission 27F ($3.90) adults; 19F ($2.70) adults over 60; free for children under 7. Tues–Sun 10 a.m.–5:30 p.m.

A Legion of Literary Landmarks

Paris is also filled with literary landmarks — and they don't all belong to Ernest Hemingway or F. Scott Fitzgerald.

Brasserie

If you're a fan of *From Here to Eternity* or *The Thin Red Line,* pay a visit to this brasserie (see also Chapter 14 for a review of the food), where novelist and regular James Jones kept his own *chope* (mug) at the bar. Not only is the location excellent — the building is situated directly off the footbridge from Ile de la Cité to Ile St-Louis with an unparalleled view of the eastern tip of Ile de la Cité (including the back of Notre-Dame) — the bar is also the last remaining independent brasserie in Paris. Jones lived with his family around the corner on Ile de la Cité, and the recent film about their lives, *A Soldier's Daughter Never Cries,* was filmed in the neighborhood.

Ile St-Louis, 55 quai de Bourbon. 1er. ☎ 01-43-54-02-59. Métro: Pont Marie.

Maison de Balzac

The very modest Honoré de Balzac lived in this very posh residential Passy neighborhood from 1840 to 1847 under a false name to avoid creditors, only allowing entrance to those who knew a password. He wrote some of his most famous novels here, including those that make up his *La Comédie Humaine* (The Human Comedy). His study is preserved, and portraits, books, letters, and manuscripts are on display. You can also see his jewel-encrusted cane and the Limoges coffee pot that bears his initials in mulberry pink — leaving you to wonder just how bad his money problems *really* were.

47 rue Raynouard, 16e. ☎ 01-55-74-41-80. Take Métro line 6 to Passy, walk one block away from the river and turn left into rue Raynouard. Admission 30F ($4.30) adults; 20F ($2.85) adults over 60; 15F ages 8–26, free for children under 8. Tues–Sun 10 a.m.– 5:40 p.m. Closed holidays.

Maison de Victor Hugo

If you or your kids have read *The Hunchback of Notre-Dame* and *Les Miserables,* you may want to visit this house. The novelist and poet lived on the second floor of this townhouse, built in 1610, from 1832 to 1848. You can see some of Hugo's furniture, samples of his handwriting, his inkwell, first editions of his works, and a painting of his funeral procession at the Arc de Triomphe in 1885. Portraits of his family adorn the walls, and the Chinese salon from Hugo's house on Guernsey has been reassembled here. The highlight is more than 450 of Hugo's drawings, illustrating scenes from his own works.

6 place des Vosges, 4e. ☎ 01-42-72-10-16. Take Métro line 1 to St-Paul. Admission: 22F ($3.15) adults; 15F ($2.15) children 8–17; free on Sunday. Tues–Sun 10 a.m.–5:40 p.m. (ticket window closes at 5:15 p.m.).

Shakespeare and Company

This is *not* the original Shakespeare and Company, even though it looks old and dusty enough to be. That original was opened in 1919 at 6 rue Dupuytren (take the Métro to Odéon, walk through the square there, and turn left) by Sylvia Beach. Two years later, Beach moved the shop to 12 rue de l'Odéon (the building is no longer there) and stayed until the United States entered into World War II (in Germany-occupied Paris, Beach was considered an enemy alien and was forced to abandon shop). The newest of the Shakespeares was opened by George Whitman in the mid-1960s and named in honor of Beach. It serves as a haven for Americans and English speakers, playing the dual role of gathering place and bookstore. On Sunday nights, poetry readings are scheduled.

37 rue de la Bûcherie, 5e. No phone. Métro or RER: St-Michel.

Brasserie Lipp and Café les Deux Magots

You can't talk about literary Paris without mentioning Hemingway, and two of his favorite hangouts are just across the street from each other on boulevard St-Germain-des-Prés. Brasserie Lipp is where Hemingway lovingly recalls eating potato salad in *A Moveable Feast,* and the Café les Deux Magots is where Jake Barnes meets Lady Brett in *The Sun Also Rises.* Tourism has driven up prices, so just go for a glass of wine or a coffee.

Brasserie Lipp: 151 bd. St-Germain, 6e. ☎ 01-45-48-53-91. Open daily 9 a.m.–1 a.m. Café les Deux Magots: 170 bd. St-Germain, 6e. ☎ 01-45-48-55-25. Open daily 7:30 a.m.–1:30 a.m. Both are less than 50 yards from the St-Germain-des-Prés stop.

La Closerie de Lilas

Author John Dos Passos and artist Picasso hung out here, and Soviet revolutionary Leon Trotsky played chess here. But the true claim to fame is that Hemingway completed *The Sun Also Rises* in just six weeks on the terrace here. Much of the novel also takes place at Closerie, which means "the courtyard of lilacs." Lilac bushes still bloom here, and the place is just as crowded as it was in the 1930s, although a new chef turns out delicious food (see Chapter 14), and the décor is decidedly upscale.

171 bd. du Montparnasse, 6e. ☎ *01-40-51-34-50. Take the RER line B to the Port-Royal stop. Open daily noon–1 a.m.*

Harry's New York Bar

They say that the Bloody Mary was invented at Harry's New York Bar, a place that's still going strong all these years after — guess who? — Ernest Hemingway and F. Scott Fitzgerald went on a few famous benders. Unfortunately, Harry's is now a high-priced tourist trap, so peek in for the ambience, but I don't recommend lightening your wallet with a drink.

5 rue Danou, 2e ☎ *01-42-61-71-14. Take the Métro to Opéra, then head down the rue de la Paix and take the first left. Open daily 10:30 a.m.–4 a.m.*

Parks and Gardens

You can visit parks for flowers and plants and parks for admiring views. Parks with puppet shows and pony rides, and parks with museums are on the grounds. Whatever parks you decide to visit, you can relax from the beauty and serenity of planted gardens, splashing fountains, and arrow straight paths — and kids love them. Most parks are open until sunset, unless otherwise noted.

Parc de la Bagatelle

The rose gardens here are sublime, while the thematic gardens reveal the art of gardening through the centuries. A water lily pond pays homage to a certain famous painter (think *Monet*). The château here, which you can view from the outside only, was built by the Comte d'Artois in 1775, after he made a bet with his sister-in-law, Marie Antoinette, that he could do it in under 90 days. It took 66 days. Under Napoléon, it was used as a hunting lodge.

16e. Take the Métro to Porte Maillot.

Parc de Belleville

Topped by the Maison de l'Air, a museum with displays devoted to, yes, the air that we breathe, the Parc de Belleville is a superb place to visit with children. You can enjoy fountains, a children's play area, and an open-air theater with many concerts during the summer, and rock formations and grottoes that evoke the days when the hill was a strategic point to fight enemies like Attila the Hun. The park is also a wonderful place to watch the sun set over western Paris. Access the park by taking the rue Piat off rue de Belleville and enter through an iron gate spelling out the words Villa Ottoz. A curved path leads you to tree-lined promenades (more than 500 trees are here), with the first of the magnificent Left Bank views peeping through the spaces between pretty houses. Beds of roses and other seasonal flowers line walks, and views of the city's Left Bank become more pronounced the higher up the terraced pathways you go.

20e. Take the Métro to Pyrénées, then walk down rue de Belleville and turn left onto rue Piat where you see arched iron gates leading into the park. You can also take the Métro to Courrones, cross bd. de Belleville and turn left onto rue Julien Lacroix where you find another entrance.

The Parc des Buttes-Chaumont

Featuring cliffs, waterfalls, a lake, and a cave topped by a temple, this former gypsum quarry and centuries-old dump is one of four man-made parks Napoléon III commissioned to resemble the English gardens which he grew to love during his exile in England.

19e. Métro:Buttes-Chaumont.

Parc Floral de Paris

The Bois de Vincennes houses the spectacular Parc Floral de Paris with a butterfly garden, library, and miniature golf, as well as the Parc Zoologique de Paris. You can rent bikes here and ride around the extensive grounds, or row a rented canoe around a winding pond. (See also Chapter 20.)

☎ 01-43-43-92-95. Métro: Porte Dorée or Chateau de Vincennes.

Parc Monceau

Kids love this park for its oddities, including a Dutch windmill, a Roman temple, a covered bridge, a waterfall, a farm, medieval ruins, and a pagoda, all designed by Carmontelle. It was a favorite place for Marcel Proust to stroll, and it contains Paris's largest tree, an Oriental plane tree with a circumference of almost 23 feet. Have a picnic here with supplies from the rue de Levis (open Tuesday through Sunday; Métro: Villiers).

Boulevard de Coucelles, 8e. ☎ 01-42-27-39-56. Métro: Ternes.

Parc Montsouris

Parc Montsouris is another of Napoléon III's English parks, and it resembles an English garden, with cascades, copses, and winding paths. Swans and ducks gather on the pond, and the bandstand is still in use.

14e. RER:Cité Universitaire.

Parc de la Villette

In the summer, you can catch an outdoor movie, listen to a concert, and your kids can play on a giant dragon slide and on a submarine. You can also visit the children's museum, the Cité des Sciences et de l'Industrie, and the Musée de la Musique, which are also located on the grounds. This modern park has a series of theme gardens, including an exotic bamboo garden and a garden featuring steam and water jets. Scattered throughout the park are playgrounds and other attractions. (See Chapter 20.)

You can get to the Parc de la Villette by Métro, but a fun, alternative route worth trying is taking a guided canal trip to the park from Pont l'Arsenal or Musée d'Orsay with **Paris Canal** (☎ **01-42-40-96-97;** Métro: Bastille). The three-hour cruises leave the Musée d'Orsay at 9:30 a.m. and end at the Parc de la Villette. The same voyage in reverse leaves the park at 2:30 p.m. Reservations are essential. The trip costs 100F ($14.30) for adults, 75F ($10.70) for seniors over 60, and 55F ($7.90) for children 4 to 11. **Canauxrama** (☎ **01-42-39-15-00;** Métro: Jaurés) offers similar tours at 9:45 a.m. and 2:30 p.m. leaving from Port l'Arsenal in the 12e and ending at the Parc de la Villette. This trip costs 75F ($10.70), and reduced prices are sometimes offered. Reservations are required.

19e. Métro: Porte de la Villette.

The Promenade Plantée

This old railroad bridge has been converted into a neat 5-km-long garden that begins at the Opéra Bastille, runs along the length of avenue Daumesnil, the Reuilly Garden, and the Porte Dorée to the Bois de Vincennes. Beneath the promenade, artisans have built boutiques and studios into the bridge, collectively known as the Viaduc des Arts. Check them out for eclectic, unusual gifts and ideas.

12e. Métro: Bel Air or Dugommier.

Chapter 18

Seeing Paris by Guided Tour

• •

In This Chapter

▶ Touring by bus

▶ Seeing Paris on foot

▶ Taking art and lecture tours

▶ Cruising down the river and canals

▶ Pedaling through Paris by bike

• •

*1*f you're a newcomer to the wonders of Paris, an orientation tour can help you understand the city's geography. But even if you've been coming to Paris for ten years or more, one of the various tours can introduce you to sides of the city you never knew existed. As you see from this chapter, you have many good reasons for taking a guided tour. Being lucky enough to be shown around by guides whose enthusiasm makes the city come to life can be the high point of your entire trip.

Orientation Tours: Get on the Bus

Paris is the perfect city to explore on your own, but if time is a priority, or your energy is sorely lacking, consider taking an introductory bus tour. The biggest company has been **Cityrama** (4 place des Pyramides, 1er. ☎ **01-44-55-61-00;** Métro: Palais-Royal–Musée du Louvre). The two-hour orientation tour is a bit pricey at 150F ($21.45), but your kids under 12 years of age get to ride free. Guided half- and full-day tours are also available for 290F ($41.45) and 500F ($71.45), respectively. Tours to Versailles for 200F ($28.60) and to Chartres for 275F ($39.30) are a better bargain because they take the hassle out of visiting these monuments. Nighttime illumination tours start at 150F ($21.45).

Paris l'Open Tour (☎ 01-43-46-52-06), from Paris's public transportation system, the RATP, has quickly come to rival Cityrama. Its bright-yellow convertible buses take you to city highlights, while recorded commentary in French and English plays over the bus's speakers. The 2-hour, 15-minute circuit covers all the sights in central Paris and offers extensions south to Bercy and north to Montmartre. A two-day pass costs 135F ($19.30), or 110F ($15.70) with a Paris Visite pass, and you can get on or off the bus as many times as you want, which, in my opinion, makes this the more worthwhile tour. The buses run daily every 25 minutes throughout the year from around 9:30 a.m. to 6:30 p.m. The pass, as well as the Paris Visite Pass (120–170F/$17.15–24.30), is on sale at the Paris Tourist Office and the RATP visitor center at place de la Madeleine.

The **RATP** (☎ 08-36-68-41-14) also runs the **Balabus,** a fleet of orange-and-white buses that only run on Sundays and holidays, noon to 8 p.m. from April to September. Routes run between the Gare de Lyon and the Grand Arche de La Défense, in both directions, and will cost you just one Métro ticket. The bus has a "Bb" symbol across its side and on signs posted along the route.

Touring by Boat: Anchors Aweigh

One of the most romantic and beautiful ways to see Paris is by taking one of the sightseeing boats that cruise up and down Paris's waterways. In addition to the Seine River cruises (see Chapter 16), try a longer and more unusual tour with **Paris Canal** (☎ 01-42-40-96-97; Métro: Bastille). Its three-hour cruises leave the Musée d'Orsay at 9:30 a.m. and end at Parc de la Villette. The boat passes under the Bastille and enters the Canal St-Martin for a lazy journey along the tree-lined quai Jemmapes. You cruise under bridges and through many locks.

If you have restless young children, the wait for each lock to let the boat pass may prove too long. The boat leaves the Parc de la Villette at 2:30 p.m. for the same voyage in reverse. Reservations are essential. The trip costs 100F ($14.30) for adults, 75F ($10.70) over 60, 55F ($7.90) children 4 to 11.

Canauxrama (☎ 01-42-39-15-00; Métro: Jaurès) offers similar tours at 9:45 a.m. and 2:30 p.m. leaving from Port l'Arsenal in the 12e and ending at the Parc de la Villette in the 19e; 75F ($10.70) adults, 55F ($7.90) reduced. Reservations are required. (See the sidebar "Paris by canal: The bridge and tunnel crowd.")

Walking Your Way across Paris

WICE (20 bd. du Montparnasse, 15e. ☎ 01-45-66-75-50; Fax: 01-40-65-96-53; Internet: www.wice-paris.com), a nonprofit cultural association for Paris's English–speaking community, gives comprehensive walking tours of Paris. These are in–depth tours for travelers who want to do more than skim the surface. Recent tours included: The Royal Squares of Paris, Creative Writing Walks of the Left and Right Banks, and a Halloween tour of Pére Lachaise Cemetery. Commentary is always excellent and guides are experts in their respective fields.

Paris by canal: The bridge and tunnel crowd

If you've toured the Seine, but still long for a boat ride, pick up the *Canauxrama* tour at pont l'Arsenal and enjoy a pleasant cruise along the Canal St. Martin, which winds for 4.5 watery kilometers (about 2½ miles) through Paris's northeast *quartiers* (quarters). In contrast to the Seine's elegant scenery, the canal passes through neighborhoods that are shabby but vibrant, filled with street life and children, where entire families sit along the banks, fishing. This is the Paris of the working class.

The canal, built by Napoleon in the early nineteenth-century, gives access to barges when high waters prevent them from passing under the bridges of the Seine. You sail into a two-kilometer-long underground vault, once lit by 37 lanterns to guide bargemen. Today, however, the vault is pitch-dark, lit only occasionally in daylight by circular grates cut into the tunnel's roof; you feel like you've stepped into Greek mythology and are taking a ferry along the River Styx to the Underworld. The tunnel passes beneath the famous *Colonne de Juillet* in the center of place de la Bastille (a landmark erected in honor of citizens killed in the less famous revolutions of 1830 and 1848) — most visitors never realize you can see it from below!

People wave as your boat passes under the many pedestrian bridges and through the canal's locks *(écluses)*. The double *écluse de Temple* in the tenth (10e) arrondissement played a role in the 1938 film *Hotel du Nord*. The cruise turns around at the Parc de la Villette, at the tip of the *bassin* (basin) *de la Villette* where the Canal St. Martin splits into two other canals — the Saint Denis and the l'Ourcq. Nineteenth-century Parisians made their Sunday outings here, and the *bassin* still provides Paris with the water for its fountains. The area is surrounded by wonderful old factories and warehouses, some restored, which artists now use as studios.

You can remain on board for the return trip or disembark to play in the sprawling park that serves as a backyard for the surrounding population, many of whom are African immigrants. This is a great place to spend an afternoon with two huge museum complexes, the Cité des Sciences et de l'Industrie and the Musée de la Musique. In the summer, free movie festivals and concerts abound. Whatever you choose, you can enjoy a nice afternoon seeing a part of Paris you may have otherwise missed.

—*Alice Alexiou*

Tours vary in length and cost, but most run between 90F ($12.90) and 150F ($21.45) for a 2- to 3-hour tour. Paris residents and returning visitors love these tours, so book a few weeks ahead to reserve a place. You can do this on their Web site or by e-mailing them at wice@ wice-paris.org.

Paris Walking Tours (☎ **01-48-09-21-40;** Internet: www.ourworld. compuserve.com/homepages/pariswalking/) were founded by Peter and Oriel Caine and have become a popular English-language

A Bullfrog's irreverent view of Paris

You say you've never heard of the hook-slide, the shrinkage statue, or "the most famous builder's bum in Paris?" They're all nicknames for famous statues throughout Paris, coined by the original, irreverent Bullfrog Bikes company. Discover these and more from one of the guides leading the twice-daily **Bullfrog Bikes** tours (☎ **01-06-09-98-08-60**). This is the tour to take if you're bored to tears by the thought of a guided tour, if you're backpacking through Paris and want to take a load off your feet (you can leave your gear in the locked garage), and, particularly if you're part of a family with bike-loving kids (children must be at least 8 years old). The slightly off-kilter perspective of the Bullfrog guides is particularly refreshing — especially since you get to hear their commentary from the comfortable seat of a Schwinn cruiser.

Relatively new on the scene, Bullfrog Bikes is the only monolingual bike outfit in Paris — their day and night tours only come in American-accented English. But jokes aside, the guides know what they're talking about. Daytime tours take riders from the Eiffel Tower, include a break for a sit-down snack (cost not included), and stop at most of the big sights of particular historical interest, except for the Louvre and Notre-Dame. These are done in a separate — and gorgeous — night tour, where bikers learn about Notre-Dame, then stop for Berthillon ice cream (see Chapter 15) on the Ile St-Louis, and cruise the courtyard of the Louvre at dusk, often to the accompaniment of a local busker playing Mozart on his flute. The night tour also includes a ride on a Bateaux Mouche river cruise boat (see Chapter 16) with wine. (Don't drink too much, though; you still have to pedal the bike back to the garage!)

outfit whose guided walks cost 60F ($8.60) — about half as much as WICE's. Specific tours concentrate on a single neighborhood (The Village of Montmartre, The Historic Marais), a particular theme (Hemingway's Paris), or perhaps a single sight (Les Invalides, the Paris Sewers). The Caines also offer a good Paris Orientation tour that includes bus, Métro, and riverboat travel for 260F ($37.15) for which reservations are required. You don't need to make a reservation for the regular daily tour. Call for the designated meeting place.

Paris Contact (☎01-42-51-08-40) offers two-hour guided walks built around themes (In Jefferson's Footsteps, The Origins of Paris) or neighborhoods (St-Germain-des-Prés, Le Marais, Montmartre). The tours cost 60F ($8.60) per person and don't have to be booked in advance — but do call ahead and ask for the full program to be faxed to your hotel. If none of the scheduled tours grab you, Paris Contact can also do custom tours. They require 48 hours advance notice, have a two–person minimum and cost 80F ($11.45) per person.

Paris à Pied (☎800-594-9535; Internet: www.parisapied.com; E-mail: parisapied@aol.com) has three 3–hour tours geared to first-time visitors to Paris. Tours cost 200F ($28.60) and are made up of no more than six people. This season's tours included: The Heart of Old Paris, The Latin Quarter, and The Marais.

Siren's Song Tours (☎01-56-24-36-00; cell phone: 06-15-11-81-32; Internet: www.OneCity.com/Paris) offers an excellent 1½–mile guided walk of Bohemian Paris. Gentry Lane, a scholar of Modernist Literature and a writer, knows so much about the era's famous expatriates that you may think she's talking about friends. Tours cost 200F ($28.60), with group discounts available, and are limited to six people.

Seeing Paris by Bike

For cyclists, **Paris à Vélo C'est Sympa** (☎ 01-48-87-60-01; Métro: Bastille) has half-day tours of Paris for 170F ($17). Reservations are required. You can rent a bike for 80F ($11.42) a day, 60F ($8.60) for a half-day, or 150F ($21.40) for Saturday morning until Sunday evening.

Also, try **Bullfrog Bike Tours** (☎01-06-09-98-08-60), with reservations optional for day and required at night. Friendly guides from Texas will take you on day or night bike tours of the city lasting three to four hours. 150F ($21.45) day, 170F ($24.30) night. Look for the Bullfrog Bikes flags under the Eiffel Tower, at the edge of the Champs de Mars. Tours are at 11 a.m. and 3:30 p.m., May 5 through August 25, 11 a.m. only August 26 through September 15. Closed July 14, and the day of the Tour de France.

Chapter 19

A Parisian Shopping Guide

*N*othing is so wonderful as browsing the shops of Paris — even the tiniest *pâtissier* (candy shop) will have an exquisite, enticing window display to lure you inside. Paris is truly a shopper's heaven, from the toniest haute couture shop, to the hidden *depot-vente* (resale shop) selling last year's Yves St-Laurent at fabulous prices. Even non-shoppers can find something to fascinate: the eye-popping hardware store in the basement of BHV, inexpensive furnishings at Conforama, and the mouth-watering *épicerie* (grocer) at Bon Marché. This chapter gives you an overview of the Parisian shopping scene, with hints about where to find the bargains, how to get it all home, and, yes, even how to get some of your money back.

Taking a Look at the Shopping Scene

Shopping in Paris has never been better. A recent upswing in France's economy has seen many new stores open, and others expand. A recent influx of American brands into the City of Lights — Tommy Hilfiger, Ralph Lauren, Calvin Klein, MAC and Bobbi Brown cosmetics, Donna Karan — has Parisians looking like . . . well, looking like stylish Parisians wearing American clothes. As for non-European Union visitors, a surging dollar and a falling euro at press time, meant that all of it was much more affordable. As I said, shopping in Paris has never been better! You still need to keep a few things in mind, however, on your hunting and gathering forays.

Paris Shopping

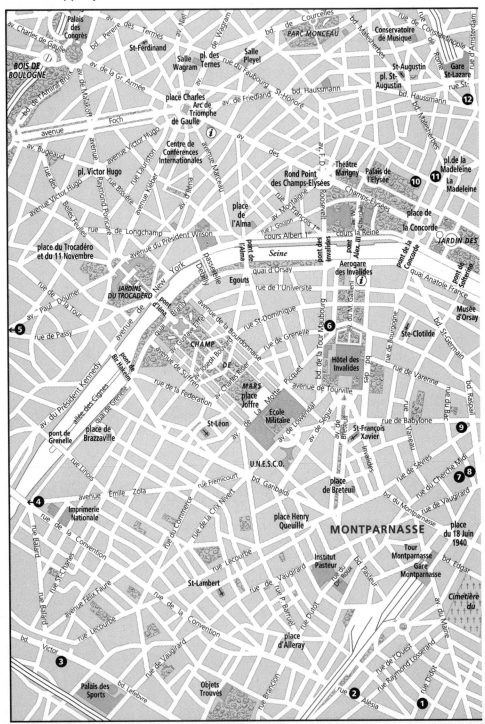

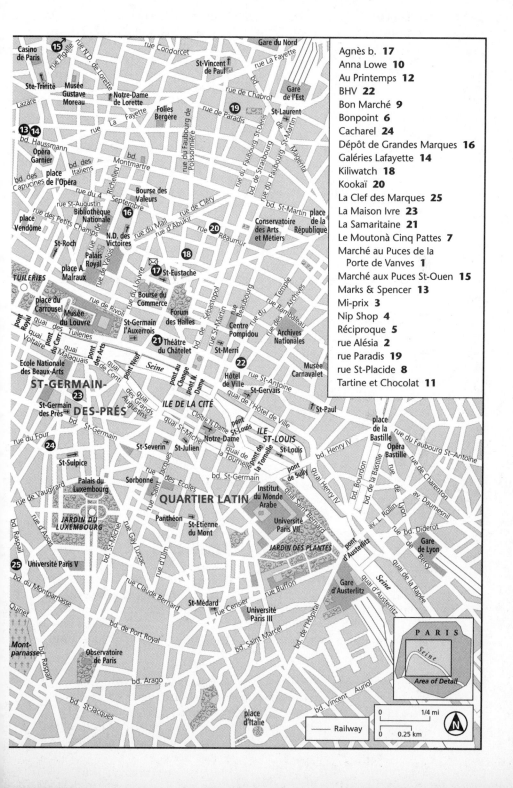

Agnès b. **17**
Anna Lowe **10**
Au Printemps **12**
BHV **22**
Bon Marché **9**
Bonpoint **6**
Cacharel **24**
Dépôt de Grandes Marques **16**
Galéries Lafayette **14**
Kiliwatch **18**
Kookaï **20**
La Clef des Marques **25**
La Maison Ivre **23**
La Samaritaine **21**
Le Moutonà Cinq Pattes **7**
Marché au Puces de la
    Porte de Vanves **1**
Marché aux Puces St-Ouen **15**
Marks & Spencer **13**
Mi-prix **3**
Nip Shop **4**
Réciproque **5**
rue Alésia **2**
rue Paradis **19**
rue St-Placide **8**
Tartine et Chocolat **11**

Remember that a 20.6-percent value-added tax (VAT) has been tacked onto the price of most products, which means that many things cost less at home. (For details on getting a VAT refund, see the following section "Getting a Refund on the VAT.") In fact, Paris is probably the worst place to buy an American or British label (and why would you want to? You're after French style, after all.) Even French-made goods are not necessarily cheaper here than elsewhere. Appliances, paper products, housewares, computer supplies, CDs, and women's clothing are notoriously expensive in France, though the cost of computers is beginning to come down. On the other hand, you can often get good deals on cosmetics such as Bourjois (a low-priced line made in the same factory as Chanel), skin care products from Lierac, Galenic, Roc, and Vichy, and some luxury goods. To recognize a bargain, it helps to check out the prices of French products before your trip.

Probably the best time to find a bargain in Paris is during the twice-annual sales *(soldes)* in January and July when merchandise can be marked down 30 to 50 percent. If you can brave the crowds, you just may find the perfect designer outfit at a fraction of the retail price.

Store hours are Monday through Saturday from 9 or 9:30 a.m. (sometimes 10 a.m.) to 7 p.m., later on Thursday evenings, without a break for lunch. Some smaller stores are closed on Monday or Monday mornings, and break for lunch for one to three hours, beginning at around 1 p.m. Small stores also may be closed for all or part of August, and on some days around Christmas and Easter. Sunday shopping is gradually making inroads in Paris but is limited to tourist areas. Try rue de Rivoli across from the Louvre, rue des Francs-Bourgeois in the Marais, the Carrousel du Louvre and the Champs-Elysées.

Politeness is imperative when you shop in Paris. Always greet the salespeople with *"Bonjour, madame"* or *"Bonjour, monsieur"* when you arrive. Whether you've bought anything or not, say, *"Merci, au revoir,"* (Thank you, goodbye) when you're leaving.

Getting a Refund on the VAT

If you spend more than 1,200F ($171.45) in a single store, you are entitled to a value-added tax (VAT), also referred to in France as TVA, refund on your purchases. The discount, however, is not automatic. Food, wine, and tobacco don't count, and the refund is granted only on purchases you take with you out of the country — not on merchandise you ship home.

To apply, you must show the clerk your passport to prove your eligibility. You then are given an export sales document (in triplicate — two pink sheets and a green one), which you must sign, and usually an envelope addressed to the store. Travelers leaving from Charles-de-Gaulle Airport may visit the Europe Tax-Free Shopping (ETS) refund point, operated by CCF Change, to receive an immediate VAT refund in cash; you pay a 30F ($4.30) fee if you take your refund in cash. Otherwise, when you depart, arrive at the airport as early as possible to allow for lines at the *détaxe* refund booth at French Customs.

If you're traveling by train, go to the *détaxe* area in the station before boarding — you can't get your refund documents processed on the train. Give the three sheets to the Customs official, who stamps them and returns a pink and a green copy to you. Keep the green copy and mail the pink copy to the store.

Your reimbursement is either mailed as a check (in French francs) or credited to your credit card account. If you don't receive your tax refund in four months, write to the store, giving the date of purchase, and the location where the forms were given to Customs officials. Include a photocopy of your green refund sheet. Department stores that cater to foreign visitors, like Au Printemps and Galeries Lafayette, have special *détaxe* areas where clerks will prepare your invoices for you.

Browsing the Department Stores

Two of Paris's major department stores, Au Printemps and Galeries Lafayette, offer visitors a 10-percent discount coupon, good in most departments. If your hotel or travel agent doesn't give you one of these coupons (they're sometimes attached to a city map), you can ask for it at the stores' welcome desks — the clerks speak English.

Au Bon Marché

This is the only department store on the Left Bank and the oldest department store in Paris. Elegant, but small enough to be manageable, much of the store's merchandise is exquisite — check out the lingerie on the third floor. The prices, however, often reflect this. If you're lucky enough to be here during the sales, you can find tons of deals. Make sure to visit the huge supermarket (it's in a separate building next door); it's the city's largest *épicerie,* and you can find nearly any kind of food. A small antiques market can be found on the second floor, as well as a café and cafeteria.

24 rue de Sèvres,7e. ☎ *01 44 39 80 00. Métro: Sèvres-Babylone.*

Au Printemps

Au Printemps is one of Paris's larger department stores, but its largeness is not very well organized, with merchandise sold in three different buildings. Fashion shows are held under the 1920s glass dome at 10:15 a.m. every Tuesday year-round, and every Friday from March through

October. Be sure to obtain one of their 10-percent discount coupons, which is good in most departments. If you haven't already received one from your hotel or travel agent (they're sometimes attached to a city map), you can ask for it at the reception desk inside the store.

64 bd. Haussmann, 9e. ☎ 01-42-82-50-00. Métro: Havre-Caumartin.

BHV

Near the Marais, BHV *(Bazar de l'Hôtel de Ville)* sells the usual clothing, cosmetics, luggage, and leatherware, but is worth a visit for its giant basement-level hardware store with everything you need to fix up your home.

52 rue de Rivoli, 1er. ☎ 01 42 74 90 00. Métro: Hôtel de Ville.

Galeries Lafayette

The crowds and crowds of tourists here attest to the fact that Galeries Lafayette makes shopping easier for foreigners — their VAT refund office is always crowded with visitors taking advantage of the service. Much of the merchandise is of excellent quality, and the January sales are famous. Plus, the store offers a 10-percent discount coupon, good in most departments, which you can ask for at the front desk. The sixth floor self-service cafeteria, Lafayette Café, offers tasty food, and has good views of the Opéra and the rooftops of Paris.

40 bd. Haussmann, 9e. ☎ 01-42-82-34-56. Métro: Opéra or Chaussée-d'Antin.

La Samaritaine

Probably the best thing about La Samaritaine, besides the fact that the prices are lower than Galeries Lafayette and Au Printemps, is its views. Look for signs in its main building to the *panorama,* a free observation point with a wonderful view of Paris that actually takes in the Eiffel Tower. Located between the Louvre and the Pont Neuf, La Samaritaine is housed in four buildings with art-nouveau touches, and has an art-deco facade on quai du Louvre. The fifth floor of store no. 2 has a nice, inexpensive restaurant.

19 rue de la Monnaie, 1er. ☎ 01-40-41-20-20. Métro: Pont-Neuf or Châtelet–Les Halles.

Marks & Spencer

These are branches of the same British stores known for their good values and slightly conservative clothes. In addition to clothes and household items, they have supermarkets offering ready-made sandwiches and salads — great for picnic items or evening snacks.

Marks & Spencer: 35 bd. Haussmann, 9e (☎ 01-47-42-42-91; Métro: Havre-Caumartin); or 88 rue de Rivoli, 4e (☎ 01-44-61-08-00; Métro: Hôtel-de-Ville).

Monoprix-Prisunic

Monoprix and Prisunic were once fierce competitors, but they recently merged, and they've passed on the advantages — mainly low prices — to customers. Clothing is stylish, and the stores are also great for accessories, low-priced cosmetics, lingerie, and housewares. Many locations also have large grocery stores.

Various locations. ☎ *01-40-75-11-02.*

Tati

For the most part, Tati is a frankly tacky store, originally opened to cater to budget-conscious shoppers. But you never know what you may find here if you dig; the occasional gem awaits for those with a good nose.

4 bd. Rochechouart, 18e. ☎ *01-55-29-50-00. Métro: Barbés-Rochechouart. Other branches are located at 172 rue du Temple, 4e (☎ 01-42-76-04-93 or 01-48-04-56-49), 13 place de la République, 3e (☎ 01-48-87-72-81), 11 Bis rue Scribe (01-47-42-20-28). A branch, Tati Or, specializes in gold (see "Jewelry," later in this chapter).*

Checking out the City's Markets

I don't think a trip to Paris is complete without a visit to the vast **Marché aux Puces de la Porte de St-Ouen,** 18e (Métro: Porte-de-Clignancourt).

Also known as *the Clignancourt flea market,* it features several thousand stalls, carts, shops, and vendors selling everything from vintage clothing to antique chandeliers, paintings, and furniture. A real shopping adventure, you need to arrive early to snag the deals — if you can find any. The best times for bargains are right at opening time and just before closing time.

Don't be put off by the stalls selling cheap junk on the market's periphery, it gets much better the farther you walk. Watch out for pickpockets. Open Saturday through Monday 9 a.m. to 8 p.m.

The market at **Porte de Vanves,** 14e (Métro: Porte de Vanves) is probably the smallest of the fleas, and a bit more upscale. (So are its prices.) Open Saturday and Sunday 8:30 a.m. to 1 p.m.

The prettiest of all the markets is the **Marché aux Fleurs,** 4e (Métro: Cité), the flower market on place Louis-Lépine on the Ile de la Cité. Visit Monday through Saturday to enjoy the flowers, even if you don't buy anything. On Sunday it becomes the **Marché aux Oiseaux,** where birds and more unusual furry creatures — on a recent visit I saw hedgehogs, a skunk, and a raccoon, as well as ferrets, mice, guinea pigs, and rabbits — are sold. If you don't mind seeing creatures in cages, it can be fascinating.

Of course, you shouldn't miss the food markets (see Chapter 15), including the ones on rue Mouffetard in the Latin Quarter, rue de Buci in St-Germain, and rue Montorguiel, near the Bourse. All three sell the freshest fruits, vegetables, meats, and cheeses. Most open-air food markets are open Tuesday through Sunday 9 a.m. to 1 p.m.

Visiting the Great Shopping Neighborhoods

Paris is arguably the shopping mecca of the world. You can score great finds for every taste and dollar amount here, if only you know the right places to look. Read this section to get a significant head start in the hunt.

The land of beauty and culture: The 8e

When people across the globe desire over-the-top luxury, they go to Paris; all you have to do is head for the 8e to see why. Nearly every elite French design houses is based on the two streets that positively ooze *haute couture* — **avenue Montaigne** (Métro: Alma-Marceau, Franklin D. Roosevelt) and **rue du Faubourg St-Honoré** (Métro: Concorde). Less well-heeled visitors should beware the snob quotient, which is quite high. But you can still have a good time window-shopping here, even if you don't have a platinum card.

Although these streets boast some of the same big designer names, they are completely different in temperament. Avenue Montaigne is wide, graceful, lined with chestnut trees, and also undeniably hip, attracting the likes of **Dolce & Gabbana** at No. 2 (☎ 01-47-20-42-43) and **Prada** at No. 10 (☎ 01-53-23-99-40). Other designers on this street include: **Céline,** 38 av. Montaigne (☎ 01-49-52-12-12); **Chanel,** 42 av. Montaigne (☎ 01-47-23-74-12); **Christian Dior,** 30 av. Montaigne (☎ 01-40-73-54-00); **Escada,** 57 av. Montaigne (☎ 01-42-89-83-45); **Ferragamo,** 45 av. Montaigne (☎ 01-47-23-36-37); **Christian Lacroix,** 26 av. Montaigne (☎ 01-47-20-68-95); **Thierry Mugler,** 49 av. Montaigne (☎ 01-47-23-37-62); **Ungaro,** 2 av. Montaigne (☎ 01-53-57-00-00); and **Valentino,** 17 av. Montaigne (☎ 01-47-23-64-61).

Rue du Faubourg St-Honoré is jammed with shoppers walking along the small, narrow sidewalks. Here you find **Gucci** at No. 2 (☎ 01-53-05-11-11), **Hermès** (pronounced "Air-mess") at No. 24 (☎ 01-40-17-47-17) and **Yves St-Laurent** at No. 38 (☎ 01-42-65-74-59).

Begin at the rue Royale intersection and head west. Other designer stores you run across here include: **Ferragamo,** 50 rue du Faubourg St-Honoré (☎ **01-43-12-96-96**); **Gianni Versace,** 62 rue du Faubourg St-Honoré (☎ **01-47-42-88-02**); **La Perla,** 20 rue du Faubourg St-Honoré (☎ **01-43-12-33-50**); **Maud Frizon,** bat. 0, 90 rue du Faubourg St-Honoré (☎ **01-42-65-27-96**); **Sonia Rykiel,** 70 rue du Faubourg St-Honoré (☎ **01-42-65-20-81**); and **Tartine et Chocolat,** 105 rue du Faubourg-St-Honoré, (☎ **01-45-62-44-04**).

Eclecticism and Art: The 4e

The Marais (4e) is a beautiful neighborhood crammed with magnificent Renaissance mansions, artists' studios, secret courtyards, and some of the most original shops in the city.

Rue des Francs-Bourgeois (Métro: St-Paul or Rambuteau) is the highlight of the area, full of small shops selling everything from fashion to jewels. And don't miss **Rue des Rosiers** (Métro: St-Paul), a fashion destination in its own right, with white-hot designers standing shoulder-to-shoulder with Jewish delis. Everything is really close in the Marais, so don't be afraid to ramble down the tiniest lane whenever whim dictates. Part of the fun of this neighborhood is that it's such a mixed shopping bag.

Marais highlights include: **Paule Ka,** 20 rue Mahler (☎ **01-45-44-92-60**), for the sort of timeless womenswear Grace Kelly and Audrey Hepburn made famous; **Autour du Monde Home,** 8 rue des Francs-Bourgeois (☎ **01-42-77-06-08**), a clothing/housewares store with everything from relaxed and sporty linen dresses, to delicate linen sheets, and nifty tableware; **Anne Séverine Liotard,** 7 rue St-Merri (☎ **01-48-04-00-38**), for candles that burn forever and double as *objets d'art;* **Lunettes Beausoleil,** 28 rue Roi du Sicile (☎ **01-42-77-28-29**), for glamorous sunglasses that flatter any face; **Extrem Origin,** 10 rue Ferdinand Duval (☎ **01-42-72-70-10**) for ultrachic interior design that uses only natural elements; and **Plein Sud,** 21 rue des Francs-Bourgeois (☎ **01-42-72-10-60**), for sexy French women's fashion that's carried only in exclusive stores in the United States.

"BCBG" Chic: The 6e

Bon Chic Bon Genre is what the French call stylish young professionals with old family money, and you see plenty of them sipping coffee, or shopping in this area of St-Germain-des-Prés between bd. St-Germain, from rue des St-Pères to place St-Sulpice. (The closest Métro stops are Mabillon and St-Germain-des-Prés.) Famed literary hangouts such as Café de Flore, and Les Deux Magots are here in case you get hungry, and lots of trendy stores in case you get bored.

Louis Vuitton has opened a huge store behind Les Deux Magots on 6, place St-Germain (☎ 01-45-49-62-32) and **Christian Dior** and **Cartier** are nearby at 18 rue de l'Abbaye (☎ 01-56-24-90-53) and 41 rue de Rennes (☎ 01-45-49-65-80) respectively. Plenty of stores here are a better value than **Emporio Armani,** 149 bd. St-Germain (☎ 01-53-63-33-50); **Céline,** 58 rue de Rennes, (☎ 01-45-48-58-55); **Christian Lacroix,** 2 place St-Sulpice (☎ 01-46-33-48-95) — check out Stefanel, 54 rue de Rennes (☎ 01-45-44-06-07) and **Comptoir des Cotonniers,** 59 rue de Bonaparte (☎ 01-43-26-07-56) — but it's always fun to see the latest fashions.

And if you thought you'd escape GAP, you were sadly mistaken. GAP and other international chain stores have taken up residence in the Marché St-Germain, a modern shopping mall that's out of place in a neighborhood known for bookstores and upscale boutiques. Visit if you need to experience air conditioning, otherwise don't waste your time.

Young and Branché: The 2e

In this technological age, *branché* means "plugged in," or hip, and the 2e is where young, hip Parisians head for the season's funkiest looks. Although it lacks atmosphere, the area doesn't lack for stores selling knock-offs of trends. The cheapest shopping is in the Sentier area, around the Sentier Métro stop, which is Paris's garment district, overlapping parts of the 3e and 1er. Prostitutes frequent the area later in the day and evening. The best, but not the cheapest, shops are found within a square formed on the south by rue Rambuteau, on the west by rue du Louvre, on the north by rue Réamur, and on the east by rue St-Martin. This is where you find hip second-hand clothes, funky clubwear, and "stock" boutiques selling last season's designs at a discount.

Don't miss **Barbara Bui,** 23 rue Etienne-Marcel, 1er (☎ 01-40-26-43-65), for sophisticated, contemporary fashion (she also has a trendy café two doors down); **Le Shop,** 3 rue d'Argout, 2e (☎ 01-40-28-95-94) for two floors of clubwear (that's nightclub) by France's hottest designers; **Kiliwatch,** 64 rue Tiquetonne 2e (☎ 01-42-21-17-37) for cool retro looks that are sure to be on next year's runways (designers come here for inspiration); **Agnès b.,** 3–6 rue du Jour (☎ 01-45-08-56-56) for timeless chic for men and women. Other stores include **Et Vous Stock,** 15 rue de Turbigo, 2e (☎ 01-40-13-04-12), for last year's unsold stock of women's clothing; **Kookaï Le Stock,** 82 rue Réamur, 2e (☎ 01-45-08-93-69), for last year's unsold stock of teen and women's clothing; and **Mon Amie Pierlot,** 3 rue Montmartre, 1er (☎ 01-40-28-45-55), for women's casual clothes.

Streets of Dreams: Paris Bargain Shopping

When you see the prices in Paris boutiques, you may wonder how Parisian women can afford to look as put-together as they do. The answer is they know where to go to find the *soldes* (sales), *dégriffés* (designer wear with the labels cut out), *stock* (overstock), and *dépot-vente* (resale). You also can find that some of the best fashion deals are found in resale shops that deal directly with designer showrooms and people in the fashion industry. Designer clothing that has been worn on a runway or for a fashion shoot is on sale for half price, along with other gently used clothes and accessories. Most *dépôts-vente* are on the Right Bank in the 8e, 16e, and 17e arrondissements. If you're itching for a bargain after shopping for full–price items, the following information is for you.

- ✔ **Rue Alésia,** 14e (Métro: Alésia), is filled with French designer discount outlets selling last year's overstock at up to 70-percent below retail. You find that these stock boutiques are more downscale than their sister shops, and be prepared to rifle through the racks to find the gems. Outlets include **Chevignon** at No. 12, **Sonia Rykiel** at No. 54, and **Cacharel** at No. 114. You can find clothing outlets, as well: **Sergent Major** at No. 82, **Toute Compte Fait** at No. 101, and **Jacadi** at No. 116.

- ✔ **Rue St-Placide,** 6e (Métro: Sèvres-Babylone), is also a street of dreams with discounted designs in five branches alone of **Le Mouton à Cinq Pattes** (8, 10, 14–18, and 48 rue St-Placide, 6e). Discounted no-name shoes, and housewares stores are also sold here.

- ✔ **Rue Paradis,** 10e (Métro: Poissonnière) is filled with wholesale china and porcelain stores such as **Paradis Porcelaine** at No. 56, and **La Tisanière Porcelaine** at No. 21.

Try also the following slate of discount stores.

Anna Lowe

This shop is a find for those who want the very best designers — Yves Saint-Laurent, Chanel, Giorgio Armani — at a steep discount. Shopping is genteel and substantially less uptight than at the same designers' retail shops.

Remember, however, that a steep discount off an incredibly expensive couture price can still mean an expensive item.

104 rue du Faubourg-St-Honoré, 8e. ☎ *01-42-66-11-32 or 01-40-06-02-42. Métro: Miromesnil or St-Phillippe-de-Roule.*

The top spots for late-night shopping

French stores tend to close early, around 7 p.m. — except on Thursday nights when they close around 9 p.m. So what do you do if you're in need of a late-night makeup, CD, clothing, book, or grocery fix? Visit the following stores, all open until midnight, with the exception of one florist, open all night.

To buy flowers 24 hours a day, 7 days a week, head for **Elyfleur,** 82 av. de Wagram, 17e (☎ 01-47-66-87-19; Métro: Charles de Gaulle-Etoile). Particularly good if you've had a fight over dinner.

FNAC, 74 av. des Champs-Elysées, 8e (☎ 01-53-53-64-64; Métro: George V.), is the place for concert tickets, film developing, and browsing for CDs, books, videos, electronics, and collectible toys. Open 10 a.m.–midnight Monday–Saturday.

For a slice of existential history, visit **La Hune,** 170 bd. St-Germain, 6e (☎ 01-45-48-35-85; Métro: St-Germain-des Prés), a bookshop sandwiched between the famous literary cafes Les Deux Magots and Café de Flore. La Hune has been a center for Left Bank intellectuals since 1945. The selection of books (most in French) is outstanding. Open 10 a.m.–midnight Monday–Saturday.

Shop for clothes, accessories, toiletries, and makeup at the reasonably priced **Monoprix,** 52 av. des Champs-Elysées, 8e (☎ 01-53-77-65-64; Métro: Franklin-D-Roosevelt). The store is sort of like an upscale Target. When you're finished, visit the supermarket downstairs. Open 10 a.m.–midnight Monday–Saturday.

For all your medicinal and toiletry needs, visit **Pharmacie des Halles,** 10 bd. de Sébastopol, 4e (☎ 01-42-72-03-23; Métro: Châtelet). Open 9 a.m.–midnight, Monday–Saturday, noon–midnight Sunday.

You can buy everything from clothing to paper plates to shampoo at **Prisunic,** 109 rue de la Boétie, 8e (☎ 01-53-77-65-65; Métro: Franklin-D-Roosevelt). Prisunic and Monoprix used to be rivals, but their management has merged, and now clothes are designed by a hip Dutch designer. Open 9 a.m.–midnight Monday–Saturday.

If you've ever had the urge to buy makeup, bath products, or perfume at 10 at night, then **Sephora,** 70 av. des Champs-Elysées, 8e (☎ 01-53-93-22-50; Métro: Charles de Gaulle-Etoile), is the store for you. It carries an extensive selection of brands from around the world and you're free to try out products first. Open 10 a.m.–midnight Monday–Saturday, noon–midnight Sunday.

English-speaking residents of Paris gather in the cluttered **Shakespeare and Company,** 37 rue de la Bûcherie, 5e (No phone; Métro or RER: St-Michel.), which sells mostly used books in English. The name is in honor of Sylvia Beach's legendary literary lair (but not the same place). Poetry readings are held on Sundays. Open noon–midnight daily.

For books (mostly in French), music, and videotapes, try a branch of the English chain **Virgin Megastore,** 52–60 ave. des Champs-Elysées, 8e (☎ 01-49-53-50-00; Métro: Franklin-D-Roosevelt.), that's open 10 a.m.–midnight Monday–Saturday, and noon–midnight Sunday.

Bonpoint

Your children are princes and princesses in your eyes; dress them in Bonpoint clothes, and they'll look the part to everyone else as well. You usually have to pay for their royal treatment. However, at this Bonpoint, you can often find the same merchandise at reduced prices, especially after the yearly sales in January and July.

82 rue de Grenelle, 7e. ☎ *01-42-84-12-39. Métro: Rue-du-Bac.*

Dépôt de Grandes Marques

Come search through racks of stylish men's suits at reduced prices.

15 rue de la Banque, 4th floor, 2e. ☎ *01-42-96-99-04. Métro: Bourse.*

La Clef des Marques

This large boutique with other branches at 86 rue Faubourg St-Antoine, 12e (☎ **01-40-01-95-15**) and 20 place Marché St-Honoré, 1er (☎ **01-47-03-90-40**) sells everything from shoes to baby clothes, lingerie and end-of-series couture items. You can unearth some real gems at these stores.

124 bd. Raspail, 6e. ☎ *01-45-48-29-57. Métro: Notre-Dame des Champs.*

Le Mouton à Cinq Pattes

You often come across extremely well-known designer names on the packed racks of women's, men's, and children's clothing, as well as shoes and accessories. The stock changes constantly. (In other words, if you see something you like, grab it. It may not be there the next day.) Other branches are located at 19 rue Gregoire de Tours, 6e (☎ **01-43-29-73-56**), and 15 rue Vieille du Temple, 4e (☎ **01-42-71-86-30**).

8, 10, 14–18, and 48 rue St-Placide, 6e. ☎ *01-45-48-86-26 for all stores. Métro: Sèvres-Babylone.*

Mi-prix

Men's designer clothes with labels from designers like Karl Lagerfeld, Alaia, Missoni, and Gianfranco Ferre are steeply discounted here.

27 bd. Victor, 15e. ☎ *01-48-28-42-48. Métro: Balard or Porte de Versailles.*

Nip Shop

Yves Saint-Laurent, Sonia Rykiel, and Guy Laroche are big labels here, though lesser-known designers are also represented.

6 rue Edmond-About, 16e. ☎ *01-45-04-66-19. Métro: Rue de la Pompe.*

Réciproque

This is the largest *depôt-vente* (resale shop) in Paris for men, women, and children. You find jewelry, furs, belts, antiques, and designer purses, (Hermès, Gucci, Vuitton were just a few of the names I saw on a recent visit). If you've always dreamed of owning a designer outfit — I've never seen so many "gently-worn" Chanel suits in one place — you may find one here that fits your budget, but prices over $1,000 are still all too common. Mid-range labels are also well represented.

89–123 rue de la Pompe, 16e. ☎ *01-47-04-30-28. Métro: Rue de la Pompe.*

The Best Shopping in Paris from A to Z

From antiques to wine (okay, so not quite to Z!), I list my favorite stores and the best values you can find in the City of Lights.

Antiques

Le Louvre des Antiquaires

This is an enormous mall filled with an amazing diversity of shops that sell everything from Jean Cocteau sketches, to silver older than the United States. Items are pricey, but rumors have it that some good deals exist here. A café and toilets are located on the second floor.

2 place du Palais-Royal, 1er. ☎ *01-42-97-27-00. Métro:Palais-Royal-Musée du Louvre. Le Village Suisse. 54 av. de la Motte-Picquet, 15e (no phone). Métro: La Motte-Picquet. About 150 stores in a two-block radius sell antiques in the middle-to high-priced range. Open Sunday.*

Bookstores

Abbey Bookshop

This small Canadian bookstore has two floors of English-language books, and also is a gathering place for expats and visiting Canadians.

29 rue de la Parcheminerie, 5e. ☎ *01-46-33-16-24. Métro: St-Michel or Cluny-Sorbonne.*

Brentano's

Part of the U.S. chain and one of Paris's leading English-language bookstores, Brentano's has a big general fiction and nonfiction stock that includes guides and maps. It usually has a shelf of discounted books, which is a good thing, because prices are high.

37 av. de l'Opéra, 2e. ☎ *01-42-61-52-50. Métro: Opéra.*

Galignani

Galignani claims to be the oldest English-language bookstore on the continent. Dark and expensive, it does have a good selection of magazines and art books in French and English.

224 rue de Rivoli, 1er. ☎ *01-42-60-76-07. Métro: Tuileries.*

Gibert Joseph

This is *the* Parisian students' bookstore, selling new and secondhand books, records, videos, and stationery on several floors and in several branches on bd. St-Michel.

26, 30, 32, and 34 bd. St-Michel, 6e. ☎ *01-44-41-88-88. Métro: Odéon or Cluny-Sorbonne.*

Librarie La Hune

This bookstore has been a center for Left Bank intellectuals since 1945 when Sartre was among its clients. Most books are in French.

170 bd. St-Germain. ☎ *01-45-48-35-85. Métro: St-Germain.*

San Francisco Book Co.

The 20,000 second-hand books in this small, four-year-old store are affordable and arranged alphabetically. If you're tired of lugging around a quality fiction or non-fiction title, you may even be able to sell it for cash (bring identification). Service can be disappointingly cold however.

17 rue Monsieur le Prince, 6e. ☎ *01-43-29-15-70. Métro: Odéon.*

Shakespeare and Company

No, this *isn't* the original, but English-speaking residents of Paris still gather in this cluttered store, named after Sylvia Beach's legendary literary lair. Poetry readings are held on Sundays.

37 rue de la Bûcherie, 5e. No phone. Métro or RER: St-Michel.

Tea and Tattered Pages

Most of the 15,000 English-language books in this cozy shop are used, and sell for around 30F ($4.30), which is as cheap as you can find in Paris. You can have tea or light fare here, and often brownies and other American treats are also available.

24 rue Mayet, 6e. ☎ *01-40-65-94-35. Métro: Falguière or Duroc.*

Village Voice

Quality fiction in English is the highlight of this small store in St-Germain-des-Prés, along with an excellent selection of poetry, plays, nonfiction and literary magazines. Owner Odile Hellier hosts free poetry and fiction readings with celebrated authors and poets.

6 rue Princesse, 6e. ☎ *01-46-33-36-47. Métro: Mabillon.*

W. H. Smith

Besides a full stock of British and American books, this store carries a wide range of British and American newspapers, some videos and magazines. You can get the most recent Sunday *New York Times* here on Tuesdays for 75F ($10.70). Prices are high.

248 rue de Rivoli, 1er. ☎ *01-42-61-58-15 or 01-44-77-88-99. Métro: Concorde.*

Ceramics, china, and glass

Baccarat

Baccarat's crystal has been world-renowned since the eighteenth-century. This store is also a museum, so even if its prices are too high, you can still enjoy browsing.

30 rue de Paradis, 10e. ☎ *01-47-70-64-30 or 01-40-22-11-00. Métro: Château-d'Eau, Poissonnière, or Gare-de-l'Est.*

Cristal Vendôme

Shop duty-free for Lalique, Baccarat, and more at this shop in the Hôtel Intercontinental. The store will even ship purchases home.

1 rue de Castiglione, 1er. ☎ *01-49-27-09-60. Metro: Concorde.*

La Maison Ivre

This charming shop sits in the heart of the antiques and gallery district (on the Left Bank between St-Germain-des-Prés and the Seine). It carries an excellent selection of handmade pottery from all over France, with an emphasis on Provençal and southern French ceramics. You find oven-ware, bowls, platters, plates, pitchers, mugs, and vases here.

38 rue Jacob, 6e. ☎ 01-42-60-01-85. Métro: St-Germain-des-Prés.

Clothing for children

Jacadi

When I worked as an *au pair,* this is where my chic employer shopped for her very proper children's clothes.

256 bd. St-Germain, 7e. (☎ 01-42-84-30-40). Many branches are located all over the city including 17 bd. Poissonière, 2e (☎ 01-42-36-69-91).

Natalys

Part of a French chain with a dozen stores in Paris, Natalys sells chil-dren's wear, maternity wear, and related products.

92 av. des Champs-Elysées, 8e. ☎ 01-43-59-17-65. Métro: Franklin-D-Roosevelt.

Tartine et Chocolat

Your children will look *très mignons* (very cute) in these very sweet, but pricey clothes.

105 rue du Faubourg-St-Honoré, 8e. ☎ 01-45-62-44-04. Métro: Concorde. Another branch is located at 266 bd. St-Germain, 7e (☎ 01-45-56-10-45).

Clothing for men

Façonnable

You can find some quality shirts and pants here, in addition to jackets, suits, and other men's furnishings.

9 rue du Faubourg-St-Honoré, 8e. ☎ 01-47-42-72-60. Métro: Sèvres-Babylone. Another branch is located at 174 bd. St-Germain, 6e (☎ 01-40-49-02-47).

Madelios

This huge store offers one-stop shopping for men, selling everything from overcoats to lighters. If companions get bored waiting, the store is part of a small mall that has some nice stores for browsing.

23 bd. de la Madeleine, 1er. ☎ 01-42-60-39-30.

Clothing for teens and the young at heart

H&M

This Swedish store, the "IKEA of fashion," has low-cost clothing for men and women in a hip atmosphere.

118 rue Rivoli, 1er. ☎ *01-55-34-38-00. Métro: Hôtel-de-Ville.*

Kiliwatch

This bright mish-mash of club clothes and vintage in a slightly psyche-delic setting, offers some surprisingly good prices. They have everything from wigs to coats, plus a few new designers. A must for club kids.

64 rue Tiquetonne, 1er. ☎ *01-42-21-17-37.*

Kookaï

Fun and funky with the latest styles, most in synthetics. Kookaï is located all over the city.

35 bd. Saint-Michel, 5e. ☎ *01-46-34-75-02. Métro: St-Michel.*

Mango

With locations throughout the city, this store is popular with young Parisian women for its inexpensive fashion-conscious clothes.

3 pl 18 Juin 1940, 6e. ☎ *01-45-48-04-96.*

Zara

Zara hails from Spain and is just starting to open branches in the U.S. It often offers well-made copies of today's hottest styles for women, men, and children at extremely low prices (think such designers as Prada), so it can be worth stopping by.

45 rue de Rennes, 6e. ☎ *01-44-39-03-50. Locations all over the place, including 2 rue Halévy, 9e (☎ 01-44-71-90-90 and 01-44-71-90-93), near the Opéra, and 44 av. Champs-Elysées (☎ 01-45-61-52-81 and 01-45-61-52-81).*

Clothing for women

1 2 3

If you don't mind synthetics or blends, you can find stylish women's suits, blouses, sweaters, and accessories at moderate prices; occasionally, you find an all-wool or all-cotton product.

42 rue Chaussée d'Antin, 9e. ☎ *01-40-16-80-06. Métro: Chaussée d'Antin. Other branches include 30 av. Italie, 13e (*☎ *01-45-80-02- 88).*

Agnès b

If you want a basic but classic French outfit, you can't do better than Agnès b. This location is targeted purely to women, but other locations around the city also sell men's and children's wear.

3–6 rue du Jour, 1er. ☎ *01-45-08-56-56. Métro: Les Halles.*

Cacharel

Beautiful and reasonably priced women's, children's, and men's clothes, some in the popular Liberty flower-printed fabrics.

64 rue Bonaparte, 6e. ☎ *01-40-46-00-45.*

Colette

The most cutting-edge fashion — much of it American (thus, cheaper in the States) — is for sale here, in *très* artistic displays. You can also find artsy chotchkes, art magazines, and art exhibits. The French love this store, so try to visit to see what all the fuss is about. Don't buy, just look, and maybe have a bite to eat, or drink one of the extensive selection of waters at the basement café and water bar.

213 rue St-Honoré, 1er. ☎ *01-55-35-33-90. Métro: Tuileries.*

Etam

The Etam chain has dozens of stores all over Paris with recent fashions at low prices. Merchandise is mostly made from synthethetic or synthetic blend fabrics. The Etam lingerie store at 47 rue de Sèvres, 6e, (☎ **01-45-48-21-33**) has some pretty and affordable nightclothes and under garments.

9 bd. St Michel, 5e. ☎ *1-43-54-79-20. Métro: St-Michel.*

La City

The selection is limited at this store, which sells young and modern styles, and everything is synthetic, but the prices are reasonable.

37 rue Chaussée d'Antin, 9e. ☎ 01-48-74-41-00. Métro: Chaussée d'Antin. Other branches are located at 18 rue St-Antoine, 4e (☎ 01-42-78-95-55) and 42 rue Passy, 16e (☎ 01-42-88-66-21).

Morgan

Sexy suits, dresses, and casual wear in synthetics and blends, at low prices for young women.

16 rue Turbigo, 2e. ☎ 01-44-82-02-00. Métro: Etienne-Marcel.

Rodier

Prices are high, but the quality of the stylish knits here is good, and you can often find bargains during sales.

72 av. Ternes, 17e. ☎ 01-45-74-17-17. Métro: Ternes. Branches include 23 bd. Madeleine, 1er (☎ 01-40-15-06-80), and 47 rue de Rennes, 6e (☎ 01-45-44-30-27).

Food

Lafayette Gourmet

This large, well-stocked supermarket in the basement of the men's store at Galeries Lafayette, is a terrific spot to browse for gifts or for yourself. They have a good selection of wines and the house-brand merchandise, often cheaper than other labels, is of very good quality. Eat at the prepared-food counters — ideal for picnics or train meals — or one of the other areas for quick meals or snacks.

52 bd. Haussmann, 9e. ☎ 01-48-74-46-06. Métro: Chaussée-d'Antin.

Les Grandes Epiceries (Luxury Supermarkets)

Au Bon Marché

This is one of the best luxury supermarkets in Paris, and is a great place to look for gourmet gifts, such as olive oils, homemade chocolates, or wine. It makes for great one-stop picnic shopping, too, offering a wide array of prepared foods and cheeses. Unfortunately, it doesn't come cheap.

38 rue de Sèvres, 7e. ☎ 01-44-39-81-00. Métro: Sèvres-Babylone.

La Maison du Chocolat

This is one of the best places in Paris to buy chocolate with racks and racks priced individually or by the kilo. Each is made from a blend of as many as six kinds of South American and African chocolate, flavored with just about everything imaginable. All the merchandise is made on the premises. If the smell doesn't lure you in, the windows will.

225 rue du Faubourg-St-Honoré, 8e. ☎ *01-42-27-39-44. Métro: Ternes.*

La Maison du Miel

This petite shop has varieties of honey you never dreamed possible (lavender, for example), identified according to the flower to which the bees were exposed. Lemon flower and pine tree have distinct tastes and make fine gifts.

24 rue Vignon, 9e. ☎ *01-47-42-26-70. Métro: Madeleine or Havre-Caumartin.*

L'Univers des Anges Gourmands

The owner calls this store a *fleuriste de chocolat* (chocolate florist), and sells chocolate made up like floral bouquets.

49, av. de la Bourdonnais, 7e. ☎ *01-45-56-13-04. Métro: École Militaire.*

Jacques Papin

Don't visit this store when you're hungry — unless you want to walk out with hundreds of dollars worth of wonderful stuff. This butcher shop has some of the most exquisite foods you can ever see, including trout in aspic, fine pâtés and salads, lobsters, and smoked salmon.

Prestige et Tradition, 8 rue de Buci, 6e. ☎ *01-43-26-86-09. Métro: Odéon.*

Gifts

Axis

If you're looking for a set of dinner plates imprinted with the cartoon character TinTin, or scrub brushes that look like people, this is the place to come. It carries a neat assortment of contemporary gifts.

14 rue Lobineau, Marché St-Germain, 6e. ☎ *01-43-29-66-23. Métro: Mabillon. A branch store is at 11 rue de Charonne, 11e (*☎ *01-48-06-79-10).*

Pylones

This boutique sells the unusual, from Simpsons collectibles, and children's umbrellas that stand on their own, to bicycle bells shaped like ladybugs. This is a fun place to browse.

57 rue de St-Louis-en-l'Ile, 4e. ☎ 01-46-34-05-02. Métro: Cité. Branches at 7 rue Tardieu, 18e. (☎ 01-46-06-37-00.) Métro: Anvers; and 54 galerie Vivienne, 2e (☎ 01-42-61-51-60), Métro: Bourse.

Housewares

Alessi

Bright and affordable kitchen implements, such as magnetized salt and pepper shakers, and wine openers that look a tad, well, *human*. Some cutlery, dishes, and linens, too.

14 rue du Faubourg St-Honoré, 8e. ☎ 01-42-66-14-61. Métro: Madéleine or Concorde.

Déhillerin

Cooks love this store filled with copper cookware, glasses, dishes, china, gadgets, utensils, pots, and kitchen appliances, especially since its prices are discounted.

18–20 rue Coquillière, 1er. ☎ 01-42-36-53-13. Métro: Les Halles.

Verrerie des Halles

All the accoutrements of the kitchen are here, at discount prices usually reserved for professionals.

15 rue du Louvre, 1er. ☎ 01-42-36-80-60. Métro: Louvre-Rivoli.

Jewelry

Bijoux Burma

Come here for some of the best costume jewelry in the city, the secret weapon of many a Parisian woman. With branches at 14 rue Castiglione, 1e (☎ 01-42-60-35-52) and 23 bd. Madeleine, 1er (☎ 01-42-96-05-00).

50 rue François 1er, 8e. ☎ 01-47-23-70-93. Métro: Franklin-D-Roosevelt.

Eric et Lydie

This shop in the arty Passage du Grand Cerf, contains unusual, beautiful, and surprisingly reasonably priced costume jewelry and accessories.

7, Passage du Grand Cerf, 2e. ☎ *01-40-26-52-59. Métro: Etienne-Marcel.*

Monic

At this store in the Marais — open Sunday afternoons — you find a wide range of affordable costume jewelry and designer creations at a discount.

5 rue des Francs-Bourgeois, 4e. ☎ *01-42-72-39-15. Métro: St-Paul.*

Tati Or

Eighteen-carat gold jewelry for up to 40 percent less than traditional jewelers and more than 3,000 bracelets, earrings, necklaces, rings, and pins are offered, with about 500 items selling for less than 400F ($67.80).

19 rue de la Paix, 2e. ☎ *01-40-07-06-76. Métro: Opéra.*

Toys

Au Nain Bleu

Au Nain Bleu is filled with toy soldiers, stuffed animals, games, model airplanes, model cars, and puppets. The store has been in business for over 150 years.

406 rue St-Honoré, 8e. ☎ *01-42-60-39-01. Métro: Concorde.*

Fnac Junior

In addition to the books, videos, and music for children, Fnac Junior has story hours and activities for its young guests.

19 rue Vavin, 6e. ☎ *01-56-24-03-46. Métro: Vavin.*

Wine

Le Jardin des Vignes

Here you find very interesting bottles of rare wine, champagne, and cognac, at reasonable prices. The owners of Le Jardin des Vignes are really excited about wine and also offer lessons.

91 rue de Turenne, 3e. ☎ *01-42-77-05-00. Métro: St-Sébastien-Froissart.*

Lescene-Dura

Perhaps the ultimate shop for oenophiles, this crowded, friendly place is a good bet for gifts. It sells an amazing array of corkscrews, glassware, and pocketknives, and everything you need to make wine at home.

63 rue de la Verrerie, 4e. ☎ *01-42-72-08-74. Métro: Hôtel-de-Ville.*

Nicolas

This is the flagship store of the wine chain, with more than 110 branches in and around Paris, and it offers good prices for bottles you may not be able to find in the United States.

31 place de la Madeleine, 8e. ☎ *01-42-68-00-16. Métro: Madeleine.*

Getting through Customs on the Way Home

And after all that shopping comes the best part of your trip — getting it home.

Returning U.S. citizens who have been away for 48 hours or more are allowed to bring back, once every 30 days, $400 worth of merchandise duty-free. You are charged a flat rate of 10-percent duty on the next $1,000 worth of purchases; on gifts, the duty-free limit is $100. You cannot bring fresh foodstuffs into the United States; tinned foods, however, are allowed.

Citizens of the U.K. who are returning from a European Union country have no limit on what can be brought back from an EU country, as long as the items are for personal use (this includes gifts), and the necessary duty and tax has been paid. Guidance levels are set at: 800 cigarettes, 200 cigars, 1kg smoking tobacco, 10 liters of spirits, 90 liters of wine and 110 liters of beer. Canada allows its citizens a $500 exemption, and you're allowed to bring back duty-free 200 cigarettes, 1.5 liters of wine, or 1.14 liters of liquor, and 50 cigars. In addition, you may mail gifts to Canada from abroad at the rate of Can$60 a day, provided they're unsolicited and don't contain alcohol or tobacco or advertising matter. Write on the package "Unsolicited gift, under $60 value." All valuables should be declared on the Y-38 form before departure from France, including serial numbers of valuables you already own, such as expensive foreign cameras. *Note:* The $500 exemption can be used only once a year.

The duty-free allowance in Australia is A$400 or, for those under 18, A$200. Personal property mailed back from France should be marked "Australian goods returned" to avoid payment of duty. Upon returning to Australia, citizens can bring in 250 cigarettes or 250 grams of loose tobacco and 1,125ml of alcohol. If you're returning with valuable goods you already own, such as foreign-made cameras, you should file form B263 before leaving Paris.

The duty-free allowance for New Zealand is NZ$700. Citizens over 17 can bring in 200 cigarettes or 50 cigars or 250 grams of tobacco (or a mixture of all three if their combined weight doesn't exceed 250 grams), plus 4.5 liters of wine or beer or 1.125 liters of liquor.

Chapter 20

Four Itineraries and a Stroll

*P*aris has so much to see and do that first- and even second-time visitors to the city can feel overwhelmed just trying to figure out where to begin. If you're short on time, or have young children with you, you want to maximize your opportunities to see the best Paris has to offer in the most efficient way possible. The following itineraries were designed to help you figure out where to start and what to do. But please feel free to branch out and explore those interesting alleyways and pretty green spaces you encounter all around you. That's what's so much fun about Paris — it reveals itself in all kinds of ways, making the trips of each independent visitor different, and special.

Spending Three Days in Paris

On **Day One,** start early by having coffee and croissants at a café. Then begin at the true center of Paris: **Notre-Dame,** on the **Ile de la Cité.** The cathedral is a great starting point for any tour. From there, take a short walk to the island's other Gothic masterpiece, **St-Chapelle,** in the **Palais de Justice.** Afterward, cross the Seine to the **Louvre.** Select just a few rooms in a particular collection for your first visit — this is one of the world's largest and finest museums, and it would take months to see everything. Take a well-deserved lunch break in the museum's comfortable **Café Marly** (see Chapter 14 for description).

From the museum, stroll through the beautiful **Jardin des Tuileries** to the **place de la Concorde,** with its Egyptian obelisk and fountains. Walk up the **Champs-Elysées** to the **Arc de Triomphe** and browse the stores (**Fnac** and **Virgin Megastore** are good places to buy music, and they each have a café on the premises for a break; **Zara** is great for the latest fashion at low prices). Walk south on avenue Marceau or take bus 92 to Alma Marceau and board the **Bateaux-Mouches** for a **Seine boat ride** (see Chapter 16). After you disembark, have dinner at the friendly and reasonably-priced **L'Assiette Lyonnaise,** 21 rue Marbeuf, 8e. (From Pont L'Alma walk down av. George V to rue Marbeuf and make a right. L'Assiette Lyonnaise is on your right.)

Explore the **Left Bank** on **Day Two.** Take the Métro to LaMotte-Picquet-Grenelle and stop into **Monoprix** just across the street for cheap picnic food. Walk down av. de Suffren until you reach the **École Militaire.** Facing this is the **Champs de Mars** and the **Eiffel Tower.** After you climb the tower, visit the **Église du Dome** (which contains the **Tomb of Napoléon**) on the other side of the Ecole Militaire. Admission also includes entrance to the **Musée d'Armée.** Across bd. des Invalides is the **Musée Rodin,** where you can picnic in the gardens before gazing at the artwork inside. Then walk down bd. des Invalides to the Seine, and head east for quai Anatole France and the **Musée d'Orsay** where you can spend a few hours with the impressionist masters. Afterward, take rue du Bac to **bd. St-Germain,** to browse in upscale shops and art galleries. You can see stately eighteenth-century mansions, many of which have been converted into government offices and embassies. Relax in Parisians' favorite park, the **Jardin du Luxembourg** off bd. St-Germain and bd. St-Michel, then walk down St-Michel into the **Latin Quarter.** The **Panthéon** is at the top of the hill on rue Soufflot. Have dinner at one of the famous cafés, **Café de Flore, Les Deux Magots,** or **Brasserie Lipp** (see Chapter 14) on bd. St-Germain, or at one of the many restaurants in the 5e, behind the Panthéon on rue Mouffetard.

On **Day Three,** get up early and hop on the Métro to St-Paul, in the heart of the **Marais.** Walk over to Paris's oldest square, the aristocratic **place des Vosges,** bordered by seventeenth-century townhouses. Then head over to rue Thorigny for the **Musée Picasso.** Try to be here when it opens at 9:30, and allow two hours for your visit. Afterward follow rue du Vieille Temple to rue des Rosiers and pick up lunch from **Florence Finkelsztajn** or **Jo Goldenberg** (see Chapter 14). Browse the stores here and on rue des Francs Bourgeois, then explore the wonderful **Centre Georges Pompidou.** Afterward, jump on the Métro and head for Père Lachaise. Spend the afternoon searching out **Cimitière Père Lachaise**'s famous residents with the 10F ($1.45) map (it's the best one) sold outside the gates on bd. de Ménilmontant. After, take the Métro to Abbesses. Walk down rue Tardieu to the base of **Sacré-Coeur.** Take the funicular (one Métro ticket) to the top, then spend 15–20 minutes inside Sacré-Coeur before climbing to its dome. After climbing down, head behind the church to the **place du Tertre,** to see how much it still resembles the picture painted of it by van Gogh. Artists may ask to paint your picture and some can be quite persuasive; just politely tell them *"non, merci."* Even though the cafés are picturesque — and more expensive — save your appetite for **Au Poulbot Gourmet,** 39 rue Lamarck (follow rue Lamarck down the hill to 39).

Spending Five Days in Paris

Spend the first three days as outlined in the "If you have three days in Paris" itinerary. Add the **Conciergerie** to your tour of Ile de la Cité; the entrance is on the Seine side of the Palais de Justice.

On **Day Four,** visit **Versailles.** On **Day Five,** take the Métro to Opéra to visit the stunning and newly-renovated **Opéra Garnier** with its mural by Marc Chagall. Cash the last of your traveler's checks at nearby **American Express,** then head over to bd. Haussmann where you can shop the rest of the afternoon away at department stores **Au Printemps** and **Galeries Lafayette.** The sixth floor cafeteria at Galeries Lafayette offers plenty of lunch or dinner choices, from a salad bar to grilled steaks and dessert.

Itineraries for Families with Kids

These itineraries take into account short attention spans, so restaurants listed tend to be on the fast-food side. I haven't broken these down into day-by-day schedules, because your kids probably have varying (and, if more than one, probably competing) interests. So feel free to mix-and-match.

Version One

Climb the **Eiffel Tower;** then cross over the Champs de Mars to visit **Napoleon's Tomb** and the **Musée de l'Armée** at **Invalides.** Afterward cross the Pont Alexandre III and pay a visit to the kid–friendly science museum, **Palais de la Découverte.** You should be more than ready to eat, and you have your pick of places on the Champs-Elysées. **Lina's Sandwiches,** 8 rue Marbeuf, is a nearby inexpensive, and delicious, choice. After lunch, continue walking up the Champs-Elysées until you face the **Arc de Triomphe.**

 Never cross the traffic circle to get to the Arc; make sure you use the pedestrian tunnel. Climb to the top and watch 12 lanes of traffic converge around the circle below. Afterward take Bus no. 83 from the Friedland-Haussmann stop across the traffic circle to the **Jardin du Luxembourg,** Parisians' favorite park. Exit the park on bd. St-Germain or bd. St-Michel for some quick shopping before having dinner at one of the many restaurants in the area. You get an authentic French meal in upscale surroundings at **Chez Maître Paul,** 12 rue Monsieur-le-Prince (see Chapter 14, "Paris's Best Restaurants.") For something a little less fancy, try **À la Bonne Crêpe,** 11 rue Grégoire-de-Tours (see Chapter 14).

Version 2

Take half of a **Canauxrama** boat trip (if they're restless or very young, your kids won't stand for more) to **Parc de la Villette,** and cross over the pedestrian bridge to visit the **Cité des Sciences et de l'Industrie.** Try to catch one of the six short films shown on the giant **Géode** screen on the grounds. Afterward, grab lunch in the complex's cafeteria, restaurant chains **Hippo** or **Quick,** or from one of the vendors in the park grounds, and watch your kids tackle the giant dragon sliding board and explore the submarine. Then, cross the pedestrian bridge to the other side where your small kids can enjoy kiddie rides, and your bigger ones can enjoy the **Musée de la Musique.** Afterward, take the Métro to the **Buttes-Chaumont** stop and admire the waterfalls, cliffs, and cave with stalactites and stalagmites (all man-made) of the park with the same name. Then have an early and light dinner — you may be too tired to pay attention to what you're eating!

Version 3

Bring a picnic lunch with you, then take the Métro to Porte Dorée and follow the signs for the **Bois de Vincennes**. Rent a bike to explore the park's extensive grounds, or rent a canoe, and lazily take in the lush surroundings. Have lunch near the cave crowned by a pseudo–Greek temple. Afterward walk over to the **Parc Zoologique** on av. St-Maurice and spend a few hours observing the animals in very natural settings. Your kids may want to climb a neat futuristic observation tower from which they get a great view of the animals, park, and surrounding city. Afterward, hop on the Métro for the Château de Vincennes stop. After a tour of the *chateau,* head over to the **Parc Floral,** which has a great playground, a butterfly garden, and a large amphitheatre where jazz musicians play on summer Saturdays. Then get on the Métro and shoot over to Châtelet. Walk over the Pont au Change and head for the Ile St-Louis's best ice cream shop, **Berthillon.** If you have any energy left, try taking one of the nearby Seine boat tours from Vedettes Pont Neuf, moored next to Pont Neuf, or take a Batobus from the Notre-Dame stop.

Indulging in an Itinerary for Shopaholics

For more on the stores I list here, see Chapter 19.

Begin at **Galeries Lafayette** on bd. Haussmann. If you haven't received a 10-percent discount coupon from your hotel or travel agent, get one at the Welcome Desk on the main floor of the main store (make sure you have your passport with you). The women's clothes on the second and third floors of the main building are worth browsing. A **Lina's**

Sandwiches is on the third floor, sushi on the fifth, but I recommend the sixth-floor cafeteria for a break or lunch — the choices are appetizing and the views over the rooftops of Paris are particularly good. The **Galeries Lafayette Men's** store is right next door; after you've had your fill of picking out presents for him, visit the mezzanine-level **Lafayette Gourmet,** one of Paris's better grocery stores. Their wine cave has a nice selection, and they ship your purchases home for you.

After you finish with Galeries Lafayette, walk down the block to **Au Printemps.** Again, stop in at the Welcome desk in the main store for your 10-percent discount coupon. Its home furnishings store, **Printemps Maison,** has three floors filled with beautiful objects — if you're here in January or July you might even get a great bargain. You can also catch a fashion show under the art nouveau dome here on Tuesdays and Fridays, from March to October at 10 a.m. If you couldn't find that special present for the man in your life at Galeries Lafayette, stop in at Au Printemps's men's store, **Brummell,** behind the main store. You can take a food break at **Café Flo** on the sixth floor of the main store, or have tea from one of Paris's premier tea salons, **Ladurée,** on the first floor.

If you're not "department-stored-out," you still have **Marks & Spencer** and **C&A** to explore. They're both across from Au Printemps and Galeries Lafayette on bd. Haussmann. Marks & Spencer is a branch of the British store, so if you're British, you probably want to skip it in favor of the lower-priced (and quality) clothing at C&A. If you're American, however, Marks & Spencer carries all the items that Brits can't live without, from the St. Michael's clothing line, to the food in the grocery store on the main floor. From C&A walk over to the place de la Madeleine (take a left at rue Tronchet) where you find gourmet food paradise, **Fauchon.** With the Madeleine behind you, keep an eye out for **Gucci.** This is where the rue du Faubourg St-Honoré is, and you can window shop, or really shop, the rest of your day away at couture stores from **Ferragamo** to **Gianni Versace.**

Strolling along the Seine

The Seine River is called the loveliest avenue in Paris, where flower vendors, seed merchants, and booksellers line the parapets, and some of the city's most important attractions, can be viewed at their best. This tour tells you how to best stroll the Seine's Left Bank from its edge, with occasional forays to the sidewalks and monuments above.

With your back to place du Louvre, facing the Seine, turn right and walk along the **Quai du Louvre.** When you come to the bridge on the quay, cross the **Passerelle des Arts,** a pedestrian bridge over the Seine which connects the Institut de France and the Louvre. You have great views of the Louvre, Sainte-Chapelle, and, in the distance, the spires of Notre-Dame. You emerge onto the: **Quai de Conti,** on the Left Bank.

Bypassing the Institut de France, head left along the river. The *bouquinistes* you see selling old books and magazines, posters, and cards, are a Paris tradition — they've had their stalls along the Seine for almost 400 years. You see stairs on your left leading down to the riverbank. Ahead of you is the **Pont Neuf,** the most famous and oldest bridge in Paris, begun in 1578 and completed in 1607. Continue along the river, where you see stairs leading up to the **Quai des Grands-Augustins,** constructed by Philip the Fair in 1313, making it Paris's oldest quay. Picasso had his studio nearby at 7 rue des Grands-Augustins, where he painted *Guernica,* as is noted on the plaque. Continue along the river to the **Pont St-Michel,** whose initial N is not for Pont Neuf, as many erroneously believe, but for Napoléon, under whose reign the bridge was constructed. Stairs lead up to the place St-Michel, where you can browse shops on the bd. St-Michel or grab a quick bite at one of many restaurants. This was where some of the most bitter fighting occurred against the Nazis in 1944; it again became a scene of turmoil during the student riots in the May Revolution of 1968.

At this point, the promenade becomes the quai St-Michel. You pass under the Petit Pont, and then stairs lead to **L'Église St-Julien-le-Pauvre,** behind the Square René Viviani. The oldest tree in Paris is here, a false acacia planted in 1601. The church was begun in the twelfth century, renovated in the sixteenth century, and completely restored in the nineteenth century, when it was given over to the Greek Orthodox church. To the right of the entrance you find a medieval iron wellhead and two paving stones from the Roman road to Orléans. Inside, a wooden screen hung with icons encloses the beautiful chancel.

Continue along quai de Montebello, with its spectacular views of Notre-Dame.

You can see three barges *(peniches)* along quai de Montebello that have been turned into open-air restaurants that are good for quick or leisurely drinks, snacks, and meals, and they each present concerts at night.

The next set of stairs leads to **Rue Haut Pavé,** across the quai de Montebello. The narrow streets that branch off from this spot take you through a particularly quiet and attractive part of the Latin Quarter. Ahead of you is the Pont de l'Archevêché, a good place for a rear-view photo of Notre-Dame. Continue along the **Quai de la Tournelle,** which used to be a port handling hay, wood, and coal. Ahead of you is the **Pont de la Tournelle,** one of the newest bridges of Paris, dating from 1928. Its art deco statue is that of St-Généviève, the patron saint of Paris.

The quai de la Tournelle becomes the quai St-Bernard after the Pont de Sully. The banks have been turned into a sculpture garden, the **Musée de la Sculpture en Plein Air,** with plenty of benches on which to rest and admire the view across the Seine. The large glass structure looming over the garden is the **Institut du Monde Arabe,** which houses a museum of Muslim civilization, and a few meters down from this is the menagerie and the entrance of the **Jardin des Plantes.** Ahead of you and on the other side of the river is the Bercy neighborhood, Paris's latest urban renewal project. After strolling through the Jardin des Plantes and/or visiting the Institute du Monde Arabe, backtrack to the stairs leading to the **Pont de Sully,** which dates from 1876 and cuts across Ile St-Louis to the Right Bank. This is a good opportunity to walk along the Ile St-Louis quay. When you cross onto the Ile St-Louis, notice on the left the **Hôtel Lambert,** 2 quai d'Anjou, where Voltaire once lived with his mistress. Turn left onto the **quai d'Anjou.** At no. 17, the **Hôtel Lauzun** was home to Baudelaire and Théophile Gautier.

Turn left on rue St-Louis-en-l'Ile and visit **Berthillon,** 31 rue St-Louis-en-l'Ile (at rue des Deux-Ponts), the best ice-cream and sorbet parlor in France, with flavors such as Grand Marnier and mocha; lime and rhubarb. Return to quai d'Anjou, turn left, and walk along quai de Bourbon. Cross the Pont Louis-Philippe and turn left on the **Quai de l'Hôtel de Ville.** The Renaissance-style Hôtel de Ville (City Hall), and its massive esplanade dotted with fountains is on your right. Next, you arrive at the **Quai de Gesvres** and the Pont Notre-Dame, then the **Pont au Change** which was the designated money-changing spot in the Middle Ages. To your right is place du Châtelet. The quay now becomes the **Quai de la Mégisserie** where seed merchants and pet shops sell their wares. You have a good view of the Conciergerie and the Law Courts. Now you're back at the Pont Neuf, that landmark bridge. If you continue along, you return to the Louvre, where you began.

Chapter 21

Traveling Beyond Paris: Five Great Day Trips

●●●

●●●

*J*ust as you're getting used to Paris, I'm sending you out of the city. Don't worry, these adventures can all be done in a day; you should be back in time to grab a good dinner.

The Château de Versailles

When you first see the royal palace of Versailles (☎ **01-30-84-74-00; Internet:** www.chateauversailles.fr), you will not be able to take it all in — "incredible" doesn't do it justice. And it attests to the incredible privilege enjoyed by royalty during the 72-year reign of Louis XIV, who truly thought his greatness would be demonstrated with a château that would be the wonder of Europe. He hired the best: Louis Le Vau and Jules Hardouin-Mansart, France's premier architects; André Le Nôtre, designer of the Tuileries gardens; and Charles Le Brun, head of the Royal Academy of Painting and Sculpture, for the interior. Construction got underway in 1661.

In 1682, Louis XIV transferred the court to Versailles to live with him — in order to prevent plots against him. Historians estimate that anywhere from 3,000– to 10,000 people, including servants, lived at Versailles. When you realize that Louis XIV truly believed that all this over-the-top magnificence was simply his due, you may understand better the anger of the revolutionaries a century later.

Day Trips from Paris

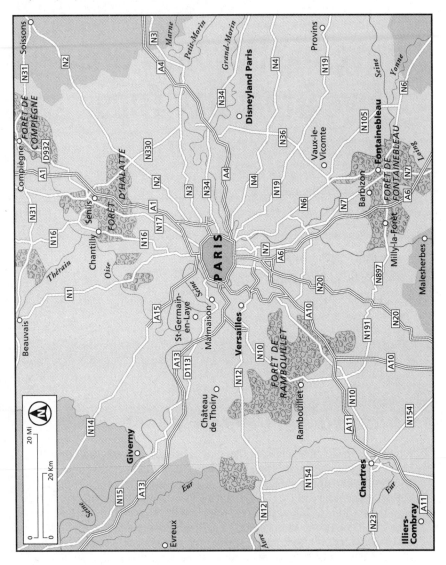

Louis XIV died in 1715 and was succeeded by his great-grandson, Louis XV, who continued the outrageous pomp and ceremony and made interior renovations and redecorations until lack of funds forced him to stop. His son and daughter-in-law, Louis XVI and Marie Antoinette, had simpler tastes and made no major changes at Versailles. But by then, it was too late. On October 6, 1789, a mob marched on the palace and forced the royal couple to return to Paris, and Versailles ceased to be a royal residence.

Louis-Philippe, who reigned from 1830 to 1848 and succeeded Louis XVIII, prevented the Château's destruction by donating his own money to convert it into a museum dedicated to the glory of France. John D. Rockefeller also contributed to the restoration of Versailles, and the work from that contribution continues to this day.

Exploring Versailles

After you've seen the Château, plan to spend at least an hour strolling through the **Formal Gardens.** Spread across 250 acres, Le Nôtre created a Garden of Eden, using ornamental lakes and canals, geometrically designed flowerbeds, and avenues bordered with statuary. Louis XV, imagining he was in Venice, used to take gondola rides with his "favorite" of the moment on the mile-long Grand Canal.

Due to the crowds and long lines, most guests are content to visit only the château and gardens, but you can see much more at Versailles if you've got the stamina. The most important of the remaining sights are the **Grand Trianon** and the **Petit Trianon,** both opulent love nests constructed for the mistresses of kings. A long walk across the park will take you to the pink-and-white-marble Grand Trianon, designed in 1687 by Hardouin-Mansart for Louis XIV. It has traditionally served as a lodging for the country's important guests, although de Gaulle wanted to turn it into a weekend retreat for himself. Napoléon I spent the night here, and U. S. President Richard Nixon slept in the room where Mme de Pompadour (a mistress of Louis XV) died. Gabriel, the designer of the place de la Concorde, built the Petit Trianon in 1768 for Louis XV. Its construction was inspired by Mme de Pompadour, who died before it was complete. So Louis used it for his trysts with Mme du Barry, his next mistress, instead. Marie Antoinette adopted it as her favorite residence, where she could escape the constraints of palace life.

Behind the Petit Trianon is the **Hamlet,** a collection of small thatched farmhouses and a water mill where Marie Antoinette could pretend she was a farmer, enchanted by the simple tasks of farm life. Near the Hamlet is the Temple of Love, built in 1775 by Richard Mique, Marie Antoinette's favorite architect. In the center of its Corinthian colonnade is a reproduction of Bouchardon's Cupid shaping a bow from the club of Hercules.

Between the Grand and Petit Trianons is the entrance to the **Carriage Museum,** which houses coaches from the eighteenth and nineteenth centuries, among them one used at the coronation of Charles X and another used at the wedding of Napoléon I and Marie-Louise. One sleigh rests on tortoiseshell runners. A ticket to the Petit Trianon also admits you to this museum.

Versailles

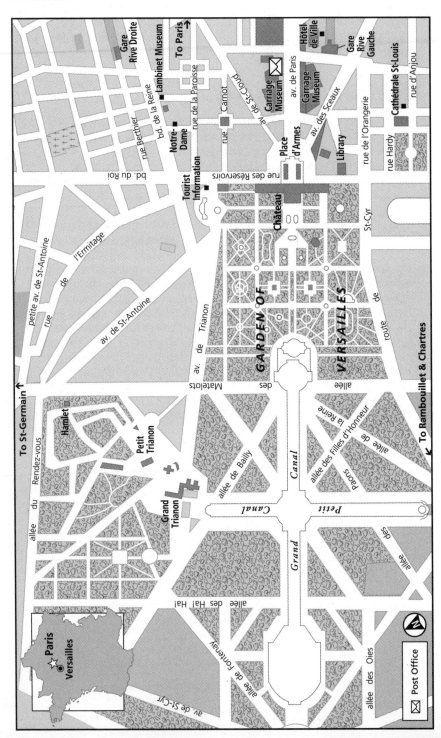

Admission to the palace is 45F ($6.45) for adults until 3:30 p.m., when the price drops to 35F ($5); 35F ($5) for ages 18 to 24 and over 60, and for all on Sunday. Admission to the Grand Trianon is 25F ($3.60), reduced to 15F ($2.15) after 3:30 p.m.; to the Petit Trianon, 15F ($2.15), lowered to 10F ($1.45) after 3:30 p.m. From May 2 to September 30, the palace is open Tuesday through Sunday 9 a.m. to 6:30 p.m.; the Grand Trianon and Petit Trianon are open the same days 10 a.m. to 6 p.m. The rest of the year, the palace is open Tuesday through Sunday 9 a.m. to 5:30 p.m.; the Grand Trianon and Petit Trianon are open Tuesday through Friday 10 a.m. to noon and 2 to 5 p.m., Saturday and Sunday 10 a.m. to 5 p.m.

Getting to Versailles

By car: Head west on the A13 highway from Porte d'Auteuil toward Rouen. Take the Versailles-Château exit, about 14 miles from Paris. Park in the visitors' parking lot at place d'Armes for 28F to 35F ($4 to $5). The drive takes about a half hour, but can take more than an hour in traffic.

By tour bus: Cityrama, 4 place des Pyramides, 1er (☎ **01-44-55-61-00;** Internet: www.cityrama.com) Métro: Palais-Royal– Musée du Louvre has different trips to Versailles ranging from 200 to 530F ($28.60 to $75.70); **Paris Vision,** 214 rue de Rivoli 1er (☎ **01-49-27-00-06;** Internet: www.parisvision.com) offers an all-day excursion leaving from Paris at 8:30 a.m. every day but Monday, for 390F ($55.70); price includes entrance ticket. **France Tourisme,** 33 Quai des Grands Augustins, 6e (☎ **01-53-10-35-35**), has a 195F ($27.90) tour that includes audio guides.

Where to dine

The town of Versailles has no shortage of places where you can break for lunch, but once you're on palace grounds, you may find it infinitely more convenient to just stay put — otherwise you have to hike back into town and back out to the palace again. Consider bringing a picnic, or try one of these other options. In the Château, you can eat at a cafeteria just off the Cour de la Chapelle.

In the Formal Gardens, you find an informal restaurant, **La Flotille,** on Petite Venise. (To get there from the Château, walk directly back through the gardens to where the canal starts. You see Petite Venise and the restaurant to your right.) Finally, several **snack bars** are located in the gardens near the Quinconce du Midi and the Grand Trianon.

The Palais de Fontainebleau

Fontainebleau (☎ **01-60-71-50-70**) contains more than 700 years of royal history from the enthronement of Louis VII in 1137, to the fall of the Second Empire in 1873. What this place is probably most famous for, however, is Napoléon's farewell to his Imperial Guard, which he delivered on the grand curved stairway before leaving for exile. If you get tired of the palace's splendor, you can walk around the beautiful gardens and then rent bikes to ride in the 42,000 acres of the kings' old hunting grounds, the Forêt de Fontainebleau.

Exploring Fontainebleu

François I transformed a run-down royal palace into Fontainebleau in 1528 for his mistress, and his successor, Henri II, left a beautiful memorial to the woman he loved, a **ballroom** decorated with the intertwined initials of his mistress, Diane de Poitiers and himself. The Mona Lisa once hung here; François I bought the painting from da Vinci, himself. Stucco-framed paintings now hanging in the **Gallery of François I** include *The Rape of Europa,* and depict mythological and allegorical scenes related to the king's life.

Make sure to see the racy ceiling paintings above the **Louis XV Staircase.** Originally painted for the bedroom of a duchess, the stairway's architect simply ripped out her floor and used her bedroom ceiling to cover the stairway. One fresco depicts the Queen of the Amazons climbing into Alexander the Great's bed.

When Louis XIV ascended to the throne, Fontainebleau was largely neglected because of his preoccupation with Versailles, but it found renewed glory under Napoléon I. You can walk around much of the palace on your own, but most of the Napoleonic Rooms are accessible only on guided tours, which are in French. Napoleon had two bed chambers; mirrors adorn either side of his bed in the grander chamber (look for his symbol, a bee), while a small bed is housed in the aptly named **Small Bedchamber.** A red and gold throne with the initial N is displayed in the **Throne Room.** You can also see Napoléon's **offices** where the emperor signed his abdication, though the document exhibited is only a copy.

After a visit to the palace, wander through the gardens, paying special attention to the lovely, bucolic carp pond with its fearless swans. If you'd like to promenade in the forest, a detailed map of its paths is available for 35F ($5) from the **Office de Tourisme** (4, rue Royale, near the palace; ☎ 01-60-74-99-99). You can also rent bikes nearby from **A la Petite Reine** (32 rue des Sablons; ☎ 01-60-74-57-57) for 80F ($11.45) a day, 100F ($14.30) on weekends with a credit card deposit. The **Tour Denencourt,** about three miles north of the palace, makes a nice ride and has a pretty view.

The Château de Fontainebleau is open Wednesday through Monday 9:30 a.m. to 6 p.m. in July and August; 9:30 a.m. to 5 p.m. in May, June, September, and October; 9:30 a.m.- 12:30 p.m. and 2- 5 p.m. November– April. Admission to the Grands Appartements is 35F ($5) for adults, 23F ($3.30) for ages 18– 24 and over 60 and for all on Sunday. Separate admission to the Napoleonic Rooms is 16F ($2.30) for adults, 12F ($1.70) for students 18 to 25 years old. Children under 18 years of age enter free.

Fontainebleau

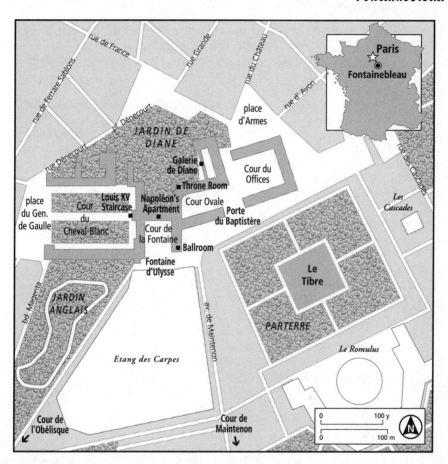

Getting to Fontainebleau

The Montargie line to Fontainebleau Avon station departs hourly from the Gare de Lyon in Paris. The trip takes 35 to 60 minutes and costs 47F ($6.70). Fontainebleau Avon station is just outside the town in Avon, a suburb of Paris. From the station, the town bus makes the two-mile trip to the Château every 10 to 15 minutes on weekdays, every 30 minutes on Saturdays and Sundays. The bus costs 8F ($1.15). By tour bus: Cityrama, 4 place des Pyramides, 1er (☎ **01-44-55-61-00;** Métro: Palais-Royal– Musée du Louvre) combines both Fontainebleau and the village of Barbizon for 335F ($47.90) per person.

Dining out

If you're arriving by train and only plan to visit Fontainebleau, consider bringing a picnic from Paris. In fine weather, the Château's gardens and the nearby forest beckon. But if you've got a car, save your appetite for Barbizon.

On the western edge of France's finest forest, lies the village of Barbizon, home to a number of noted landscape artists — Corot, Millet, Rousseau, and Daumier, among others in the nineteenth century. The colorful town has a lively mix of good restaurants, boutiques, and antiques shops — the perfect place to while away an afternoon.

For lunch, try the **Relais de Barbizon,** 2 av. Charles-de-Gaulle (☎ 01-60-66-40-28), whose 145F ($20.70) lunch menu features hearty, home-style dishes such as duckling in wild cherry sauce or braised lamb with thyme. The restaurant is closed for dinner Tuesday, and for lunch and dinner Wednesday. MasterCard and Visa are accepted.

The Cathedral at Chartres

The Cathédrale de Notre-Dame-de-Chartres (☎ **02-37-21-56-33**), one of the world's greatest Gothic cathedrals and one of the finest creations of the Middle Ages, comes second in importance to a majority of its visitors. Instead, a small scrap of material — said to be worn by the Virgin Mary when she gave birth to Jesus — draws the masses here.

Seeing the cathedral

Take one of the excellent guided tours (40F/$5.70) of the cathedral — especially those by Malcolm Miller, an Englishman (☎ **02-37-28-15-58**). He gives fascinating tours daily, except Sunday, at noon and 2:45 p.m. from Easter to November; he's sometimes available in winter as well. French-language tours of the crypt are given at 11 a.m. and 2:15, 3:30, and 4:30 p.m. (also at 5:15 p.m. in summer). The crypt tour costs 10F ($1.45) for adults, 7F ($1) for ages 18 to 24 and over 60.

A good time to visit is on Sunday afternoons when free organ concerts (4:45 to 5:45 p.m.) and the filtered light coming in from the western windows make the church come wonderfully alive.

The cathedral that you see today dates principally from the thirteenth century, when it was built with the combined efforts and contributions of kings, princes, church officials, and pilgrims from all over Europe. This Notre-Dame was among the first to use flying buttresses.

Notre-Dame de Chartres

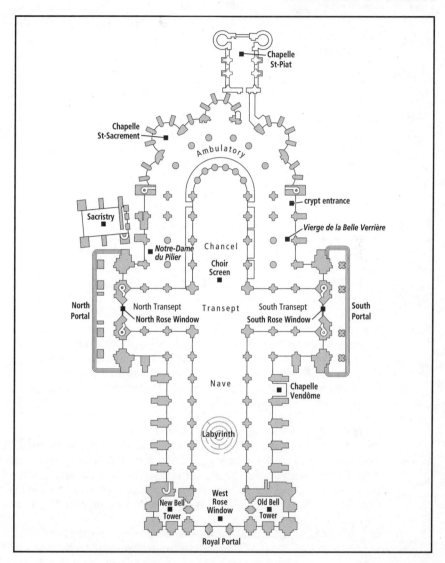

Begin at the beginning — with the **entryway.** People say that Rodin sat for hours on the edge of the sidewalk, contemplating the portal, spellbound by its sculptured bodies draped in long, flowing robes with amazingly lifelike faces. Before entering, walk around to both the north and south portals, which date from the thirteenth century. The bays depict such biblical scenes as the expulsion of Adam and Eve from the Garden of Eden, and episodes from the life of the Virgin.

Next, just inside, are the **Clocher Vieux** (Old Tower) with its 350-foot steeple dating from the twelfth century, and the **Clocher Neuf** (New Tower). Originally built in 1134, the new tower's elaborate ornamental tower was added between 1507 and 1513 following one of the many fires that swept over the cathedral.

You can climb to the top of the Clocher Neuf, but make sure your shoes aren't slippery — parts of the tower are without a railing and are quite steep and narrow.

The cathedral is also known for its celebrated **choir screen**. Don't let the term fool you; this is a carved wood structure that took nearly 200 years to complete. The niches, 40 in all, contain statues illustrating scenes from the life of Mary. The screen is in the middle of the cathedral toward the back.

Few of the rushed visitors ever notice the screen; they're transfixed by the **stained-glass windows**. Bring a pair of binoculars to better focus on the panes covering more than 3,000 square yards. The glass is unequaled anywhere in the world and is truly mystical. It was spared in both world wars because of a decision to remove it — piece by piece.

Most of the stained glass dates from the twelfth and thirteenth centuries. Many visitors find it difficult to single out one panel or window of particular merit; however, the oldest is the twelfth-century **Notre Dame de la belle verrière** (Our Lady of the Beautiful Window, sometimes called the Blue Virgin) on the south side. The colors from the glass are such a vibrant, startling blue, many find it hard to believe that the window is 1,000 years old.

Look down in the **nave** — the widest in France — at the thirteenth-century labyrinth. It was designed for pilgrims to navigate on their hands and knees as a form of penance, all 1,000 feet of it. These days, much of it is covered with fold-up chairs for mass. The **Sancta Camisia,** the holy relic that some people believe Mary wore during the birth of Jesus, is behind the choir screen in a chapel to the left of the church's treasury.

Entrance to the cathedral is free and is open daily April through September 7:30 a.m. to 7:30 p.m.; October through March 7:30 a.m. to 7 p.m. French-language tours of the cathedral are given in summer, Tuesday through Saturday at 10:30 a.m. and daily at 3 p.m.; in winter, daily at 2:30 p.m. Ask at the Chartres tourist office (☎ **02-37-21-50-00**) outside the cathedral for information about tours in English and a schedule of masses that are open to the public. From April to September, the tower is open Monday to Saturday 9:30 to 11:30 a.m. and daily 2 to 5:30 p.m.; October to March, Monday to Saturday 10 to 11:30 a.m. and daily 2 to 4 p.m. Admission to the tower is 25F ($3.60) for adults, 15F ($2.15) for seniors and students, and children under 12 are free.

Getting to Chartres

To get to Chartres **by train,** pick up one of the hourly SNCF trains from Paris's Gare Montparnasse to the town of Chartres. A round-trip ticket costs about 144F ($20.60); the trip takes about an hour.

By car: Take the A10/A11 highway from Porte d'Orléans and follow the signs to Le Mans and Chartres. The drive takes about 75 minutes.

By tour bus: Cityrama, 4 place des Pyramides, 1er (☎ **01-44-55-61-00;** Métro: Palais-Royal– Musée du Louvre) offers 5–hour excursions leaving from Paris every Tuesday, Thursday, and Saturday for 285F ($40.70).

Dining out

You can find plenty of restaurants, cafés and snack bars around town, but just a stone's throw from the cathedral is **Le Buisson Ardent,** 10 rue au Lait (☎ 02-37-34-04-66). The restaurant serves up well–prepared fare made with farm-fresh ingredients in a quaint, wood-beamed dining room. A variety of fresh fish dishes are available, though the roast pigeon with lemon juice, served with potato pancakes and fresh vegetables, is also recommended. *Calvados* (a cider brandy) is a specialty of the Normandy region, and for dessert, try the crispy hot apples with sorbet and Calvados-flavored butter sauce. Choose from three fixed-price menus, at 138F, 188F and 225F ($19.70, $26.90, $32.15). The restaurant is open daily for lunch, and Monday through Saturday for dinner. MasterCard and Visa are accepted.

If you have extra time, spend it by exploring the medieval cobbled streets of the **Old Town.** At the foot of the cathedral are lanes with gabled and turreted houses and humped bridges spanning the Eure River. One house, on rue Chantault, dates back nine centuries.

Stop in to the **Musée de Beaux-Arts de Chartres,** 29 Cloître Notre-Dame (☎ 02-37-36-41-39) to see paintings by old masters such as Watteau, Brosamer, and Zurbarán. The museum is open Wednesday through Monday, 10 a.m. to noon, and 2 to 5 p.m. Admission is 10F ($1.45).

Disneyland Paris

Disneyland Paris (☎ 01-64-74-30-00) opened in 1992 to much contro-versy (Remember how much resistance there once was to the park?). It may be hard to imagine, but it's now France's No. 1 attraction, with more than 50 million visitors a year — 40 percent of them French, and half of those Parisian. Set on a 5,000-acre site (about one-fifth the size of Paris) in the suburb of Marne-la-Vallée, the park incorporates the ele-ments of its Disney predecessors but gives them a European flair. Allow a full day to see Disneyland Paris.

Exploring the park

The Disneyland Paris resort is conceived as a total vacation destination, clustering together five "lands" of entertainment (Main Street, U.S.A; Frontierland; Adventureland; Fantasyland; and Discoveryland), six massive and well-designed hotels, a campground, a nightlife center (Le Festival Disney), swimming pools, tennis courts, and a 27-hole golf course, as well as dozens of restaurants, shows, and shops. The latest attraction is Space Mountain, which sends riders on a virtual journey from the earth to the moon through the Milky Way.

If your kids are under 7 years old, they'd be best suited for Main Street, U.S.A.; Fantasyland; Sleeping Beauty's Castle; and the afternoon parade. Children 7 through 12 years old will enjoy Frontierland, the Phantom Manor ghost house, the Big Thunder Mountain roller coaster, Adventureland, Indiana Jones and the Temple of Doom roller coaster, and the Pirates of the Caribbean ride. Teens will like Discoveryland, the Space Mountain roller coaster, and the Star Tours simulated spacecraft ride.

Guided tours in English cost 45F ($6.45) for adults, 35F ($5) for children aged 3 to 11 years old. Tours last 3½ hours, and group size is generally 20 or more. The tours offer one of the best opportunities for a complete visit. Ask at the information desk for details.

Admission to the park for one day is 210F ($30) for visitors over 11 years old, 170F ($24.30) for children 4 to 11 years of age, children under four enter free. Admission for two days is 385F ($55) adults, 330 ($47.15) children. Off-season (early November to late March) prices for one day are 160F ($22.90) adults, 130F ($18.60) children; 310F ($44.30) and 250F ($35.70), respectively, for two days. Entrance to Le Festival Disney (the consortium of shops, dance clubs, and restaurants) is free; a cover charge is usually in order for the dance clubs.

Disneyland Paris is open June 12 to September 12, daily 9 a.m. to 11 p.m.; September 13 to June 11, Monday to Friday 10 a.m. to 6 p.m., and Saturday and Sunday 9 a.m. to 8 p.m. Hours vary with the weather and season, so call ☎ 01-64-74-30-00 before setting out.

 Wheelchairs and children's strollers can be rented for 30F ($4.30) per day, with a 50F ($7.15) deposit. For more information, contact the Disneyland Paris Guest Relations office, in City Hall on Main Street, U.S.A. (☎ 01-64-74-30-00).

Getting to Disneyland Paris

To get to Disneyland Paris

By train: Take the RER Line A from the center of Paris (Invalides, Nation, or Châtelet– Les Halles) to Marne-la-Vallée/Chessy, a 45-minute ride. The fare is 38F ($6.35) one-way or 76F ($10.90) round-trip. Trains run every 10 to 20 minutes, depending on the time of day. The station is at the entrance to the park.

By bus: Shuttle buses connect the resort's hotels with Orly Airport (every 45 minutes daily between 9 a.m. and 7 p.m.) and Roissy–Charles-de-Gaulle (every 45 minutes daily between 8 a.m. and 8 p.m.). One-way transport to the park from either airport costs 80F ($11.45). Within the park, a free shuttle bus connects the various hotels with the theme park, stopping every 6 to 15 minutes, depending on the time of year. Service begins an hour before the park opens and stops an hour after closing.

By car: Take the A4 highway east and exit at "Park Euro Disney." Guest parking at any of the thousands of spaces costs 40F ($5.70). A series of moving sidewalks speeds up pedestrian transit from the parking areas to the theme park entrance.

Staying at Disneyland

If you want to stay at Disneyland overnight or for a few days, you need to book well in advance. Plenty of hotels are available at different price levels, and you can explore the options and book accommodations on the park's Web site at www.disneylandparis.com.

Monet's Gardens at Giverny

Monet moved to Giverny (☎ **02-32-51-28-21**) in 1883, and the water lilies beneath the Japanese bridge in the garden, as well as the flower garden, became his regular subjects until his death in 1926. In 1966, the Monet family donated Giverny to the Académie des Beaux-Arts in Paris, perhaps the most prestigious fine arts school in France, which subsequently opened the site to the public. Giverny has since become one of the most popular attractions in France, but even the crowds can't completely overwhelm the magic.

Even before you arrive at Giverny, you likely already have some idea of what you're going to see. The gardens are usually at their best in May, June, September, and October. Should you yearn to have them almost to yourself, plan to be at the gates when they open. Plan to spend at least a half day at Giverny, longer if you plan to eat lunch and visit the American Museum.

The gardens are open April to October, 10 a.m. to 6 p.m. Tuesday through Sunday. Admission to the house and gardens is 35F ($5.85) adults, 25F ($4.15) students, 20F ($3.35) children 7 to 12; admission to the gardens only is 25F ($4.15).

Giverny: It's not just for Monet any more

It's estimated that at one point, more than 50 American artists lived in Giverny with their families, and you can see much of their work at the **Musée d'Art Américain Giverny** (☎ 02-32-51-94-65), just 100 yards from Monet's house and gardens. Some say Monet's influence was responsible for the influx of American artists into the village of Giverny in the late 1880s. Others say that Monet had little contact with the Americans, and it was Giverny's beauty that captured the hearts of painters like John Singer Sargent and William Metcalf, who began spending their summers there. The museum is open April to October 10 a.m. to 6 p.m., Tuesday to Sunday. Admission 35F ($5) adults, 25F ($3.60) students and others.

Getting to Giverny

To get to Giverny

By train: Pick up an SCNF train at the Gare St-Lazare in Paris approximately every hour for the 45-minute trip to Vernon, the town nearest the Monet gardens. The round-trip fare is about 134F ($22.35). From the station, buses make the three-mile trip to the museum for 12F ($2), or you can go on foot — the route along the Seine makes for a nice walk.

By car: Take Autoroute A13 from the Porte d'Auteuil to Bonnières, then D201 to Giverny. The whole trip takes about an hour.

By tour bus: Cityrama, 4 place des Pyramides, 1er (☎ 01-44-55-61-00; Internet: www.cityrama.com) Métro: Palais-Royal–Musée du Louvre has two trips to Giverny: a Tuesday through Saturday five-hour trip at 350F ($42.90), and Sunday or Wednesday all-day Giverny–Auvers-sur-Oise trip at 600F ($85.70) that includes lunch at the American Museum. Call for specific dates. **Paris Vision**, 214 rue de Rivoli 1er (☎ 01-49-27-00-06; Internet: www.parisvision.com) offers two trips: a Versailles-Giverny all-day trip on Tuesday, Thursday, and Saturday that includes lunch at the **Moulin de Fourges** for 795F ($112.90), and Tuesday through Sunday trip without lunch for 440F ($ 62.90) per person. **France Tourisme**, 33 Quai des Grands Augustins, 6e (☎ 01-53-10-35-35) has a 280F ($40) tour Tuesday through Sunday from March through October.

Dining out

Your entry ticket is no longer valid once you leave Monet's home, so think ahead about whether you want to eat lunch before or after your visit. Most people arrive in early afternoon, so crowds are slightly lighter in the mornings.

The square directly across from Monet's house, as well as the adjacent street, has many little cafés and crêperies. But if you're in the mood for more substantial fare, walk back to town and treat yourself to **Le Relais Normand,** an old Norman manor house with fireplace and terrace. It serves delicious dishes like Neufchâtel cheese in pastry, stewed beef à la Provençal, and young rabbit in green peppercorn sauce. The four-course, prix-fixe menu at 175F ($25) is the best deal in the house. The restaurant is open for lunch Tuesday through Sunday from 12 p.m. to 3 p.m. Visa and MasterCard are accepted.

Part VI

Living It Up after Sundown: Paris Nightlife

The 5th Wave   By Rich Tennant

"It serves you right for requesting a lap-dance from someone doing the can-can."

In this part . . .

Paris is just as fabulous after the sun sets as it is during the day. The city brims with culture — everything from French-language, English-language and avant-garde theater productions to ballet, opera and symphony. But beware! Events can sell out quickly. The Ménilmontant neighborhood is still a haven for bar hoppers, and more and more clubs are opening up in barges on the Seine. And you can always check out the overpriced can-can cabaret spectacles at venues like the Moulin Rouge, the Lido, and the Crazy Horse — even though Parisians wouldn't be caught dead at 'em, there's still plenty of healthy business from visitors. Chapter 22 gives you the lowdown on Paris's vibrant theater scene, while Chapter 23 previews the symphony, opera, ballet, and cabaret. Chapter 24 hits the clubs and bars with recommendations for hot jazz spots, live music venues, classy cocktail joints, *boites des nuits* (nightspots), and gay and lesbian clubs.

Chapter 22

The Play's the Thing: Paris's Theater Scene

• •

In This Chapter

▶ Saving money on tickets

▶ Attending the national theaters

▶ Tracking down English-language theater

• •

*T*he theater scene is alive and flourishing in Paris — but if your French is rusty or not up to par, you may want to consider alternatives to French-language productions. Fortunately, Paris is also home to thriving English-language companies. The city also stages many avant-garde productions in which language is secondary, or not spoken at all, so theater buffs should be able to find something that suits. In this chapter, find out where to go to save money on tickets, where to catch a classic performance, and the best spots for English-language theater.

Saving Money on Tickets

Theater lovers take note: On Thursdays, the four national theaters in Paris sell all seats for 50F ($7.15). For half-price theater tickets for all other venues (and for the national theaters the rest of the week), go to the **Kiosque-Théâtre** at the northwest corner of the Madeleine church (Métro: Madeleine) to buy tickets for same-day performances. The panels all around the kiosk indicate whether the performance is sold out (little red man) or tickets are still available (little green man). The Kiosque-Théâtre is open Tuesday through Saturday, 12:30 to 8 p.m., Sunday 12:30 to 4 p.m. A second branch of the discount-ticket counter is in front of the Gare Montparnasse. Try to arrive no later than noon, because lines are usually long.

Students may be able to pick up last-minute tickets by applying at the box office an hour before curtain time. Have your International Student Identity Card (ISIC) with you.

National Theater in Paris

The theaters listed here are "national theaters," supported by the government, but many private ones also exist. For full listings, consult *Pariscope.*

At the **Comédie Française,** 2 rue de Richelieu, 1er (☎ 01-44-58-15-15; Métro: Palais-Royal– Musée du Louvre), the classic tragedies and comedies of Corneille, Racine, Molière, and other French playwrights, come alive in wonderful performances. Foreign playwrights, such as Shakespeare, weren't performed at the Comédie Française for nearly a century. These days, you can find a good mix of classic and modern works, and plays translated from other languages. If you don't understand very advanced French, chances are you won't enjoy the performances. Tickets are between 70 and 190F ($10 to $27.15); last-minute seats (on sale 30 minutes before start of performance) sell for 30F ($4.30).

For popular, contemporary plays, come to **Théâtre National de Chaillot,** place du Trocadéro, 16e (☎ 01-53-65-30-00; Métro: Trocadéro), part of the art deco Palais de Chaillot and located directly across the Seine from the Eiffel Tower. Tickets are 160F ($22.85) adults, 120F ($17.15) people under 26 years old, and 80F ($11.45) students.

If you like modern drama from around the world, **Théâtre National de la Colline,** 15 rue Malte-Brun, 20e (☎ 01-44-62-52-52; Metro: Gambetta), is the place to see it. Performances are from French and European names. The Petit Théâtre, located upstairs, has short plays and offerings from international theater's less famous and up-and-coming playwrights. Tickets cost 160F ($22.85) for adults, 130F ($18.60) for seniors, and 80F ($11.45) for students and people under 30.

Théâtre National de l'Odéon, place de l'Odéon, 6e (☎ 01-44-41-36-36; Métro: Odéon), is in a beautiful early-nineteenth-century building, and its row of columns overlooks a pretty semicircular square near bustling bd. St-Germain. Home of the Comédie Française until the Revolution, the Odéon is now very much a European stage. Tickets average from 30 to 180F ($4.30 to $25.70) and usually go on sale two weeks before performance.

English-Language Theater

Summer is a good time to catch English-language theater in Paris. Try the **Théâtre de Nesle,** 8 rue de Nesle, 6e (☎ 01-46-34-61-04; Métro: St-Michel) or the **Théâtre des Déchargeurs,** 3 rue des Déchargeurs, 1er (☎ 01-42-36-00-02; Métro: Châtelet).

Or, for comedy in English, try **Laughing Matters,** in the historic Hôtel du Nord, 102 quai de Jemmapes, 10e (☎ 01-53-19-98-98; Métro: Jacques Bonsergent). This company is thriving; the lineups are always terrific, featuring award-winning comics from the United States, the United Kingdom, Ireland, and Australia. Shows start at 8:30 p.m.; admission costs 100F ($14.30) at the door. (See also the sidebar "*Parlez-vous Anglais?* English-language theater in Paris," elsewhere in this chapter.)

Parlez-vous Anglais? English-language theater in Paris

On any given day, close to 100 theatrical productions may be going on in Paris and the surrounding area. However, without a firm grip on the French language — or at least the plays written by Molière — a night at the Comédie Française is likely to confuse more than entertain. What's a traveling theater fan to do? Fear not — English speakers of all types flock to Paris. Because Paris is just a hop, skip, and Eurostar Channel Tunnel train away from London, some of that city's finest actors have found their way across the Channel and into the city's English-language theater community, where they've joined up with American, Australian, and even some bilingual French *confrères* (colleagues). Productions may not be plentiful, but quality is high, and a wide range of styles are offered.

Your easiest (and cheapest) ticket is the weekly play reading at the **Café de Flore,** 172, bd. St-Germain, 6e (☎ 01-45-48-55-26; Métro: St-Germain-des-Prés). Every Monday night at 8:15, **Brava Productions** (☎ 01-45-56-01-03 or 01-48-28-00-46) rounds up a group of talented actors to present works by authors such as Tom Stoppard, David Mamet, and George Bernard Shaw. The evening is free, although you might end up paying $4 for a cup of coffee. The company also does full-blown productions in English at various theaters around town. Plays produced in their most recent season included *Love Letters, Waiting for Godot,* and *A Girl's Guide to Chaos.*

Those with a modern bent might check out **Glasshouse** (☎ 01-40-36-55-83), whose *Take the Fire,* a critically acclaimed adaptation of short Jean Cocteau texts, had an extended run last year. Other English-language theaters include **Dear Conjunction** (☎ 01-42-41-69-65), known for its interpretations of Harold Pinter; and **Paris Festival Theatre Company** (☎ 01-53-01-45-22), which performs musicals. You can find listings for English language productions in the *Paris Voice* or the *Time Out Paris* section of *Pariscope* — just be sure to call the theater ahead of time to double-check the curtain time.

And don't forget — some theater is not meant to be understood. In fact, sometimes not understanding the language can actually be a bonus. Several well-known avant-garde theater companies are located in Paris, including **Les Bouffes du Nord** (☎ 01-46-07-34-50), run by the legendary Peter Brook, and **Le Théâtre du Soleil** (☎ 01-43-74-24-08), known for its stunning adaptations of both classics and original works. Even though these performances are usually in French, the scope of these productions is so large, and the visuals are so profound, you may not even notice that you haven't understood a single word.

— *Margie Rynn*

Chapter 23

The Performing Arts

In This Chapter

▶ Finding out the latest performance info

▶ Seeing the best opera and ballet

▶ Catching on to cabaret

*P*aris is a great place to pursue culture; the mega-expensive construction of the Opéra Bastille and the multimillion dollar renovations of the Opéra Garnier and Châtelet, home to Théâtre Musical de Paris, are just some examples of the interest its citizens take in enlightening themselves. Many performances sell out in advance. This chapter helps you find out what's going on and then get you there.

Finding Out What's Playing

Several local publications provide up-to-the-minute listings of performances and other evening entertainment. *Pariscope: Une Semaine de Paris* (3F/42¢), is a weekly guide with thorough listings of movies, plays, ballet, art exhibits, clubs, and more, and contains an English-language insert with selected listings. It can be found at any newsstand. *L'Officiel des Spectacles* (2F/30¢) is another weekly guide in French. *Paris Nuit* (30F/$5.10) is a French monthly that contains good articles as well as listings. You can pick up the free music monthlies, *La Terrasse* and *Cadences,* outside concert venues. The *Paris Free Voice* is a free monthly publication that spotlights events of interest to English speakers, including poetry readings, plays, and literary evenings at English-language bookstores and libraries.

You can also get information on the Web from the **French Government Tourist Office** (www.francetourism.com), the **Office de Tourisme et de Congrès de Paris** (www.paris-touristoffice.com), and the **Maison de la France** (www.franceguide.com). Try also **Culture Kiosque** (www.culturekiosque.com) for excellent magazine-style sites about opera and dance, including schedules, reviews and phone numbers for ordering tickets. The *Paris Free Voice* also has a Web site (http://parisvoice.com), featuring an events calendar and reviews of current opera, dance, and theater.

Ticket prices in this chapter are approximate; costs vary, depending on who is performing what on which day of the week. Call the theaters for information, or consult *Pariscope* and other entertainment listings. Many concert, theater, and dance tickets are sold through **FNAC** department stores as well as at the box office. You can find a dozen or so FNAC outlets throughout Paris; the most prominent is 74 av. des Champs-Elysées (Métro: George V). You can also reserve by phone (☎ 01-49-87-50-50) Monday through Friday from 9 a.m. to 8 p.m., Saturday 10 a.m. to 5 p.m. **Virgin Megastore,** 52 av. des Champs-Elysées (☎ 01-49-53-50-00; Métro: Franklin-D-Roosevelt), is another reputable ticket seller. The store is open Monday through Saturday 10 a.m. to midnight.

Attending Classical Music and the Symphony

Many classical music concerts occur throughout the year, and many of them are quite affordable. Look for flyers attached to most of the churches announcing schedule times, prices, and locations.

More than a dozen Parisian churches regularly schedule inexpensive or free (tickets between $20) **organ recitals** and concerts. Among them are **Notre-Dame** (☎ 01-42-34-56-10; Métro: Cité); **St-Eustache,** 1 rue Montmartre, 1er (☎ 01-42-49-26-79; Métro: Châtelet); **St-Sulpice,** place St-Sulpice (☎ 01-46-33-21-78; Métro: St-Sulpice), which has the largest organ; **St-Germain-des-Prés,** place St-Germain-des-Prés (☎ 01-44-62-70-90; Métro: St-Germain-des-Prés); the **Madeleine,** place de la Madeleine (☎ 01-42-77-65-65; Métro: Madeleine); and **St-Louis en l'Ile,** 19 rue St-Louis-en-l'Ile (☎ 01-46-34-11-60; Métro: Pont-Marie). In a less magnificent setting, the Sunday concerts at 6 p.m. at the **American Church,** 65 quai d'Orsay (☎ 01-47-05-07-99; Métro: Invalides), are friendly and inviting.

Free concerts are staged occasionally in the parks and gardens. (See Chapter 2 for a calendar.) Call ☎ 01-40-71-75-95 for information. **Maison de la Radio,** 116 av. du President Kennedy, 16e (☎ 01-56-40-15-16), offers free tickets to recordings of some concerts. Tickets are available on the spot an hour before the recording starts. The **Conservatoire National de Musique** at the Cité de la Musique, 209 av. Jean Jaurés, 19e (☎ 01-40-40-46-46), also stages free concerts and ballets performed by students at the conservatory.

The concert hall **Salle Pleyel**, 252 rue du Faubourg-St-Honoré, 8e (☎ 01-45-61-53-00; Métro: Ternes), holds programs throughout the year, including the Agora music festival during the month of June, sponsored by IRCAM (*Institut de Recherche et Coordination Acoustique/Musique*), which highlights a particular sound each night.

Tickets are 50 to 400F ($7.15–$57.15). Salle Pleyel is the official concert hall of the Orchestre de Paris, which performs from September to the end of June. The hall also welcomes internationally renowned orchestras and soloists. Major events for the 2000-2001 season included Brahms' Requiem and a recital by pianist Christian Zimmerman.

Seeing Opera and Ballet

The 2001 season offers operas such as Othello, Falstaff, and the Verdi requiem, and ballets choreographed by Pina Bausch and Charles Jude at **Châtelet, Théâtre Musical de Paris,** 1 place du Châtelet, 1e (☎ **01-40-28-28-40;** Internet: www.chatelet-theatre.com; Métro: Châtelet). Tickets for opera and ballet range from 70 to 670F ($10 to $95.70); tickets for concerts and recitals are 30 to 595F ($4.30 to $85). The box office is open daily 11a.m. to 7p.m. You can also check out the concert series performed on Mondays, Wednesdays, and Fridays at 12:45 p.m. for only 55F ($7.85).

The radiant, recently cleaned **Palais Garnier,** place de l'Opéra, 9e (☎ **08-36-69-78-68** for reservations; Fax: 01-40-01-25-60; Internet: www.opera-de-paris.fr; Métro: Opéra; RER: Auber), has a 2001 program schedule dazzling enough to match its brilliant new façade, with operas such as *The Magic Flute* and *La Clémence de Titus,* and ballets from choreographers Jerome Robbins and Jiri Kylian. Opera tickets are priced 30 to 670F ($4.30 to $95.70); dance tickets range from 30 to 395F ($4.30 to $95.70).

Although not as impressively *grand* as the Opéra Garnier, **the Opéra de la Bastille** offers first-class comfort, and magnificent acoustics at each level of the auditorium. The opera house is located at the place de la Bastille, 12e (☎ **08-36-69-78-68** for reservations; Fax: 01-40-01-16-16; Internet: www.opera-de-paris.fr; Métro: Bastille). *Nabucco, Tosca, Don Giovanni,* and *Parsifal* were just some of the operas scheduled here by the Opéra National de Paris for the 2001 season, as well as ballet favorites like *The Nutcracker* and *Romeo and Juliet* and some lesser known productions, including a feature on Flamenco dancing. Opera tickets can be bought for 45 to 670F ($6.45 to $95.70); dance tickets are priced 45 to 670F ($6.45 to $95.70).

The **Opéra-Comique/Salle Favart,** 5 rue Favart, 2e (☎ **08-25-00-00-58** for reservations; Fax: 01-49-26-05-93; Internet: www.opera-comique.com; Métro: Richelieu Drouot), offers magnificent shows in a turn-of-the-nineteenth-century building known as Salle Favart. Although the Salle Favart is smaller than its concert hall counterparts (the auditorium is so intimate that you can hear people whispering on stage), a new program by Jerome Savary promises highly entertaining shows. Tickets are priced from 50 to 370F ($7.15 to $52.85). The box office is open daily 11 a.m. to 7 p.m.

The **Ballet de l'Opéra de Paris** also schedules some performances at the Opéra de la Bastille. In both venues, reduced-price tickets for students and people under 25 or over 65 *may* be available at the box office 15 minutes before performance time, but most performances sell out far in advance.

Taking in an Evening of French Cabaret

Parisian cabarets had a reputation for sensual naughtiness long *before* Josephine Baker danced in a G-string adorned with bananas back in the 1930s, causing a stir throughout the city. Though the club names Lido, Crazy Horse Saloon, and Moulin Rouge conjure up images of performances by the likes of actor Maurice Chevalier and comedienne Mistinguett, the saucy cancan dancers draw in the crowds these days. The dancers are often overshadowed by light shows, special effects, and recorded music, but if you're expecting to see lots of flesh in today's Parisian revues, you won't be disappointed; breasts and buns abound. In fact, the rumor is that Crazy Horse dancers are chosen for the uniformity of their breast size.

When seeing a Parisian cabaret show, have dinner somewhere else and save yourself some cash. For the $35 to $45 you'd spend at the cabaret, you can have an absolutely fabulous meal at one of my pricier suggestions. (See Chapter 14.) Be aware that none of the cabaret shows is suitable for children, and that every other member of the audience may be from another country — these are some of the least "Parisian" experiences you can have while still being in Paris.

You find the sexiest acts at **Crazy Horse, Paris,** 12 av. George V, 8e (**☎ 01-47-23-32-32;** Métro: George V). Dancers, who have names like Chica Boum, Pussy Duty-Free, and Zany Zizanie, appear on swing seats or slithering and writhing in cages — you get the picture. Cover and two drinks cost from 290F ($41.45), with additional drinks from 100F ($14.30). Two shows nightly at 8:30 p.m. and 11 p.m.

At the **Lido,** 116 av. des Champs-Elysées, 8e (**☎ 01-40-76-56-10;** Métro: George V), award-winning chef Paul Bocuse designed the above-average menu, but you still should not pay the money to have dinner here. Its revue, *C'est Magique,* offers "flying" dancers, and an ascending stage that periodically delivers befeathered women, fountains, and an ice rink, as well as high-tech laser lighting and video projections. Other acts include a magician who does astonishing bird tricks. A seat at the bar is 385F ($55). The show with a half bottle of champagne is 560F ($80) Fri and Sat, and 460F ($65.70) Sun through Thurs (midnight show only). Dinner with a half bottle of champagne is 815F ($116.45). Two shows nightly at 10 p.m. and midnight.

Probably the most famous of the cabarets is the **Moulin Rouge,** place Blanche, Montmartre, 18e (☎ **01-53-09-82-82**; Métro: place-Blanche). The place has been packing in crowds since 1889, and singers such as Edith Piaf, Yves Montand, and Charles Aznavour made their reputations here. Its show, *Formidable,* features comedy, animal, and magic acts with the requisite scantily clad women bumping and grinding around the stage. A bar seat and two drinks cost 370F ($52.85) Sunday through Thursday; the revue and champagne costs 560F ($80) at the 9 p.m. show, and 500F ($71.45) at the 11 p.m. show. Dinner is available at the 9 p.m. show and costs from 790F ($112.85) to 990F ($141.45); you must arrive for dinner by 7 p.m.

Even the waiters get into the act at the **Paradis Latin**. 28 rue Cardinal-Lemoine, 5e (☎ **01-43-25-28-28**; Métro: Cardinal-Lemoine). A genial master encourages audience participation during a show that's less gimmick-filled than the others. To save money, forego dinner for the lower-priced Champagne Revue, which includes a a half bottle of bubbly and costs 465F ($66.45); dinner plus show packages range from 680 to 1,250F ($97.15 to $178.60). Performances are Wednesday through Monday, with a 9:30 p.m. showtime.

Chapter 24

Hitting the Hot Clubs and Bars

● ●

In This Chapter

▶ Getting the lowdown on the latest hot spots

▶ Searching out your kind of music and dancing

▶ Unwinding over cocktails

● ●

*W*hether you want to spend the evening chatting over cocktails, chatting up the beautiful people, or dancing till you drop, Paris has a bar or club for you. Paris may not be another "city that never sleeps" — witness the Métro closing at a mere 1 a.m. — but you can still live *la vie en rose* and paint the town a lovely shade of *rouge*. Bars usually close around 2 a.m., but most clubs don't open until 11 p.m., and the music doesn't stop pumping until dawn. Check the listings in *Night Life, Nova* magazine, or the English *Time Out Paris* section of the weekly *Pariscope* magazine for special theme nights at clubs.

Heading to the Hot Spots for Cool Jazz

The city's longstanding love affair with American jazz music dates back to the years between the world wars, when legions of African-American musicians fled segregation at home and came to Paris to perform. At the time, the Montmartre neighborhood was home to a number of thriving jazz clubs. The scene is still vibrant as new generations develop a taste for the sound. Look through the current *Pariscope* for the artists you admire. If you don't care who's playing, and you're just out for a night of good music, follow my suggestions.

A noisy crowd of foreigners and locals appreciates **Caveau de la Hûchette,** 5 rue de la Hûchette, 5e (☎ 01-43-26-65-05; Métro or RER: St-Michel) for what it is — a terrific time. Cover Sunday through Thursday is 65F ($9.30); Friday through Saturday, the price is 75F ($10.70). Music starts at 9:30 p.m. **Le Baiser Salé,** 56 rue des Lombards, 1er (☎ 01-42-33-37-71; Métro: Châtelet) specializes in fusion jazz and is a good value, too. Cover Tuesday and Thursday through Sunday varies from 50 to 80F ($7.15–$11.42), Monday through Wednesday is free admission. The club is open daily from 6 p.m. to 6 a.m.

The crowd is casual and down to earth, and the sound is some of the most interesting jazz around at **Le Duc des Lombards,** 42 rue des Lombards, 1er (☎ 01-42-33-22-88; Métro: Châtelet–Les Halles). Cover ranges from 80 to 120F ($11.45–$17.15). You can dine as well as drink at **Le Petit Journal Saint-Michel,** 71 bd. St-Michel, 5e (☎ 01-43-26-28-59; Métro: Cluny-La-Sorbonne, RER: Luxembourg) with its warm, relaxed, and French atmosphere. The Claude Bolling Trio visits regularly, as do the Claude Luter Sextet and the Benny Bailey Quartet. Cover (including a drink) is 100F ($14.30).

New Morning, 7–9 rue des Petites-Ecuries, 10e (☎ 01-45-23-51-41; Métro: Château-d'Eau), is one of Paris's best jazz clubs, and the best perform here, from Archie Shepp, Bill Evans, and Elvin Jones, to Kevin Coyne, and Koko Ateba from Cameroon. Cover is 120F ($17.15). **Slow Club,** 130 rue de Rivoli, 1er (☎ 01-42-33-84-30; Métro: Châtelet–Les Halles) is a self-styled "jazz cellar" favorite with big American and European artists who perform swing, Dixieland, and classic jazz. Cover Tuesday through Thursday is 60F ($8.60); on Friday and Saturday, cover is 75F ($10.70).

Listening to Live Music

If you love live music but don't have the time or money to get concert tickets, head to a bar known for great live gigs, usually for free. **The Chesterfield Café,** 124 rue La Boétie, 8e (☎ 01-42-25-18-06; Métro: Franklin D. Roosevelt), is the place to find up-and-coming or just-arrived rock and blues bands, as well as the occasional oldie. Alanis Morrissette, The Spin Doctors, and Eagle Eye Cherry have all played here. Concerts start at 11:30 p.m. You can also check out Sunday gospel at 2 p.m. Open 10 a.m to 5 a.m. daily.

Reasonable prices and an eclectic mix of world, jazz, and funk bands Wednesday through Saturday keep **Le Cithéa,** 114 rue Oberkampf, 11e (☎ 01-40-21-70-95; Métro: Parmentier), sizzling. A DJ spins whenever the bands aren't playing, and you have room to dance if the mood strikes. Cover is 60F ($8.55) Friday and Saturday, including two drinks. Open 9:30 p.m. to 5 a.m. daily.

World music acts reign at **La Divan du Monde,** 75 rue des Martyrs, 18e (☎ 01-44-92-77-66; Métro: Pigalle), with everything from Brazilian samba to British pop. Concerts start at 7:30 p.m. Monday through Saturday, and at 4 p.m. Sunday. On weekends a DJ spins music after the concerts. Call for closing hours.

Only two Métro stops from Père-Lachaise cemetery (take the 2 to Alexandre Dumas; see Chapter 16), **La Flèche d'Or,** 102 rue de

Bagnolet, 20e (☎ **01-43-72-04-23;** Métro: Alexandre-Dumas), is worth a visit on the weekend. Its live concerts on Friday and Saturday nights may be reggae, alternative rock, Celtic rock, or blues rock. Sundays at 5 p.m., a live dance band usually plays salsa or swing, and on other nights there could be, well, anything. This cavernous space — once a train station — pulls in a funky, artsy, racially mixed crowd. Open from 10 a.m. to 2 a.m. Tuesday through Sunday; 6 p.m. to 2 a.m. Monday. Cover ranges from 20 to 30F ($2.90–$4.30).

Getting Down: The Best Dance Clubs

Paris clubs change their programming from night to night. The current fad is salsa music, which suddenly seems to be everywhere. One fun addition to the club scene are the barges that are springing up in Paris's south, around the 13e arrondissement. Playing everything from house to blues, you can have a rip-roaringly good, though often crowded, time right on the Seine. Check the Time Out Paris section in *Pariscope* magazine (in English) for barge concert schedules. But whether you like dancing to techno, house, salsa, world, classic rock, or swing, you're sure to find it somewhere in Paris.

To club on a budget, go out during the week when cover charges may be (officially or unofficially) waived. Women often get in free, especially if they're dressed in something slinky, low-cut, short (or all three). Black clothes are *de rigueur* for men and women, and the later one goes, the more fashionable.

The Irish light ship (a boat that lights the path for other ships) *Batofar,* 11 quai François Mauriac, 13e (☎ **01-56-29-10-00;** Métro: Bibliothèque François Mitterand or Quai de la Gare), has concerts Tuesday through Sunday, starting around 8 p.m., and the party can go on all night. Drinks are reasonable, the clientele in their young 20s, and it can get crowded, but still a lot of fun can be had. Music can be anything from drum-and-bass to rock and happy house. Open Tuesday to Sunday, hours vary (check listings in *Pariscope*). Cover ranges from 20 to 60F ($2.90–$8.60), depending on the band or DJ for the night.

Well-dressed French yuppies make up the crowd at **Bus Palladium,** 6 rue Fontaine, 9e (☎ **01-53-21-07-33;** Métro: Pigalle), a club that used to play Motown, but now concentrates more on house and techno music. People who come here like to party, and everyone gets down as the night goes on. Cover on Tuesday is determined by gender — men pay 100F ($14.30), while women get in free with free champagne. No cover is charged Wednesday, but Thursday through Saturday, cover is 100F ($14.30)(including one drink). Open 11 p.m. to 6 a.m.

A festive tropical ambience and diverse music — everything from salsa to reggae — attract a lively crowd to **La Chapelle des Lombards,** 19 rue de Lappe, 11e (☎ **01-43-57-24-24;** Métro: Bastille), a hip, but cramped, club near the Bastille. To really enjoy this place, you have to dress the part, which means no sneakers or jeans, but rather your sophisticated best. Cover Thursday is 100F ($14.30), Friday and Saturday is 120F ($17.15). Open 10:30 p.m. to dawn.

La Coupole, 102 bd. du Montparnasse, 14e (☎ 01-43-27-56-00; Métro: Montparnasse-Bienvenüe), has a basement dance hall — a retro venue with plush banquettes and old-fashioned sounds — that's a big draw for out-of-towners. Come on Friday to hear the orchestra hum out some rhythm and blues. On Tuesday, salsa swings out the evening, with dance classes starting at 8:30 p.m. for 140F ($20, including a drink). Regular cover (including two drinks) on Sunday from 3 to 9 p.m. is 80F ($11.45); Saturday from 5 to 7 p.m. is 40F ($5.70) and from 9:30 p.m. to 4 a.m. 100F ($14.30)(including one drink); Tuesday from 9:30 p.m. to 3 a.m. is 100F ($14.30)(including one drink); and Friday 9:30 p.m. to 4 a.m. is 100F ($14.30)(including one drink).

La Guinguette-Pirate, quai François Mauriac, 13e (☎ 01-53-61-08-49; Métro: Bibliothèque François Mitterand or Quai de la Gare), is an old wooden boat that hosts world music concerts. A recent act was the Rageous Gratoons who played funky jazz and reggae. A lot of fun can be had, and the crowd is young. Cover is 20 to 60F ($2.90 to $8.60). Open sunset to 2 a.m.; occasional concerts are held on Saturday or Sunday at 3 or 5 p.m. (check *Pariscope*).

At **La Java,** 105 rue du Faubourg-du-Temple, 10e (☎ 01-42-02-20-52; Métro: Belleville), a diverse crowd comes to dance without restraint to mostly Cuban and Brazilian music, played by a live band on Friday and Saturday nights. If you have a taste for something fun, funky, and very authentic, and you like Latin music, this charming old dance hall may be your great night out. Salsa classes are held Thursday nights. Cover Thursday is 40F ($5.70); on Friday and Saturday the cover is 100F ($14.30) (including one drink). Open 10:30 p.m. to dawn.

The tri-level **La Locomotive,** 90 bd. de Clichy, 18e (☎ 08-36-69-69-28; Métro: place-Clichy), is popular with American students, and is especially busy on Sundays. People dance to rock and techno, though occasionally metal concerts are held. Graffiti art and psychedelic flowers decorate the walls. This is a very big place and in the lower level you can even see the remnants of an old railway line. Beers start at 25F ($3.60), drinks at 50F ($7.15). Cover Monday through Thursday and Sunday is 55F ($7.85) and 70F ($10), respectively (includes one drink); Friday's cover is 60F ($8.60) before midnight and 100F ($14.30) (includes one drink) after midnight; Saturday night the cover is 100F ($14.30) (includes one drink). Women get in free on Sunday before 12:30 a.m. Open 11 p.m. to 5 a.m.

Formerly one of the most famous rock dance clubs in Paris, **Le Gibus,** 18 rue du Faubourg-du-Temple, 11e (☎ 01-47-00-78-88; Métro: République), has changed its style. Artistic director Bitchy José books top-level DJs who spin house music to a predominantly, but not exclusively, gay crowd. Watch for the monthly "Queer Nation" and "Nuits Blanches" parties. Cover (includes one drink) is 100F ($14.30); entrance is free Wednesday nights. Open midnight to noon.

Queen, 102 av. des Champs-Elysées, 8e (☎ **01-53-89-08-90;** Métro: George V), is the busiest gay disco in Paris and one of the hottest clubs in town, with nightly crowds so thick you can find it difficult to get a drink. Clientele is about two-thirds gay, with the remaining third composed of attractive couples, models trying to escape the pickup scene, and straight men clever enough to have figured out where the beautiful women are. To get past stringent admission control at the door, it helps to have a great face and body, or at least the ability to disguise your faults with great clothes. Women usually get in only with male friends. Cover (including one drink, with or without alcohol) is 50F ($7.15) Sunday, Monday, and Thursday; Wednesday's cover (including one nonalcoholic drink) is 30F ($4.30); Friday and Saturday the charge (including one drink, with or without alcohol) is 100F ($14.30). Open daily midnight to dawn.

Kicking Back for Classy Cocktails

If you're looking for a quiet, romantic place to unwind with a drink — or if you're on the prowl for where the hip, hot, cutting-edge folks hang out — these places should fit the bill. Most bars and lounges in Paris open daily at 9 p.m., but no one arrives until after midnight. They generally close around 4 a.m.

At **Alcazar,** 62 rue Mazarine, 6e (☎ **01-53-10-19-99;** Métro: Odéon), elements of traditional brasserie style, such as banquettes and mirrors, are slicked up and mixed with innovations such as a glassed-in kitchen theatrically installed along the left wall. The comfortable upstairs bar is great for a view over the bustling downstairs restaurant. (See Chapter 14 for a review of the restaurant.)

At **Buddha Bar,** 8 rue Boissy d'Anglas, 8e (☎ **01-53-05-90-00;** Métro: Concorde), the music is spacey, the atmosphere electric, and you can see the prettiest people in Paris. A giant, impassive Buddha presides over the very un-Zenlike doings in this cavernous bar and restaurant. From the upstairs balcony you can observe the fashionable diners below, or mix with the swanky international crowd at the balcony bar. The point is to see and be seen, and then say you saw it. Drink prices start at 35F ($5).

The colonial decor at the atmospheric **China Club,** 50 rue de Charenton, 12e (☎ **01-43-43-82-02;** Métro: Bastille), just a few steps from the Bastille, is a perpetual draw. If you hate cigars, avoid the trendy upstairs *fumoir* (smoking room). All cocktails are well made (prices start at 40F/$5.70), but the Chinese food is overpriced.

Beautiful people dressed in black come to **La Fabrique,** 53, rue du Faubourg St-Antoine, 11e (☎ 01-43-07-67-07; Métro: Bastille), to be seen, drink at the minimalist bar, and eat the delicious Alsatian specialty, *Flammekueche* — large, square, thin-crusted pizzas topped with cream, herbs, and toppings of your choice, including salmon, ham, and goat's cheese. Although the bar is open until around 5 a.m., depending on the crowds, food is only served to midnight. Be ready to stand in line on the weekends, and look out for private parties when the restaurant is closed to the public.

Only a few steps from the now-passé Barfly (49 av. George V), **La Veranda,** 40 av. George V, 8e (☎ 01-53-57-49-49; Métro: George V), is the latest hot spot to target the fashion crowd. Glossy wood floors and paneled walls provide an unobtrusive setting for the glamorous clientele. Drink prices start at 70F ($10).

At **The Lizard Lounge,** 18 rue du Bourg-Tibourg, 4e (☎ 01-42-72-81-34; Métro: Hôtel-de-Ville), the music is loud, but the heavy-gauge steel balcony overlooking the main bar offers a chance for quieter conversation. This stylish but easygoing bar is a pleasant place to hang out with an arty, international crowd. You can also come early in the evening for a reasonably priced light meal prepared in the open kitchen. A DJ spins dance music in the refurbished basement Wednesday to Saturday.

Don't look for a sign — the entrance to **Man Ray,** 34 rue Marbeuf, 8e (☎ 01-56-88-36-36; Métro: Franklin-D-Roosevelt), is marked only by a Chinese character and big wrought-iron doors. The vast downstairs restaurant is dominated by statues of two winged Asian goddesses who appear concerned — possibly about the food. The upstairs bar area is spacious, and the music leans to jazz early in the evening. As the restaurant winds down around 11 p.m., the music takes on a harder edge, and a sleek international crowd stands shoulder-to-shoulder along the curving bar. American artist and photographer Man Ray's photos adorn several walls. Drinks start at 25F ($3.60).

Popular with Anglophone expatriates, **O'Sheas,** 10 rue des Capucines, 2e (☎ 01-40-15-00-30; Métro: Opéra), is busy every night with a mixed crowd that runs from stockbrokers to *au pairs* on their night off. Note that in addition to fine Irish and foreign brews, O'Sheas also serves excellent food in the first-floor restaurant. Drinks cost 25F ($3.60) and up.

Part VII

The Part of Tens

In this part . . .

*H*ere you find a few little extras that won't make or break your trip, but just might make it a little more fun. In Chapter 25, I tell you about ten places to go for a fabulous picnic — for natural beauty, for people-watching, for artistic opulence, or for all three. And in Chapter 26, I describe ten wonderful books that have Paris at their heart — books that will move you, thrill you, and inspire you to create your very own Paris adventure.

Chapter 25

Ten Great Places for a Picnic

● ●

In This Chapter

▶ Finding that special place to enjoy a meal in *plein air*

● ●

*P*aris abounds with parks and green spaces in which to picnic, and you can get delicious meats, sweets, and wine (see Chapter 15 for recommendations) from plenty of open air markets, *traiteurs* (gourmet food shops), and grocery stores. Try to make the time — you can take as long or as short as you'd like — and you won't need to worry about tipping, dressing to dine, or speaking the language once you've chosen your spot.

 A word of advice, however: Some parks, such as the Luxembourg Gardens or the Tuileries, jealously guard their lawns; you may have to walk a bit before you find a spot where you can spread out on the grass. But chairs are everywhere — some even have reclining backs! — and you can pull a few chairs right up to a fountain and eat amidst the spray from the water. If this seems too public, your best bet is to try the vast Bois de Vincennes or Bois de Boulogne where you can picnic nearly anywhere. Don't forget to clean up afterward.

Jardin du Luxembourg

The 6e arrondissement's **Jardin du Luxembourg** is one of the most beloved parks in Paris. You can sit on metal chairs near the boat pond or spread out on grass open to picnickers directly across from the Palais de Luxembourg, on the park's south edge. Not far from the Sorbonne and just south of the Latin Quarter, the large park is popular with students and children who love it for its playground, toy-boat pond, pony rides, and puppet theater. Besides pools, fountains, and statues of queens and poets, there are tennis and *boules* (lawn bowling) courts. See if you can find the miniature Statue of Liberty. (Métro: Odéon; RER: Luxembourg.)

Bois de Boulogne

A former royal forest and hunting ground, the Bois de Boulogne is a vast reserve of more than 2,200 acres with jogging paths, horseback riding paths, cycling (rentals are available), and boating on two lakes. The **Longchamp** and **Auteuil racecourses** are located here, as is the **Jardin Shakespeare** in the Pré Catelan, a garden containing many of the plants and herbs mentioned in Shakespeare's plays. (Métro: Porte Maillot, Porte Dauphine or Porte Auteuil.)

Bois de Vincennes

Rent canoes or bikes or visit the **parc zoologique** and petting zoo after your picnic on the extensive grounds at the Bois de Vincennes, which also has a Buddhist center, complete with temple, as well as the Chateau de Vincennes, where early monarchs like Charles V and Henri III sought refuge from wars. The **Parc Floral de Paris** (☎ **01-43-43-92-95**) is here with its spectacular amphitheatre (and jazz concerts on summer Saturdays), a butterfly garden, library, and miniature golf. (Métro: Porte Dorée or Château de Vincennes.)

Jardin des Tuileries

The Tuileries is a restful space in the center of Paris that houses the Orangerie and the Jeu de Paume at its western edge and plays home to 40 beautiful Maillol bronzes scattered among the trees to its east. This is the city's most formal garden, with pathways and fountains that invite you sit on the metal chairs provided and munch on picnic treats while cooling off in the breeze off the waters. The name means *tuiles* (tiles) — the clay here was once used to make roof tiles. The gardens were originally laid out in the 1560s for Catherine de Medici in front of the Tuileries Palace, which burned down during the 1871 Paris Commune. A century later, landscape artist André Le Nôtre, creator of the gardens at Versailles, redesigned a large section. (Métro: Tuileries or Concorde.)

Parc de Belleville

The Parc de Belleville is a wonderful place to visit with children, watch the sun set over western Paris, or nosh on a baguette with *saucisson sec* (cured sliced sausage, a bit like French salami). It has fountains, a children's play area, an open-air theater with concerts during the summer, rock formations, and grottoes that evoke the long-ago days when the hill was a strategic point to fight enemies like Attila the Hun. Beds of roses and other seasonal flowers line the walks, and views of the city's Left Bank become more pronounced the higher up the terraced pathways you go. Access the park by taking the rue Piat off rue Belleville and enter through an iron gate spelling out the words Villa Ottoz. A curved path leads you to tree-lined promenades (more than 500 trees are here) with the first of the magnificent Left Bank views peeping through the spaces between pretty houses. Take the Métro to Pyrénées; then walk down rue de Belleville and turn left onto rue Piat, where you see arched iron gates leading into the park. You can also take the Métro to Courrones, cross bd. de Belleville, and turn left onto rue Julien Lacroix where there is another entrance.

Parc des Buttes-Chaumont

Parc des Buttes-Chaumont is one of the four man-made parks Napoléon III commissioned to resemble the English gardens that he grew to love during his exile in England. Built on the site of a former gypsum quarry and a centuries-old dump, it features cliffs, waterfalls, a lake, and a cave topped by a temple. You have plenty of places to lay out your picnic spread here. (Métro:Buttes-Chaumont.)

Parc de la Villette

Picnic at Parc de la Villette in the summer while watching an outdoor movie or listening to a concert. Afterward, you and your kids can visit the children's museum, the **Cité des Sciences et de l'Industrie** (Museum of Science and Industry), and the **Musée de la Musique** (Music Museum), located on the grounds. This modern park has a series of theme gardens and includes an exotic bamboo garden and a garden featuring steam and water jets. Scattered throughout the park are playgrounds and other attractions (see Chapter 20). The most fun way to get here is to take a canal trip from Pont l'Arsenal or the Musee d'Orsay (see Chapter 18). You can also take the Métro to Porte de la Villette.

Parc du Champs de Mars

Once a parade ground for French troops, Parc du Champs de Mars is a vast green esplanade beneath the Eiffel Tower, extending to the École Militaire (Military Academy), at its southeast end, where Napoléon was once a student. You have plenty of places to relax and contemplate the tower. After your picnic, take a boat tour of the Seine from the nearby Bateaux Mouches. (Métro: Bir-Hakeim.)

Banks of the Seine near the Musée de Sculpture en Plein Air

Wander amid the sculptures before you spread out your meal in this waterside park that's really a museum (the name **Musée de Sculpture en Plein Air** translates to *Open-Air Sculpture Museum*). Twenty-nine artists created abstract works that compliment the meditative mood that the banks of the Seine inspire (kids will still climb all over them). Sculptures include *César* and *Zadkine*. (Métro: Sully-Morland or Gare d'Austerlitz.)

Parc Monceau

The painter Carmontelle designed several structures for Parc Monceau, including a Dutch windmill, a Roman temple, a covered bridge, a waterfall, a farm, medieval ruins, and a pagoda. Garnerin, the world's first parachutist, landed here. In the mid–nineteenth century, the park was redesigned in the English style. A favorite place for author Marcel Proust to stroll, the park contains Paris's largest tree, an Oriental plane tree with a circumference of almost 23 feet. (Métro: Ternes.)

Versailles

Imagine having a picnic in one of the world's greatest gardens. The gardens at Versailles, outside the city, are all that and more. Spread across 250 acres, they were laid out by renowned architect André Le Nôtre in 1661. At the peak of their glory, 1,400 fountains splashed, including those containing statues of Apollo, Neptune, and Latona (keep an eye out for the statues of people being turned into frogs). You see ornamental lakes and canals, geometrically designed flowerbeds, and avenues bordered with statuary, as well as the mile-long "Grand Canal." (See Chapter 21 for directions to Versailles.)

Chapter 26

Ten Great Books about Paris

- -

In This Chapter

▶ Some great fiction (and nonfiction) that will stay in your memory as long as your trip.

- -

*I*n keeping with the rules of this part of the book, I'm only naming ten books, but my list could easily contain three times as many. Scores of authors have lived (and still live) in Paris, and all have been enchanted by the city's charms (or in the case of George Orwell, its seedier side). As a result, you have countless terrific books to enjoy. This is a subjective list — I'm not saying these are the ten best books ever written about Paris; they're just an excellent place to start. I have listed them alphabetically by author.

A Tale of Two Cities, Charles Dickens

Set during the French Revolution in the late eighteenth century, this is a love story about a Englishman, Sydney Carton, who sacrifices his own life to save his French friend, Charles Darnay; Darnay is married to Lucie Manette, the woman Sydney loves. The book is perhaps best known for its famous opening lines: "It was the best of times, it was the worst of times . . ." The "two cities" Dickens refers to in the title are peaceful, quiet London and unstable, revolutionary Paris.

Paris Was Yesterday, Janet Flanner

This collection of articles comes from a *New Yorker* magazine writer who was there during the heyday of Hemingway and the "Lost Generation," between 1925 and 1939. Flanner wrote under the pen name "Genet," and she was more than a "fly on the wall" journalist; she became intimately involved in the Parisian scene she wrote about. There is lots of literary gossip and humor here, with the inside scoop on, among others, authors Gertrude Stein and James Joyce, singer Josephine Baker, actress Marlene Dietrich, and philosopher Jean-Paul Sartre.

A Moveable Feast, Ernest Hemingway

A chronicle of the author's years with his first wife, Hadley, in 1920s Paris, these stories encompass a whole cast of famed literary expatriates: F. Scott and Zelda Fitzgerald, James Joyce, Ezra Pound, T. S. Eliot, Gertrude Stein, and more. Hemingway describes everything so vividly — from his chilly writing studio on rue Cardinal Lemoine, to his marathon writing sessions at Closerie des Lilas — you may want to take the book with you to see whether his destinations still exist (many of them do). In the end, however, this book is a tribute to his love for Hadley. Written at the end of Hemingway's life and published with the permission of his fourth wife, Mary, after he committed suicide, the book exudes a palpable nostalgia for the happy, magical memories.

The American, Henry James

A *nouveau riche* American visiting Europe falls in love with a beautiful but impoverished Frenchwoman of nobility, shocking her family when he proposes. This novel of manners is wry and sometimes humorous, and a well-observed social portrait. The story takes place in late nineteenth-century Paris, giving the reader a feel for Paris of a bygone era. Readers will be happy that many sights James described in this novel still exist as they did then.

The Pleasing Hour, Lily King

A young American woman travels to Paris to be an *au pair* to a family with three children. But is she really fleeing something else? An evocative story about a young woman's search for a family and ultimately herself. Set mostly in Paris, the author realistically describes Paris and the life of some of its late twentieth-century upper class.

Honeymoon, Patrick Modiano

Set in the 1940s during World War II, this novel is about a documentary filmmaker who becomes fed up with his life and pretends to leave Paris on assignment. He remains in his neighborhood and reflects back to Paris of 20 years before when he met the love of his life.

Henry and June, Anaïs Nin

Anaïs Nin is known for the staggeringly comprehensive diaries that chronicle her life — and, famously, her sexual awakening — in the first half of the twentieth century. *Henry and June* tracks her fascination and affairs with both writer Henry Miller and his wife, June. You find terrific descriptions of the Montparnasse neighborhood in the 1930s. The book was made into a 1990 film starring Fred Ward and Uma Thurman as the couple in the title.

Down and Out in Paris and London, George Orwell

Many know George Orwell for his savvy political critiques *Animal Farm* and *1984,* but this, his first book, has a more autobiographical bent. An unemployed writer becomes one of the desperately poor of Paris and London in the 1920s, working as a dishwasher in a series of hotels and restaurants. A shockingly sad, funny, and scary look at society and poverty — a piece of Paris's less palatable past.

The Alice B. Toklas Cookbook, Alice B. Toklas

Gertrude Stein's lifelong companion packs this book with 300 recipes — including the one for her infamous hashish fudge — and intersperses her memories of the artists (Picasso, Matisse) and writers (Hemingway, James Joyce) who enjoyed her food. Even if you don't cook (and perhaps especially if you don't, because some of the recipes are quite challenging), Toklas's recollections are worth reading.

The Way I Found Her, Rose Tremain

Lewis, a young British teenager, travels to Paris's 8e arrondissement during the 1980s with his mother, who is hired to translate a romance novel for a Russian expatriate writer. The boy falls in love with Valentina, the writer. His mother, Alice, falls in love with a roofer. And when Valentina is kidnapped, Lewis takes it upon himself to solve the crime in this poignant mystery/coming-of-age tale.

Appendix A

Quick Concierge

• •

American Express: The grand Paris office, 11 rue Scribe, 9e (☎ 01-47-14-50-00; Métro: Opéra Chaussée-d'Antin or Havre-Caumartin; RER: Auber), is open weekdays 9 a.m. to 6 p.m. The bank is open 9 a.m. to 5 p.m. on Saturday, but the mail pickup window is closed.

ATM locators: ATMs are widely available; there is a bank on many a Paris corner. If you'd like to print out a list of ATMs that accept MasterCard or Visa cards before you leave home, ask your bank, or print out lists from the following sites: www.visa.com/pd/atm or www.mastercard.com/atm.

Baby-Sitters: Ababa, 8 av. du Maine, 15e (☎ 01-45-49-46-46), **Allo Maman Poule?,** 7 villa Murat, 16e (☎ 01-45-20-96-96), or **Kid Services,** 17 rue Molière, 9e (☎ 01-42-61-90-00). Specify when calling if you'd like a sitter who speaks English.

Business Hours: The **grands magasins** (department stores) are generally open Monday through Saturday 9:30 a.m. to 7 p.m.; **smaller shops** close for lunch and reopen around 2 p.m., but this is rarer than it used to be. Many stores stay open until 7 p.m. in summer; others are closed on Monday, especially in the morning. **Large offices** remain open all day, but some close for lunch. **Banks** are normally open weekdays 9 a.m. to noon and 1 or 1:30 to 4:30 p.m. Some banks also open on Saturday morning. Some currency-exchange booths are open very long hours; see "Currency Exchange," below.

Climate: From May through September you can expect clear sunny days and temperatures in the 70s and 80s. But be prepared for rainy or searingly hot summers, too. From late

October through April the weather is often gray and misty with a dampness that gets into your bones. Always bring an umbrella. Temperatures average about 45 degrees Fahrenheit in winter, and the low 60s in spring and autumn. Note: Ignore the song, "April in Paris," and pack layers for your early spring trip to the City of Light. It is often quite chilly.

Collect calls: For an AT&T operator: ☎ 0800-99-00-11; MCI: ☎ 0800-99-00-19; Sprint: ☎ 0800-99-00-87. See also Telephone, later in this Appendix.

Credit Cards: Visa, MasterCard, American Express, and the Diner's Club cards are all accepted in Paris, but not at all establishments. See also Lost Property later in this section.

Currency Exchange: Banks and *bureaux de change* (exchange offices) almost always offer better exchange rates than hotels, restaurants, and shops, which should be used only in emergencies. For good rates, without fees or commissions, and quick service, try the **Comptoir de Change Opéra,** 9 rue Scribe, 9e (☎ 01-47-42-20-96; Métro: Opéra; RER: Auber). It is open weekdays 9 a.m. to 6 p.m., Saturday 9:30 a.m. to 4 p.m. The bureaux de change at all train stations (except Gare de Montparnasse) are open daily; those at 63 av. des Champs-Elysées, 8e (Métro: Franklin-D-Roosevelt), and 140 av. des Champs-Elysées, 8e (Métro: Charles-de-Gaulle–Étoile), keep long hours. (See "Money" in Chapter 2 for exchange rates.)

Despite disadvantageous exchange rates and long lines, many people prefer to exchange their money at **American Express** (see the listing earlier in this Appendix).

Customs: Non-EU nationals can bring into France duty-free 200 cigarettes or 100 cigarillos or 50 cigars or 250 grams of smoking tobacco; 2 liters of wine and 1 liter of alcohol over 38.80 proof; 50 grams of perfume, one-quarter liter of toilet water; 500 grams of coffee, and 100 grams of tea. Travelers ages 15 and over can also bring in 1,200F ($171.45) in other goods; for those 14 and under, the limit is 600F ($85.75). **EU citizens** may bring any amount of goods into France as long as it is for their personal use and not for resale.

Returning **U.S. citizens** who have been away for 48 hours or more are allowed to bring back, once every 30 days, $400 worth of merchandise duty-free. You'll be charged a flat rate of 10-percent duty on the next $1,000 worth of purchases; on gifts, the duty-free limit is $100. You cannot bring fresh foodstuffs into the United States; tinned foods, however, are allowed.

Citizens of the U.K. who are **returning from a European Union country** have no limit on what can be brought back from an EU country, as long as the items are for personal use (this includes gifts), and the necessary duty and tax have been paid. There are guidance levels set at: 800 cigarettes, 200 cigars, 1kg smoking tobacco, 10 liters of spirits, 90 liters of wine and 110 liters of beer. **Canada** allows its citizens a $500 exemption, and you're allowed to bring back duty-free 200 cigarettes, 1.5 liters of wine or 1.14 liters of liquor, and 50 cigars. In addition, you may mail gifts to Canada from abroad at the rate of Can$60 a day, provided they're unsolicited and don't contain alcohol, or tobacco, or advertising matter. Write on the package "Unsolicited gift, under $60 value." All valuables should be declared on the Y-38 form before departure from Canada, including serial numbers of valuables you already own, such as expensive foreign cameras. *Note:* The $500 exemption can be used only once a year.

The duty-free allowance in **Australia** is A$400 or, for those under 18, A$200. Personal property mailed back from England should be marked "Australian goods returned" to avoid payment of duty. Upon returning to Australia, citizens can bring in 250 cigarettes or 250 grams of loose tobacco, and 1,125ml of alcohol. If you're returning with valuable goods you already own, such as foreign-made cameras, you should file form B263.

The duty-free allowance for **New Zealand** is NZ$700. Citizens over 17 can bring in 200 cigarettes or 50 cigars or 250 grams of tobacco (or a mixture of all three if their combined weight doesn't exceed 250 grams), plus 4.5 liters of wine or beer or 1.125 liters of liquor.

Dentists: You can call your consulate and ask the duty officer to recommend a dentist. For dental emergencies, call **SOS Dentaire** (☎ 01-43-37-51-00) daily from 9 a.m. to midnight.

Doctors: Call your consulate and ask the duty officer to recommend a doctor, or call **SOS Médecins** (☎ 01-43-37-51-00), a 24-hour service. Most doctors and dentists speak some English.

Drugstores: Pharmacies are marked with a green cross and are often upscale affairs that sell toiletries in addition to prescription drugs and over-the-counter remedies. If you're shopping for products other than drugs, it's almost always cheaper to buy them elsewhere, such as a *supermarché* (supermarket).

Electricity: The French electrical system runs on 220 volts. Adapters are needed to convert the voltage and fit sockets, and are cheaper at home than they are in Paris. Many hotels have two-pin (in some cases, three-pin) sockets for electric razors. It's a good idea to ask at your hotel before plugging in any electrical appliance.

Embassies/Consulates: If you have a passport, immigration, legal, or other problem, contact your consulate. Call before you go:

they often keep strange hours and observe both French and home-country holidays. Here's where to find them: **Australia,** 4 rue Jean-Rey, 15e (☎ 01-40-59-33-00; Métro: Bir-Hakeim); **Canada,** 35 av. Montaigne, 8e (☎ 01-44-43-29-00; Métro: Franklin-D-Roosevelt or Alma Marceau); **New Zealand,** 7 ter rue Léonard-de-Vinci, 16e (☎ 01-45-00-24-11, ext. 280 from 9 a.m. to 1 p.m.; Métro: Victor-Hugo); **Great Britain,** 35 rue Faubourg St-Honoré, 8e (☎ 01-44-51-31-02; Métro: Madeleine); **United States,** 2 rue St-Florentin, 1er (☎ 01-43-12-22-22; Métro: Concorde).

Emergencies: Call ☎ **17** for the **police.** To report a **fire,** dial ☎ **18.** For an **ambulance,** call ☎ **15,** or call ☎ **01-45-67-50-50** for **SAMU** (*Service d'aide médicale d'urgence,* or "emergency services"). For help in English, call **SOS Help** at ☎ **01-47-23-80-80** between 3 and 11 p.m. The main police station, 9 bd. du Palais, 4e (☎ **01-53-71-53-71;** Métro: Cité) is open 24 hours a day.

Holidays: See "When to Go," in Chapter 2.

Hospitals: Two hospitals with English-speaking staff are the **American Hospital of Paris,** 63 bd. Victor-Hugo, Neuilly-sur-Seine (☎ **01-46-41-25-25**), just west of Paris proper (Métro: Les Sablons or Levallois-Perret), and the **British Hospital of Paris,** 3 rue Barbes Levallois-Perret (☎ **01-46-39-22-22**), just north of Neuilly, over the city line northwest of Paris (Métro: Anatole-France). Note that the American Hospital charges about $600 a day for a room, not including doctor's fees. The emergency department charges more than $60 for a visit, not including tests and x-rays.

Information: Before you go: **French Government Tourist Office** (Fax: 212-838-7855; Internet: www.francetourism.com), 444 Madison Ave., 16th floor, New York, NY 10022-6903. This office does not provide information over the phone. When you arrive: **Office de Tourisme de Paris,** 127 av. des Champs-Elysées, 8e (☎ 08-36-68-31-12 2.23F/32¢min, or 01-49-52-53-35.)

Internet Access: To surf the net or check your e-mail, open an account at a free-mail provider, such as Hotmail (hotmail.com) or Yahoo! Mail (mail.yahoo.com) and all you need to check e-mail while you travel is a Web connection, easily available at Net cafés around the world. After logging on, just point the browser to your e-mail provider, enter your username and password and you'll have access to your mail.

The following Paris Web bars, listed by arrondissement, charge modest fees (25–60F/$3.60–$8.60 per hour) to their customers.

Cybercafé de Paris. 11 and 15, rue des Halles, 1er. ☎ 01-42-21-11-11. Métro: Châtelet.

CA&RI Télémation. 72-74, passage de Choiseul, 2e. ☎ 01-47-03-36-12. Métro: Palais Royal-Musée du Louvre.

Web Bar. 32, rue de Picardie, 3e. ☎ 01-42-72-66-55. Métro: République or Temple.

Café Orbital. 13, rue de Medicis, 6e. ☎ 01-43-25-76-77. Métro: Odéon, RER: Luxembourg.

TOPWIN Cyber Café. 10 rue Veronèse, 13e. ☎ 01-43-31-86-55. Métro: place d'Italie. (Charging only 25F/$3.60 per hour, this is one of the cheapest cybercafés in Paris. Also open Sundays.)

Laundry & Dry Cleaning: To find a laundry near you, ask at your hotel or consult the Yellow Pages under *Laveries pour particuliers.* Take as many 10F, 2F, and 1F pieces as you can. Washing and drying 6 kilos (13¼ lbs.) usually costs about 35F ($5.85). Dry cleaning is *nettoyage à sec;* look for shop signs with the word pressing.

Liquor Laws: Supermarkets, grocery stores, and cafés sell alcoholic beverages. The legal drinking age is 16. Persons under 16 can be served an alcoholic drink in a bar or restaurant if accompanied by a parent or legal guardian. Wine and liquor are sold every day of the year. *Be warned:* The authorities are very strict about drunk-driving laws. If convicted, you face a stiff fine and a possible prison term of two months to two years.

Lost Property: The central office is **Objets Trouvés,** 36 rue des Morillons, 15e (☎ 01-55-76-20-20; Métro: Convention), at the corner of rue de Dantzig. The office is open Monday, Wednesday, and Friday 8:30 a.m. to 5 p.m., Tuesday and Thursday 8:30 a.m. to 8 p.m. For Lost and Found on the **Métro,** call ☎ 01-40-06-75-27. If you lose your **Visa** card, call ☎ 08-36-69-08-80; for **MasterCard,** call ☎ 01-45-67-53-53. To report lost **American Express** cards, call ☎ 01-47-77-72-00.

Luggage Storage/Lockers: Most hotels will store luggage for you free, and that's your best bet, especially if you plan to return to Paris after a tour of the provinces. Otherwise, try the *consignes* at railway stations.

Mail: Large **post offices** are normally open weekdays 8 a.m. to 7 p.m., Saturday 8 a.m. to noon; small post offices may have shorter hours. There are many post offices (PTT) scattered around the city; ask anybody for the nearest one. Airmail letters and postcards to the United States cost 4.40F (65¢); within Europe, 3F (45¢); and to Australia or New Zealand, 5.20F (75¢).

The city's **main post office** is at 52 rue du Louvre, 75001 Paris (☎ 01-40-28-20-00; Métro: Louvre-Rivoli). It's open 24 hours a day for urgent mail, telegrams, and telephone calls. It handles Poste Restante mail: sent to you in care of the post office and stored until you pick it up; be prepared to show your passport and pay 3F (45¢) for each letter you receive. If you don't want to use Poste Restante, you can receive mail in care of **American Express.** Holders of American Express cards or traveler's checks get this service free; others have to pay a fee.

Maps: Maps printed by the department stores are usually available free at hotels, and they're good for those visiting Paris for only a few days and hitting only the major attractions.

But if you plan to really explore all the nooks and crannies of the city, the best maps are those of the *Plan de Paris par Arrondissement,* pocket-sized books with maps and a street index, available at most bookstores. They're extremely practical, and prices start at around 40F ($5.70). Most Parisians carry a copy because they, too, get lost at times.

Newspapers & Magazines: Many newsstands carry the latest editions of the *International Herald Tribune,* published Monday through Saturday, and the major London papers. *Time* and *Newsweek* are readily available in Paris. So is *USA Today*'s International edition. The weekly entertainment guide *Pariscope,* which comes out on Wednesdays, has an English-language insert that gives you up-to-the-minute information on the latest cultural events. You can also get the New York Times in some of the bigger English-language bookstores.

Police: Dial ☎ **17** in emergencies; otherwise, call ☎ 01-53-71-53-71.

Post Office: See "Mail," previously in this Appendix.

Rest Rooms: Public rest rooms are plentiful, but you usually have to pay for them. Every café has a rest room, but it is supposed to be for customers only. The best plan is to ask to use the telephone; it's usually next to the *toilette.* For 2F (29¢) you can use the streetside toilets, which are automatically flushed out and cleaned after every use. Some Métro stations have serviced rest rooms; you are expected to tip the attendant 2F (29¢).

Safety: Paris is a relatively safe city, and violent crime is rare. Your biggest risks are pickpockets and purse snatchers, so be particularly attentive on the Métro and on crowded buses, in museum lines and around tourist attractions. Women should be on guard in crowded tourist areas and on the Métro against overly friendly men who seem to have made a specialty out of bothering unsuspecting female tourists. Tricks include asking your name and nationality, then sticking like a burr to you for the rest of the day. They're usually more harassing than harmful, but if you're too nice, you may be stuck spending time with someone with whom you prefer not to. A simple "leave me alone", (*laissez-moi tranquille* ["lay-say mwa tran-*keel*"]) usually works.

Smoking: Although restaurants are required to provide nonsmoking sections, you may find yourself next to the kitchen or the rest rooms. Even there, your neighbor may light up and defy you to say something about it. Large brasseries, expensive restaurants, and places accustomed to dealing with foreigners, are most likely to be accommodating.

Taxes: *Watch out:* You could get burned. As a member of the European Community, France routinely imposes a standard 20.6-percent value-added tax (VAT) on many goods and services. The tax on merchandise applies to clothing, appliances, liquor, leather goods, shoes, furs, jewelry, perfume, cameras, and even caviar. You can get a refund — usually 13 percent — on certain goods and merchandise, but not on services. The minimum purchase is 1,200F ($171.45) in the same store for nationals or residents of countries outside the European Union.

Taxis: Alpha Taxis (☎ 01-45-85-85-85); **artaxi** (☎ 01-42-03-50-50); **TaxisG7** (☎ 01-47-39-47-39); **Taxis Bleus** (☎ 01-49-36-10-10) Be aware that the meter starts running as soon as you call a cab, so they're more expensive than regular cabs. You can hail taxis in the street (look for a taxi with a white light on; an orange light means it's occupied), but most drivers will not pick you up if you are in the general vicinity of a taxi stand (look for the blue "taxi" sign).

Telephone/Telex/Fax: Most **public phone booths** take only telephone debit cards called **télécartes,** which can be bought at post offices and at *tabacs* (cafes and kiosks that sell tobacco products). You insert the card into the phone and make your call; the cost

is automatically deducted from the "value" of the card recorded on its magnetized strip. The télécarte comes in 50- and 120-unit denominations, costing 49F ($7) and 96F ($13.70), respectively, and can only be used in a phone booth.

Cashiers will almost always try to sell you a card from France Télécom, the French phone company, but cards exist that give you more talk time for the same amount of money. Instead of inserting the card into a public phone, you dial a free number and tap in a code. The cards come with directions, some in English, and can be used from public and private phones, unlike France Télécom's card. Look for *tabacs* that have advertisements for Delta Multimedia or Kertel, or ask for a *télécarte international avec un code*. The coin-operated pay phones that are left are almost exclusively in bars, cafes, and restaurants, and take 1F, 2F, and 5F pieces; the minimum charge is 2F (29¢).

For placing **international calls from France,** dial 00, then the country code (for the United States and Canada, 1; for Britain, 44; for Ireland, 353; for Australia, 61; for New Zealand, 64), then the area or city code, and then the local number (for example, to call New York, you'd dial 00 + 1 + 212 + 000-0000). **To place a collect call to North America,** dial 00-33-11, and an English-speaking operator will assist you. Dial 00-00-11 for an American AT&T operator; MCI 0800-99-00-19; Sprint 0800-99-00-87.

For **calling from Paris to anywhere else in France** (called *province*), the country is divided into five zones with prefixes beginning 01, 02, 03, 04, and 05; check a phone directory for the code of the city you're calling.

If you're **calling France from the United States,** dial the international prefix, 011; then the country code for France, 33; followed by city code and the local number, but leave off the initial zero (for example, 011 + 33 + 1-00-00-00-00).

Avoid making phone calls from your hotel room; many hotels charge at least 2F (29 ¢) for local calls, and the markup on international calls can be staggering.

You can send **telex** and **fax** messages at the main post office in each arrondissement of Paris, but it's often cheaper to ask at your hotel or to go to a neighborhood printer or copy shop.

Time: Paris is 6 hours ahead of eastern standard time; noon in New York is 6 p.m. in Paris.

Tipping: Service is supposedly included at your hotel, but the custom is to tip the **bellhop** about 7F ($1) per bag, more in expensive (splurge) hotels. If you have a lot of luggage, tip a bit more. Don't tip housekeepers unless you do something that requires extra work. Tip a few dollars if a reception staff member performs extra services.

Although your *addition* (restaurant bill) or *fiche* (café check) will bear the words *service compris* (service charge included), always leave a small tip. Generally, 5 percent is considered acceptable. Remember, service has supposedly already been paid for.

Taxi drivers appreciate a tip of 2F to 3F (29¢ to 43¢). On longer journeys, when the fare exceeds 100F ($14.30), a 5- to-10-percent tip is appropriate. At the theater and cinema, tip 2F (29¢) if an usher shows you to your seat. In **public toilets,** there is often a posted fee for using the facilities. If not, the maintenance person will expect a tip of about 2F (29¢). Put it in the basket or on the plate at the entrance. **Porters** and **cloakroom attendants** are usually governed by set prices, which are displayed. If not, give a porter 5F to 8F (70¢ to $1.15) per suitcase, and a cloakroom attendant 2F to 4F (29¢ to 57¢) per coat.

Trains: The telephone number for reservations on France's national railroads (SNCF) is ☎ **08-36-35-35-35** (2.23F/32¢/minute). Open 7 a.m.–10 p.m. daily. Remember, you must validate your train ticket in the orange ticket *composteur* on the platform or pay a fine.

Water: Tap water in Paris is perfectly safe, but if you're prone to stomach problems, you may prefer to drink mineral water.

Weather updates: ☎ 08-36-70-12-34 (2.23F/ 32¢/minute) for France and abroad; ☎ 08-36-68-02-75 (2.23F/32¢/minute) for Paris and Ile de France.

Toll-Free Numbers and Web Sites

Major Airlines

Air Canada
☎ 800-630-3299
Internet: www.aircanada.ca

Air France
☎ 800-237-2747
Internet: www.airfrance.com

American Airlines
☎ 800-433-7300
Internet: www.aa.com

British Airways
☎ 800-247-9297
Internet: www.british-airways.com

Continental Airlines
☎ 800-525-0280
Internet: www.continental.com

Delta Air Lines
☎ 800-221-1212
Internet: www.delta-air.com

Iceland Air
☎ 800-223-5500
Internet: www.icelandair.com

Northwest/KLM
☎ 800-225-2525
Internet: www.nwa.com

TWA
☎ 800-221-2000
Internet: www.twa.com

United Airlines
☎ 800-241-6522
Internet: www.united.com

US Airways
☎ 800-428-4322
Internet: www.usairways.com

Car Rental Agencies

Auto Europe
☎ 800-223-5555
Internet: www.autoeurope.com

Avis
☎ 800-331-1212;
Internet: www.avis.com
In Paris: place Madeleine, 8e;
☎ 01-42-66-67-58

Budget
☎ 800-527-0700;
Internet: www.drivebudget.com
information on Paris locations:
☎ 08-00-10-00-01; 1.29F/18¢ min

Hertz
☎ 800-654-3131
Internet: www.hertz.com
In Paris: 123 rue Jeanne d'Arc, 13e
☎ 01-45-86-53-33

Kemwel Holiday Auto (KHA)
☎ 800-678-0678
Internet: www.kemwel.com

National
☎ 800-CAR-RENT
Internet: www.nationalcar.com
In Paris: 23 bd Arago, 13e.
☎ 01-47-07-87-39

Where to Get More Information

The information sources I list in this section are the best of the bunch; dig in before you go and you'll be well prepared for your trip.

Tourist Offices

For general information about France, contact an office of the **French Government Tourist Office** at one of the following addresses:

✔ **In The United States:** Phone numbers aren't listed because offices prefer to be in touch via e-mail or fax. The **French Government Tourist Office** (Fax: 212-838-7855; Internet: www.francetourism. com), 444 Madison Ave., 16th floor, New York, NY 10022-6903; 676 N. Michigan Ave., Chicago, IL 60611-2819 (Fax: 312-337-6339); or 9454 Wilshire Blvd., Suite 715, Beverly Hills, CA 90212-2967 (Fax: 310-276-2835).

✔ **In Canada: Maison de la France/French Government Tourist Office,** 1981 av. McGill College, Suite 490, Montréal PQ H3A 2W9 (Fax: 514-845-4868).

✔ **In The United Kingdom: Maison de la France/French Government Tourist Office,** 178 Piccadilly, London W1V 0AL (☎ 0891-244-123; Fax: 0171-493-6594).

✔ **In Australia: French Tourist Bureau,** 25 Bligh St. Level 22, Sydney, NSW 2000 Australia (☎ 02-231-5244; Fax: 02-231-8682).

✔ **In New Zealand:** You won't find a representative in New Zealand; contact the Australian representative.

✔ **In Paris:** The **Office de Tourisme et des Congrès de Paris,** 127 av. des Champs-Elysées, 75008 Paris (☎ **08-36-68-31-12** [2.23F/min.]; Fax: 01-49-52-53-00; Métro: Charles-de-Gaulle–Étoile or George V).

Surfing the Web

You'll find a lot of excellent information about Paris on the Internet — the latest news, restaurant reviews, concert schedules, subway maps, and more.

✔ **Aeroports de Paris** (www.paris-airports.com). Click the American flag on this site's home page for an English version that provides transfer information into Paris, and lists terminals, maps, airlines, boutiques, hotels, restaurants, and accessibility information for travelers with disabilities.

✔ **Arthur Frommer's Budget Travel Newsletter** (www.frommers.com/newsletters). Click here for travel tips, reviews, online booking, "Ask the Expert" bulletin boards, travel bargains and travel secrets for hundreds of destinations.

✔ **Bonjour Paris** (www.bparis.com). Utilize this fun and interesting site chock full of information about the city. You'll find everything from cultural differences to shopping to restaurant reviews, all written from an American expatriate point of view.

✔ **French Government Tourist Office** (www.francetourism.com). Here you'll find information on planning your trip to France, as well as practical tips, family activities, events, and accommodations.

✔ **ISMAP** (address locator) (www.ismap.com). Type in an address in Paris on this site and ISMAP will map it, including nearby sights of interest and the closest Métro stops.

✔ **Paris.Com** (www.paris.com). The lodging section of this site includes photos of rooms; you can also find restaurant reviews and descriptions of the sights here.

✔ **Paris Digest** (www.parisdigest.com). Paris Digest selects "the best sights in Paris" and provides photos and links to them, as well as restaurants with views and good décor, and information on shopping, hotels, and things to do.

✔ **Paris France Guide** (www.parisfranceguide.com). This site has lots of useful information about Paris, with current nightlife, restaurant, music, theater, and events listings. This guide is brought to you by the publishers of the *Living in France, Study in France,* and *What's on in France* guides.

✔ **Paris Free Voice** (www.parisvoice.com or www.thinkparis.com). This is the online version of the free Paris monthly, *The Paris Voice*. It's hip and opinionated with lots of listings for the performing arts, music, and theater.

✔ **Paris Pages** (www.paris.org). There's so much information on this site, you won't know where to begin. Lodging reviews are organized by area and the monuments standing nearby, and you'll also find photo tours, shop listings, and a map of attractions with details.

✔ **Paris Tourist Office** (www.paris-touristoffice.com). The official site of the Paris Tourist Office provides information on the year's events, museums, accommodations, nightlife, and restaurants.

✔ **RATP (Paris Urban Transit)** (www.ratp.fr/index.eng.html). Find subway and bus line maps, timetables and information, as well as routes and times for Noctambus, Paris's night buses that run after the Métro closes.

✔ **Smartweb: Paris** (www.smartweb.fr/paris). The big attractions, such as the Louvre and the Eiffel Tower, are featured, in addition to shop and gallery listings organized by arrondissement. Airport terminal information and click-on subway maps are also posted here.

✔ **SNCF (French Rail)** (www.sncf.fr). The official Web site of the French railway system, this site sells seats online for trips through France. You'll also find timetables and prices here.

✔ **Subway Navigator** (metro.ratp.fr:10001/bin/cities/english). This site provides detailed subway maps for Paris and other French cities, plus 60 other cities around the world. You can select a city and enter your arrival and departure points, and then Subway Navigator will map out your route and estimate how long your trip will take.

Hitting the Books

Most bookstores will have several shelves devoted entirely to Paris-related titles, given that the city is one of the most-visited on the planet. Here are a few other books that might be useful for your trip. All Frommer's guides are published by Hungry Minds, Inc.

- ✔ *Frommer's Paris,* updated every year, is an authoritative guide that covers the city and its surroundings.

- ✔ *Frommer's Paris from $85 a Day* is the guide for travelers who want to visit Paris comfortably, but don't want to spend a fortune doing it.

- ✔ *Frommer's Portable Paris* is the pocket-sized version of Frommer's Paris.

- ✔ *Frommer's Memorable Walks in Paris* is for those who want to explore the city in depth and on foot with easy directions and descriptions of important sights.

- ✔ *Frommer's Irreverent Paris* is a fun guide for sophisticated travelers who want the basics without a lot of excess.

Appendix B

A Glossary of French Words and Phrases

Basic Vocabulary

English	French	Pronunciation
Yes/No	**Oui/Non**	wee/nohn
Okay	**d'accord**	dah-*core*
Please	**S'il vous plaît**	seel-voo-*play*
Thank you	**Merci**	mair-*see*
You're welcome	**De rien**	duh ree-*ehn*
Hello (during daylight hours)	**Bonjour**	bohn-*jhoor*
Good evening	**Bonsoir**	bohn-*swahr*
Goodbye	**Au revoir**	o ruh-*vwahr*
What's your name?	**Comment vous appellez-vous?**	ko-mahn-voo-za-pell-ay-*voo*
My name is . . .	**Je m'appelle . . .**	jhuh ma-*pell* . . .
Happy to meet you	**Enchanté(e)**	ohn-shahn-*tay*
Miss	**Mademoiselle**	mad mwa-*zel*
Mr.	**Monsieur**	muh-*syuh*
Mrs.	**Madame**	ma-*dam*
How are you?	**Comment allez-vous?**	kuh-mahn-tahl-ay-*voo*
Fine, thank you, and you?	**Très bien, merci, et vous?**	tray bee-ehn, mare-ci, ay *voo?*
Very well, thank you	**Très bien, merci**	tray bee-ehn, mair-*see*

(continued)

Basic Vocabulary (continued)

English	French	Pronunciation
So-so	Comme ci, comme ça	kum-*see*, kum-*sah*
I'm sorry/excuse me	Pardon	pahr-*dohn*
I'm so very sorry	Désolè(e)	day-zoh-*lay*
Do you speak English?	Parlez-vous anglais?	par-lay-voo-ahn-*glay*
I don't speak French	Je ne parle pas français	jhuh ne parl pah frahn-say
I don't understand	Je ne comprends pas	jhuh ne kohm-*prahn* pah
Could you speak more slowly?	Pouvez-vous parler un peu plus lentement?	Poo-*vay* voo par-*lay* uh puh ploo lan-te-*ment*
Could you repeat that?	Répétez, s'il vous plaît	ray-pay-tay, seel voo play
What is it?	Qu'est-ce que c'est?	kess-kuh-*say*
What time is it?	Qu'elle heure est-il?	kel uhr eh-*teel*
What?	Quoi?	kwah?
Pardon?	Pardon?	par-*doh*?
Help!	Aidez-moi!	*Ay*-day moi!
How? or What did you say?	Comment?	ko-*mahn*?
When?	Quand?	cohn?
Where is . . . ?	Où est . . . ?	ooh-eh?
Who?	Qui?	kee?
Why?	Pourquoi?	poor-*kwah*?
Here/there	ici/là	ee-*see*/lah
Left/right	à gauche/à droite	ah goash/ah drwaht
Straight ahead	tout droit	too-drwah
I'm American/ Canadian/British	Je suis américain(e)/ canadien(e)/ anglais(e)	jhe swee a-may-ree-*kehn*/ canah-dee-*en*/ ahn-*glay* (*glaise*)

English	French	Pronunciation
I'm going to	**Je vais à . . .**	jhe vay ah
I want to get off at . . .	**Je voudrais descendre à**	jhe voo-*dray* day-son-drah-ah

Health Terms

English	French	Pronunciation
I'm sick	**Je suis malade**	jhuh swee mal-*ahd*
I have a headache	**J'ai une mal de tête**	jhay oon mal de tet
I have a stomachache	**J'ai une mal de ventre**	jhay oon mal de *vahn*-trah
I would like to buy some aspirin	**Je voudrais acheter des aspirines**	jhe *voo*-dray *ash*-tay days as-peh-*reen*
hospital	**l'hôpital**	low-pee-*tahl*
insurance	**l'assurances**	lah-sur-*ahns*

Travel Terms

English	French	Pronunciation
airport	**l'aéroport**	lair-o-*por*
bank	**la banque**	lah bahnk
bridge	**le pont**	luh pohn
bus station	**la gare routière**	lah gar roo-tee-*air*
bus stop	**l'arrêt de bus**	lah-*ray* duh boohss
by means of a bicycle	**en vélo/par bicyclette**	ahn *vay*-low/par bee-see-*clet*
by means of a car	**en voiture**	ahn vwa-*toor*
cashier	**la caisse**	lah *kess*
driver's license	**permis de conduire**	per-*mee* duh con-*dweer*
elevator	**l'ascenseur**	lah sahn *seuhr*

(continued)

Travel Terms *(continued)*

English	French	Pronunciation
entrance (to a building or a city)	**la porte**	lah port
exit (from a building or a freeway)	**une sortie**	ewn sor-*tee*
ground floor	**le rez-de-chausée**	luh ray-duh-show-*say*
highway to . . .	**la route pour . . .**	lah root por
luggage storage	**la consigne**	lah kohn-*seen*-yuh
museum	**le musée**	luh mew-*zay*
no entry	**sens interdit**	sehns ahn-ter-*dee*
no smoking	**défense de fumer**	day-*fahns* duh fu-may
on foot	**à pied**	ah pee-*ay*
one-day pass	**ticket journalier**	tee-kay jhoor-nall-ee-*ay*
one-way ticket	**aller simple**	ah-*lay sam*-pluh
police	**la police**	lah po-*lees*
round-trip ticket	**aller-retour**	ah-*lay* re-*toor*
second floor	**le premier étage**	luh prem-ee-*ehr* ay-*taj*
slow down	**ralentez**	rah-lahn-*teer*
store	**le magasin**	luh ma-ga-*zehn*
street	**la rue**	lah roo
suburb	**le banlieu, environs**	luh bahn-*liew*, en-veer-*ohns*
subway	**le Métro**	luh may-tro
telephone	**le téléphone**	luh tay-lay-*phun*
ticket	**un billet**	uh *bee*-yay
ticket office	**le vente de billets**	luh vahnt duh bee-*yay*
toilets	**les toilettes**	lay twa-*lets*
I'd like . . .	**Je voudrais . . .**	jhe voo-*dray*
a room	**une chambre**	ewn *shahm*-bruh
the key	**la clé (la clef)**	lah clay

Shopping Terms

English	French	Pronunciation
How much does it cost?	**C'est combien?/ Ça coûte combien?**	say comb-bee-*ehn?/* sah coot comb-bee-*ehn?*
That's expensive	**C'est cher/chère**	say share
That's inexpensive	**C'est raisonnable/ C'est bon marché**	say ray-son-*ahb*-bluh/ say bohn mar-*shay*
Do you take credit cards?	**Est-ce que vous acceptez cartes de credit?**	es-kuh voo zaksep-*tay* lay kart duh creh-*dee?*
I'd like to buy . . .	**Je voudrais acheter . . .**	jhe voo-dray ahsh-*tay* . . .
aspirin	**des aspirines**	deyz ahs-peer-*eens*
cigarettes	**des cigarettes**	day see-ga-*ret*
condoms	**des préservatifs**	day pray-ser-va-*teefs*
contraceptive suppositories	**des ovules contraceptive**	days oh-*vyules* kahn-trah-cep-*teef*
a dictionary	**un dictionnaire**	uh deek-see-oh-*nare*
a gift (for someone)	**un cadeau**	uh kah-*doe*
a handbag	**un sac à main**	uh sahk ah man
a magazine	**une revue**	ewn reh-*vu*
a map of the city	**un plan de ville**	uh plahn de *veel*
matches	**des allumettes**	dayz a-loo-*met*
lighter	**un briquet**	uh *bree*-kay
a newspaper	**un journal**	uh zhoor-*nahl*
a phonecard	**une carte téléphonique**	ewn cart tay-lay-fone-*eek*
a postcard	**une carte postale**	ewn carte pos-*tahl*
a road map	**une carte routière**	ewn cart roo-tee-*air*
shoes	**des chaussures**	day show-*suhr*
soap	**du savon**	dew sah-*vohn*
socks	**des chaussettes**	day show-*set*
a stamp	**un timbre**	uh *tam*-bruh
writing paper	**du papier à lettres**	dew pap-pee-*ay* a *let*-ruh

Elements of Time

English	French	Pronunciation
Sunday	**dimanche**	dee-*mahnsh*
Monday	**lundi**	luhn-*dee*
Tuesday	**mardi**	mahr-*dee*
Wednesday	**mercredi**	mair-kruh-*dee*
Thursday	**jeudi**	jheu-*dee*
Friday	**vendredi**	vawn-druh-*dee*
Saturday	**samedi**	sahm-*dee*
Yesterday	**hier**	ee-*air*
Today	**aujourd'hui**	o-jhord-*dwee*
This morning	**ce matin**	suh ma-*tan*
This afternoon	**cette après-midi**	set ah-preh mee-*dee*
Tonight	**ce soir**	suh *swahr*
Tomorrow	**demain**	de-*man*
Now	**maintenant**	mant-*naw*

Making Dollars and Sense of It

Expense	Amount
Airfare	
Car Rental	
Lodging	
Parking	
Breakfast	
Lunch	
Dinner	
Babysitting	
Attractions	
Transportation	
Souvenirs	
Tips	
Grand Total	

Notes

Fare Game: Choosing an Airline

Travel Agency: _____ Phone: _____

Agent's Name: _____ Quoted Fare: _____

Departure Schedule & Flight Information

Airline: _____ Airport: _____

Flight #: _____ Date: _____ Time: _____ a.m./p.m.

Arrives in: _____ Time: _____ a.m./p.m.

Connecting Flight (if any)

Amount of time between flights: _____ hours/mins

Airline: _____ Airport: _____

Flight #: _____ Date: _____ Time: _____ a.m./p.m.

Arrives in: _____ Time: _____ a.m./p.m.

Return Trip Schedule & Flight Information

Airline: _____ Airport: _____

Flight #: _____ Date: _____ Time: _____ a.m./p.m.

Arrives in: _____ Time: _____ a.m./p.m.

Connecting Flight (if any)

Amount of time between flights: _____ hours/mins

Airline: _____ Airport: _____

Flight #: _____ Date: _____ Time: _____ a.m./p.m.

Arrives in: _____ Time: _____ a.m./p.m.

Notes

Sweet Dreams: Choosing Your Hotel

Enter the hotels where you'd prefer to stay based on location and price. Then use the worksheet below to plan your itinerary.

Hotel	Location	Price per night

Menus & Venues

Enter the restaurants where you'd most like to dine. Then use the worksheet below to plan your itinerary.

Name	*Address/Phone*	*Cuisine/Price*

Menus & Venues

Enter the restaurants where you'd most like to dine. Then use the worksheet below to plan your itinerary.

Name	Address/Phone	Cuisine/Price

Places to Go, People to See, Things to Do

Enter the attractions you would most like to see. Then use the worksheet below to plan your itinerary.

Attractions	Amount of time you expect to spend there	Best day and time to go

Places to Go, People to See, Things to Do

Enter the attractions you would most like to see. Then use the worksheet below to plan your itinerary.

Attractions	Amount of time you expect to spend there	Best day and time to go

Going "My" Way

Itinerary #1

- ☐ _____
- ☐ _____
- ☐ _____
- ☐ _____

Itinerary #2

- ☐ _____
- ☐ _____
- ☐ _____
- ☐ _____

Itinerary #3

- ☐ _____
- ☐ _____
- ☐ _____
- ☐ _____

Itinerary #4

- ☐ _____
- ☐ _____
- ☐ _____
- ☐ _____

Itinerary #5

- ☐ _____
- ☐ _____
- ☐ _____
- ☐ _____

Itinerary #6

- ☐ _____
- ☐ _____
- ☐ _____
- ☐ _____

Itinerary #7

- ☐ _____
- ☐ _____
- ☐ _____
- ☐ _____

Itinerary #8

- ☐ _____
- ☐ _____
- ☐ _____
- ☐ _____

Itinerary #9

- ☐ _____
- ☐ _____
- ☐ _____
- ☐ _____

Itinerary #10

- ☐ _____
- ☐ _____
- ☐ _____
- ☐ _____

Going "My" Way

Itinerary #1

- ☐ _____
- ☐ _____
- ☐ _____
- ☐ _____

Itinerary #2

- ☐ _____
- ☐ _____
- ☐ _____
- ☐ _____

Itinerary #3

- ☐ _____
- ☐ _____
- ☐ _____
- ☐ _____

Itinerary #4

- ☐ _____
- ☐ _____
- ☐ _____
- ☐ _____

Itinerary #5

- ☐ _____
- ☐ _____
- ☐ _____
- ☐ _____

Itinerary #6

❑ _____
❑ _____
❑ _____
❑ _____

Itinerary #7

❑ _____
❑ _____
❑ _____
❑ _____

Itinerary #8

❑ _____
❑ _____
❑ _____
❑ _____

Itinerary #9

❑ _____
❑ _____
❑ _____
❑ _____

Itinerary #10

❑ _____
❑ _____
❑ _____
❑ _____

Notes

Index

See also separate Accommodations and Restaurant indexes at the end of this index.

• C •

• *M* •

• *Q* •

• *R* •

Discover Dummies Online!

The Dummies Web Site is your fun and friendly online resource for the latest information about *For Dummies* books and your favorite topics. The Web site is the place to communicate with us, exchange ideas with other *For Dummies* readers, chat with authors, and have fun!

Ten Fun and Useful Things You Can Do at www.dummies.com

1. Win free *For Dummies* books and more!

2. Register your book and be entered in a prize drawing.

3. Meet your favorite authors through the Hungry Minds Author Chat Series.

4. Exchange helpful information with other *For Dummies* readers.

5. Discover other great *For Dummies* books you must have!

6. Purchase Dummieswear exclusively from our Web site.

7. Buy *For Dummies* books online.

8. Talk to us. Make comments, ask questions, get answers!

9. Download free software.

10. Find additional useful resources from authors.

Link directly to these ten fun and useful things at **www.dummies.com/10useful**

For other technology titles from Hungry Minds, go to www.hungryminds.com

Not on the Web yet? It's easy to get started with *Dummies 101: The Internet For Windows 98* or *The Internet For Dummies* at local retailers everywhere.

Find other *For Dummies* books on these topics:
Business • Career • Databases • Food & Beverage • Games • Gardening
Graphics • Hardware • Health & Fitness • Internet and the World Wide Web
Networking • Office Suites • Operating Systems • Personal Finance • Pets
Programming • Recreation • Sports • Spreadsheets • Teacher Resources
Test Prep • Word Processing

FOR DUMMIES
BOOK REGISTRATION

Register This Book and Win!

We want to hear from you!

Visit **dummies.com** to register this book and tell us how you liked it!

✔ Get entered in our monthly prize giveaway.

✔ Give us feedback about this book — tell us what you like best, what you like least, or maybe what you'd like to ask the author and us to change!

✔ Let us know any other *For Dummies* topics that interest you.

Your feedback helps us determine what books to publish, tells us what coverage to add as we revise our books, and lets us know whether we're meeting your needs as a *For Dummies* reader. You're our most valuable resource, and what you have to say is important to us!

Not on the Web yet? It's easy to get started with *Dummies 101: The Internet For Windows 98* or *The Internet For Dummies* at local retailers everywhere.

Or let us know what you think by sending us a letter at the following address:

For Dummies Book Registration
Dummies Press
10475 Crosspoint Blvd.
Indianapolis, IN 46256

™

BESTSELLING BOOK SERIES